Intimate Modernism

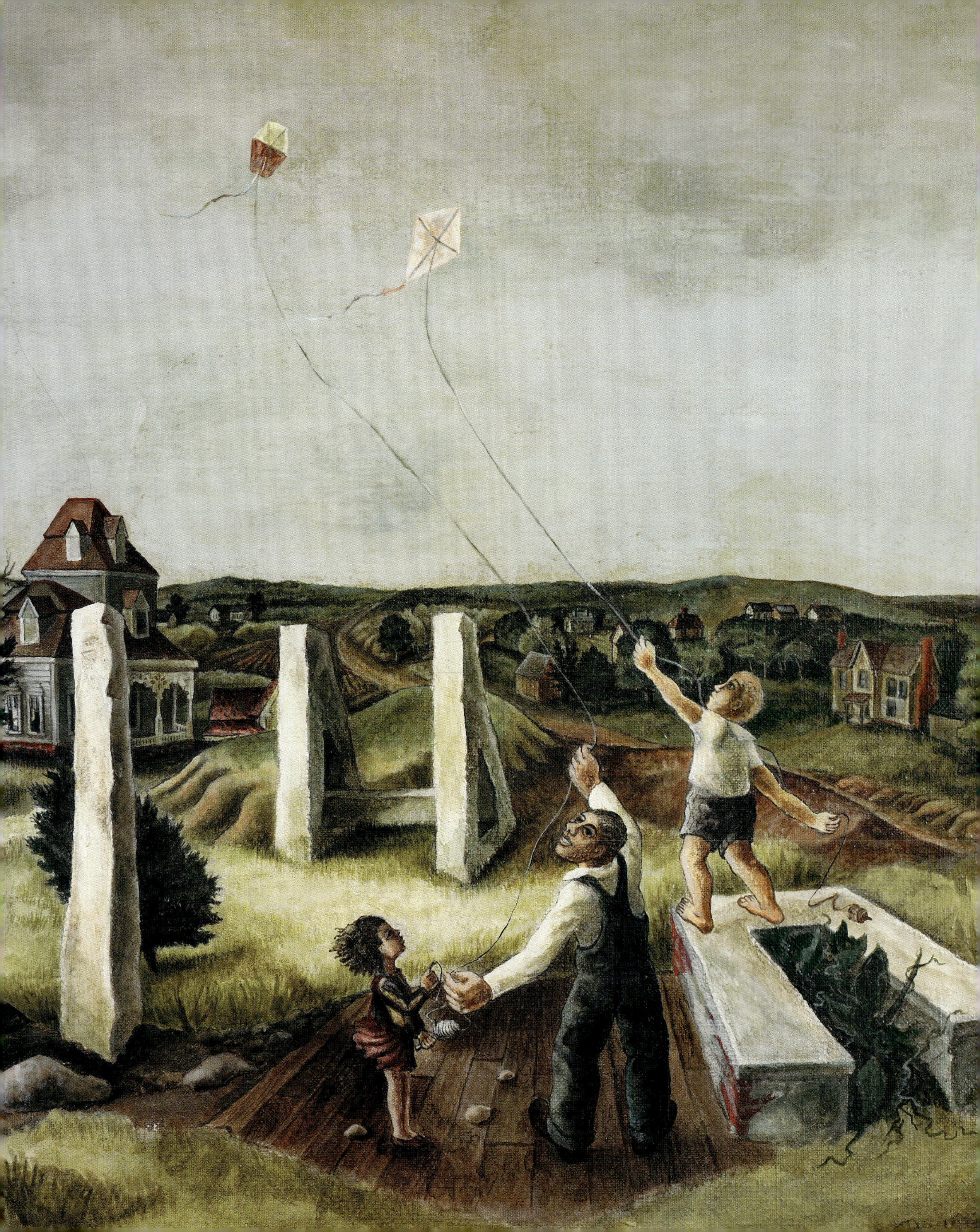

SCOTT GRANT BARKER AND JANE MYERS

Intimate Modernism

FORT WORTH CIRCLE ARTISTS IN THE 1940S

Amon Carter Museum, Fort Worth

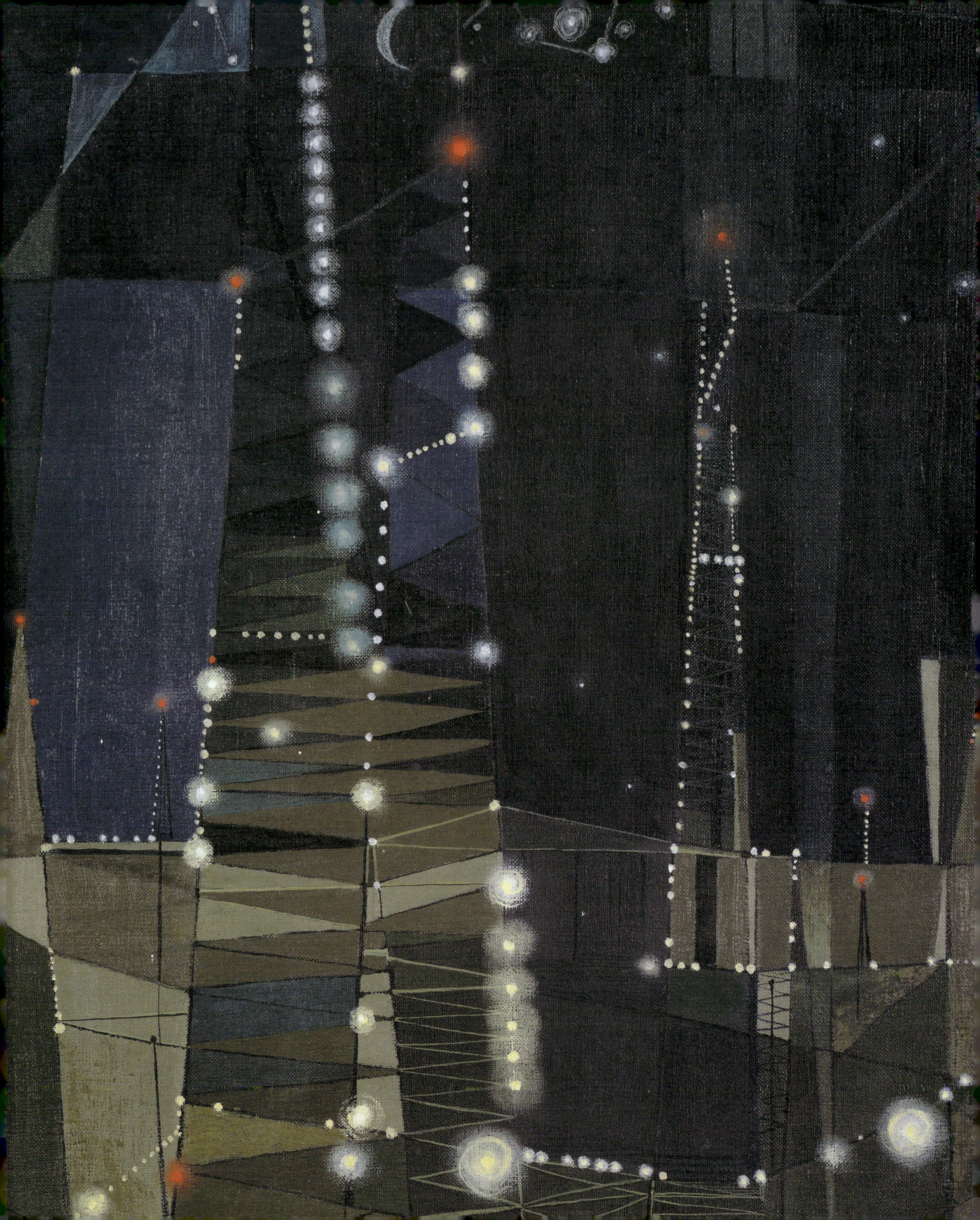

ACKNOWLEDGMENTS

Endless fascination and a heightened sense of connection await anyone who chooses to embrace their community through the study of its art. There is not a more enjoyable vehicle for traveling into your city's past than the one called art history. As this history of a community is revealed, so too are a thousand other stories, each one shining new light on the city and region in which you live. This I know to be true.

The exhibition documented in these pages was the dream of J. O. "Dutch" Phillips Jr. Dutch was born in Fort Worth in 1944 and grew up in the close company of the artists of the Fort Worth Circle. Bill Bomar was his godfather. He attended the Reeder School. As an adult, he carried the torch of the Fort Worth Circle as a well-known art dealer in Fort Worth and Dallas. In 1992, it was Dutch's enthusiasm for the work of the Circle, and his belief in their uniqueness, that set me on a personal path of discovery.

In 2005, Jane Myers, senior curator of prints and drawings at the Amon Carter Museum, made the decision to go forward with the Fort Worth Circle exhibition. Jane had served on the Carter's curatorial staff for many years and had become versed in the lore and legend of the Fort Worth Circle. If drawn to a cultural life, one cannot live in Fort Worth long without hearing the stories. Jane heard them and took them to heart. Because of Dutch Phillips, who died in 2000, and Jane Myers, the artists of the Fort Worth Circle will, through this exhibition and publication, live again.

My contributions to this exhibition would have been impossible without the friendship and confidence of those who lived the story. I am eternally grateful for the enjoyable times we spent together. My fond thanks to those now departed: Flora Reeder, Marjorie Johnson Lee, Sara Shannon Steel, Cynthia Brants, and Reilly Nail. And to those still living and working: Kelly Fearing, George Grammer, and Pat Steel.

Family members and friends of the Circle artists were an invaluable resource over the years. They include Nell Reeder Branch, W. Ernest Chilton Jr., Sharon Conger, Judy Cordell, Jane Cranz, Pen Cranz, Don Dow, Charles DuBuis, Caroline Dulle, Bea Dunning, Hank Green Jr., Eleanor Harris, Lydia Hughes, Murray James, Don Keaton, Hedwig Helfensteller Marshall,

Connie Messing, Linda Mixson, Brooks Morris, Polly and Ocky Phillips, Susie Pritchett, Howard Ross, Ruth Ross, Frances Spiller Scott, Stanley Shepelwich, Shannon Steel, Camilla Thompson, and Kevin Vogel.

My sincere thanks to the professional guardians of our past: Ken Hopkins and Max Hill at the Fort Worth Public Library; Sam Ratcliffe at the Hamon Arts Library at Southern Methodist University; Dr. Gerald Saxon, Ann Hodges, Brenda McClurkin, Cathy Spitzenberger, and Gary Spurr at the University of Texas at Arlington, Special Collections; Margaret Blagg at the Old Jail Art Center; and the professional staff of the Amon Carter Museum.

Ken Jackson, Larry Kleinschmidt, Morris Matson, and A. C. Cook, all fellow admirers of Fort Worth art, are constant sources of support and inspiration. Rick Selcer, Dalton Hoffman, Quentin McGown, and Susie Pritchett are my role models for what local historians can and should be.

The unwavering support of my dear wife, Linda Jo, has been and remains the source of my ability to happily immerse myself in the history of this great community. The joy of discovery and the satisfaction of giving back are feelings we would not trade for anything.

Scott Grant Barker
November 2007

ACKNOWLEDGMENTS

The exhibition *Intimate Modernism: Fort Worth Circle Artists in the 1940s* and the related publication were made possible by an enthusiastic and supportive group of collectors, funders, colleagues, and members of the Amon Carter Museum staff. We are particularly indebted to Scott Barker for his wide-ranging expertise in all aspects of the Fort Worth Circle. His avid interest in local art and his gracious willingness to share his knowledge and insight enabled the Carter to realize this project.

We are also deeply grateful to the private and institutional lenders of works that appear in the exhibition and publication. (For a comprehensive list, refer to the List of Plates at the back of this publication.) All were perfectly willing to share their paintings, prints, pastels, and watercolors with the broad audience who will see this exhibition and enjoy the publication for many years to come.

Outside funding has made the project possible. To these individuals and corporations, we extend our gratitude: Center for the Advancement and Study of Early Texas Art (CASETA), Collectors of Fort Worth Art (COFWA), David Dike, Fifth Avenue Foundation, Shirlee and Taylor Gandy, Mrs. W. K. Gordon Jr., Humanities Texas, Marty Leonard, Kathryn and Morris C. Matson, Mary Belle and J. Olcott Phillips, Quicksilver Resources, RBC Dain Rauscher, Betty Sanders Family, William E. Scott Foundation, Mac Shafer, Texas Commission on the Arts, and the Valley House Gallery and Sculpture Garden in memory of Margaret and Donald S. Vogel.

In addition to the forty-four lenders and the funders, we extend special thanks to two of the artists whose work is featured in the exhibition: Kelly Fearing and George Grammer. Similarly, we thank Pat Steel, the husband of Sara Shannon, who graciously accommodated our requests for his wife's work. These individuals were also invaluable resources regarding the personalities that comprised the cultural scene in Fort Worth during the 1940s.

Prior to his death in 2000, Dutch Phillips, owner of a local art gallery and champion of the Fort Worth Circle, convinced Amon Carter Museum curators that the artists of the Circle deserved a place in the museum's holdings of nineteenth- and twentieth-century American art. Due to his guidance, fifteen of the works in this exhibition are owned by the Carter.

In addition to the lenders, there are other individuals who should be acknowledged for providing key research assistance and warm hospitality: Daniel Alonzo, Mr. and Mrs. Stephen Alton, Chuck Bailey, Linda Baird, Cynthia Bell, Margaret Blagg, Ambler Cantey and Russell Blair, Roger Blanc, Mr. and Mrs. James Branch, Peter Briggs, W. Ernest Chilton Jr., Emily Clark, Sharon Conger, David Conn, Pen Cranz (Mr. Edmund P.), Leslie Davis, Mr. and Mrs. Donald P. Dow, Gregory Dow, Charles DuBuis, Rick Floyd, Dr. Harry Froeshke, Mr. and Mrs. Patrick Gordon, Henry Sterling Green, Judie Greenman, Dr. and Mrs. Kenneth Hamlett, Dale Harper, Dick Harris, Larry Kleinschmidt, Carol Lampier, Michelle Locke, Hedwig Marshall, Brenda McClurkin, Mr. and Mrs. Quentin McGown III, Mr. and Mrs. Quentin McGown IV, Mr. and Mrs. Virgil Miller, Rebekah Morin, Brooks Morris Jr., Claire Myers, Diana Nail, Emily Neff, Atlee Phillips, Mary Frances Phillips, Jeff Reeder, Ruth Ross, Mr. and Mrs.Tom Rouse, William Rudolph, Stanley Shepelwich, Laverne Stanley, Robert Summers, Nancy Tockey, Elizabeth Weinman, Mr. and Mrs. Otis T. Welch, Mitch Whitten, and Lyle Williams.

Finally, the staff at the Amon Carter Museum is to be commended for their professionalism and extensive talents specific to seeing this project to fruition. Our gratitude to them all.

Jane Myers
Senior Curator of Prints and Drawings

Ron Tyler
Director
November 2007

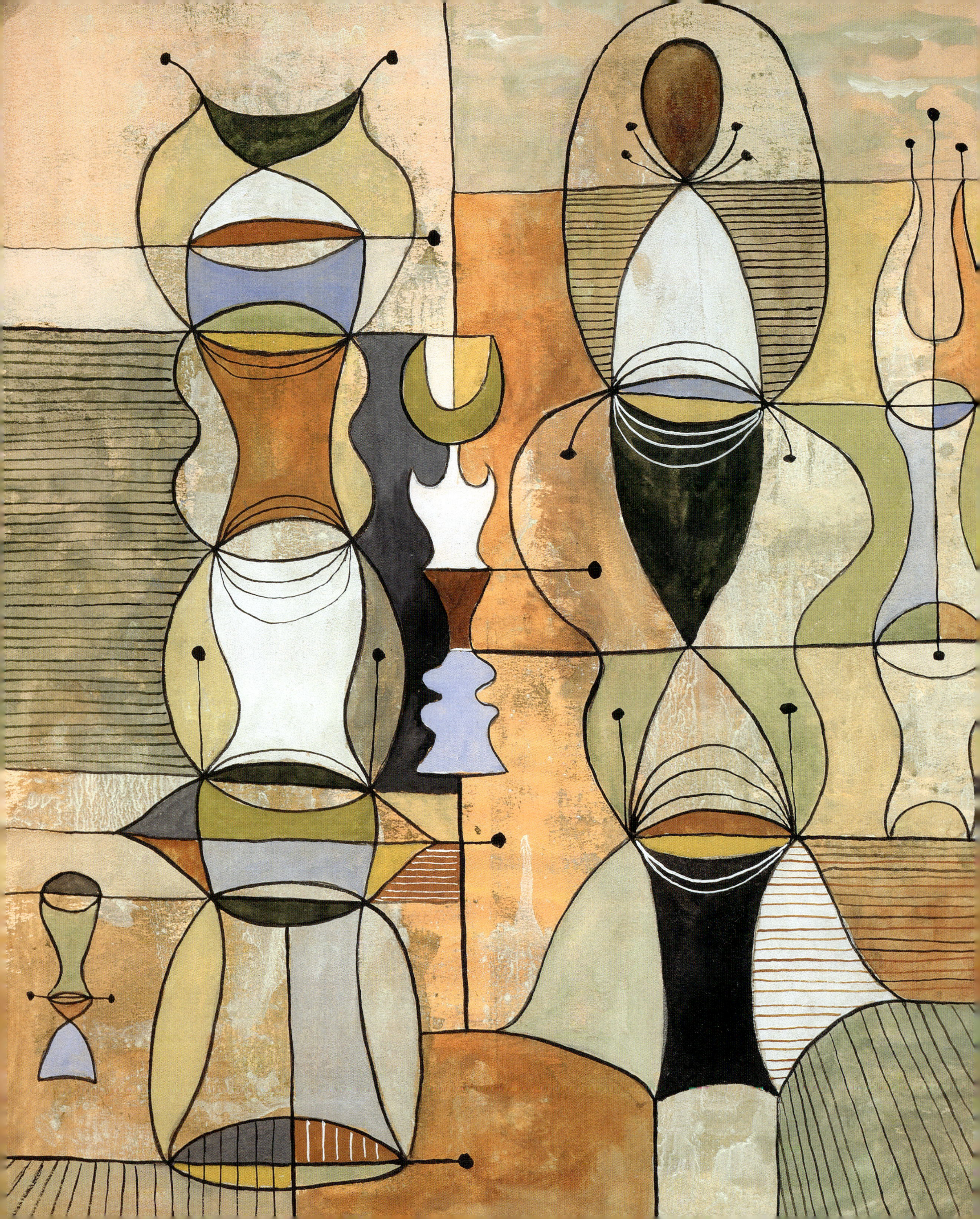

In the Fort Worth art world of the 1930s, tensions were building just below the surface. For decades, the city's leading artists had focused their creative endeavors on traditional and reassuring themes. The placid Trinity River views by Samuel P. Ziegler, lush still lifes by Anastasia Salt, and spacious Texas landscapes of Dwight C. Holmes reflected an approach to art acceptable both to the artists and their admirers. Most other artists in the city were likewise guided by public taste and convention. Although much of their work was accomplished, it was so thematically conservative that in 1936 Dallas painter Alexandre Hogue chided, "artistically, Fort Worth is enjoying poor health."[1]

Hogue's criticism proved prescient, for in the minds of a few young Fort Worth artists the conventions of the day were no longer acceptable. By 1941, the hierarchy of Fort Worth's most prominent painters had completely shifted. Almost overnight, artists who had enjoyed wide popularity during the Great Depression found themselves overshadowed by a small group with a very different view of art. The determination of these new artists and the dominance they established in the public mind became the driving forces of the Fort Worth art world throughout the years of World War II and the decade beyond. Among the legends and legendary figures in Fort Worth's past – and there are many – the artists of the Fort Worth Circle occupy a special place as pioneers of modern art in a city that is today "a center of innovative architecture, art, music, ballet, and opera."[2]

An Unconventional Vision

REMEMBERING THE FORT WORTH CIRCLE SCOTT GRANT BARKER

The cords of truth and myth have intertwined in the years since the Fort Worth Circle was at its zenith, and two matters specific to their legacy call for clarity. One version of the Circle's story holds that this small group of artists brought modern art to Texas, or that they were the state's first modern painters. In fact, modernism in Texas art was not a development unique to any one painter or group of painters. Pockets of modernist work arose simultaneously in widely scattered areas of the state during the last half of the 1930s. Sometimes this work was the product of a single artist working alone, as in the case of Houston's Robert Preusser. What is true is that the Fort Worth Circle was the state's first colony of artists to embrace and manifest a clearly nonregional aesthetic.[3]

A second issue in need of clarification involves the label "Fort Worth School," a signature designation that has followed these artists for half a century. The notion that a school of art could emerge in the Southwest was broached early in 1946 by Bror Utter,[4] considered by many to be the most important of the Circle artists. Two years later, John Rosenfield of the *Dallas Morning News* published a column placing the focus of the Texas art scene squarely in Fort Worth by suggesting that a "school" was at work: "Fort Worth is the only city [in Texas] with what might be called a 'school' of artists."[5] Modernism in Fort Worth art, he suggested, was driven by this group of painters who displayed an advanced aesthetic and possessed the gifts to express it.

The romance and raw power of the concept of a school was a direct compliment to the artists of the Circle, and the moniker was immediately embraced by their Fort Worth supporters. Indeed, "Fort Worth School" entered the lexicon throughout the city and state, and as the postwar talent pool of contemporary Fort Worth artists inevitably deepened, members of the Circle were perceived collectively with others as artists of the Fort Worth School.

But was there in fact a Fort Worth School? In the 1990s artist Cynthia Brants, a later member of the 1940s Circle, began arguing for a different characterization, one based on the unique visions and diversities of style inherent in the group. "At first, we were referred to as a 'school,'" she wrote, "but that is misleading in that we did not share a common school of thought."[6] In truth, the primary interests of the individuals within the Circle were expressed through an array of themes and genres, ranging from portraiture to abstraction, and in a variety of mediums. In addition, the social, collegial, and competitive nature of the group, as described by Brants and others, suggests a circle of highly talented and enlightened friends rather than a school of painters united by a common view of art's purposes.[7]

By the turn of this century, and largely at Brants' urging, the name "Fort Worth Circle" had gained acceptance over the older designation, and both enjoy ardent support today. Clearly, though, in the 1940s a small and somewhat exclusionary community of artists, undeniably compatible and intimate, coalesced in Fort Worth and worked and thrived as a creative group. It is this handful of original players who, for the purposes of this publication, are referred to as the Fort Worth Circle.

The emergence of the Fort Worth Circle in the 1940s was the continuation of a process begun years earlier. The origin of the Circle can be defined as a nucleus of four people in their mid-twenties who met as art students at the Fort Worth School of Fine Arts: Lia Cuilty, Veronica

Helfensteller, Marjorie Johnson, and Bror Utter. Just prior to America's involvement in World War II, Edward Dickson Reeder, a high school classmate of Utter's, assumed leadership of the small band. It was Reeder and his New York–born wife, Flora Blanc, who provided the social glue that bonded the group together. Also in the Reeder sphere were Sara Shannon and William P. (Bill) Bomar Jr. Reeder, Bomar, and Helfensteller all received private art instruction as teenagers from the same teacher, Sallie Mummert.[8] Kelly Fearing was assimilated into the group after moving to Fort Worth during the war. Cynthia Brants became in 1945 the youngest female member of the Circle, and the following year George Grammer, the youngest of the artists, was the last to join the group when Fearing and the Reeders, who had followed his work, looped him into the network.

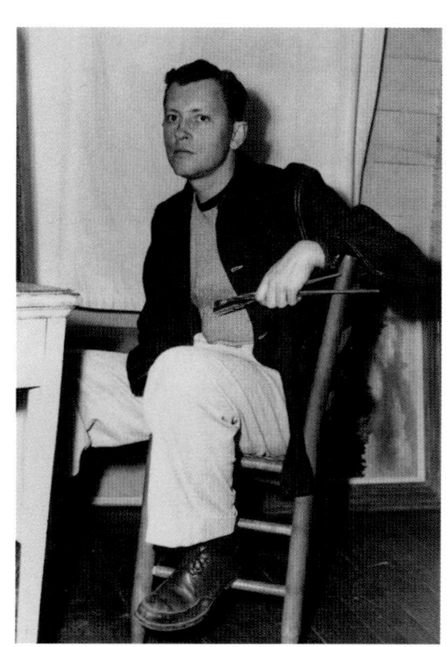

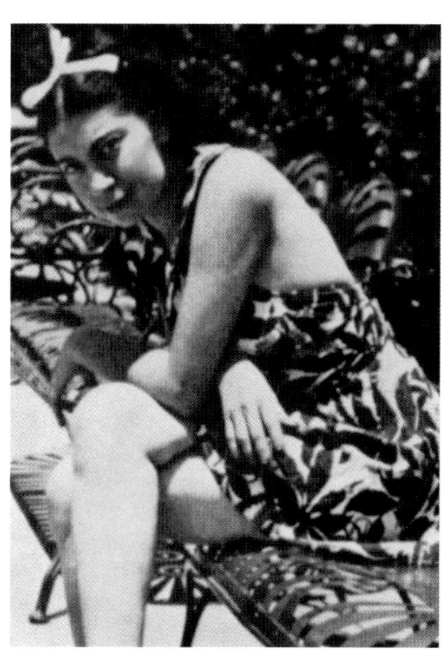

FIGURE **1** Bror Utter, n.d.

FIGURE **2** Lia Cuilty, n.d.

The Circle's rise to prominence – and a main reason for the acceptance of progressive art in Texas – began in a house on Lipscomb Street in Fort Worth. The Texas School of Arts opened in 1932 in the home of artist Sallie Gillespie.[9] The school was owned and operated by Gillespie and two Fort Worth colleagues, Blanche McVeigh and Evaline Sellors. All three were alumnae of the Pennsylvania Academy of the Fine Arts.[10] Gillespie taught painting, McVeigh taught etching and figure drawing, and Sellors taught sculpture. The school offered courses throughout the day, including night and weekend classes, making it a primary training ground for people who held jobs. In the second year Gillespie withdrew, triggering a change in name and location. New space was rented, and Evaline Sellors hired Wade Jolly, a friend and fellow student from her academy days, to become the school's painting instructor. Renamed the Fort Worth School of Fine Arts, the institution soon became a magnet for aspiring artists from all parts of the city.[11] At the school, students received rigorous training, critical assessments, and exhibition opportunities.[12]

It was in the Fort Worth School of Fine Arts that core friendships were formed between Cuilty, Helfensteller, Johnson, and Utter. Utter, the son of a print shop owner, found in the school kindred spirits who were as interested in learning as he was (fig. 1). Helfensteller, the daughter of a construction superintendent, had abandoned art studies for several years, but the lure of the school drew her back. She, Utter, and Johnson, who worked full-time as an operator for Southwestern Bell Telephone and attended classes as she could, became close friends and sketching partners.[13] Lia Cuilty, the fourth member of the sketching group, was employed by a Fort Worth produce wholesaler and took courses at the Art Institute of Dallas before she enrolled at the school (fig. 2).

Another rising artist at the Fort Worth School of Fine Arts was Frank Preston Fisher Jr., who emerged in 1936 when his painting *The Fence* was

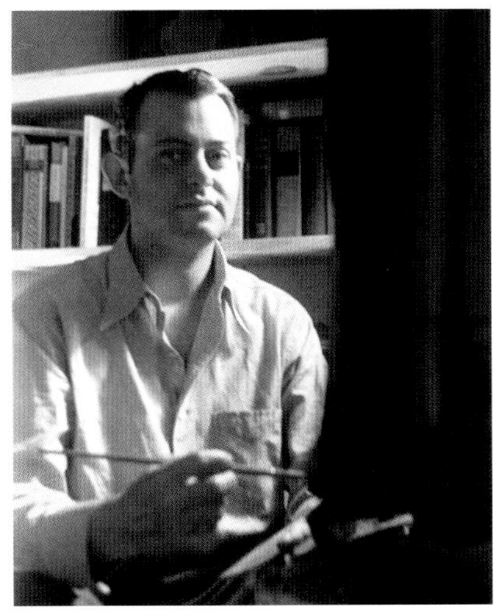

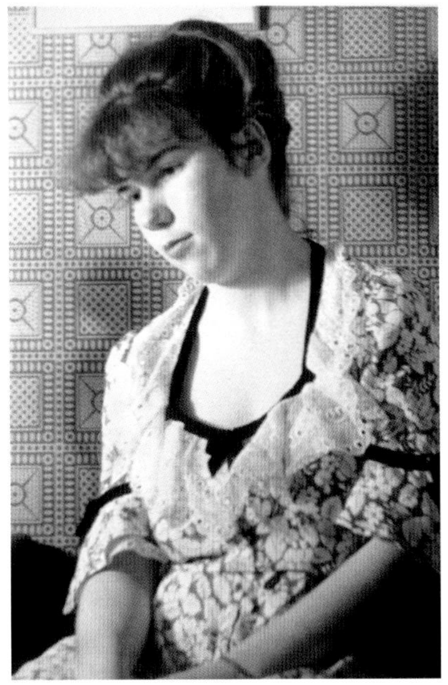

FIGURE **3** Dickson Reeder, 1943

FIGURE **4** Flora Reeder, ca. 1940

shown in the Texas Centennial Exposition in Dallas. Two years later, while they were still students at the school, Fisher and Utter exhibited paintings described by the *Fort Worth Star-Telegram* as "abstractions...forms that have never been seen on land or sea."[14] That article marked the first time works by Fort Worth artists had ever been characterized as abstract. In November 1938, Fisher, Utter, Helfensteller, and Johnson exhibited together.[15] Johnson later recalled Fisher as a man of unnerving eccentricity whose visibility fostered resentment among the artists who would go on to form the Fort Worth Circle. Indeed, as Fisher won recognition he became, in Johnson's view, more an obstacle to circumvent than a kindred spirit to embrace.[16]

Dickson Reeder, the Circle's eventual leader, was an art prodigy with a gift for portrait painting (fig. 3). Following high school, he trained extensively with portraitist Wayman Adams in New York and briefly operated a portrait studio in downtown Fort Worth. During an extended tour of Europe beginning in 1936, Reeder spent about a year in Paris, where he met Flora Blanc, a young painter from New York City (fig. 4). Through Blanc he met expatriate Englishman Stanley William Hayter, whose studio, Atelier 17, was famous as a laboratory and training ground for cutting-edge approaches to intaglio printmaking. Under Hayter's guidance, Reeder acquired printing skills that he would later use in Fort Worth.[17] Reeder and Blanc married in 1937 and settled in New York City, where she had family and he had high ambitions.

The vehicle that propelled these emerging artists into the public eye did not exist until 1939. During the Great Depression, Fort Worth's highest-profile exhibition space was located in the Carnegie Public Library (fig. 5). Through a shared arrangement, the library served as a home to the Fort Worth Art Association and its permanent collection of American paintings.[18] Exhibitions in the public art gallery were tightly controlled, and shows featuring local artists were not permitted.[19] This changed in 1938, however, when the Carnegie Library's board of trustees paved the way for the building to be razed so that a new, larger library could be built in its place. This led to the reorganization of the association's leadership group, a tumultuous affair that swept the earliest, entrenched leaders from office and replaced them with younger, more open-minded people. In June 1939, under the leadership of Edwin Bewley Sr., the Fort Worth Art Association opened its doors to local artists by inaugurating the gallery in the new Fort Worth Public Library with the first citywide *Fort Worth Artists Exhibition*.[20] Ninety-nine paintings, prints, and sculptures were displayed, making it the largest showing of local art ever assembled in the city (fig. 6). The publicity and public interest generated by the exhibition convinced the leaders of the association to adopt an annual, competitive exhibition. The *Local Artists*

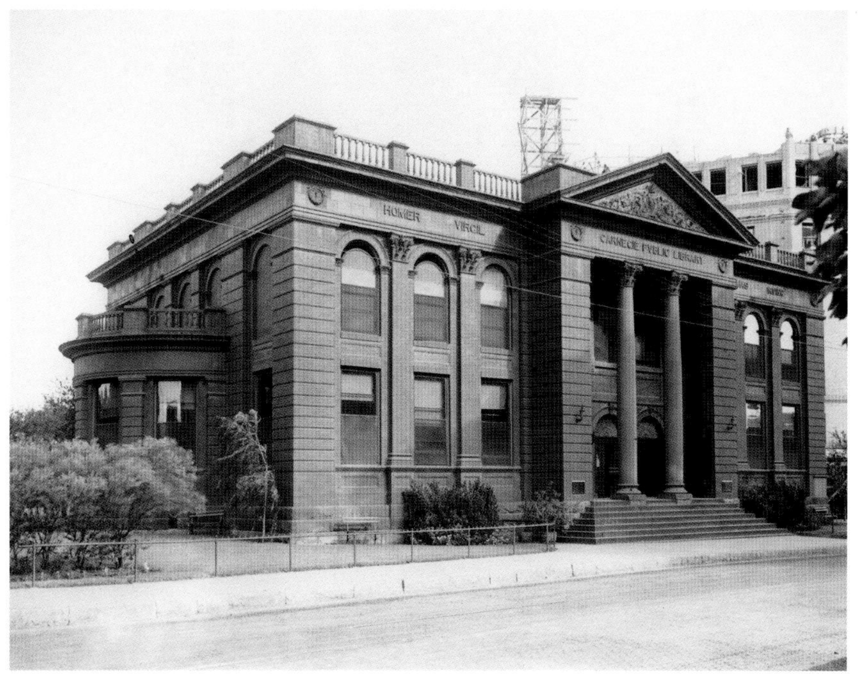

FIGURE 5 Carnegie Public Library, Fort Worth, Texas, ca. 1910

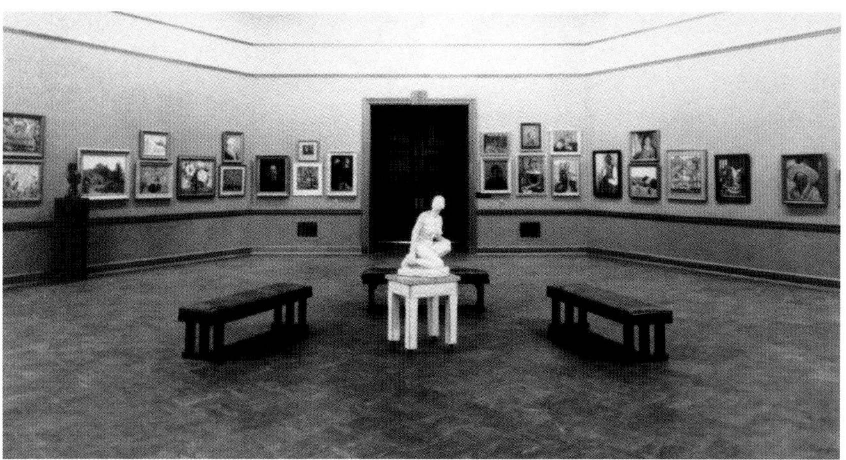

FIGURE 6 The Fort Worth Public Library Art Gallery, where much of the Circle's art was displayed throughout the 1940s, ca. 1940

Show, or the *Local* as it came to be known, would be the springboard that catapulted the restless and eager artists of the Fort Worth Circle into full view. For the next fifteen years, through the worst and best of times, the gallery of the public library served as a prime mover in changing the art of the city.

Frank Fisher became the first alumnus of the Fort Worth School of Fine Arts to receive critical scrutiny when he was awarded First Prize in the inaugural exhibition. Of his entry, *Still Life* (pl. 5), the *Fort Worth Star-Telegram* reported, "In making the award, the jury stated that the picture, a still life in oil, was cited as outstanding because it represented the most creative and imaginative work, and they considered it the type of painting that should be encouraged."[21] Lia Cuilty, Veronica Helfensteller, Marjorie Johnson, Sara Shannon, and Bror Utter also exhibited works in the show.

The Fort Worth Art Association's new openness to exhibiting local art seemed to forecast an even broader range of opportunity for Texas artists. In February 1940 a juried competition, open to artists statewide, debuted: the *Texas General Exhibition*. The show was conceived by the Museum of Fine Arts of Houston, the Dallas Museum of Fine Arts (now known as the Dallas Museum of Art), and the Witte Museum in San Antonio, and it traveled to all three venues. Acceptance into the *Texas General*, as it was called, offered a degree of exposure previously unavailable to Texas artists, so inclusion in the exhibition was widely sought. Four Fort Worth artists were accepted into the first *Texas General*, including Blanche McVeigh, Evaline Sellors, and Veronica Helfensteller, who received a Special Mention for her watercolor *Old Theatre*. Helfensteller won Second Prize in the *Local* that year as well for her watercolor *K. of C. General Store*. First Prize for oil painting in the 1940 *Local* went again to Frank Fisher for his *Farm at Early Morning*, a regionalist work marked with a modernist sensibility.[22]

In the fall of 1940, Dickson Reeder returned to his hometown, where he quickly secured portrait commissions, renewed old friendships, and assumed a teaching position at Texas Wesleyan College in east Fort Worth.[23] Once settled, he and Flora initiated the salon lifestyle they had enjoyed in Paris and New York. Their bohemian attitudes, sociability, and refined views on art and music quickly attracted followers. Every Saturday night the Reeders' home filled with artists, musicians, and friends eager to imbibe and debate. A gifted dancer, Flora frequently starred in impromptu ballets, and she and Dickson often played instruments while others performed (fig. 7). The atmosphere — perpetually enlivened by recorded strains of Shostakovich, Stravinsky, and Ravel — along with the ongoing parade of interesting characters marked the home as a destination for people seeking to experience and enjoy the Reeders' liberated ways. Their most frequent houseguests were the artists and painters Dickson knew and considered his peers, the artists of the burgeoning Circle. In this crucible of socialization, a remarkable closeness between Bomar, Cuilty, Helfensteller, Shannon, Utter, and the Reeders was forged (fig. 8).

If a particular point in time was seminal in the rise of Fort Worth modernism, it was the fateful year of 1941. In the final *Local Artists Show* held before the war, Reeder won First Prize for his commissioned portrait *The Shannon Children* (pl. 33). With Glenn and Ogden Shannon as his subjects, Reeder painted two figures situated in a starkly geometric space, then rendered the composition with an unconventional perspective. The painting was quite unlike anything seen in Fort Worth to that time. In

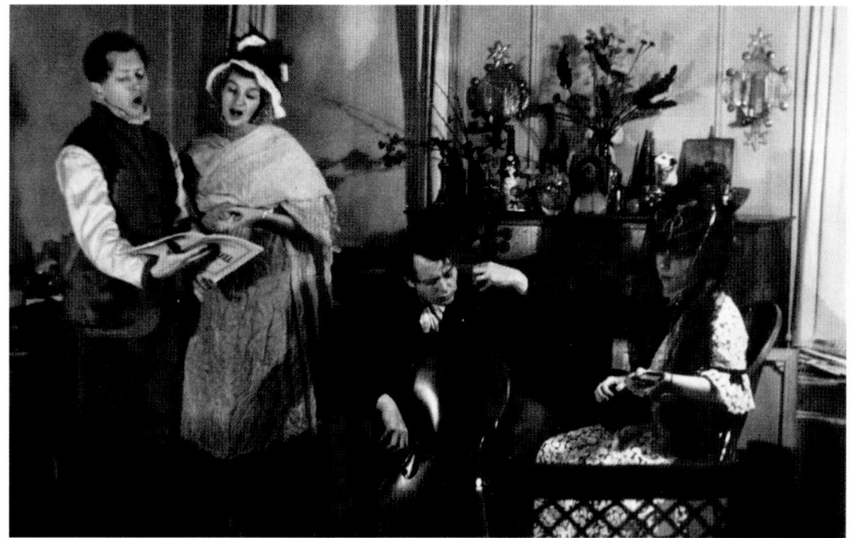

FIGURE **7** At their parties, the Reeders often played instruments while their guests sang, 1943

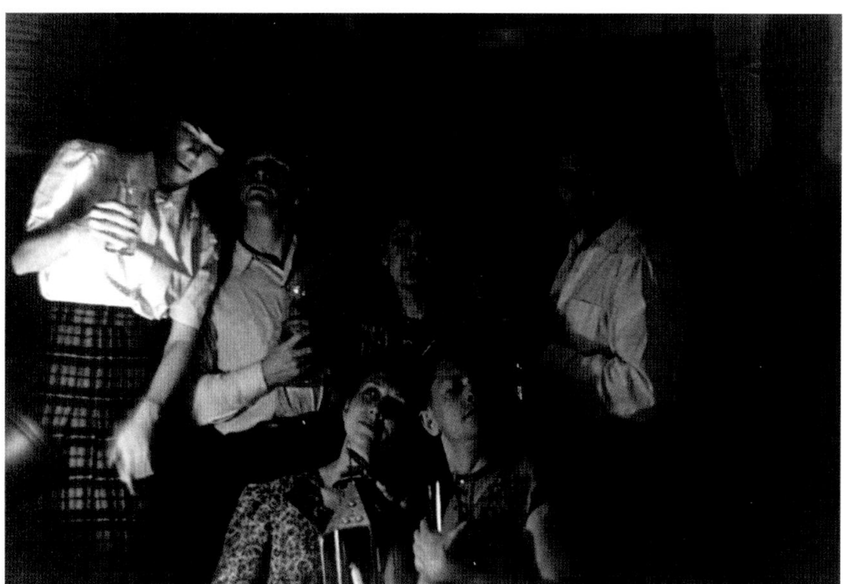

FIGURE **8** Front row: Veronica Helfensteller, Bror Utter; back row: Flora Blanc Reeder, Kelly Fearing, Lia Cuilty, and Dickson Reeder, n.d.

retrospect, the work can be considered an attempt at American surrealism, but in truth Reeder regarded this artistic style as a European fad.[24] Clearly, the artist was searching for a fresh approach to portraiture. The painting's success established Reeder's reputation as a visionary and, with its eccentric originality, pointed in a direction his peers in the Circle would eagerly follow. Over the next several years Reeder and others in the group, particularly Bror Utter, produced numerous figural studies set in imaginary space.

Flora Blanc, Helfensteller, Marjorie Johnson, and Utter also exhibited works in the 1941 *Local*. Notably absent was Frank Fisher. That January, Fisher had resigned as president of the Allied Artists Club, and the last exhibition of his work took place in November, when a group of his abstract paintings was shown at Texas Wesleyan College.[25] As word of mental illness circulated, Frank Fisher quietly disappeared from public view.[26] It was a tragic and irreversible conclusion to the career of a highly experimental painter.

In March 1941 Dickson Reeder wrote, "But now, due to the chaotic state of the world, there seems to be the beginning of the long-awaited courtship of art and America."[27] He was right. But on December 7 that courtship was rendered virtually invisible against the black sky of Pearl Harbor. In the weeks and months following the Japanese attack, every cultural organization in every city across the country was faced with the hard decision of how to operate in the wartime environment. The Fort Worth Art Association's incoming president, Samuel Benton Cantey III, took the view that the public interest would be better served by maintaining a semblance of normalcy than by suspending the association's activities. Though chronically short of money,[28] the association over the next four years consistently presented exhibitions and art education programs for the city of Fort Worth. Mirroring the association's tack, the *Texas General Exhibition*, still sponsored by the state's three major art museums at the time, was presented every winter from 1942 to 1945.

The *Local* also continued to be held every spring throughout the duration of the war, and for his enigmatic figure study *Waiting Lady*, Bror Utter was awarded First Prize in the 1942 show, the first held during the global conflict. Second Prize that April went to Veronica Helfensteller for her pastel *Etcher's Glove and Conch Shell*. The 1942 *Local* was also noteworthy for the first appearance of work by Bill Bomar, who had three paintings accepted by the jury.

The priorities and daily lives of almost everyone were reshaped by the hard realities of World War II. Dickson Reeder was among a number of area artists hired to work as illustrators at Consolidated Vultee Aircraft in west Fort Worth.[29] Veronica Helfensteller (fig. 9) worked as the personal secretary to Fort Worth general contractor James T. Taylor, assisting him in completing numerous war-related construction contracts.[30] Marjorie Johnson (fig. 10) served for three years with the WAVES, or Women Accepted for Volunteer Emergency Service. Bror Utter appeared before the draft board but was not selected for military service; he continued to work in his father's lithographic printing business for the duration of the war.[31] Bill Bomar, a cerebral palsy victim from birth, was not a candidate for the military. During the war, he divided his time between his parents' home in Fort Worth and his studio apartment in the Chelsea Hotel in New York City (fig. 11). Despite the upheaval in their lives, each of the Circle artists continued to produce and exhibit work as time allowed.[32]

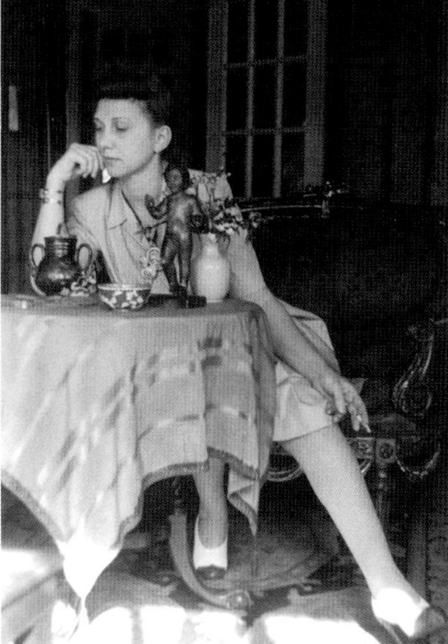

FIGURE **9** Veronica Helfensteller, ca. 1945

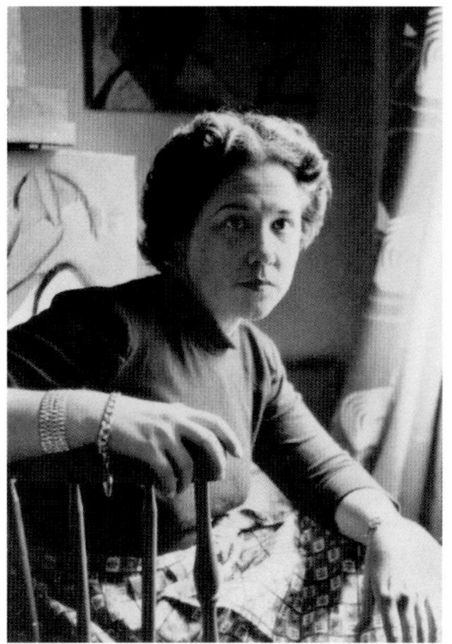

FIGURE **10** Marjorie Johnson, 1949

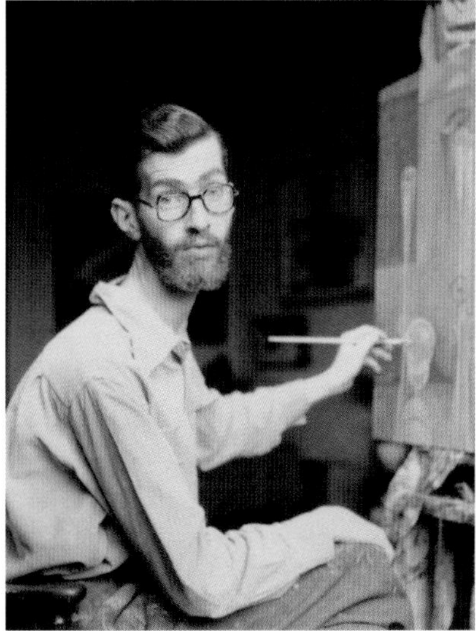

FIGURE **11** Bill Bomar, New York City, 1948

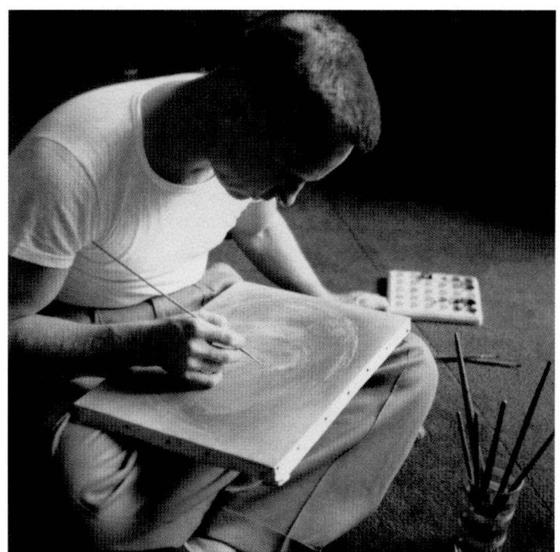

FIGURE **12** Kelly Fearing in Bill Bomar's Chelsea Hotel apartment, 1948

The war would also introduce a new member into the Circle. Kelly Fearing (fig. 12), a meditative artist with an experimental bent, was employed as a middle-school teacher in Winnfield, Louisiana, when war broke out. In 1943, through government placement, Fearing was sent to train as a draftsman at Consolidated Vultee Aircraft, paving the way for his introduction to Dickson Reeder.

Among the ranks of Fort Worth painters, all significant awards and serious recognition during the final years of the war went to artists considered the new elite. Two of the top three paintings from the 1943 *Local Artists Show*, works by Helfensteller and portraitist Emily Guthrie Smith, were acquired for the permanent collection of the Dallas Museum of Fine Arts.[33] First Prize was again awarded to Dickson Reeder, but the highest prize in that year's statewide *Texas General Exhibition* went to Bror Utter for *The Visitors*. In May 1943, the Fort Worth Art Association claimed a larger role in promoting local talent by initiating an annual solo exhibition in the galleries of the Fort Worth Public Library. Blanche McVeigh, the pioneering etching and drawing instructor at the Fort Worth School of Fine Arts, was the first artist featured in this way, followed in 1944 by her student Veronica Helfensteller. The Helfensteller exhibition solidified that artist's reputation as the region's leading practitioner of what Patricia Peck, art critic for the *Dallas Morning News*, called "reasonable unreality.... There are giraffes at lunch and performing baboons and ladies riding through the woods on beautiful horses," Peck wrote. "The small paintings...are entirely charming."[34] Bill Bomar was the First Prize winner in the 1944 *Local*.

During the war, the *Local Artists Show* was faithfully covered in the pages of the *Fort Worth Star-Telegram* by art critic Ida Belle Hicks. But it was Peck at the *Dallas Morning News* who came closer than anyone to quantifying some of the essential and mystifying characteristics of the art of the Fort Worth Circle. Her review of the 1944 *Local* hinged on the observation that "there is a curious in-turned quality about the show. The pictures have sharpness and life but it is the vitality of introspection and the energy of escape."[35]

The 1944 *Local* was the most volatile of the wartime shows. "Conservatives will be shocked," Hicks wrote of the show. "But those who have kept in step with the upper-bracket artists of the day will feel that Fort Worth artists are staying abreast of the modern movement."[36] Visitors to the exhibition were not confronted by gritty scenes of battle or comforted by images of patriotic zeal. Instead, they were challenged by baffling figure paintings from Bror Utter, difficult abstractions by Bill Bomar and Dickson Reeder, and fanciful

FIGURE **13** Sara Shannon, 1943

FIGURE **14** Installation photograph of *Six Texas Painters*, Weyhe Gallery, New York City, September 1944

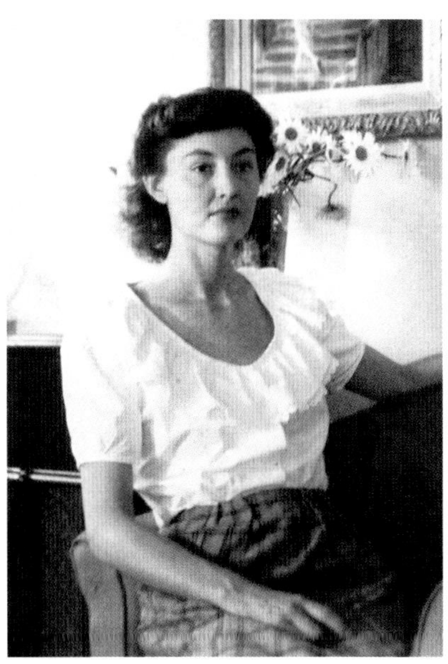

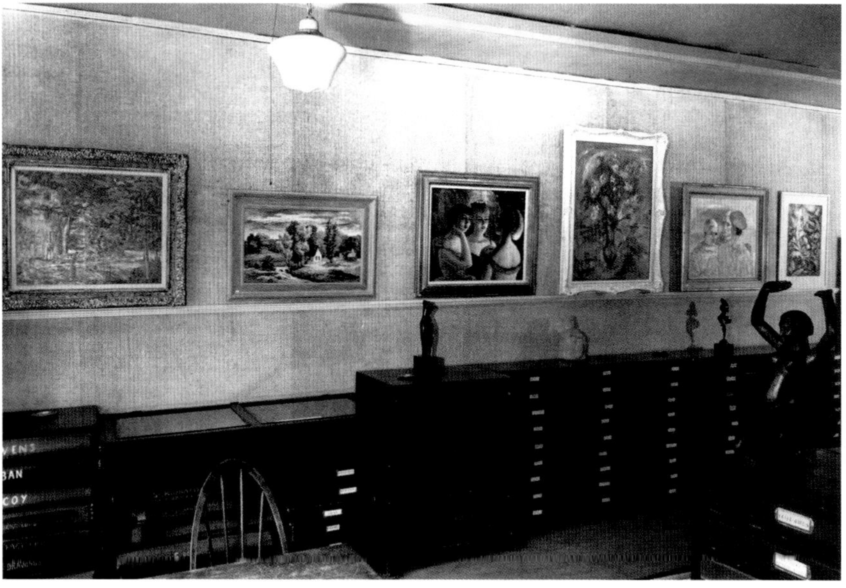

landscapes by Veronica Helfensteller and Sara Shannon (fig. 13). Alongside Kelly Fearing's memory painting of servicemen dancing the night away with partners furnished by the USO, viewers encountered unconventional portraits by Bomar and Flora Blanc. Patricia Peck predicted the show would be "controversial" for its "new modes of expression."[37] These fresh expressions seemed to baffle and almost disgust *Fort Worth Press* columnist Edith Guedry, who referred in her review to "exhibitionistic plaques that say nothing in particular, portraits that suggest boogie woogie music, masque still lifes that are unexplainable, and figure groups playing around a coffin." The viewer will ask some "rather harsh questions" about this artwork, she wrote, "and can be pretty certain that he is right in his answers."[38] There was clearly an evocative power in the personal nature of the Circle's art. Each artist was concerned not with what others would think about their work, but rather with what they themselves felt compelled to create. It was this fundamental disposition that made their work a kind of art that few in Fort Worth had ever seen.

Six Texas Painters — an exhibition featuring the work of Bomar, Helfensteller, the Reeders, and Utter, plus artist Donald Vogel from Dallas — is a watershed in the Circle's history and generated extensive publicity when it opened in New York City in September 1944. The exhibition of thirty paintings was held at the Weyhe Gallery on Lexington Avenue (fig. 14). The media coverage in Fort Worth and New York marked the first time that the Fort Worth artists were portrayed as a compatible and independent-minded group. "The paintings by the six young Texas artists...appear at once individualized and congenially related," the reviewer Edward Jewell wrote in the *New York Times*, "and the joyousness of the ensemble effort proves infectious."[39] This idea of a group of artists working together while maintaining distinct identities was introduced by an insightful Patricia Peck commentary on the back cover of the exhibition catalogue: "A small group of non-specific regionalists have been busily painting.... The drama of form in bizarre and fanciful settings, the excitement of texture, and the endless elegance of color have been their principal preoccupations. They are closely knit. They have known each other for years, have worked and painted together. They criticize each other without restraint and admire each other freely and deeply. Each has studied and traveled outside of Texas, but each is a Texan, either by birth or adoption."[40] The *Fort Worth Star-Telegram* ran two extensive articles on the show, and Guedry of the *Press* seems to have come around to the Circle's "new ways" in her complimentary article on the exhibition.[41] The show also earned a brief but favorable mention in the *New York Sun*,[42] and Maude Riley of *Art Digest* marveled at the show's variety and lack of regional influence.

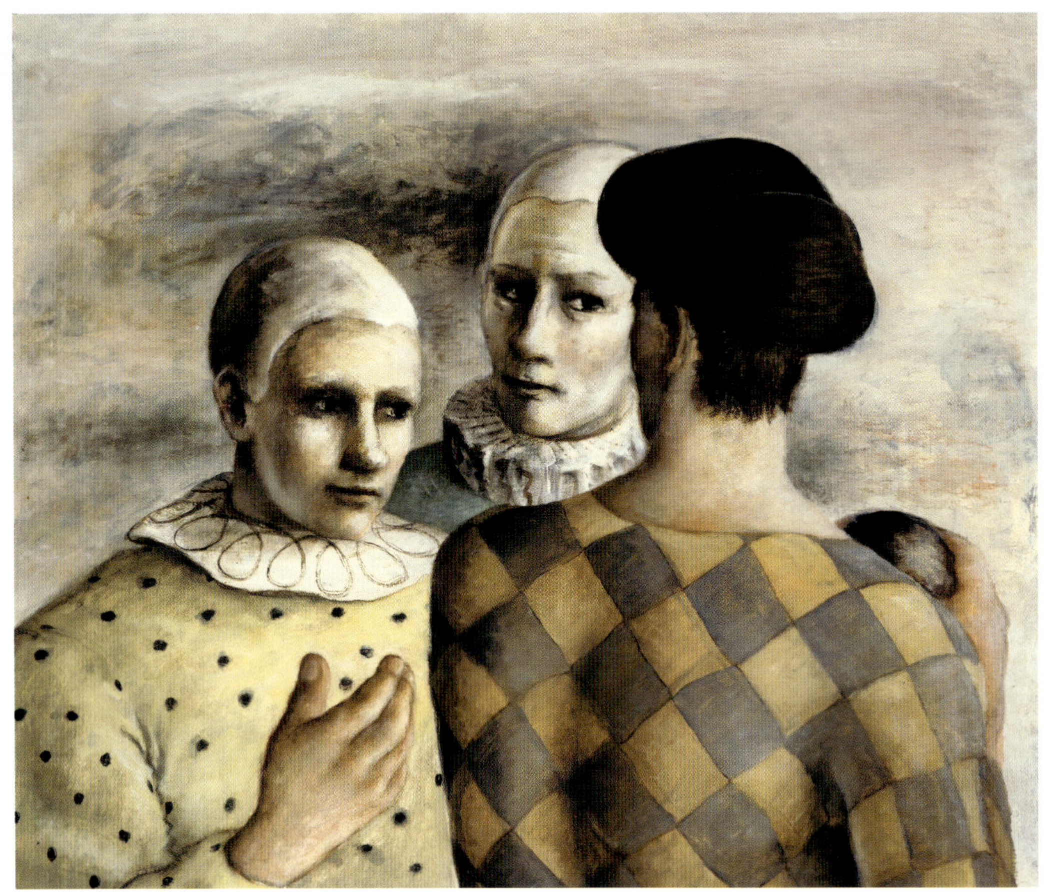

FIGURE **15**
Dickson Reeder,
The Dispute,
1944

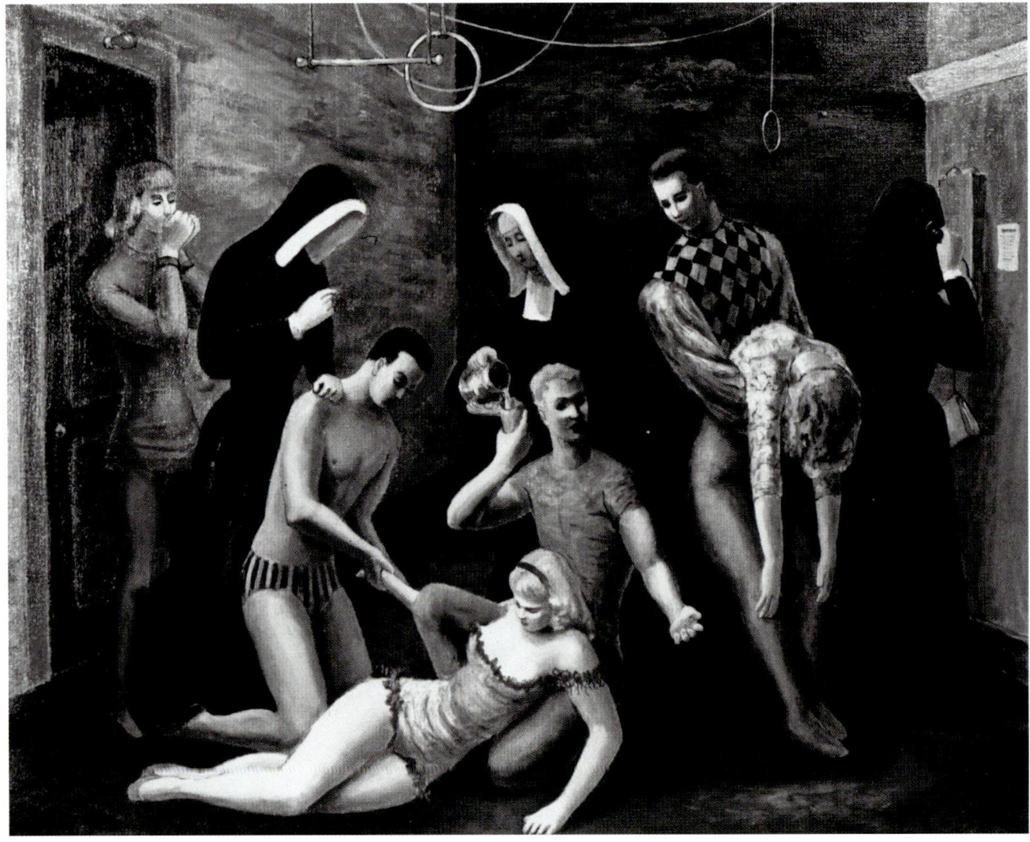

FIGURE **16**
Bror Utter,
Accident at Rehearsal,
1944

The Dispute (fig. 15), Reeder's image of bloodless conflict, drew particular attention from Riley, as did Bror Utter's peculiar and richly narrative *Accident at Rehearsal* (fig. 16): "Something amusingly illusory has been added to surrealism's repertoire," she observed.[43]

In the same year as the Weyhe Gallery show, six members of the Circle were turning their voracious curiosity and energy to printmaking. Spearheaded by Veronica Helfensteller and fueled by the Reeders' technical knowledge, these three, along with Lia Cuilty, Kelly Fearing, and Bror Utter, entered a white-hot period of experimental printmaking.[44] Their weekly sessions, held in Helfensteller's studio, produced an astonishing and innovative array of images. Using techniques the Reeders had learned from Stanley William Hayter; ink, paper, and plates furnished by Utter; and Helfensteller's small etching press, the group explored the elastic and intrinsic worlds of surrealism and abstraction. Their prints, many of which are reproduced for the first time in these pages, manifest an advanced esthetic. They were shown together only once, at the Fort Worth Public Library in February 1945. In her review in the *Star-Telegram*, Hicks dutifully published a detailed list of the exhibition's contents, but suggested that her readers seek out "an expert analyst, schooled in the psychological aspects of art," to explain the works.[45]

The Circle's peculiar brand of modernism was again on full display in the 1945 *Local*, the last held during wartime. Like Dickson Reeder's First Prize winner four years earlier, Kelly Fearing's *The Kite Flyers*, which took First Prize in this exhibition, situates its figures in imaginary space (pl. 69). Fearing placed his young subjects in a landscape filled with upright triangular stones, an obelisk, and Victorian-era farmhouses. Reeder took Second Prize with his painting *The Explanation*, which portrays three female dancers interacting in a windowless, featureless room illuminated by a bright, mysterious light. Lia Cuilty took Third Prize for her unusual work *The Grapevine Swing*, a painting that depicts a tiny redheaded girl playing beneath a canopy of stark, dead trees. In her review of the show, Hicks published photographs of each prizewinning artwork, but again offered only limited commentary, using imagery over critical assessment to inform her readership of the Circle's strange creative inclinations.[46]

The surrender of Germany on May 7, 1945, and Japan the following September birthed an unbridled optimism across the country, and in this spirit the citizens of Fort Worth turned their collective attention to the future. Core supporters of the Fort Worth Art Association, eager to realize the long-held dream of "the establishment and maintenance of a free public Art Museum in Fort Worth,"[47] backed an issuance of municipal bonds to fund the construction of a new building. But even with the support of many of Fort

Worth's most influential citizens, the process proved slow and difficult. As a result, the home of the association and the center of its activities remained housed on the second floor of the Fort Worth Public Library for eight more years. The day-to-day administration of the association's programs was taken over in 1945 by Sallie Gillespie, an old friend to most of the Circle artists, and though Sam Cantey was succeeded as president by O. P. Newberry in 1944, he remained at the center of the association's leadership. During the postwar years, the unconditional faith of these three in the value of local art never wavered, and association resources were consistently dedicated to promoting it.

Soon after the war ended, Bror Utter's ascendance in the Texas art world went into high gear. For his provocative masterwork *The Dreamer* (pl. 82), Utter was awarded First Prize in the 1946 *Local*. That same year his art was the subject of a solo exhibition mounted by the Fort Worth Art Association. Utter soon entered an explosive period of creative experimentation with what he termed "embellished forms,"[48] or abstract constructions based on the human figure. It was an innovation that made him famous among art groups across the state.[49] Sometimes he rendered the figures male and female, at other times he depicted them as androgynous. Regardless, they appear animated and alive on the picture plane. These forms were a vehicle of abstract design unique to Utter's art, and while he continued to produce expressive landscapes, the majority of his paintings in the postwar 1940s reflect a deep fascination with the human form. With his rise in popularity, Utter was one of the first artists hired to conduct regularly scheduled art classes in the Fort Worth Public Library, where he quickly discovered an innate talent for teaching.

The 1946 *Local* launched the careers of two young artists who would become the last to be associated with the Fort Worth Circle, Cynthia Brants (fig. 17) and George Grammer (fig. 18). Beautiful, socially prominent, fiercely independent, and a trained and gifted painter, Brants had attended Sarah Lawrence College in Bronxville, New York, because the school offered a four-year degree in painting. Her paintings reflected the influences of Cézanne and the cubists and introduced a new dimension into the body of local work. As her work matured, Brants' paintings became perennial favorites among the judges of the *Local*. George Grammer was a 1945 graduate of Fort Worth's Paschal High School. He would enjoy his best years as a painter in the 1950s and beyond, but at the age of nineteen he was recognized by Dickson Reeder and Kelly Fearing as a talent to be admired. Although he was inexperienced, Grammer possessed a rich imagination and exercised meticulous execution in

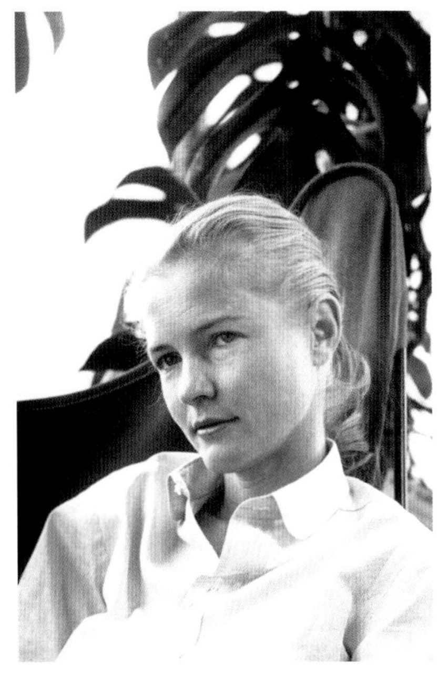

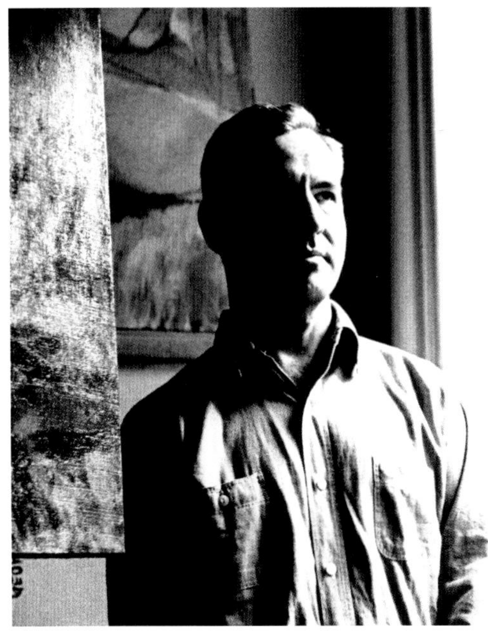

FIGURE 17 Cynthia Brants, 1954

FIGURE 18 George Grammer, ca. 1955

his work. He would become known for complex, abstracted images of cityscapes and night scenes.

Following the war, Dickson Reeder worked to solidify his reputation as a top-tier portraitist, a turn that would produce one of his finest likenesses, *Portrait of Bill Bomar* (pl. 36). Reeder's task was complicated by the presence of the gifted Emily Guthrie Smith. While she never ventured into abstraction with the members of the Circle, Smith was an excellent portraitist and friendly competitor in the local market, particularly with Reeder. Reeder's career trajectory altered significantly, however, when he and his wife committed to launching the Reeder Children's School of Theater and Design. With Dickson creating sets and costumes and Flora in charge of training the school's young actors, none older than fourteen, the Reeder School presented its first production, William Makepeace Thackeray's *The Rose and the Ring*, in the Paschal High School auditorium in 1946. The Reeders' cultural prominence and the excellence of the program paid off in good publicity and encouraging community support. Thus began an enterprise that, during the next twelve years, consumed the bulk of the Reeders' time and energy and enabled hundreds of Fort Worth youth and their parents to experience a panoramic view of the interrelation of "the arts" (fig. 19).

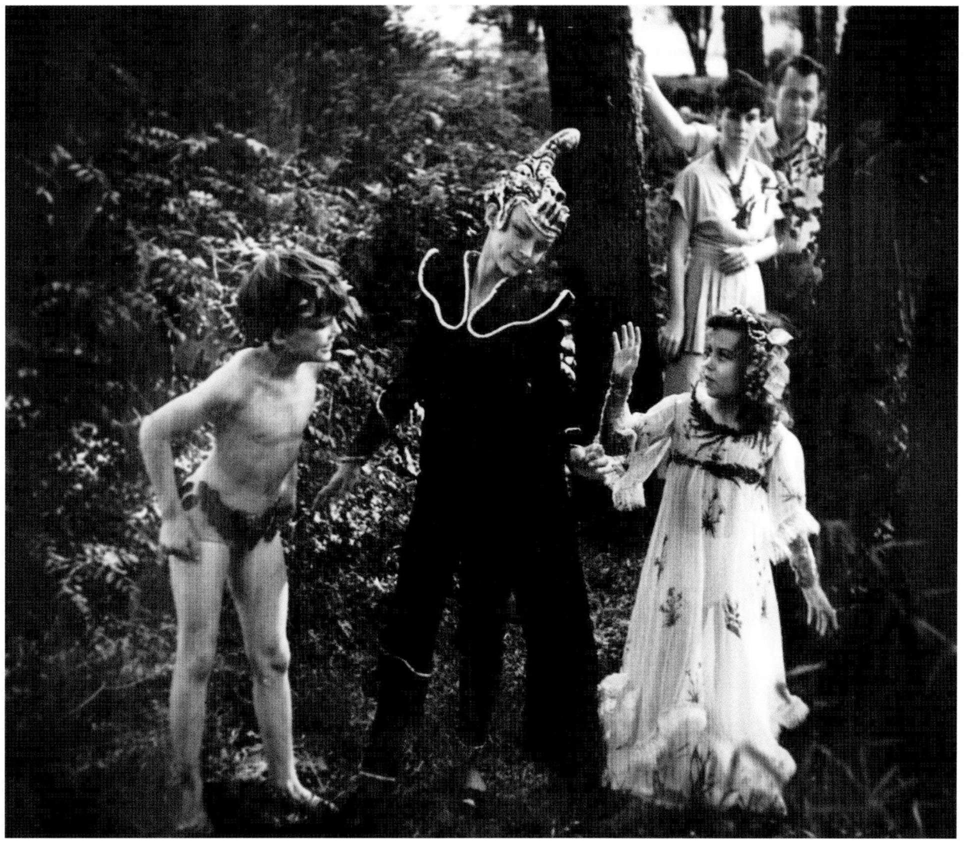

FIGURE **19**
With Dickson and Flora looking on, a trio of actors performs in the Reeder Children's School production of *A Midsummer Night's Dream*, 1948

For his part in the postwar years, Bill Bomar attained a notable level of visibility through several well-publicized exhibitions in New York and Fort Worth. He was the only artist of the Circle to enjoy full-time representation in a New York gallery.[50] His first solo exhibition opened at the Weyhe Gallery in September 1946 to a good review in the *New York Times*: "The paintings are...unaffected by any isms of any kind and they carry conviction," the critic Howard Devree wrote. "Bomar introduces an almost mystical touch reminiscent of some of Blake's verse.... It is a very interesting first show."[51] Interest in Bomar gained momentum when the Fort Worth Art Association organized a solo show of his work in December the following year.[52] Despite his physical affliction and limitations, Bomar produced exacting portraits and energetic landscapes and still lifes; but it was on his abstractions that he built his reputation. His early works, such as *Between Streets*, were based largely on empirical imagery. As he matured, he filled his paintings with recurring shapes and symbols, the meanings of which only Bomar understood. As a man of wealth, he collected art at a high level. His Chelsea Hotel apartment became famous among other artists of the Circle as a destination where works by Klee, Kandinsky, and Modigliani could be admired and studied (fig. 20). Bomar was joined in New York City after the war by Marjorie Johnson and newlywed Sara Shannon Steel, both of whom became full-time Manhattan residents. Bomar's desire to remain close to the artists in the Circle prompted frequent visits home, which were the keys to his being regularly invited to compete in the *Local*. In 1948, he won First Prize for his *Web and Roses* (pl. 64).

A genuine and symbiotic friendship between the artists of the Circle and Sam Cantey was fundamental to the avant-garde image of both and to the continued rise of the artists. Cantey and his wife, Betsy, were the earliest and most ardent of the group's admirers (fig. 21). Following his term as president of the Fort Worth Art Association, Cantey was deeply involved in the postwar drive for a public art museum in Fort Worth. He was unusually receptive to art's complexities and perfectly positioned socially to encourage others to be open-minded as well. He was the chief organizer and relentless promoter of the *Local*, and it was largely through his efforts that the show became one of Fort Worth's most highly anticipated social events and the year's best opportunity for acquiring the work of area artists.[53] Cantey collected paintings, prints, and drawings of the Circle and actively lobbied others to do the same. He created additional interest among Fort Worth's monied collectors by holding small, solo exhibitions in his home. It was through such an arrangement that Cantey raised funds for Kelly Fearing's entry into the Master's program at Columbia University in 1947, an opportunity the artist ultimately bypassed in favor of an offer to join the art faculty at the

FIGURE **20** Lia Cuilty, Marjorie Johnson, and Bill Bomar in New York City, 1949

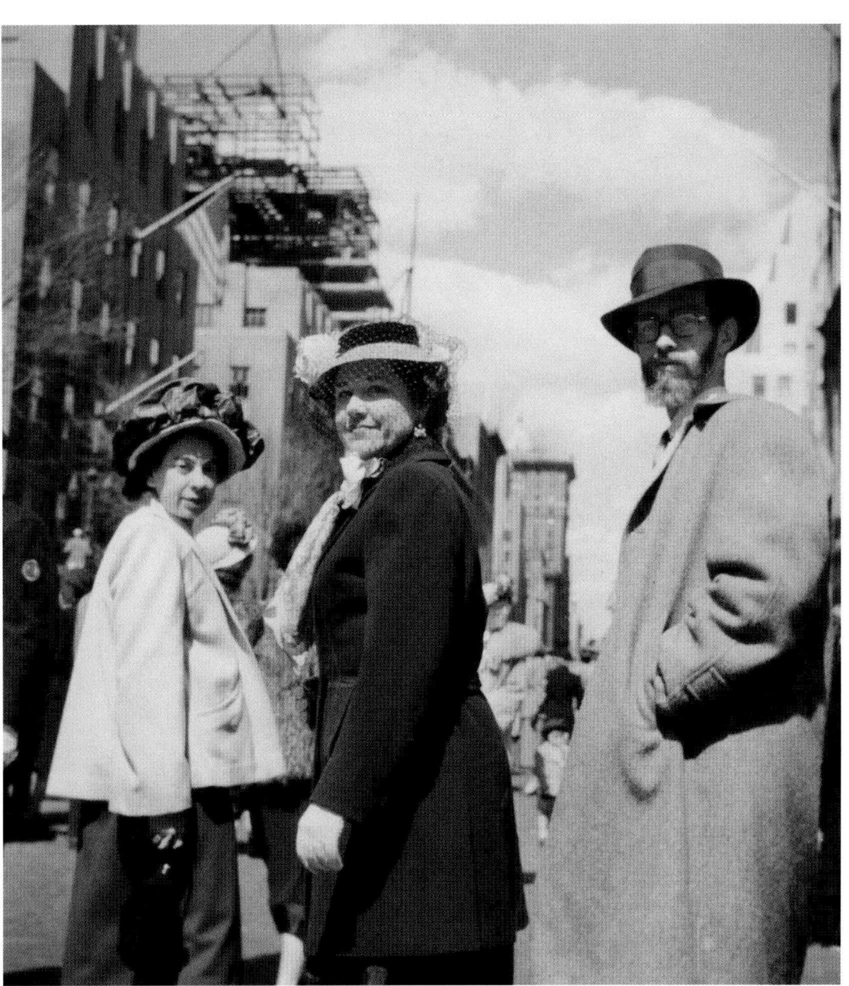

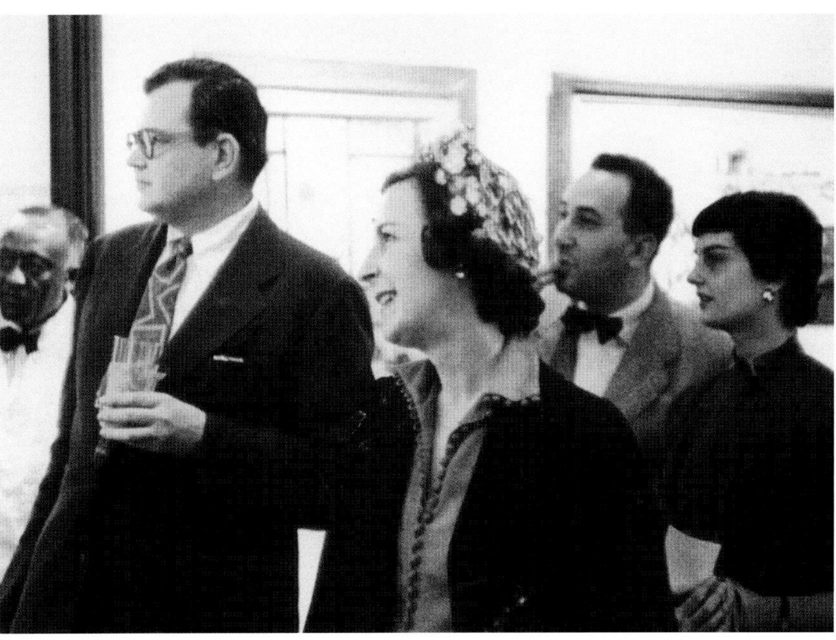

FIGURE **21** Sam and Betsy Cantey, ca. 1950s

University of Texas, Austin. Cantey counted Bill Bomar, Cynthia Brants, Lia Cuilty, Kelly Fearing, the Reeders, and Bror Utter among his closest friends, and he in turn was viewed by them as a peer and indispensable friend.

With the publication of *Dallas Morning News* columnist John Rosenfield's observation that a "school" of artists was at work in Fort Worth, Cantey had the tool he needed to hammer home this tantalizing concept. His admiration for the artists of the Circle was already well known, and with this nod from Rosenfield, Cantey began to encourage collectors to pay attention to new artists as well, particularly war veteran McKie Trotter. A painter from Georgia, Trotter carried a deep commitment to modernism when he joined the art faculty of Texas Wesleyan College in 1948. Within a few short years, and due largely to Cantey's efforts through the *Local*, a new family of names — including Jack Boynton, David Brownlow, John Erikson, and Charles T. Williams — would also become known to collectors as artists of the "Fort Worth School."

Dickson Reeder and Bror Utter dominated the 1949 *Local*, the last of the decade. Featuring beautifully rendered figures posed within arched compartments, Utter's First Prize painting, *Cloisters* (fig. 22), was recognized as a clear summation of the artist's output to that time. Reeder took Second Prize for *Charles*, an insightful and utterly engaging portrait of Charles McCally, a student at the Reeder School (pl. 38). Marjorie Johnson won Third Prize for *Still Life with Blue Pitcher*.

In 1950, ten years after the Circle artists first exhibited their work, the young Cynthia Brants took center stage, and the Fort Worth art world began to steadily transform around her. Brants' distinctive color-space theory of painting garnered many admirers. She was awarded First Prize in the *Local* in 1950 for *Rooftops of Florence*, and she benefited greatly from a successful solo show in December of that year. Edith Halpert selected paintings by Brants and George Grammer for inclusion in a prestigious group exhibition at Halpert's Downtown Gallery in New York City in 1951.[54] That same year, Betty McLean founded the first contemporary art gallery in Dallas, and six of her stable of nine artists, including Brants and George Grammer, were recruited from the original Fort Worth Circle.[55]

The Circle's era of dominance was near an end. The final generational change took place in the early 1950s with the appearance of a new group of modernist painters centered at Texas Christian University in Fort Worth. The group included TCU art instructor John Erickson and his student Jack Boynton. Both quickly became First Prize winners in the *Local*. McKie Trotter moved from Texas Wesleyan College to join the TCU art department faculty in 1954, which further bolstered this shift of activity. Perhaps the most significant figure to appear from the TCU environment was the

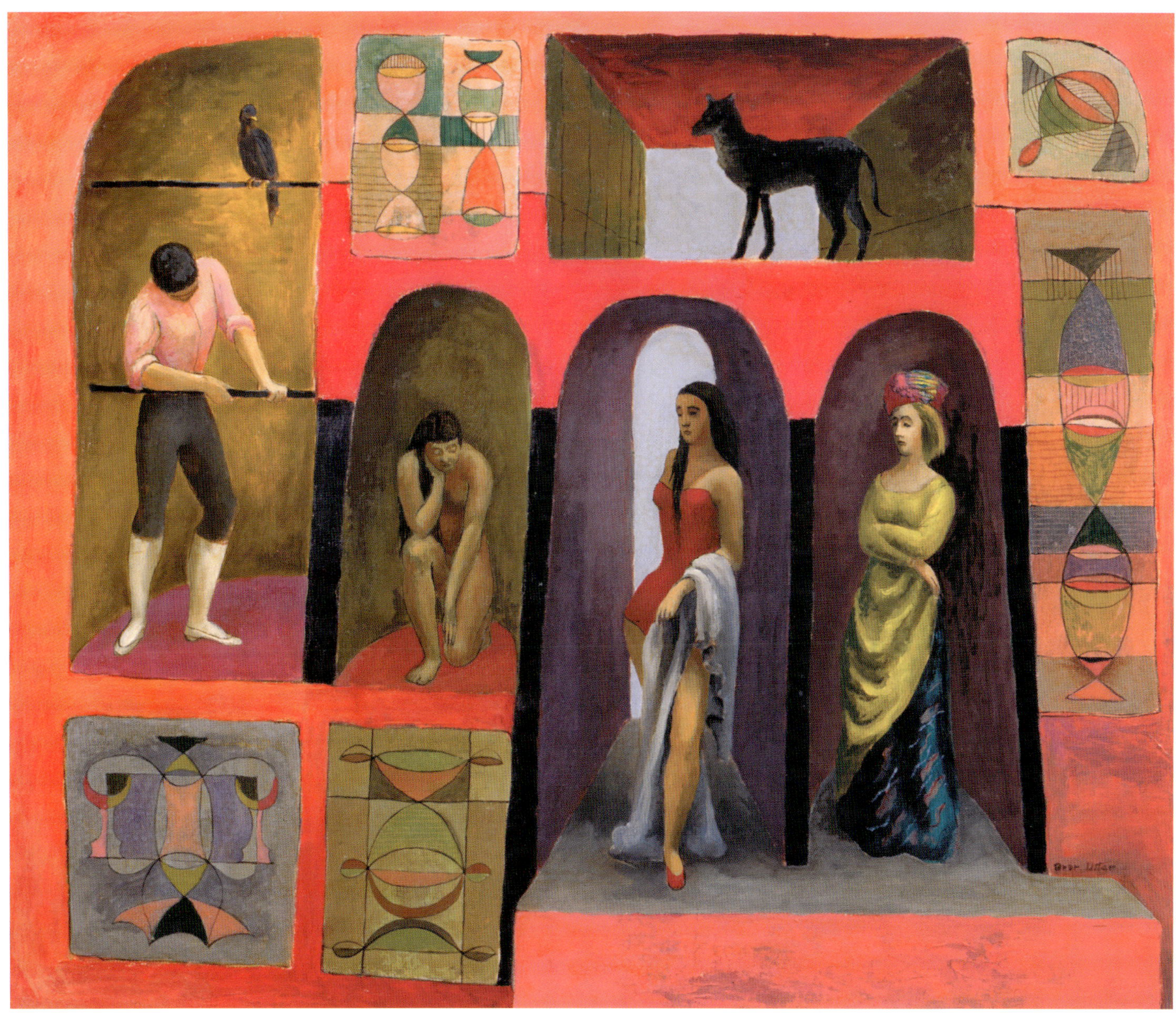

FIGURE **22** Bror Utter, *Cloisters*, 1948

brilliant sculptor Charles T. Williams. Boynton, Trotter, and Williams were all awarded solo shows by the Fort Worth Art Association in the 1950s.

On October 8, 1954, in elaborate ceremonies, the city's first public art museum was dedicated. The occasion marked the culmination of eight years of fundraising and lobbying by Sam Cantey, Dan Defenbacher, Robert Windfohr, and other Fort Worth Art Association leaders. The Fort Worth Art Center was inaugurated with an enormous exhibition covering five centuries of Occidental art. Works representing the Italian Renaissance through Abstract Expressionism were borrowed from across the country and brought to Fort Worth for the occasion.[56] NBC affiliate WBAP broadcast the gala Saturday night opening on live TV.

Set aside in one small gallery of the new building hung a more tranquil show, one with its own theme and its own catalogue. In this gallery, seventeen years of prizewinning artworks from the *Local Artists Show* were shown together for the first time.[57] Sam Cantey had looked for them all summer.[58] The exhibition, *Seventeen Years*, was a reminder of the critical role local artists had played in keeping an appreciation for the visual arts alive and growing, even during times of great trial and even greater uncertainty. Most importantly, it was his way of acknowledging the influence of the members of the Fort Worth Circle on himself and many others. Looking back, Cantey could clearly see that the Circle's unconventional vision had presaged art's direction when no one knew exactly where it was going.

By the mid-1950s, in parallel with the rise of the New York School in the East, the center of the Texas art world shifted to Houston.[59] The intimate modernism favored by the artists of the Fort Worth Circle was pushed aside by newer, more hard-edged ideas. But the Circle's legacy of change and openness to the unlimited boundaries of art was firmly planted. The interest of collectors and the support of Sam Cantey remained strong, and so the work of the Circle continued to sell. Their artworks, on display in homes throughout the city and state, still serve as unwavering reminders of the Circle's pioneering uniqueness.

In the long afterglow of their dominance, the Circle artists remained remarkably close-knit, even as the group largely dispersed: Bomar, Grammer, Johnson, and Shannon to New York; Fearing to Austin; and Helfensteller to Santa Fe. Cynthia Brants, Lia Cuilty, the Reeders, and Bror Utter remained in Fort Worth. For each one, many years of productivity remained ahead. For them, the life of an artist was sometimes glamorous, often maddening, but the only life they ever wanted and the only path they ever intended to follow. In their work, and for the rest of their lives, none ever tired of the joy of creation or bringing new meaning to the ethereal language called art.

1 Alexandre Hogue, "Progressive Texas," *Art Digest*, 10:17, 1 June 1936, pp. 17–18. In the article, Hogue berates newspapers in Fort Worth and other Texas cities for devoting too much space to "mediocre works." He softens his comments by noting that there are "progressive artists" at work in Fort Worth, but he provides no names.

2 Suzanne Hamlin, "Journeys; 36 Hours | Fort Worth," *New York Times*, 25 June 2004.

3 Michael R. Grauer, *First Light: Local Art and the Fort Worth Public Library, 1901–1961*. (Fort Worth: Fort Worth Public Library Foundation, 2001), xi.

4 Ida Belle Hicks, "Bror Utter Thinks Southwest Ready to Form New School of Painting," *Fort Worth Star-Telegram*, 3 February 1946.

5 John Rosenfield, "Notes on the Passing Show," *Dallas Morning News*, 17 September 1948.

6 Cynthia Brants, from the Foreword in "The Fort Worth Circle and the 1940s," Lecture for Retrofest, 23 April 1998, Amon Carter Museum Archives, n.p.

7 The Circle artists "were *extraordinary* in their mutual support of each other." Reilly Nail, "About This Exhibition," *Beyond Regionalism: The Fort Worth School (1945–1955)* (Albany: The Old Jail Art Center, 1986), n.p.

8 *Sallie Mummert and Her Students, 1925–1945* (Fort Worth: Collectors of Fort Worth Art, 2006).

9 Jerry Harwell Jr., "Fort Worth Holds Interest in Fine Art, School Proves," *Fort Worth Press*, 4 November 1932.

10 Cheryl Leibold, archivist, Pennsylvania Academy of the Fine Arts, in an e-mail to the author, 3 January 2007. Sellors attended the academy from 1924 to 1929, with several interruptions due to illness; she was twice awarded the William Emlen Cresson Traveling Scholarship for European study. McVeigh attended the academy's Chester Springs summer school in 1926, where she studied printmaking with Daniel Garber. Gillespie attended Chester Springs painting classes during the summers of 1925 and 1926.

11 Resa C. Oglesby, *History of the Fort Worth Art Association* (MA thesis, Texas Woman's University, 1950), 90–1.

12 Sallie Blyth Mummert, "Fort Worth Artists Organize Guild," *Fort Worth Star-Telegram*, 3 February 1935. One of the most important offshoots of the Fort Worth School of Fine Arts was the formation of the Fort Worth Artists Guild (also known as the Artists Guild of Texas). McVeigh and Jolly both served as early presidents. Most group exhibitions organized by the guild were competitive and selected by jury. The guild's activities provided artists with a public forum denied them at the Carnegie Public Library (see note 19).

13 Marjorie Johnson, interview with the author, 9 November 1994, n.p., collection of the author.

14 Mummert, "Art Association Receives 8 Original Drawings in Color by E. W. Deming," *Fort Worth Star-Telegram*, 20 February 1938.

15 "7 Artists Are to Exhibit in Sunday Show," *Fort Worth Press*, 18 November 1938.

16 Marjorie Johnson, interview with the author, 23 November 1994, n.p., collection of the author.

17 Stephen Pinson, "Regionalism Redux: Fort Worth's Utopian Experiment in Modernism," *Prints of the Fort Worth Circle, 1940–1960*. (Austin: Archer M. Huntington Art Gallery, 1992), 9.

18 Preeminent among the association's holdings were George Inness' *Approaching Storm* (1875, Modern Art Museum of Fort Worth) and Thomas Eakins' *Swimming* (1885, Amon Carter Museum).

19 Oglesby, *History of the Fort Worth Art Association*, 77, 89–90, 95, 111–5. Complete control of the library gallery was exercised by head librarian Jennie Scott Scheuber, whose personal standards favored artists with established national or regional reputations. Given the limited space and availability of the Carnegie Library art gallery, Scheuber saw little reason to devote library resources to the work of lesser-known or emerging talents. Only in her annual exhibition of selected Texas paintings were works by area artists shown. Undercurrents of resentment against Scheuber and her policies were factors in the formation of the Fort Worth Artists Guild in 1935 (see note 12).

20 "57 Artists Represented in First Citywide Exhibition," *Fort Worth Star-Telegram*. The day of publication is not known, but the article appeared in the paper sometime between May and June 1939.

21 "First Prize in Citywide Art Exhibit Goes to Still Life," *Fort Worth Star-Telegram*, 1 June 1939. The jury consisted of Olin Travis, head of the Dallas Art Institute; Howard Joyner, head of the art department of what would become the University of Texas at Arlington; and Ronald Williams, an instructor in the art department of North Texas State Teachers College in Denton. Throughout the 1940s, a three-person jury, composed of professional artists, was used by the Fort Worth Art Association to judge the *Local*.

22 "First Prize Winner in Local Artists Show," *Fort Worth Star-Telegram*, 7 April 1940. Jurors included Ward Lockwood, head of the art department at the University of Texas, Austin; Delmar Pachl, art instructor at what would become the University of Texas at Arlington; and Edith Brisac, art instructor at Texas State College for Women in Denton. *Old Theatre*, *K. of C. General Store*, and *Farm at Early Morning* are all unlocated.

23 "Artist to Join Staff at TWC," *Fort Worth Star-Telegram*, 4 January 1941.

24 Dickson Reeder, "An Artist Views the Show," *Fort Worth Star-Telegram*, 23 March 1941.

25 Hicks, "Art Season Here Nears Height," *Fort Worth Star-Telegram*, 9 November 1941.

26 Marjorie Johnson, interview with the author, 29 January 1996, n.p., collection of the author.

27 Reeder, "An Artist Views the Show," *Fort Worth Star-Telegram*, 23 March 1941.

28 "Art Association Is 'Broke'; Needs $2500 for Year," *Fort Worth Press*, 13 September 1942.

29 "Right in der Fuehrer's Face — Artists Manning Battle Stations," *Fort Worth Star-Telegram*, undated clipping from 1943, Amon Carter Museum Archives.

30 "James T. Taylor Funeral Will Be Held Thursday," *Fort Worth Star-Telegram*, 12 March 1947.

31 Johnson interview, 1996.

32 Hicks, "Wartime Pressure Fails to Slow Artists in Work," *Fort Worth Star-Telegram*, 12 December 1943.

33 *Catalogue of Texas Painting and Sculpture in the Collection of the Dallas Museum of Fine Arts* (Dallas: Dallas Museum of Fine Arts, 1951). Jerry Bywaters, just months away from being named director of the Dallas Museum of Fine Arts, was lead juror for the 1943 *Local Artists Show* in Fort Worth. Bywaters acquired the Helfensteller and Smith paintings for the DMFA permanent collection in 1945.

34 Patricia Peck, "Fact and Fancy in Fort Worth," *Dallas Morning News*, 17 May 1944.

35 Peck, "Art from the Local Painters Out Where the West Begins," *Dallas Morning News*, 16 April 1944.

36 Hicks, "Works of 22 Fort Worth Artists Are on Exhibit in Local Show at Library," *Fort Worth Star-Telegram*, 9 April 1944.

37 Peck, "Art from the Local Painters Out Where the West Begins," *Dallas Morning News*, 16 April 1944. Peck's review of the 1944 *Local* contains the best account of the exhibition's controversial nature.

38 Edith Guedry, "Modern Art May Not Be Pleasing, But It Is Typical of Era in Which We're Living," *Fort Worth Press*, 13 April 1944.

39 Edward Jewell, "Art Plans of Local Museums," *New York Times*, 24 September 1944.

40 *Six Texas Painters* (New York: Weyhe Gallery, September 1944).

41 Hicks, "Three Exhibitions Soon to Draw Widespread Attention to Work of Texas Artists," *Fort Worth Star-Telegram*, 10 September 1944. See also Guedry, "Fort Worth Eyes Are on Show of Five Local Painters Opening in New York Monday," *Fort Worth Press*, 15 September 1944, and Hicks, "Six Texas Artists Show in New York Includes Many Fort Worth Paintings," *Fort Worth Star-Telegram*, 17 September 1944.

42 Melville Upton, "Art of Soviet Children," *New York Sun*, 24 September 1944. The title of the article refers to the principal exhibition addressed in Upton's review; he reviewed several concurrent shows, including *Six Texas Painters*.

43 Maude Riley, "Art Digest Editor Says Work of 6 Texans Is Interesting and in No Sense Regional," *Fort Worth Star-Telegram*, 23 September 1944.

44 Elizabeth G. Seaton, ed., *Paths to the Press: Printmaking and American Women Artists, 1910–1960* (Manhattan: Marianna Kistler Beach Museum of Art, Kansas State University, 2006), 150–51.

45 Hicks, "Two New Shows Are of Contrasting Interest," *Fort Worth Star-Telegram*, 25 February 1945.

46 "Kelly Fearing Oil Is Chosen for Purchase," *Fort Worth Star-Telegram*, 22 April 1945. See also Hicks, "Exhibits, Not Regional, Marked by Individuality," *Fort Worth Star-Telegram*, 29 April 1945, and "Progress of Fort Worth Artists Gillespie Topic," *Fort Worth Star-Telegram*, 6 May 1945.

47 Jennie Scott Scheuber, *Catalogue of Paintings in the Permanent Collection* (Fort Worth: Fort Worth Art Association, 1928), 5.

48 Hicks, "Utter's Art Provocative But Highly Interesting," *Fort Worth Star-Telegram*, 27 January 1946. See also Hicks, "Bror Utter Thinks Southwest Ready to Form New School of Painting," *Fort Worth Star-Telegram*, 3 February 1946. Both articles offer enlightening insight into Utter's concept of "embellished form."

49 "Utter's Show," *Texas Week*, 18 January 1947.

50 In the late 1940s, paintings by Helfensteller were sold through the American British Art Center in New York City; the exact span of the center's relationship with the artist is not known.

51 Howard Devree, "Among the New Exhibitions," *New York Times*, 29 September 1946.

52 Nedra Jenkins, "Bomar's Works Didn't Disappoint Homefolks," *Fort Worth Star-Telegram*, 7 December 1947.

53 Reilly Nail, "About This Exhibition," *Beyond Regionalism: The Fort Worth School (1945–1955)* (Albany: The Old Jail Art Center, 1986), n.p.

54 *Newcomers: First Showing of a New Generation* (New York: The Downtown Gallery, 1951).

55 *Exhibition No. Five* (Dallas: Betty McLean Gallery, 1951).

56 *Catalogue of the Inaugural Exhibition of the Fort Worth Art Center* (Fort Worth: Fort Worth Art Association, 1954).

57 *Seventeen Years: An Exhibition of the First Prize Winners in Painting, Drawing, Printmaking, and Sculpture in the 17 Annual Exhibitions of Work by Fort Worth Artists Held by the Fort Worth Art Association* (Fort Worth: Fort Worth Art Association, 1954).

58 Jenkins, "Local Artists Will Get Important Roles at Center Opening on Oct. 8," *Fort Worth Star-Telegram*, 2 October 1954.

59 Grauer, *First Light: Local Art and the Fort Worth Public Library (1901–1961)* (Fort Worth: Fort Worth Public Library Foundation, 2001), xi.

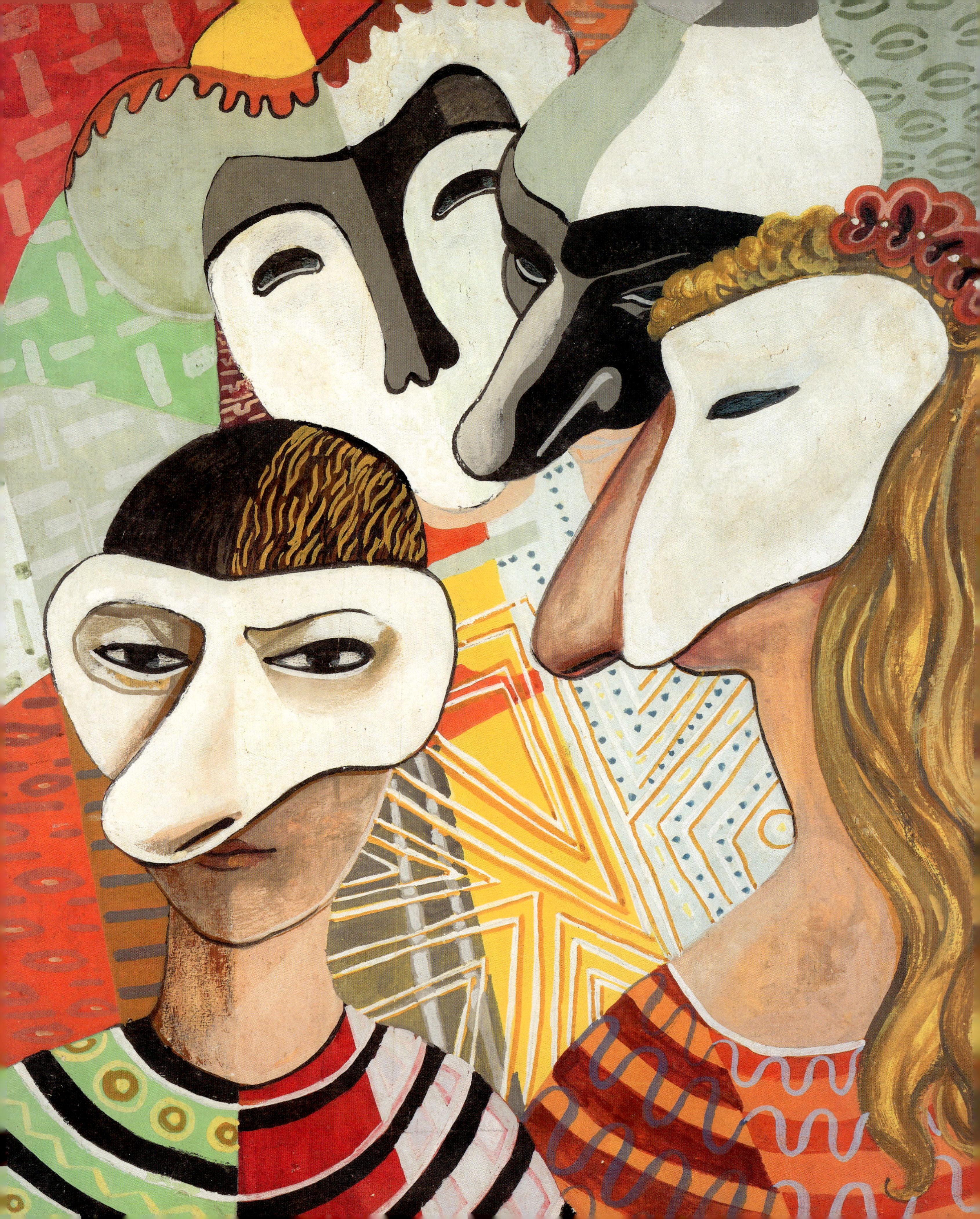

"It is reassuring to me personally, and I would hope to others as well, just to know that for one swift decade in this part of the country a group of functioning, contemporary artists who believed in the seriousness of their endeavor, lived and flourished in a community which believed in them, attended their exhibitions, and purchased their work." DAVE HICKEY

Progressive Rebels and True Believers

HOW THE FORT WORTH CIRCLE MADE ART NEW

JANE MYERS

INTRODUCTION Far away from the grim arenas of World War II, a group of emerging young artists – bound by friendship, mutual respect, and a passion for unconventional visual idioms – gathered in the city of Fort Worth, Texas, a once scrappy town on the western frontier but in their day a rapidly expanding commercial and urban center. For these individuals, who were at the outset of their careers, the growing prosperity of the community was attended by few exhibition opportunities and, for those who did not travel, limited firsthand exposure to high art. A single gallery space at this time, located in the public library, would fortell the city's great art institutions of the twenty-first century: the Amon Carter Museum, the Kimbell Art Museum, and the Modern Art Museum of Fort Worth. Operated by the Fort Worth Art Association (the forerunner to the Modern Art Museum of Fort Worth), this library space offered regular, rotating art exhibitions from sources both inside and outside the state.

In the late 1930s, some of these artists began to join forces to oppose what they perceived as the prevailing provincialism of the Fort Worth Art Association exhibitions and would find that the city's geographical remoteness did not preclude a fertile creative environment. Fiercely proud of their individuality, these "genuine citizens of the world"[1] — Bill Bomar, Lia Cuilty, Kelly Fearing, Veronica Helfensteller, Marjorie Johnson, Dickson Reeder and Flora Blanc Reeder, Sara Shannon, and Bror Utter — availed themselves of an increasingly expanded range of aesthetic choices offered by the rich veins of abstract and surreal art that emanated from Paris and the expanding art scene in New York City.[2] Along with Cynthia Brants and George Grammer, who would join the circle in the late 1940s, this group of artists would become known as the Fort Worth Circle or the Fort Worth School, labels that have carried a range of imprecise associations over the years. In this publication, Fort Worth Circle is the preferred term to characterize this initial group of artists who coalesced to create "Texas' first genuinely cosmopolitan moment."[3] The designation accurately reflects their unity of spirit, while avoiding the implication that the artists' alliance carried a more formal affiliation. The group lacked a fixed nomenclature, but during the war years, they were unequivocal in their dismissal of what Utter called the "Bluebonnet schools and all that awful stuff. It wasn't truly primitive…just rank amateurs mostly."[4] Fort Worth was not ostensibly positioned to embrace art as a vital force in modern life, but the city soon would be noticed for the Circle's pioneering efforts.

Six of the artists were born in Fort Worth: Bomar, Brants, Grammer, Helfensteller, Dickson Reeder, and Utter. Two others, Johnson and Shannon, were born in Texas (Upland and Burleson), and three were born out of state: Cuilty in Mexico, Fearing in Arkansas, and Flora Reeder in New York City. Fueled by a spirited camaraderie and iconoclasm, they generated a surge of artistic expression that included the performing arts of dance, music, and drama. A lively, albeit cliquish, enclave, they were the fierce standard-bearers of all that was modern on the Fort Worth cultural scene. The group's social center was the salon hosted by Dickson and Flora Reeder at their home at 2411 Sixth Avenue. Upon moving to Fort Worth from New York City in 1940, the Reeders mingled with participants in the performing and visual arts, and it was not long before the weekly soirees at their home on the city's south side became a destination. According to Kelly Fearing, "During those years there was always somebody coming through Fort Worth who was in the [armed] forces, but who was [also] an artist or a musician. And the Reeders somehow or another always invited them to their house for a Saturday night gathering."[5]

Essential to the early success of the Circle was their ability to create a progressive artistic language respecting both representation and abstraction, two imprecise yet fertile concepts that often polarized American critics and artists during the 1930s. The North Texas art world was open to the Circle artists who began to repeatedly win exhibition prizes, not only at the annual *Local Artists Show*, or *Local* as it came to be known, held at the Fort Worth Public Library under the auspices of the Fort Worth Art Association, but also in statewide juried events. Several organizations, most notably the Dallas Museum of Fine Arts (now known as the Dallas Museum of Art) and the Fort Worth Art Association, regularly added to their collections by purchasing exhibition prizewinning works. The Circle's experimentation with contemporary artistic styles provoked responses more quizzical than scathing. A local writer critiqued the 1944 *Local* in which works by Bomar, Fearing, Helfensteller, Johnson, the Reeders, Shannon, and Utter were exhibited: "If you are a layman when it comes to art and want to get the most out of the show, better take a professional artist along with you to tell you what some of the paintings mean."[6] Throughout the 1940s, the Circle rose in prestige and visibility. Such perspicacious collectors as Fort Worth banker Samuel Benton Cantey III and his wife, Betsy, became primary advocates for the Circle and spread enthusiasm for their work among fellow society figures, thus providing a vital link between affluent old Fort Worth families and the artists, most of whom relied on outside income to supplement their artistic careers.[7]

Together, the essays in this catalogue and the works in the accompanying exhibition tell the story of a unique cultural moment in the city's history. Some of the players are peripherally discussed, such as Frank Fisher, an influential figure to be sure, though he disappeared from the scene by 1940 and his style had more to do with early French modernism than the art of the moment (pl. 5). Sara Shannon (fig. 13) was certainly part of the Circle and exhibited works with other Circle artists, but she was not a prolific painter herself. Marjorie Johnson moved to New York following the war but continued to exhibit with her Circle counterparts. Emily Guthrie Smith moved within the Circle's orbit but, unlike her cohorts, had no desire to challenge traditional approaches; she became the city's most popular portraitist. The works of Cynthia Brants and George Grammer are treated at the end of this discussion as art generated by the Circle's youngest acolytes, who, in the late 1940s, were just forming their mature styles. Subsequent undertakings in the field of art history will undoubtedly elucidate how their works of the late 1940s and early 1950s paved the way for the next constellation of artists — such as Jack Boynton, David Brownlow, McKie Trotter, and Charles T. Williams — to be embraced by the same community that fostered the Fort Worth Circle.

> "We thought regionalism was old hat…. We thought regionalism had been exhausted, and we wanted to go beyond it, so we were influenced by the school of Paris." BROR UTTER

REGIONALISM AND BEYOND In 1939, the year of the first *Local Artists Show*, the future Circle members who had remained in their native South and Southwest – Cuilty, Fearing, Helfensteller, and Utter – were not yet predisposed toward modern experimentation. Initially, they worked in the predominant regional style, an aspect of their early work that some of them would come to denounce. These artists shared a focus on rural, small-town, and, sometimes, urban life, tinged with the measured optimism that accompanied difficult times. During the mid-1930s, Veronica Helfensteller rendered St. Louis in her watercolor views of a brick apartment house (pl. 6) and the thick masonry arches of Eads Bridge (pl. 7). Executed during a brief residency there, and characteristically regionalist in subject and style, these watercolors are distinguished by Helfensteller's trademark use of deep color applied with a spontaneity that she maintained to the end of her life.[8] An equally expressive use of watercolor is seen in Kelly Fearing's *Jitterbuggers* (pl. 3), which captures the spirit of small-town Ruston, Louisiana, where the artist lived as a young man. A celebration of the Texas landscape, Lia Cuilty's *The Day's at Morn* (pl. 2), provides an affectionate portrayal of her family's ranch west of Fort Worth. Her sanguine view of rural life contrasts markedly with her contemporaneous *Arrested Flight* (pl. 68), an inventive work comprised of dynamic abstracted forms. In the spirit of the French surrealists, the allusive title reflects the often baffling content that came to be associated with the Circle. Similarly, Bror Utter created work that evokes a regional sensibility, such as his 1944 *Going Home* (pl. 13), while at the same time he created bewildering abstractions. In *Going Home*, expressive brushstrokes in a pastel-hued palette of creamy green and yellow pigments animate the buildings and landscape, as does the slightly out-of-kilter perspective and the scrupulous opposition of light and dark tonal bands. One critic applauded the painting's characteristics after viewing it in a 1944 solo exhibition: "Of the landscapes which make up about half of the show, *Going Home* is one of the best. Pleasantly composed and beautifully colored, it is vivid without the use of bright shades. The flowing motion of a road provides life and liveliness to

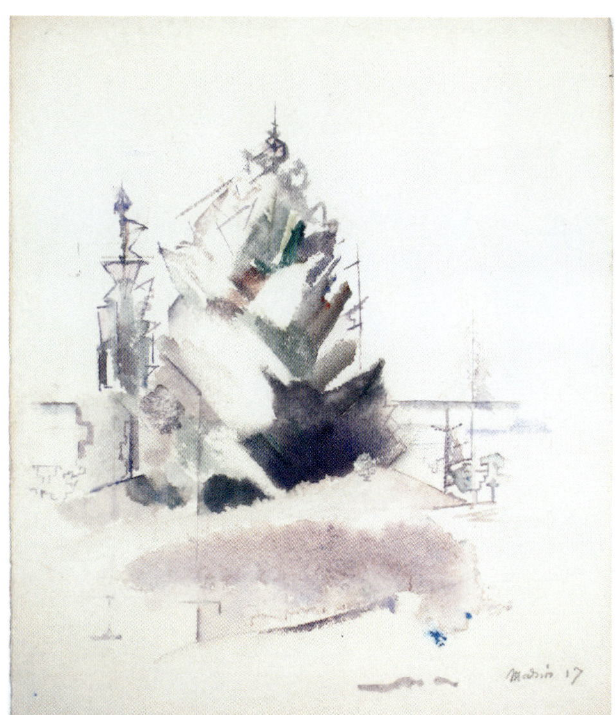

FIGURE **23**
John Marin,
Tree, Maine, 1917

the scene."[9] Mindful of his patrons' taste, Utter was reluctant to ever entirely forego this type of painting.[10]

In contrast, the formative years for those living outside the region – Bomar and Dickson and Flora Reeder – meant access to a more stimulating range of artistic possibilities, and their stories entail a broader appreciation for art trends of the time. Bomar's study at the Cranbrook Academy of Art in Bloomfield Hills, Michigan, where he participated in a modern art and design curriculum formulated by Eero Saarinen, helped frame his developing artistic vision. By 1940, he had moved to New York City and was painting complex images, such as his 1942 watercolor *Santa Fe View* (pl. 1). Like modernist John Marin, who had spent two summers in New Mexico some ten years earlier, Bomar was fascinated by the use of translucent watercolor to transform and energize the dry Southwest landscape. Also like Marin, he dug beneath the surface of the heavy sheet to create highlights, an approach that heralded Bomar's lifelong fascination with the properties of paper.[11] Whereas Marin's slashing strokes broke down conventional landscape perspective, Bomar embellished his more conventional composition through colorful patterns of dots and cross-hatching. Bomar acquired two watercolors by Marin at Alfred Stieglitz's An American Place in New York City: *Movement Casco Bay* (1915) and *Tree, Maine* (1917) (fig. 23).[12] Together, Bomar and his mother, Jewel Nail Bomar, collected paintings, sculptures, and works on paper by other leading European and American painters and sculptors including Charles Demuth, Arthur Dove, Morris

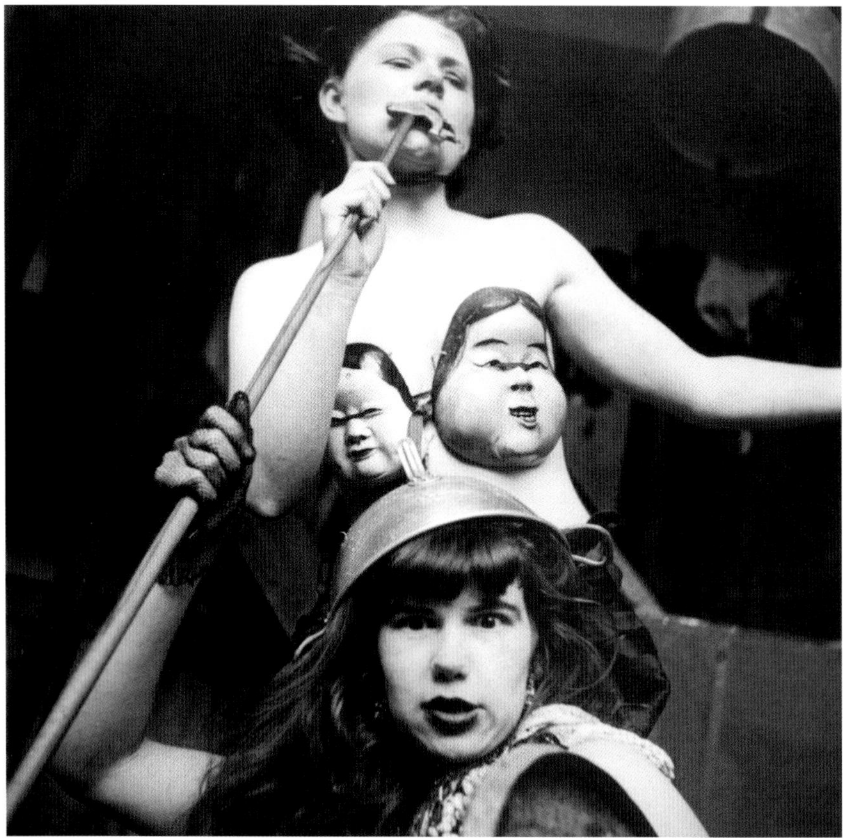

FIGURE **24** Flora Blanc as the Goddess of War and friend Helen Phillips as Peace, Paris, ca. 1937

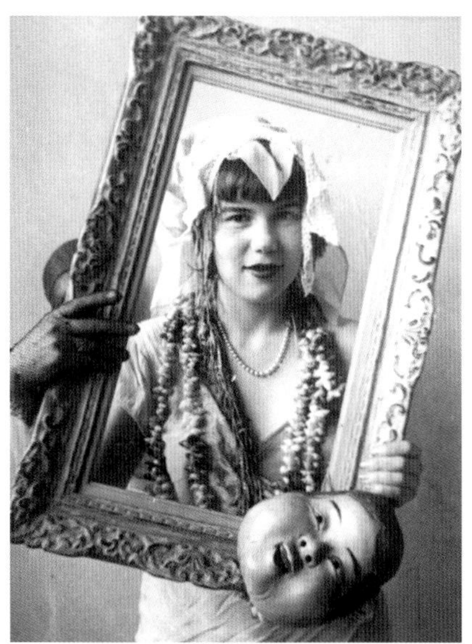

FIGURE **25** Flora Blanc, Paris, ca. 1937

Graves, Paul Klee, Gaston Lachaise, Wilhelm Lehmbruck, Aristide Maillol, Henri Matisse, Amedeo Modigliani, and Pablo Picasso, an inspired collection that informed Bomar's own work as well as that of his Fort Worth colleagues.[13]

Dickson and Flora Reeder's firsthand familiarity with the Parisian and New York art worlds during the late 1930s also would serve as a conduit of inspiration for those in Fort Worth. A love of art attracted each to Paris in 1936. Following classes at the Art Students League in her native New York City, Flora Blanc, then just twenty, made an extended trip to Paris to study with Fernand Léger. There, she met her future husband, Dickson Reeder, five years her senior, who was likewise engrossed in the contemporary art scene. In Paris, the Reeders, who would marry in December 1937, reveled in the bohemian pleasures of expatriate students, moving in creative circles and meeting intellectual celebrities like writer Henry Miller (1891–1980), who was writing the follow-up to his subversive novel *Tropic of Cancer*.[14]

Flora rented a flat a short distance from Miller's famed Villa Seurat and resided in the same building as Hans Reichel, a German painter and close friend to the controversial writer. Period snapshots reveal the young Americans' lighthearted antics: Flora, sporting a colander as helmet, acting as Goddess of War to friend Helen Phillips' personification of Peace (fig. 24) and Flora posing as a classic beauty within an empty picture frame (fig. 25).

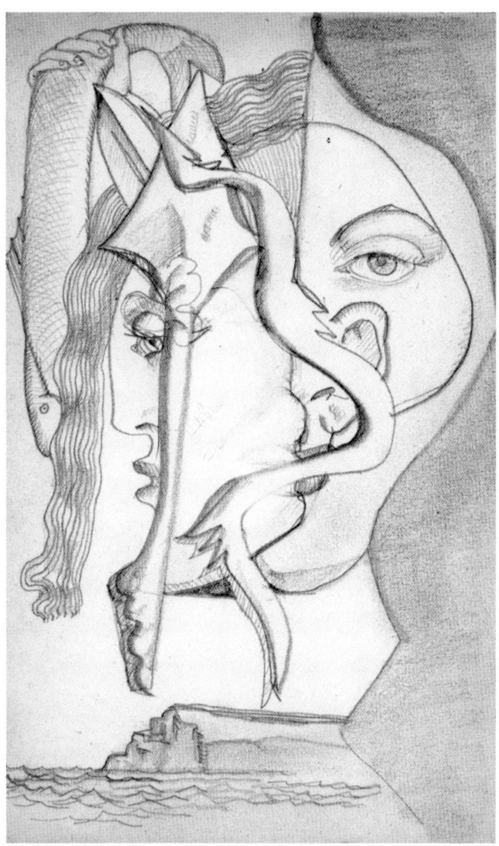

FIGURE **26** A drawing (1937) from one of Dickson Reeder's sketchbooks showing the influence of Picasso, Léger, and surrealism

Key to the evolution of the Fort Worth Circle would be Dickson's introduction by Flora to Englishman Stanley William Hayter (1901–1988), the leading innovator in contemporary printmaking.[15] Both Reeders became Hayter's devoted acolytes at Atelier 17, the studio he had established in Paris in 1925. Graphite drawings from Dickson's Paris sketchbooks reveal his initial exposure to the visual language of the modern French art of Picasso and Léger as well as that of the surrealists, many of whom then were making prints at Hayter's studio (fig. 26). Reeder translated a handful of these drawings into the intaglio medium, including a study in abstraction (pl. 10) and the flat, abstract visage of a woman, Mazy. Mazy was the nickname of Helen Phillips (1913–1995), a California art student who would become Hayter's wife and a fast friend of the Reeders'. Maintaining Hayter's emphasis on the preeminence of line, Reeder transformed the sketch (pl. 11) into a linear engraving, solidifying the composition in the process (pl. 8). In the final state, Reeder filled the interstices with the contrasting tonal textures of soft-ground etching Hayter had taught him were achievable (pl. 9). A similar procedural sequence would become habitual for the Circle members when they began their spate of printmaking a few years later in Fort Worth. Though the Reeders' work is distinctly their own, they were under the sway of Hayter not only as a technician but also as an adherent to the surrealist fascination with the netherworld of myth and fantasy. Flora, whose career as a fine artist would be overshadowed by that of her husband's, also experimented with printmaking while in Paris. *The Dragon and Saint George* (pl. 12) depicts the ancient tale of a Christian martyr and was a running theme for the artist as indicated by the numerous related drawings in her Paris sketchbooks. The Circle's pursuit of intaglio printmaking had its genesis in such works, but their greatest success with etching was yet to come.

Back in Fort Worth, Frank Fisher's painting *Still Life* (pl. 5), the First Prize winner at the 1939 *Local*, intimated a new era for artists working within the traditionally conservative environs of Fort Worth. The jurors — consisting of two university art instructors, Ron Williams of North Texas State and Howard Joyner of North Texas Agricultural College in Arlington, and Olin Travis, head of the Dallas Art Institute and a prominent member of Dallas' Lone Star Printmakers — deemed the painting a "creative and imaginative work," and the "type of painting they thought should be encouraged."[16] The work reflects the strong influence of French Post-impressionism and European modernism on American art and, although such experimentations were already decades old, the painting's simplified forms, vivid colors, and distorted perspective represented a startlingly new direction for local artists and helped pave the way for the innovative endeavors to come.

"The pictures have sharpness and life, but it is the vitality of introspection and the energy of escape. This is no condemnation, for in wartime escapism has proved to be a dominant factor in all the arts." PATRICIA PECK

THE ENERGY OF ESCAPE: ART, THEATER, AND DANCE When the Reeders returned to live in Fort Worth in 1940, their experiences abroad brought fellow Fort Worth artists closer to the seductions of prewar Paris. Young artists and musicians were entranced by the Reeders' milieu — an apparent embodiment of Paris in the 1920s — which as their friend Dallas artist

Donald Vogel recalled, "encompassed the world."[17] By the 1944 *Local*, the Reeders' coterie was perceived in Fort Worth as a singular force. In her review of the exhibition, art critic Patricia Peck characterized the Fort Worth artists as a "closely knit and kindred group," whose works demonstrate a "fearless freedom of line and color...uniqueness of subject matter [and] a gaiety, obliviousness and imagination."[18] To viewers accustomed to more accessible imagery, many of the works appeared edgy and esoteric. They include Bill Bomar's paintings *The Cat in Portia's Garden* and *Flora* (pl. 29), Dickson Reeder's *Three Fish in a Net*, and Bror Utter's *Rivals* and *Accident at Rehearsal* (fig. 16). The Circle's intellectual and artistic synergy was fueled by love of art, theater, and dance. At the same time, as Peck suggests at this chapter's beginning, their lives were being played out against the backdrop of terrible global conflict. Years later, Fearing remained thoughtful about the war's impact on the Circle, referring to a "kind of fantasy/romanticism that existed with all of [us] during World War II. A kind of escapism."[19]

Fearing was the only Circle member to depict overt subject matter from the war, but those works, such as *Attic Piece* (pl. 4), date prior to his arrival in Fort Worth in the summer of 1943 to work in the art department of Consolidated Vultee Aircraft, a plant opened by the War Department to manufacture B-24s. Fearing's poignantly topical painting, like those of contemporaries such as Yasuo Kuniyoshi, adapted a metaphorical viewpoint using the genre of still life to address contemporary events.[20] One in a small series of paintings made in 1941 devoted to contemporary global events, *Attic Piece* captures the catastrophic fallout of a nation swerving toward war. The artist singles out forlorn objects discarded in an attic to invoke lives abruptly interrupted — a man's ties drooping on a bent hanger and a lampshade in the form of a woman. The headlines of a crumpled newspaper allude to Germany's surprise invasion of Russia and Japan's menacing activities in the Pacific during the summer of 1941 when the painting was executed.[21]

When the Circle made forays into contemporary narratives, they centered on their own bohemian lifestyle. Their escapist sensibility is illustrated in three early works — a gouache, a pastel, and an oil — depicting melodramatic tableaus inspired by a single evening's revelry in October 1943.[22] A Halloween costume party set in the stately Fort Worth home of Bill Bomar's parents provided a colorful subject for three female artists associated with the Circle. Emily Guthrie Smith's *The Halloween Party* (pl. 24), Veronica Helfensteller's *The Host in the Coffin* (pl. 14), and Sara Shannon's *Ballet on the Stairs* (pl. 23) depict their friends as self-conscious poseurs. In the first two images, figures surround the "corpse" of host Bill Bomar, who frostily receives his guests from his drapery-swagged coffin.[23]

Shannon's painting arrays three of the guests, their appendages forming graceful arabesques, along the sweeping staircase that appears in all three images.

Such theatrical conceptions abound in their early work that fall at the juncture of the fine and dramatic arts, and the primary players were often each other. Set in stagelike environments, Flora Reeder's *Reading the Cards* (pl. 22) and Dickson Reeder's portrayal of Sara Shannon (pl. 15) display a compressed zone with an illusionistic floor canting toward the back of the pictorial space. *Reading the Cards*, set at the Reeders' home, depicts a friend divining the fortunes of Dickson Reeder and Veronica Helfensteller, a favorite Circle activity. A single electric light in Flora Reeder's painting theatrically spotlights the three figures crowded into the foreground, while her husband employs more even lighting for his portrayal of Sara Shannon as she slyly reveals to the viewer the ace of spades. Reeder merges the real space of Shannon's figure and the illusional recession of a hall and doorway by rendering her arm at rest on a protruding ledge. Such works not only demonstrate their employment of stagelike artifice as an artistic language, but also underscore the Circle's emotional intimacy.

Lady with a Box (pl. 25) by Bror Utter also transpires in a proscenium setting and, further, indicates the Circle's fascination with investigating a variety of paper mediums. The Circle's predilection for this figure type — a melancholic, expressionless woman — was so pervasive that a critic lamented in 1944: "Again the feminine figures are typically wide-hipped, narrow shouldered, with single-planed faces of unrealistic loveliness."[24] *Lady with a Box* exhibits an impressive array of lithographic effects: the repetitive fluttering pattern of the woman's ruffled sleeves created by the sharp edge of the litho crayon; the fine white lines incised with a sharp instrument to demarcate details; and a mottled, textural skirt resulting from the erasure of black areas. Utter studied lithography in the summer of 1941 at the Colorado Springs Fine Arts Center, where he also took classes in painting and portraiture.[25] This lithograph, which was awarded the Purchase Prize at the first annual Texas Print Exhibition at the Dallas Museum of Fine Arts in 1941, reflects an unusually complicated application of a difficult medium in contrast to the artist's other lithographic endeavors, which focused more on conventional draftsmanship coupled with the inherent grainy quality of the limestone (fig. 27). By virtue of his position with his father's Fort Worth printing company, where he rinsed enormous glass plates with collodion in the photolithographic process used by commercial firms, Utter was already familiar with some of the technical intricacies of lithography.[26] But in Colorado Springs, Utter was exposed to advanced techniques in an atelier setting as part of an acclaimed program with such instructors as the school's director, Boardman Robinson; master lithographer Lawrence Barrett; Adolf Dehn; Arnold Blanch; and Dallas artist Otis Dozier.[27]

Fearing, Dickson Reeder, and Utter, in particular, also employed this stylized figurative type during the 1944–45 period for subtle narratives that contained neither detailed representation nor truly vanguard sensibilities. These lyrical, generalized figures, bearing uniform, vague visages, were familiar to the Circle from works by such artists as American Guy Pène du Bois (1884–1958) and French artist Marie Laurencin (1883–1956), the latter a favorite of Fort Worth collectors.[28] The figures in Kelly Fearing's enigmatic narratives, such as *The Aquarist* (pl. 72) and *The Lifters* (pl. 70) are broadly defined, although the physiognomy of the foreground lifter is sufficiently distinctive to recognize the man as the artist himself. It is tempting to ascribe autobiographical meaning to these multifigured paintings of actors and entertainers, so close was the Circle's identification with the world of performance. Bror Utter's *The Aerialists* (pl. 26), which depicts a woman in nineteenth-century historical costume, as well as trapeze artists and stagehands behind massive proscenium curtains, mirrors the number of men and women most active in the Circle. A related painting, now lost, entitled *Accident at Rehearsal* (fig. 16), provides another behind-the-scenes view of hardworking performers. Two stricken women, apparently victims of a fall from the trapeze bars and ropes suspended overhead, are attended by three nuns (presumably costumed actors) and other members of the performing troupe.[29] Personal affinities, however,

FIGURE **27**
Bror Utter, *Colorado Springs*, 1941[27]

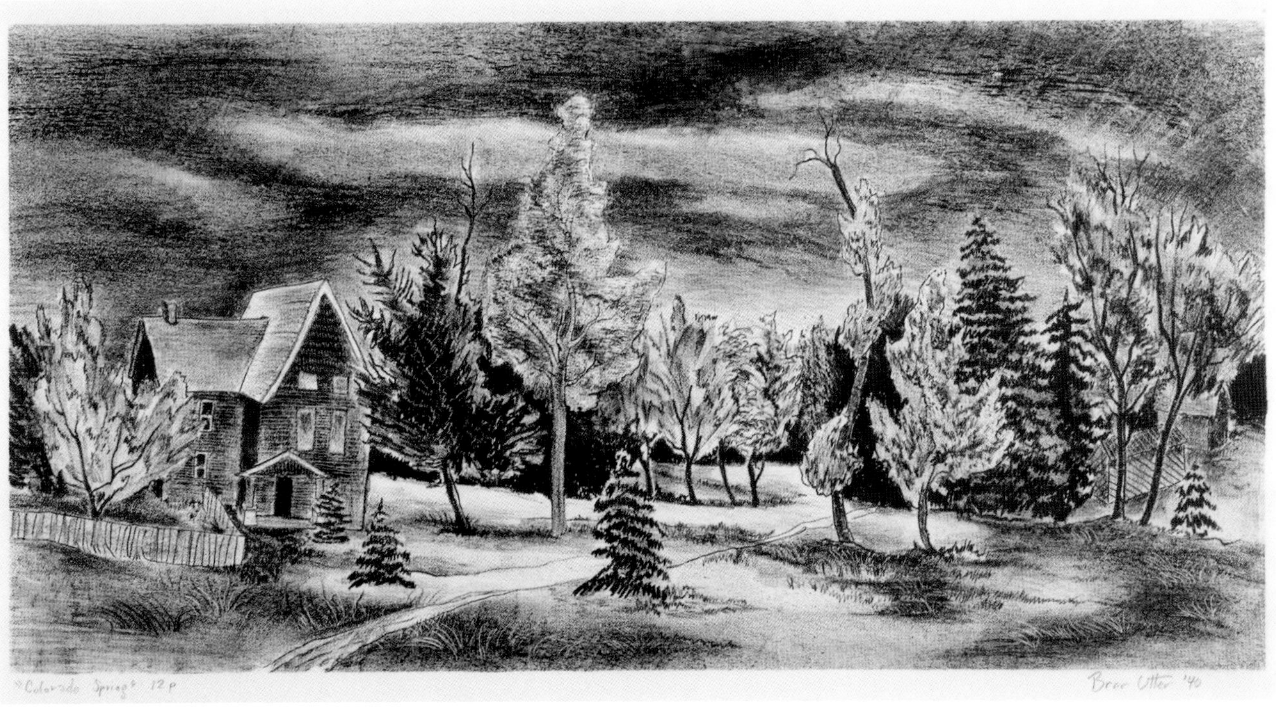

can only be inferred. Whether members of the Circle projected their interpersonal dynamics in such narratives may never be fully understood, but they were clearly enamored of the physical self-expression of the trapeze artists, dancers, and other entertainers. Utter's predilection for vaudeville performers dated to his youth, when he attended shows at Fort Worth's popular Majestic Theater. Such halls featured short acts, many of them involving acrobatics, a subject reflected in the titles of Utter's early works such as *Aerial Fantasy*, *Wobbly Rings*, and *Acrobats Embracing*.[30]

Donald Vogel recalled the theatrical flair of the Reeders, who "had a costume box...we would dress in the most outlandish ways to act out pantomime and dance."[31] Reeder's *Masquerade* (pl. 17) and *All Hallow's Eve* (pl. 16), although stylistically divergent, depict the festival-like atmosphere of masked revelers in costume.[32] In both works, the gathered ensemble reflects elements of commedia dell'arte, the distinctive theatrical form established in the mid-sixteenth century involving troupes of pantomime entertainers who wore half masks similar to those in the paintings.[33] The marginalization of clowns and other performers was a broad theme shared by European and American artists from Picasso to Charles Demuth. American artists like Demuth and Walt Kuhn, for example, were among those modern painters who empathized with the creative personages who lived in the limelight while rejecting transparency either as individuals or as artists. The mask as a means of concealment was also central to the French surrealists active in prewar Paris.[34] "Activities prohibited in everyday life may surface behind the temporary sanctuary of the mask. The role of such masks...is to reaffirm at regular intervals the true and immediate presence of myth in everyday life...art of a choreographic ensemble."[35] Contrasting with the bright color and lively decorative pattern of *Masquerade*, the cluster of masked figures pressing upon a masked woman in the emotionally resonant *All Hallow's Eve* is unsettling.

Physicality was also reflected in the Circle's affinity for dance. Kelly Fearing studied gymnastics and was drawn to ballet and tap from an early age. He recalls being profoundly moved by a production of Agnes de Mille's *Rodeo*, which premiered in 1942, with the Ballet Russe de Monte Carlo on one of its nationwide tours.[36] As young men, Utter and Reeder similarly enjoyed the Ballet Russe during a Dallas appearance.[37] Utter became acquainted with German-born Hanya Holm (1893–1992), a pioneer of modern dance, in Colorado Springs during the summer of 1941,[38] and the Reeders knew famed ballet dancer Tanaquil Le Clercq (1929–2000). Fearing recalls the impromptu productions at the Reeders' as they listened to the music of contemporary composers, including Shostakovich and Ravel: "With a bit of liquor, we all let our hair down and were always listening to the latest recordings. At that time Stravinsky was one of the most played composers.... And we finally would let ourselves go into a ballet to [this music]. And of course I fell right in with this because I had studied dance and I adored it.... We would really try to do the whole ballet. We would improvise it on the spot."[39]

The Circle's fascination with performance was realized even more literally through the theatrical school for children founded by the Reeders in 1945, known as the Reeder Children's School of Theater and Design, which continued until 1958.[40] The school was born of a successful staging of the medieval romance *Aucassin and Nicolette* in the backyard of Texas Christian University English professor Lorraine Sherley, famous locally for her interdisciplinary approach to teaching the humanities. The school's curriculum allowed children, ages four to fourteen, to undertake the study of a single play over the course of each school year, their efforts culminating in a public spring performance. Flora, gifted with musical talent and an exuberant personality, applied a firm but engaging pedagogical method she had learned as a child at the rigorous King-Coit School (1923–59) in New York[41] (fig. 28). Students learned about the mechanics of performance and the broader cultural context in which the play transpired. Classes covered history, literature, art, dance, and music: "As the child's imagination becomes infused with the elements of the play, he is stimulated to interpret it in many different ways — pantomime, dancing, painting, and invention of dialogue."[42] Each detail of the play was carefully scripted, with Flora

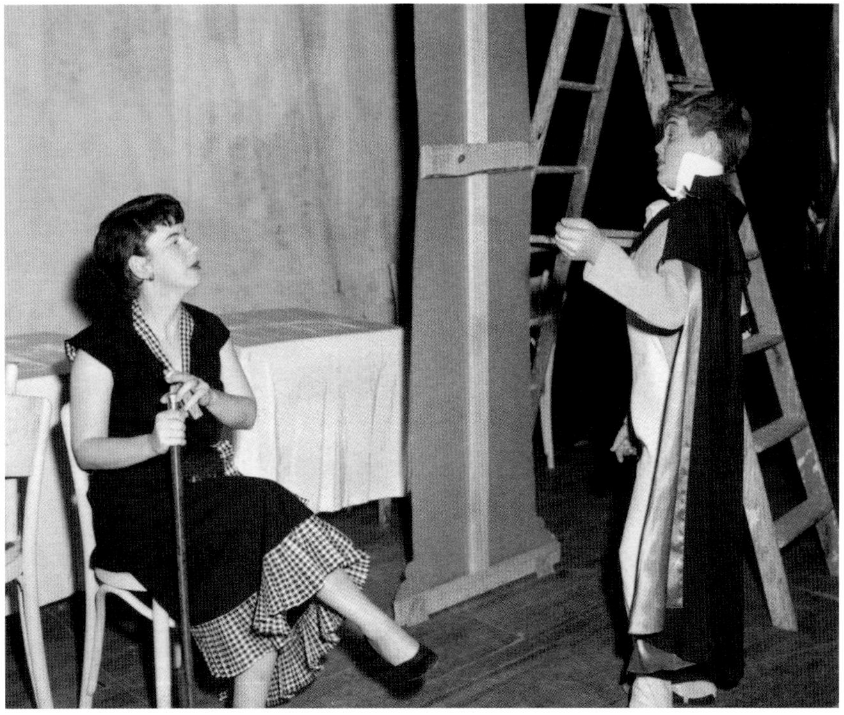

FIGURE **28** Flora applying her firm but engaging pedagogical method with a young actor, mid-1950s

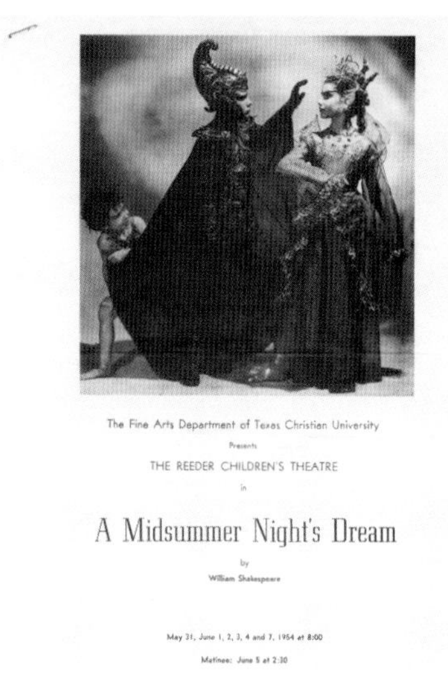

FIGURE **29** The program cover for the Reeder Children's School production of *A Midsummer Night's Dream*, 1954

employing storytelling techniques to teach each student the entire script, triggering their lines through musical themes and physical movement. Her directorial duties also involved procuring musical scores appropriate to the period, be it Elizabethan dance music or Italian lyric song. Artist friends of the Reeders contributed their creative talents by painting the sets and fabricating the costumes, all designed by Dickson. The children of Fort Worth became rapt pupils as they entered the rarefied world of Shakespeare and other classic literary figures (fig. 29).

The selection of adult plays set the school apart from other children's theaters of the period, where the preferred programming was classic fairy tales.[43] Dickson Reeder's training with famed Russian avant-garde theater designer Alexandra Exter (1882 – 1949) in Paris during the 1930s also contributed to the sophistication of the productions.[44] In their stridently architectonic and geometrical aspects, Exter's revolutionary stage designs of the 1920s drew heavily upon Cubism and Russian Constructivism. Reeder, however, responded most fully to Exter's use of bright, harmonious colors and indigenous Ukrainian folk textiles. The hot red and yellow tones of Reeder's curtain study and the robes worn by the King and Queen of Paflagonia in *The Rose and the Ring* (pls. 18 and 19) aptly convey the spirit of parody in William Makepeace Thackeray's lighthearted 1855 tale. Similarly, the cool blues and lavenders of King Oberon's costume exemplify the nocturnal fairyland that serves as the primary setting for Shakespeare's *A Midsummer Night's Dream*[45] (pls. 20 and 21). Reeder's palette choices were but one component of his careful calculation to bring the entire performance, including lighting, set, and costume, in alignment to further the spirit of the original play.

A high profile venue presented itself for the expression of the Circle's joint identity in the fall of 1944. Dallas artist Donald Vogel joined five from the Fort Worth group for an exhibition entitled *Six Texas Painters* at Weyhe Gallery in New York (fig. 14).[46] This opportunity arose through the auspices of Flora's mother, Elliot Blanc, a widow who had fashioned her own salon of artists, writers, and musicians in her Upper East Side home in Manhattan.[47] Vogel, Utter, Helfensteller, the Reeders, and Bill Bomar exhibited five works each, among them Bomar's *Jay's Pool* (pl. 62), Helfensteller's *The Host in the Coffin* (pl.14), Dickson Reeder's *The Explanation*, and Utter's *Accident at Rehearsal* (fig. 16). Critical reviews highlighted the artists' youth and their palpable spirit of camaraderie — Helfensteller and Dickson Reeder were in their early thirties, the other four in their twenties. The critics pronounced the works promising, with more mature efforts sure to come, and expressed surprise that the artwork, grounded in Texas, contained no references to the native landscape.[48]

"This is the realm of art where the subject must somehow engage in the act of imagination along with the painter and runs the risk of creating too." DICKSON REEDER

MODERN PORTRAITS Bill Bomar and Dickson Reeder, the leading portraitists within the Circle, took an individualized approach to the genre, describing their subjects not only through personal attributes, but also through the filter of the artists' own perceptions. They allowed the psychological vicissitudes of modern portraiture to form a more complex emotional identification of artist with subject. The intimacy of reciprocated friendships was particularly in evidence in their paintings of their friends, families, and one another: Bill Bomar (pl. 36), Lia Cuilty (pl. 32), Veronica Helfensteller (pl. 37), Dickson Reeder (pl. 28), Flora Reeder (pl. 29), and Sara Shannon (pl. 30).

While he was dependent on the income he generated through portrait commissions, Reeder was still keenly sensitive to the modernist's desire to transcend traditional portrait genres. Having studied both in Mexico and New York City with Wayman Adams (1883–1959), an established and conservative portrait painter, Reeder was highly skilled in the methods of popular portraiture. It is all the more surprising then that not long after he returned to Fort Worth, Reeder undertook an ambitiously unconventional group portrait. *The Shannon Children* (pl. 33), a depiction of Glenn Shannon and her brother Ogden featured in the 1941 *Local*, centers on the children's penetrating stares as they confront the viewer in a strangely knowing manner. The overall staid quality of the picture speaks to both folk art and a range of twentieth-century portraiture, specifically in the flat patterns and bold designs of the floor and rug.

Unlike his portrait mentor who employed flattering Rembrandtesque lighting and painterly brushwork to embellish his sitters, Reeder used evenhanded lighting and an understated application of paint to impart a psychological remoteness in the portrait of Sara Shannon (pl. 15). Reeder sought not to probe her inner essence, but to mirror the mutual sensibilities of artist and subject. He often was captivated by such waiflike women who bore the "ethereal other-worldliness" of Ellaraye Morse, a friend of the Circle's, whose noncommissioned portrait was the purchase prizewinning painting at the 1945 *Texas General Exhibition* (pl. 34).[49] Ellaraye's willowy figure, long neck, elongated hands, and diaphanous dress all accentuate her delicate femininity. Seated with a musical score resting on her lap, she is portrayed as momentarily entranced, perhaps by a piece at one of the Reeder salon's many impromptu performances.

Some years later, Reeder spoke of the artist's dominant role in the creation of emotionally resonant portraits: "The real thing is the artist's notion of the sitter's appearance and not the sitter's notion."[50] This was a difficult balancing act for someone who was not always enamored of his portrait subjects. Individuals for whom Reeder felt an affinity, however, garnered sympathetic and warm likenesses, such as *Portrait of Veronica Helfensteller* (pl. 37) and two works executed in 1948: *Charles* (pl. 38), a student in the Reeder School, and *Joe Harris* (pl. 39), an intimate of the Circle.[51] Each sets the figure informally against a background loosely rendered in colors complementing the sitter's attire. *Portrait of Bill Bomar*, 1946 (pl. 36), is an incisive portrayal of Reeder's friend and fellow artist. Bomar was greatly restricted by his physical disabilities, a fact of life that Reeder concealed by making his right hand, normally clenched into a fist, a natural prop against which to lean his head, rendering the image a poignantly silent understanding between friends.[52]

Reeder drew artistic sustenance from his immediate domestic sphere as well and, since his days in Paris, had found his wife an alluring subject. Much less frequent are portraits of his son, Michael (b. 1942). *Conversation Piece* (pl. 35), a work of 1945, depicts Michael and his older playmate, Ruth Ann, the daughter of the Reeders' African-American maid.[53] Vivid and colorful components like the Dick Tracy and Little Orphan Annie comic strips hanging from the wall are the tangible evidence of innocent childhood pastimes. This presentation of a family unit within their domestic environs strengthens the title's allusion to "conversation piece" paintings by eighteenth-century English artists that staged the life of the landed gentry. The young girl seems to be integral to the Reeder family — her figure is the more highly finished and sensitively rendered of the two — but the painting leaves intriguing conceptual questions about the nature of childhood friendship during a period of severe racial prejudice.

The only child of a wealthy family, Bill Bomar was not dependent on outside income and could freely choose his portrait subjects. As a result, he focused predominantly on those with whom he enjoyed close relationships. In two portraits (pls. 28 and 29), he captured the dramatic bent of friends Flora and Dickson Reeder dressed in simple European folk attire — she in a blue-gray dress with crossed laces and Dickson in a loden coat — they may have acquired while living abroad. The portrait of Flora, portrayed as a poised young woman with (atypically for her) impassive countenance, shows the influence of the portraits by Amedeo Modigliani that Bomar admired and eventually would own. Dickson Reeder's bold and strident features intimate a strong personality, while his restive brow suggests a pensive mood.

Bomar's portrayal of Reeder exposed a rare intimacy, for the later portraits by Bomar favored structure and design over immediacy. Emphasizing select attributes in the portrait of Sara Shannon (pl. 30), he drew upon her innate grace and physical beauty and accentuated her striking facial features. She is posed to engage the viewer with her vitality, reinforced by the bold shapes of solid silver earrings and a brightly colored striped blouse. The shallow, sparely defined space within which the figure is placed continues throughout Bomar's portraits of the 1940s, the geometric backdrops increasing in angular emphasis. *Jewel's Feathered Hat* (pl. 31), a portrait of his mother, Jewel Nail Bomar (1895 – 1965), reflects the elegance and understated aloofness for which she was known.[54] The palette, a narrow range of cool intensities contrasting with the sitter's colorful blue-green hat and eyes, may reflect Bomar's conflicted relationship with his mother, who could be distant and difficult. Bomar positioned the background's overlapping angular shapes at strategic points, coinciding with her sharp cheekbone, a reinforcement of a severe demeanor. To different effect, he used a similar figure and ground relationship in his portrait of Lia Cuilty (pl. 32). Raising her arm above her head, eyes closed as if in reverie, Cuilty assumes a less static pose as a sympathetically feminine and private individual within her rather rigorous setting.

> "We weren't thinking that we would get fame from what we were doing — we were doing prints because we really loved doing them." KELLY FEARING

PRINTS: A HOTBED OF INNOVATION Most in the Circle demonstrated a facility in the paper mediums, and several were involved in the unprecedented wave of printmaking that began in 1944, the year of their New York debut at Weyhe Gallery. Simultaneously, Hayter and his Atelier 17, now relocated to New York in the wake of the war, were asserting their revolutionary presence on the American art scene by exhibiting sixty intaglio prints, the work of thirty-one European and American artists, at the Museum of Modern Art.[55] For the first time, Americans were exposed to the potential of contemporary intaglio printmaking and experimentation with the unique qualities of soft-ground etching. The works of Alexander Calder, Jacques Lipchitz, Joan Miró, and Hayter himself, represented by ten prints, were featured. By the time the Hayter exhibition had traveled to Fort Worth in September 1945 as part of a two-year national tour, the Circle had already held a major exhibition of their graphic work in the Print Room of the Fort Worth Public Library, having adapted Hayter's cooperative working methods and embraced his tenet that printmaking could be a creative enterprise separate from painting. While a small percentage of the Circle's prints relate directly to paintings (pls. 71 and 73), most are unique manifestations of the artists' ideas, reflecting the creative freedom and sense of experimentation that Hayter espoused.

The exhibition, the only one to exclusively feature the Circle's prints, was an amalgam of traditional narratives and the Circle's idiosyncratic fantasies. Organized by established Fort Worth printmaker Blanche McVeigh, it featured her own work in addition to that of younger artists — Kelly Fearing, Veronica Helfensteller, Dickson Reeder, Flora Blanc Reeder, and Bror Utter. The show offered an impressive array of intaglio methods whose range and novelty elicited notice: "Aquatints, line etchings, soft ground etchings, engravings, mezzotints and dry points are to be found. And some of the artists (so they tell us) have combined several of these methods in one print."[56] Further exposure occurred a few months later when Donald Vogel installed an exhibition of Texas art at the Telenews Theater in Dallas, where the local critic found the prints praiseworthy: "We found the softground etchings by Fort Worth Artists the most interesting... and single out Dickson Reeder, Bror Utter, Helfensteller, Flora Blanc Reeder and Kelly Fearing."[57]

Considering the time and place, the Circle's printmaking activity was nothing short of revolutionary. Between 1944 and 1947, in the garage behind Veronica Helfensteller's small bungalow on Fort Worth's west side, a group of artists, comprised primarily of Cuilty, Fearing, Helfensteller, Dickson Reeder, and Utter, with occasional visits from Bill Bomar, met several times a week to make intaglio prints on Helfensteller's press.[58] Despite the demands of their regular jobs, they worked hard, imbibing sherry until the early hours of the morning.[59] Bror Utter's small oil painting *Party* captures their intimate conviviality (pl. 27) with Helfensteller presiding over her gathered friends.[60] Colorfully silhouetted against the window is her collection of glass bottles whose shapes so fascinated her that she often incorporated them into her work (pl. 49). At her studio, the printmakers created a number of intimately scaled intaglio prints signified by technical complexity and distinctive iconography.

Choosing intaglio over lithography as the predominant print medium was a rebellious act in and of itself. Characterizing the *Third Annual Texas Print Exhibition* in 1943, a Dallas newspaper proclaimed: "Texas Takes to Lithography for Annual Print Exhibition"; forty-four of the fifty-nine prints and ten of the twelve prizewinners were lithographs. Of the exhibition, held in Dallas and juried by Carl Zigrosser, an influential print curator at the Philadelphia Museum of Art, critic Patricia Peck wrote in her indomitable prose: "Lithographs stormed the portal and finished in a walk, crowding other mediums into chilly, if often charming minority."[61] Helfensteller was awarded the purchase prize for her "texturally exciting" lithograph *The Three Guardians*

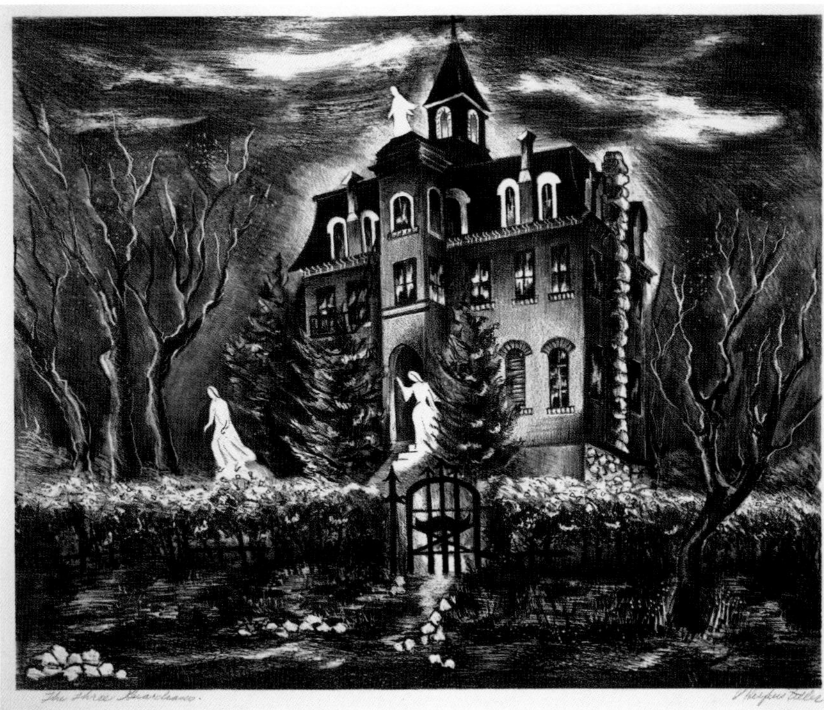

FIGURE **30** Veronica Helfensteller, *The Three Guardians*, 1943

(fig. 30), which depicts the Victorian-era St. Ignatius Academy in downtown Fort Worth transformed from sanctuary to haunted house.

The Circle's intaglio prints generally followed less illustrational formats than Helfensteller's lithograph, for the prints served as catalysts for expanded artistic expression. The printmakers took to heart Hayter's belief in the transformative power of printmaking: "Inherent in [his] spirit was the belief that printmaking was not a static process but an experimental one. The making of a plate should allow the artist to advance into the realm of the unknown."[62] Their prints seem to reflect Carl Jung's beliefs about the collective unconscious, the theory that all humans share common mythologies.[63] One local critic referred to the works in a 1945 installation as possessing a "diverting range of subject matter includ[ing] contemporary realism and studies in abstraction and non-objectivity." She wrote that "only an expert analyst, schooled in the psychological aspects of art, could give a comprehensive criticism of the library's Print Room show."[64]

Circumstances of war necessitated prints small in scale, for both metal and paper were scarce. In comparison with the generous margins and quality paper that typified the Reeders' Paris etchings, for example, the Circle printed on irregularly cut paper, averaging seven by eight inches, the entire sheet barely exceeding the dimensions of the plate mark. Fearing recalled that Utter obtained zinc plates from his father's firm, cutting one large sheet into pieces for each of the artists. The number of prints

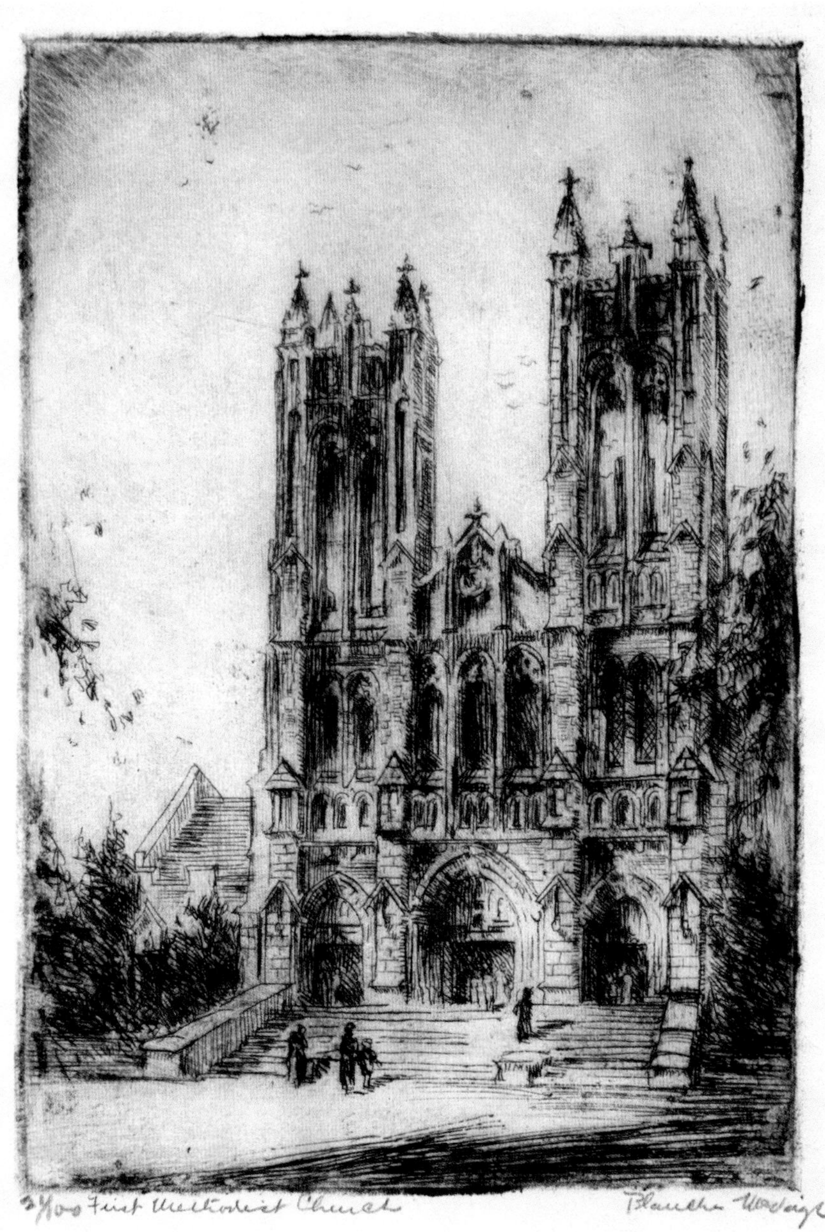

FIGURE **31** Blanche McVeigh, *First Methodist Church*, ca. 1936

pulled from each plate was small; edition sizes ranged from twelve to twenty. They sometimes added aquatint to create tonal areas, (pls. 55 and 57). More often, they employed the soft-ground etching technique to similar effect, in part for its greater technical ease but also for its own distinctive properties.[65] They made richly complex prints by pressing flexible materials into the plate's tacky ground then pulling them away. The printmakers worked with a creative freedom devoid of the financial pressure to find sympathetic collectors, for they had little intent to sell; their most active commerce was trading prints among themselves.

Complementing the artists' already advanced ideological and technical foundation was a resource near at hand. Blanche McVeigh, a nationally known intaglio printmaker, lifelong resident of Fort Worth, and neighbor of Helfensteller, had enjoyed a remarkable career, beginning with studies at the Pennsylvania Academy of the Fine Arts, the School of the Art Institute of Chicago, Washington University, and the Art Students League. The 1939 New York World's Fair's exhibition, *American Art Today*, featured her masterful aquatints, and she was an annual prizewinner in the Society of American Etchers' national tours from 1939 to 1944. Though she may not have produced prints in tandem with the Circle artists – she preferred working on the large press she kept in her living room – she was an occasional presence, and her well-honed technical abilities cannot be discounted (fig. 31). As a member of an older and more conservative generation, however, she would never share the experimental bent of her younger protégés whom she had once taught at the Fort Worth School of Fine Arts.[66]

The Circle's favored iconography was far removed from McVeigh's landscapes and cityscapes. It ranged from the world of classical myth: *Hercules and the Hydra* (pl. 44) to the Bible: *Fishermen* (pl. 47) and *Tree of Knowledge* (pl. 61). Other prints, like Dickson Reeder's *The Keyhole Extraordinary (Extraordinary Keyhole)* (pl. 54) and Utter's *Woman Combing Her Hair (Lady Combing Her Hair)* (pl. 60), are set in a strange netherworld of mythical lore and magic. Printmaking may have been a form of salvation for Reeder for, since returning to Fort Worth from Europe and New York, he had endeavored to establish himself as a portraitist, which, in the local climate, necessitated representation over experimentation. Through printmaking, Reeder was able to continue his investigations into surrealism; the guiding hand of Hayter is evident in prints such as *Mysterious Pool* (pl. 53), which incorporates the effect of wood grain perfected by Hayter and his followers. The tightly interconnected and highly textured components of Reeder's *The Keyhole Extraordinary (Extraordinary Keyhole)* and *Graffitage* (pl. 56) emulate collage, an art form the surrealists made their own. *Keyhole*'s rectilinearity contrasts with the fluid and delicate draftsmanship in *Graffitage*, which contains a lively allover design of tiny capricious shapes. Reeder would continue his acquaintance with Hayter in New York during the 1940s, and the English artist commended his work, calling Reeder's *Fish* (pl. 55) one of his finest.[67]

In comparison, Bror Utter achieved striking clarity among varied shapes, even in such small formats as *Cacti* (pl. 58), *Cells* (pl. 59), and *Tree of Knowledge*[68] (pl. 61), by contrasting crisp individualized linear elements with shaded passages. He experimented with superimposed panels of rich gradations: "We used soft ground and used fabric on the plate and pulled them up so that the acid would leave the pattern where we wanted it when we stopped out. And I used a collage method of combining line and textured pattern."[69] Utter filled the globular compartments with elements both natural and manmade to express the organic interconnections between humankind and the aquatic and the subterranean realms. Two assertively figural narrative works, *Man in the Pit* (pl. 57) and *Lady Combing Her Hair* (pl. 60), each containing incongruous clustered elements, are equally nonspecific in meaning. While the iconographic source for the man in the earthen hole remains a mystery, the woman languidly combing her hair before a mirror evokes numerous art historical traditions, including the idealized Pre-Raphaelite images of Dante Gabriel Rossetti. The representation of fragmented body parts appropriated from sculptures appears often in work of the surrealists.

Fearing looked to the delicate abstractions and esoteric forms of Paul Klee in his prints, including *Floating Objects* (pl. 45) and *Tribulations* (pl. 43).[70] Subtly echoing his series of war-related paintings of 1941, *Tribulations* carries a rare allusion to martial forms: tiny vertical strokes representing military figures bearing arms are visible in the lower right corner and through a hole in the trompe l'oeil effect of torn netting. Fearing's engraving *The Birds* (pl. 46) reveals his reverence for the delicate cipherlike forms and spare compositions of Klee, whose work served as a leitmotif for like-minded Circle artists. Bill Bomar acquired several paintings by Klee, and, at Fearing's urging, local collector Ann Windfohr, a collector of Picasso and Braque, would eventually own over a dozen. Fearing's deep admiration for Klee was instrumental in freeing him to move toward more abstract visualizations.[71]

> "Regardless of the influences, the Fort Worth artists set the mold that made all that followed possible. Their openness and pervasive goodwill was contagious. It reached out to the whole community at all levels. They made art exciting and entertaining while holding to a respectable standard." DONALD VOGEL

REASONABLE UNREALITY Over the course of the decade, the Circle further developed individualized themes resulting in some of their most heartfelt and innovative works. Dickson Reeder's continued focus on portraits, born of economic necessity, would be an exception, and his creative desires were met most rigorously through his elaborate staging of the children's theater school productions. Throughout the 1940s, however, all Circle artists benefited from their mutual search for more imaginative visual expression. In 1944, Patricia Peck applied the phrase "reasonable unreality" to the work of Veronica Helfensteller, though the description is indirectly apt for the work of her Fort Worth compatriots as well: "There probably is no painter in this part of the country who can capture quite the aura of reasonable unreality."[72] The Circle's wellspring of imagery drawn from the intangible worlds of symbol and myth, dreams and imagination, nonetheless was sufficiently recognizable to resonate with their audiences.

From the early 1940s, Bomar applied himself to the expression of dark symbolism while simultaneously producing more realistic portraits and still lifes. His 1944 Weyhe debut in the *Six Texas Painters* exhibition featured one portrait, but also included several paintings like *Jay's Pool* (pl. 62), which anticipate later depictions of the artist's idiosyncratic private universe. This luminous description of a well-manicured yard seen from several perspectives contains a pool with concentric ripples, fish, aquatic plants, tufts of grass, fieldstone rock walls, and the dominant eponymous bird.[73] The *New York Sun* review of the Weyhe Gallery exhibition singled out Bomar as "more imaginatively endowed" than colleague Bror Utter, calling *Jay's Pool* one of the artist's best.[74] Bomar would be the only one of the Circle invited to join the New York-centric artists' stable at Weyhe.[75]

Bomar's surrealist-inspired imagery continued to find a receptive audience in New York, where the European surrealists had resettled at the outset of the war and where Bomar maintained an apartment at the Chelsea Hotel, a mecca for artists, composers, and writers in lower Manhattan. Surrealism may well have accounted for the slyly subversive aspect of Bomar's and his friends' work, which held tantalizing suggestions of an impenetrable, deeply personal world. Speculation about the role of Bomar's psyche in his choice of imagery has followed the arc of his career since the 1940s. Friends and acquaintances have remarked upon the pressures he experienced as the scion of a prosperous Fort Worth family, compounded by his status as an only child with a distant mother and a father with whom he shared little in common. Titles of paintings alone denote the anxiety-laden content of his inner world: *Persistence Above Dark Water*, *Death of a Bird*, *Eternal Attempt*, *Tears*, and *When I Dream of Death*. *Web and Roses* (pl. 64) is a brooding image highlighted by deep, fluorescent colors. The work is one of many replete with self-referential motifs, most especially spiders, arrows, snakes, and thorns, that suggest themes of pain, entrapment, conflict, and loss.[76] Contemporary critics were alert to Bomar's focus on his dark internal landscape: "Most striking is their remoteness and depth of feeling...serious, inward visions composed of recurrent symbols."[77]

By the late 1940s, Bomar ventured further than his Circle colleagues by experimenting with nonobjective imagery whose content and meaning is obscure, such as that in *Day Observation for a Harlequin* (pl. 63). The intertwined linear and volumetric forms in a nondescript, cosmoslike setting represent the ever-expanding artistic boundaries and radical experimentation of the postwar period. Specifically, it references the nonobjective art promoted by Hilla Rebay (1890–1967) through the Solomon R. Guggenheim collection, which opened its Museum of Non-Objective Painting in New York in 1939.[78] Rebay, a rabid proselytizer for modern art, sought broad exposure for these works and circulated touring exhibitions drawn from this collection, one of which the Fort Worth Art Association hosted in February 1945.[79] Although the Guggenheim collection had deep holdings of works by the great modernist Wassily Kandinsky, the exhibition in Fort Worth featured only American artists who practiced geometric abstraction, such as Emil Bisttram, Harry Bertoia, and Rebay herself. *Day Observation* shares the sensibility of these nonobjective artists and exemplifies their "cryptic vocabulary, new hieroglyphs that for initiates might be decoded as a key to a parallel universe."[80] *Day Observation* exemplifies Rebay's own fervent belief that these works are "created intuitively," adding that "they are alive with spiritual rhythm and organic with the cosmic order which rules the universe."[81]

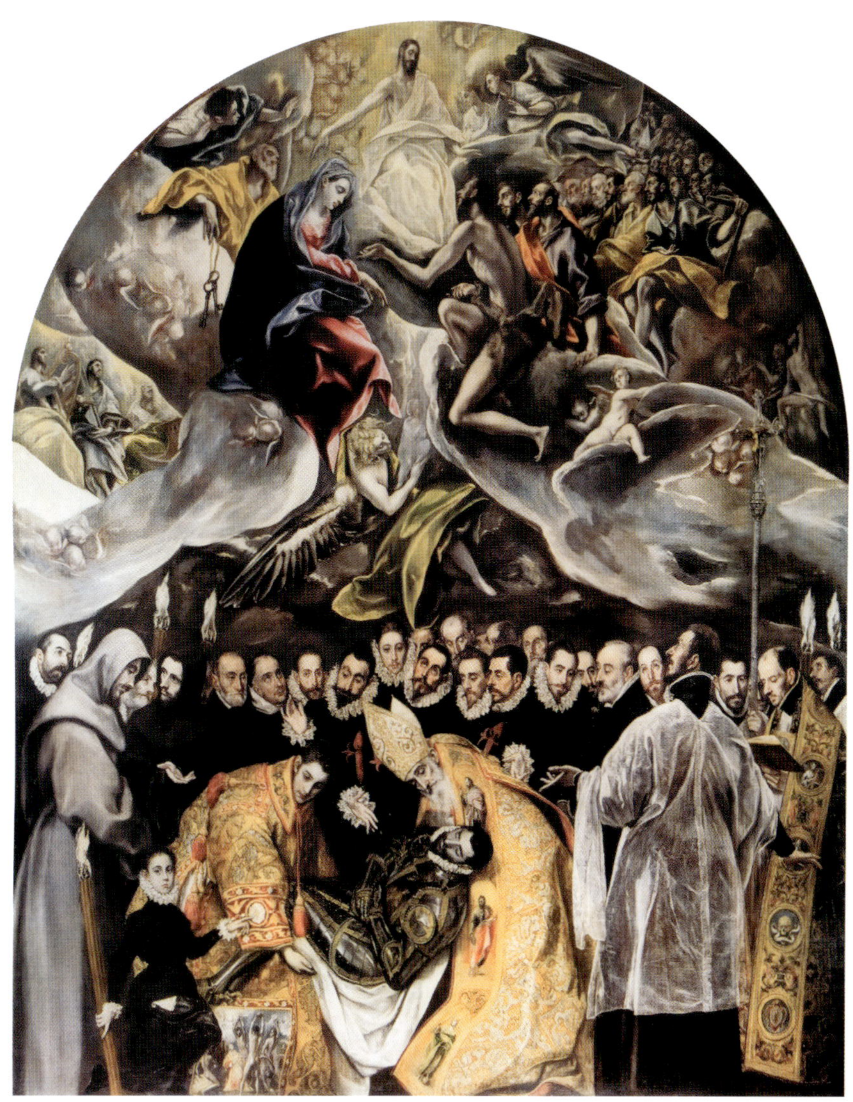

FIGURE **32** El Greco (1541–1614), *Burial of Count Orgaz*, 1586–88

Other works convey more emotive and topical references. Bomar's 1949 oil *Burial in Spain* (pl. 65) may be an oblique allusion to the Spanish Civil War of the late 1930s, for which many American artists and writers, including Bomar, felt humanitarian sympathies.[82] Perhaps during travels in Europe he saw El Greco's masterpiece, the *Burial of Count Orgaz* (1586–88) (fig. 32). Bomar's *Burial* bears a striking relationship to El Greco's massive painting: both are unified by elegant, sweeping arcs, and the same palette – gold, white, magenta, and black – dominates. Otherworldly forms lean over the burial in Bomar's painting, including one resembling a robed religious figure. A childlike figure attempts to keep the lid of a casket from closing on him as one of the other figures presses down on it. The combination of vivid colors and sections of rough, uneven surface treatment in Bomar's painting helps separate components within the crowded narrative. Bomar exhibited this painting widely, and most critics remarked on its powerful presence despite its baffling content: "His philosophical aims, not always easily interpreted, are never superficial and never waver.... This purposefulness plus expert execution command respect and admiration even from the observer who fails to find all his color schemes and patterns appealing in themselves."[83]

Within a few years of Kelly Fearing's arrival in Fort Worth, his reality-based regionalism, as in *Jitterbuggers* (pl. 3), began to assume more subtle layers of meaning as his interest turned toward depictions of figures in peculiarly still environments. *The Kite Flyers* (pl. 69), *The Lifters* (pl. 70), and the Aquarist series (pls. 71, 72, and 73), executed in 1945 and 1946 while he was rooming in a boarding house with army personnel, combine the gravity of art history with a contemporary interest in subverted content.[84] Though the imagery is drawn from the artist's immediate experiences, it emulates the fundamentals of quattrocento tempera painting – small, jewel-like scenes rendered in classical perspective. *The Kite Flyers* recalls the crispness of rock-strewn landscapes of early Italian Renaissance painters as translated to the rolling hills around Fort Worth, wherein vernacular Victorian architecture is juxtaposed with strange monolithic rock formations. *The Lifters*, *The Collector*, and *The Aquarist* are set in unadorned sparsely appointed rooms divided by interior walls, which, in *The Lifters*, contain a chart depicting gymnastic positions.[85] The peculiar iconography of the latter two works features a female associate at Consolidated Vultee Aircraft (the

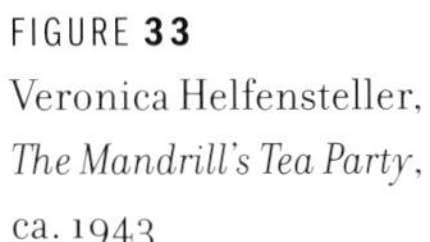

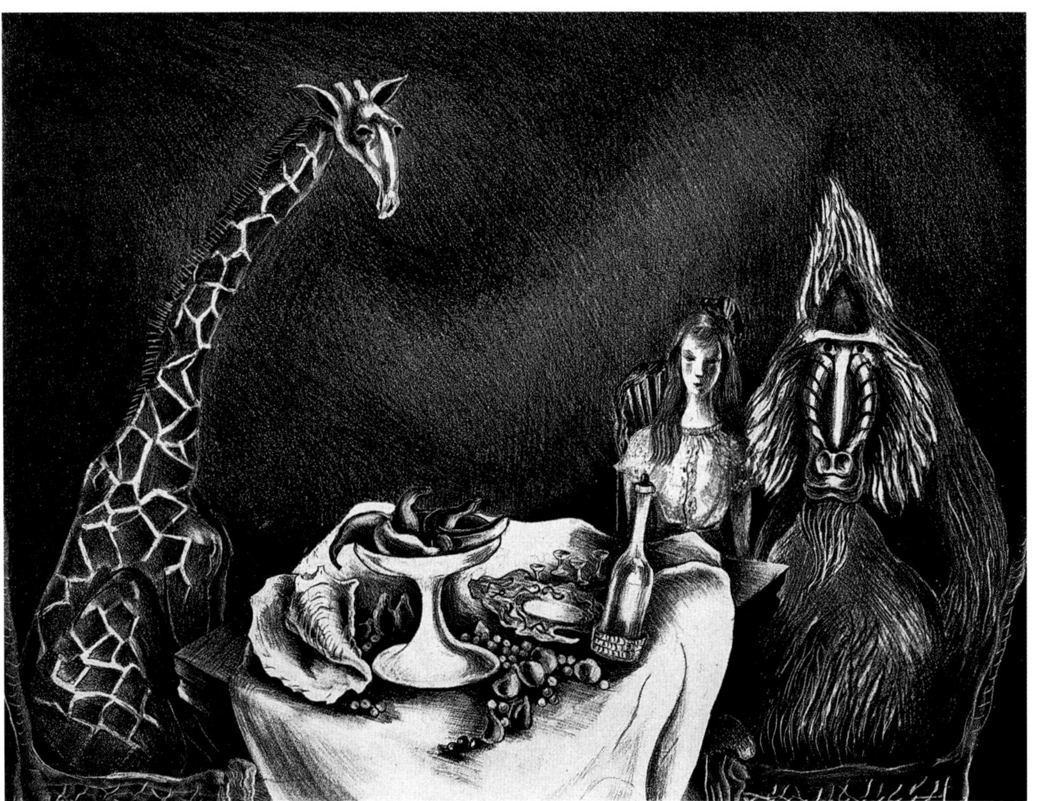

FIGURE **33**
Veronica Helfensteller,
The Mandrill's Tea Party,
ca. 1943

defense plant where he and Dickson Reeder were employed), whom Fearing asked to pose with his small aquarium of tropical fish. As it was for Paul Klee and Morris Graves, two artists he admired, the appearance and habits of fish captured Fearing's whimsy, as he explained the work: "Like flounders sometimes get. Head down before they swim around. And their eyes on one side of their head."[86]

Helfensteller made animals, both real and imagined, the center of her repertoire.[87] Following her early regionalist endeavors, she, like Fearing, turned to more modern narratives, hers overlaid with allegorical allusions. By the mid-1940s, Helfensteller's facility in lithography and watercolor had led to considerable professional achievement. In 1938, she held a solo exhibition of her watercolors and prints at the Fort Worth School of Fine Arts, and many exhibition opportunities, as well as recognition, followed.[88] Her keen fascination with the animal kingdom extended to her writing of fictional tales, but as she wrote to Corrine McNeir, "I could clothe myself in the rejection slips from magazines."[89] Like Helfensteller's artist friends, her imagination served as the point of departure: "Before I paint a picture I know exactly how it is going to look when finished. I don't draw any sketches, I don't even draw on the paper, or stone, or whatever it is to be executed on – I know so well in my mind's eye how it is to go on that preliminary preparation is unnecessary. In fact, I write a little story about every picture before I begin it."[90] A Mother Goose rhyme was the ostensible source for her etching *The House that Jack Built* (pl. 51), but the menagerie of domestic animals recounted in the original story – rat, cat, dog, cow – are nowhere to be seen in the jumble of storybook-like elements. The giraffe, an animal absent from the fable, dominates the image and, as if personifying the artist's alter ego, appears throughout her work. Placing animals in incongruous settings as they interface with humans was a significant part of the artist's invented universe. Creatures are docile and playful bystanders in *The Mandrill's Tea Party* (fig. 33) and the rare print *Three Virgins, Three Giraffes and a Turtle* (pl. 50). Animals make unexpected appearances in other venues like the still life *Rock Formation* (pl. 48), where a diminutive horse is eclipsed by a sizable butterfly and bird. Helfensteller was admired for the dramatic edge of her imaginative scenes. *Animals at the Zoo* (pl. 76) and the intensely colored untitled pastel (pl. 75) are among those works derived from visits to the Fort Worth Zoo. Her fascination with birds equaled her affection for giraffes and led to such fully conceived works on paper as *Doorway Aviary* (pl. 77), a work probably dating to Helfensteller's 1948 trip to Mexico, depicting a motley assemblage of stacked birdcages set within a rough-hewn archway.[91] The blazing red-orange gouache outlining the masonry typifies her predilection for accents of brilliant color.

Helfensteller's tales could be strangely cautionary when applied to the female gender. The beleaguered protagonist in *Poor Little Girl Who Swallowed the Seeds* (pl. 78), who turns into a vine as a result of her action, echoes the mythological transformation of the nymph Daphne, Apollo's beloved, into a tree. Another tragic female victim is a central figure in the artist's illustrations for a bizarre Gothic tale set in 1884. *"Reclining under a tree (they) played at chess and cards ..."* and *"'Horace,' she cried ..."* (pls. 79 and 80) are two in a series of eight drawings commissioned by Sam and Betsy Cantey and based on the story "The Centaur Plays Croquet," published in 1927 by New Orleans writer Lyle Saxon (1891 – 1946).[92] In an archly ironic tone, the story recounts a doomed love affair between the young mistress of a Louisiana plantation and a centaur she calls Horace. *"Reclining under a tree ..."* features the telling details of the original narrative, as the beast and Ada indulge in drinking wine, playing cards, and learning French. *"'Horace,' she cried ..."* presents the story's denouement when the centaur leaps out the window into a stormy night after the cuckolded husband tantalizes him with information about a beautiful new mare grazing nearby. Helfensteller's dense images illustrating this dark tale are as disquieting as the story.[93]

Bror Utter, too, expressed the Circle's penchant for exploring the complexities of male and female relationships. In 1946 he placed Adam and Eve in the *Garden of Earthly Delights* (pl. 83), a work that relates to his earlier prints in its lively fluid calligraphic line laying out the primary compositional elements, then completed with the addition of mottled textures. Verdant, writhing vegetation and snakelike forms await the biblical couple, who, cast in the visual vocabulary of Cubism, contrast sharply: Eve, who bears a rosy appendage portending a new life, pales beside the larger, darker, and hirsute Adam. Related to this work is a body of distinctive images also executed in opaque watercolor (gouache) that Utter created in the same year. Christened "embellished forms" by the artist, they addressed the mystical boundaries between man and woman and man and beast through a startlingly new formal language. Given the works' radical appearance, the local paper's announcement of his new aesthetic proved a patent understatement: "It will be different from the true regionalism such as that created by Grant Wood, Thomas Benton and others of their group."[94] The series, featuring colorful and varied anthropomorphic forms, debuted in Utter's solo exhibition at the Fort Worth Art Association in January 1946. On exhibit was *The Dreamer (Embellished Forms No. 2)* (pl. 82), the winner of a purchase prize at the *Local Artists Show* later the same year. *The Dreamer*, like the related etching *The Altar of the Dead* (pl. 94), isolates fragments of the natural world into discrete units. Mankind is presented in three small figure drawings that increasingly progress toward a higher degree of finish: from the flat silhouette of a man's head, to a kneeling figure, to a reclining female whose figure casts the only shadow of the three.

As the gouache's title indicates, Utter fixed on dreams as his creative source: "It's more or less like dreaming. It comes from the subconscious."[95] A bright and fanciful palette defined the strange forms, which were sufficiently individualized to suggest beasts (fanciful animals grazing in a rudimentary landscape) (pl. 86); man (a corpulent figure with heraldic feathers) (pl. 84); and women (their gender determined by their nipped waists, flowing contours, and ornamental decorations) (pl. 85). Although the heavily mottled environment is nonspecific, Utter imparted a sense of horizon and sky that intimates landscape by defining upper and lower compositional registers. By the following year, Patricia Peck hailed the artist's increasingly sophisticated handling of these curious motifs, writing that "Mr. Utter shows the most consistent growth and development of any of his colleagues."[96]

Utter's audience seemed to appreciate the Embellished Forms series on purely aesthetic terms. Upon presentation of a group of eighteen gouaches in Dallas in early 1947, Peck noted that the descriptive titles of the works were not essential to their meaning: "They are all carefully named. This may be helpful, but it is not altogether necessary.... He has achieved painting that is arresting if not profound, often exciting and that arouses in the spectator some anonymous understanding that skirts the realm of the literal and lands squarely in the imagination."[97] Today, the titles frequently have become separated from their respective images, leaving to speculation which images link with *Warrior*, *Perception*, *Extra Sensory*, *Awed*, and *Anthropomorphic Weather*. One carries the title *Presence* (pl. 87), a somewhat generic title that Utter favored for a number of works. The emotive content is palpable in such images as *Untitled* (pl. 88), where two figures with monstrous body parts are apparently engaged in mortal combat, clashing against a suspended wall with their bizarre protuberances. In 1948, the Embellished Forms series reached its apogee (pls. 89 and 91). These architectonic spaces suggest more benign environs, mysterious in their quietude.

Having played out the inventive Embellished Forms around 1948, Utter inaugurated new pictorial efforts, combining more representational figures with hard-edged architectural abstraction. That he did not find abstraction and figuration mutually exclusive is obvious in *Cloisters* (1948) (fig. 22), where he presents both styles within a structural context he increasingly favored. His works are filled with metamorphic imagery, some stylized, some figurative; a literal expression of their close alignment is represented by a figure hanging clothes in his 1952 sketchbook (fig. 34). In works as disparate as *Evening Reflections* (pl. 92), *Untitled [Two Women]* (pl. 90), and *Near and Farsighted Readers* (pl. 93), Utter embraced the duality both representation and abstraction offered. *Near and Farsighted Readers*, with its bright colors and literal title, is rendered even more accessible by virtue of its humorous content.

In the late 1940s and into the 1950s, building upon a few favored shapes — the Roman arch, calipers, flags, and birds — Utter reinvented motifs over and over and, in the process, found the inherent geometries in the human form (pl. 95).[98] As he repeated these favored idioms, his work grew more austere – unusual, perhaps, for the fact that his sketching method, as revealed in a series of sketchbooks he had kept beginning in 1940, was spontaneous.[99] First he loosely applied watercolor, allowing the resultant unstructured shape to inform the image. As Utter's forms evolved, some, as seen in a series he called Metamorphosis, became birds with pointed, beaky heads and wings (pl. 96). Some, like the large *Signals* (pl. 97), display the stylized pageantry of muscular, taut, and lithe performers. Here, nine figures — only attentive examination reveals that two are female — hold

FIGURE **34** Bror Utter, Sketchbook *[Woman hanging clothes]*, 1952

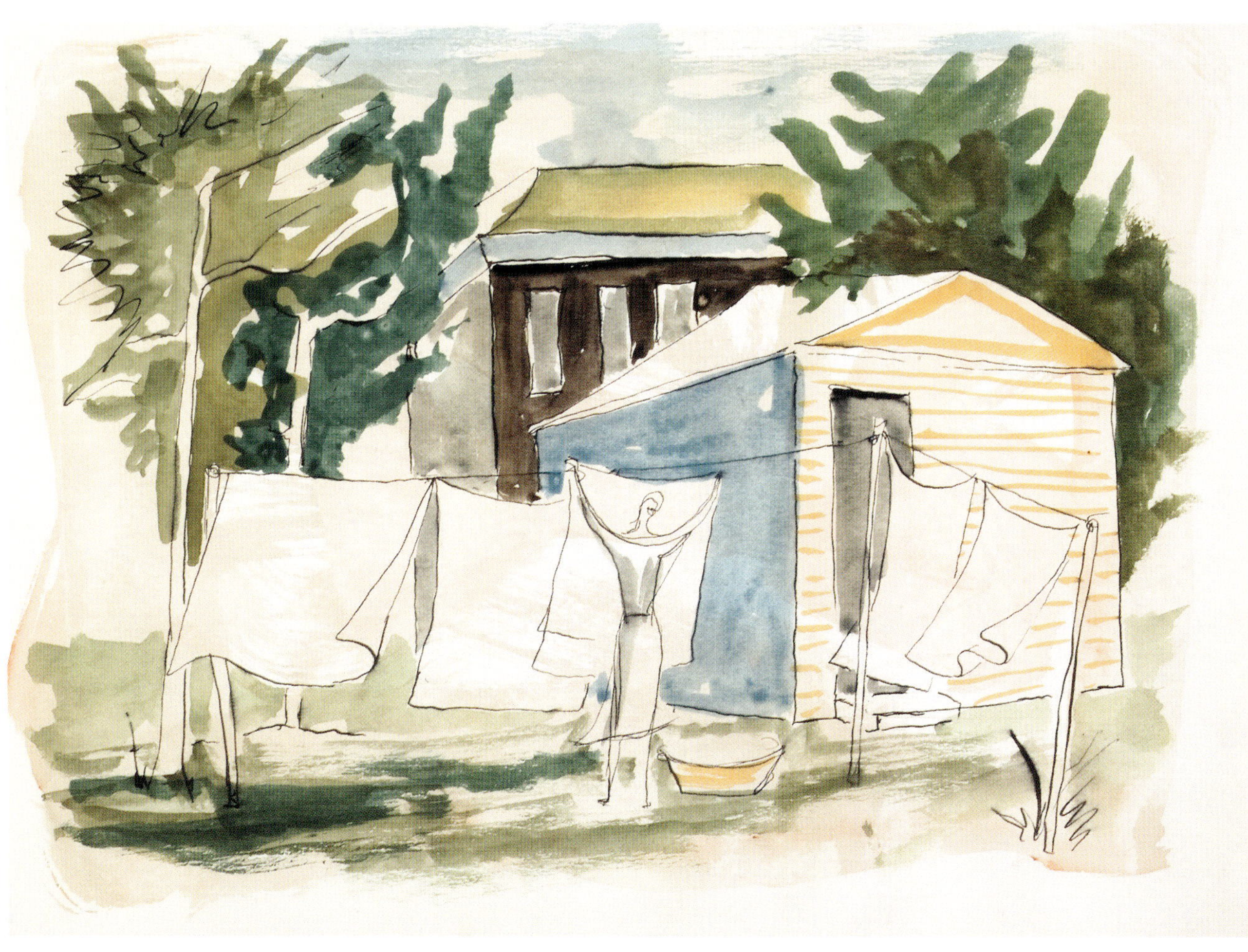

flags and banners in an exerise of semaphore. A series of stacked, arched openings expresses Utter's underlying classical aesthetic while the elaborate presentation recalls the Circle's keen theatrical sensibilities.

The careers of all members of the Circle would continue well beyond the 1940s, a decade that served as a catalyst for further artistic achievement. As the 1950s dawned, the members of the Circle who had worked together during the war were geographically dispersed, and their exchanges less frequently depended upon close proximity to Fort Worth. Kelly Fearing moved to Austin in 1947 to take a teaching position at the University of Texas. The Reeders began an extended period abroad and eventually closed their children's theater school. Severely sensitive to the Fort Worth climate, an asthmatic Veronica Helfensteller moved to Santa Fe in 1948. Bror Utter began to satisfy his wanderlust, traveling to Europe on a regular basis. Lia Cuilty remained in Fort Worth, where she actively exhibited her work into the late 1950s. Bill Bomar continued to live away for extended periods, eventually giving up his rooms at the Chelsea Hotel to permanently relocate in New Mexico.

Despite this fragmentation, they remained active, and the reputations they had established opened up new commercial and institutional avenues. Betty McLean, who operated her own gallery showcasing modern art in Dallas from 1951 to 1954, hosted a major group exhibition of the Circle in the fall of 1951 and subsequently treated individual Fort Worth artists in solo exhibitions. In the summer of 1952, Knoedler Galleries in New York City held a large exhibition of contemporary Texas painting, including the work of Bomar, Brants, Cuilty, Dickson Reeder, and Utter.[100] Prestigious museum venues also provided high visibility: Dickson Reeder's *Charles* (pl. 38) was one of 307 works selected from over 6,000 submissions for the acclaimed Metropolitan Museum of Art's *American Painting Today — 1950*. It had already entered the collection of McLean Junior High School in Fort Worth and so was one of only five marked not for sale.[101] Bror Utter's print *Monolith* was chosen for the Brooklyn Museum's prestigious Fifth National Print Annual in 1951.

The Circle's collective identity began to change as the artists moved into their mid-to-late careers and new artists broadened the individuality of expression even further. In the late 1940s, the Circle added two young artists, Cynthia Brants and George Grammer, who quickly became serious, accomplished professionals. Brants enjoyed a long career in the Fort Worth area, while Grammer continues to live and work in New York City. Like the Reeders, Brants was stimulated by direct contact with Stanley William Hayter. A student at Sarah Lawrence College, she commuted to the New School of Social Research in New York City where, since the outset of the war, Hayter had taught intaglio printing. His strong influence would continue for the rest of her life as she moved into color intaglio printing, a medium the Reeders would thoroughly investigate as well. Brants' aquatint *New England Harbor* (pl. 40) highlights the quaint contours of a seaside town and reflects the idiom of the Fort Worth prints in its receding tonal planes and beautiful residual plate tone. Her early oils are typified by robust brushwork and brilliant colors: *The Cocktail Party*, a seminal work of impressive scale and perspective, provides the viewer entree into a Fort Worth social event, while *The Centaur* (pl. 67) recalls the mythological themes of the Circle, its camouflaged rearing subject bearing some of the abstruse meaning they favored.[102] Grammer's work evolved in a more rigid and geometric direction, and he began his career with paintings like *Oil Wells at Night* (pl. 74), in which he captured the glowing lights of the state's oil fields at night. In 1951, the same year that Grammer was given a solo show at Collins Art Gallery in Fort Worth, he was already exhibiting on the national stage, when he, Brants, and Fearing were chosen for New York's Downtown Gallery's *Newcomers: First Showing of a New Generation*. Featuring artworks personally selected by Edith Halpert, the renowned gallery director, the exhibition opened to impressive reviews.

The work of Marjorie Johnson remained somewhat of a separate entity due to her departure during the war when she joined the Navy WAVES and moved to New York. Her striking print *Untitled [Woman at Table]* (pl. 52) mirrors the Circle's interest in flat pattern and texture, but departs from their midcentury prints in its greater emphasis on the human figure. Johnson trained at the Art Students League, where she not only received instruction in the human figure, but evolved her own modern idiom based on her study with Vaclav Vytlacil (1892–1984). Her brilliantly colored *Studio Corner* (pl. 81) displays her signature structural geometries and was featured in her 1949 homecoming when she was honored by the Fort Worth Art Association with a solo exhibition.

Responding to sweeping cultural factors, the Circle brought a cosmopolitan outlook to a local setting, marking a progressive turning point in Texas art history. Without question, their ability to create a dynamic atmosphere for both creativity and collecting foreshadowed today's vibrant Fort Worth artistic community. Thousands of their works remain in Dallas and Fort Worth, in various locations around the country, and even abroad, providing ample material for further evaluations of their role as a mid-twentieth-century regional art phenomenon. Largely apolitical in an era rife with vast global changes, the Circle remained ideologically charged by their unyielding belief in the transformative power of art.

INTRODUCTION

EPIGRAPH Dave Hickey, "Beyond Regionalism: The Fort Worth School (1945–1955)," *Artspace* 11:1 (Winter 1986–1987): 46.

1 Ibid.

2 Cynthia Brants, an associate of the group after the war, recalled: "The possibilities of Cubism, Surrealism, Non-Objective Abstraction, and Abstract Realism as in the work of Picasso, Braque, Klee, Kandinsky, Miro, and Mondrian, intrigued us all." Cynthia Brants, "'The Fort Worth Circle' and the 1940s," lecture for Retrofest, 23 April 1998, Amon Carter Museum Archives. Brants advocated the designation Fort Worth Circle rather than Fort Worth School and took the position that over the years the group expanded and contracted to embrace not only artists but other figures in Fort Worth's cultural history. See also Cynthia Brants, interview with Scott Barker, 9 March 2002, transcript p. 18, Amon Carter Museum Archives.

3 Hickey, "Beyond Regionalism," p. 45.

4 Bror Utter, interview with Lisa Laughlin Ferguson, February 1979, Archives of American Art, roll 3753. The press sometimes identified the group by their number. For example, in the summer of 1945, the *Dallas Morning News* referenced a group centered in Fort Worth, formerly known as "The Six" (Bill Bomar, Veronica Helfensteller, Flora and Dickson Reeder, Bror Utter, and Dallas artist Donald Vogel), that had recently added Kelly Fearing to their number, becoming "The Seven." "Chuck Wagon Art Carnival in September," *Dallas Morning News*, 31 August 1945. The following year, the same newspaper cited a recent exhibition of "Eight," including Bomar, Fearing, Helfensteller, the Reeders, and Utter, who were then exhibiting in Dallas along with Dallas artists Bertha Landers and Donald Vogel. Peggy Louise Jones, "Art Galleries to Have Two New Exhibits," *Dallas Morning News*, 24 February 1946. See also "DeForest Judd Debut Here; a Local Eight," *Dallas Morning News*, 3 November 1946.

5 Kelly Fearing, interview with Scott Barker, 26 October 2002, transcript p. 7, Amon Carter Museum Archives. The local paper referenced the weekly soirees in their multipurpose home, which was described as "a comfortable combination of studio, music room and practical living quarters." Ida Belle Hicks, "Transition of an Artist Is Reflected in Exhibit," *Fort Worth Star-Telegram*, 20 May 1945.

6 Ida Belle Hicks, "Works of 22 Fort Worth Artists Are on Exhibit in Local Show at Library," *Fort Worth Star-Telegram*, 9 April 1944.

7 Early collectors included Mrs. C. O. Moore, Mr. and Mrs. W. P. Cranz, Mr. and Mrs. Edmund Schenecker, and Mrs. W. P. Bomar (Bill Bomar's mother).

REGIONALISM AND BEYOND

EPIGRAPH Quoted in Susan Freudenheim, "Art: The 50-Year Career of Painter Bror Utter Tracks the Artistic Revolution of his Time," *Texas Homes* 9:1 (January 1985): 30.

8 Veronica Helfensteller letter to Corinne McNeir, 14 January 1944, curatorial files, Museum of Fine Arts, Houston. Although earlier in her career Helfensteller had studied commercial art at the St. Louis School of Fine Arts, she subsequently returned to the same institution for a summer session, at which time she probably executed these watercolors.

9 Nadene Walker, "Bror Utter Show Opening Monday Made Up of Careful and Conscientious Work," *Fort Worth Star-Telegram*, 11 June 1944. The exhibition was held at Fort Worth's Collins Gallery.

10 In later life, Utter spoke of meeting patrons' preference for representation over abstraction. Bror Utter, unidentified interviewer, 20 February 1986, Bror Utter Papers, Amon Carter Museum Archives. See also Freudenheim, p. 30.

11 John Marin summered in New Mexico in 1929 and 1930. Bomar's colleague Bror Utter recalled seeing Marin's watercolors of New Mexico as a teenager in Santa Fe. "They left me a little baffled because of their lack of conventional techniques." Utter interview, 1979 (transcript revision by the artist), p. 12, Amon Carter Museum Archives.

12 See Sheldon Reich, *John Marin Part II Catalogue Raisonné* (Tucson: The University of Arizona Press, 1970), 15.27 and 17.49. Both watercolors are located at the Old Jail Art Center in Albany, Texas. Bomar is credited with bringing the first work by Marin to Fort Worth. Rual Askew, "Dallas to Host Show Evolved 'Next Door,'" *Dallas Morning News*, 2 January 1959. Bror Utter recalled seeing works by Arthur Dove, John Marin, and Georgia O'Keeffe at Stieglitz's gallery with Bomar in the mid-1940s. See Dutch Phillips' recollection, panel discussion, Modern Art Museum of Fort Worth, 14 April 1992, Amon Carter Museum Archives.

13 The collection is located at the Old Jail Art Center, Albany, Texas.

14 Miller wrote *Tropic of Capricorn* in Paris from mid-1936 to mid-1938. A 1937 pen-and-ink drawing with watercolor wash by Miller, dedicated to "Dickson Reeders... from Henry...," is in a private collection. The drawing was featured as *Seated Figure* in the exhibition *The Museum and the Private Collector*, held at the Fort Worth Art Center, April 4–May 1, 1966.

15 See P. M. S. Hacker, ed., *The Renaissance of Gravure: The Art of S. W. Hayter* (Oxford: Clarendon Press, 1988); *Hayter e l'Atelier 17* (Milano: Electa, 1990); *Hayter et l'Atelier 17* (Gravelines: Musée du dessin et de l'estampe originale, 1993).

16 "First Prize in Citywide Art Exhibit Goes to Still Life," *Fort Worth Star-Telegram*, 1 June 1939.

THE ENERGY OF ESCAPE: ART, THEATER, AND DANCE

EPIGRAPH Patricia Peck, "Art from the Local Painters Out Where the West Begins," *Dallas Morning News*, 16 April 1944.

17 Brooks Morris, interview with the author, 6 November 2006, Amon Carter Museum Archives. See also Donald Stanley Vogel, *Memories and Images: The World of Donald Vogel and Valley House Gallery* (Denton, Texas: The University of North Texas Press, 2000), 60.

18 Peck, "Art from the Local Painters," 16 April 1944.

19 Fearing interview, 2002, p. 28.

20 Several years prior to Fearing's arrival in Fort Worth, Dickson Reeder singled out Kuniyoshi's work for special praise in a review of an exhibition of contemporary American painting held at the Fort Worth Public Library. Dickson Reeder, "An Artist Views the Show," *Fort Worth Star-Telegram*, 23 March 1941. Kuniyoshi had been one of Flora Reeder's teachers in New York.

21 In addition to being dated 1941 by the artist in the lower right corner, the work is inscribed on the verso: "August 25, 1941."

22 Fearing interview, 2002, pp. 27–28.

23 In *Halloween Party*, Smith placed herself center stage, gaily attired in a vibrant red gown and elaborate headdress. Among the others who inhabit her scene are Lia Cuilty (to the artist's left); Veronica Helfensteller (kneeling before the casket); patrons Betsy and Sam Cantey attired in royal accoutrements to the far left of the composition; Dickson Reeder in blackface; and Smith's husband, Toby, wearing a black cape and mask. *Ballet on the Stairs* features the artist herself wearing an ornate floral mask; a leotard-clad and stockier Flora Reeder, who is also identifiable in the other two images of merriment by her long pink gloves and roller skates; and a largely nude Bror Utter, who appears in the other versions of the scene wearing a tall cylindrical mask. Bomar, now freed from his casket, attired in shorts, and holding Flora's feathered hat, gazes into a shadowy background softly illuminated by the crescent moon and inhabited by a mystifying cloaked figure. The massive columns that recede up the sweeping staircase are also visible as background elements in the other two images, all of which are set in the Bomars' generously proportioned entrance hall, a signature motif associated with the house's architect, David Adler (1882–1949), of Chicago.

24 Walker, "Bror Utter Show," 11 June 1944.

25 Adolf Dehn and Lawrence Barrett outline the lithographic methods evident in this print in *How to Draw and Print Lithographs* (New York: American Artists Group, Inc.,1950). The artist likely shipped the stone on which he had drawn the image back to Colorado Springs for printing, a practice he shared with Helfensteller, who would attend the program at the Colorado Springs Fine Arts Center in 1942.

26 Utter interview, 1979, pp. 15–16.

27 Although Utter later asserted that he had gone to Colorado Springs in the summer of 1940 (see Utter interview, 1979, p. 21), other evidence indicates the trip actually took place during the summer of 1941. See, for example, "Lithograph of the Grocery Store by Georgia Artist," *Dallas Morning News*, 4 September 1941, and Ida Belle Hicks, "Bror Utter's 1-Man Show Opens Today," *Fort Worth Star-Telegram*, 30 November 1941. Photographs taken in Colorado dated 1941 and located in the Bror Utter Papers in the Amon Carter Museum Archives depict Blanch, Dehn, Otis and Velma Dozier, Robinson, and Yasuo Kuniyoshi, who visited Colorado Springs that year. Extant lithographs by Utter bearing a 1940 date were likely incorrectly dated by the artist at a later time.

28 Sam Cantey noted that "Marie Laurencin was and has remained one of the sturdier bridges that leads the way into modern art." Askew, "Dallas to Host," 2 January 1959.

29 The nuns impart a satirical element also favored by artist Adolf Dehn, whom Utter knew in Colorado Springs in 1941. The ninth-grade winner of a contest to write an essay reviewing the 1944 *Local Artists Show* precociously observed the similarity of Utter's *Accident at Rehearsal* to Guy Pène du Bois' *Carnival Interlude* (1935). Robert Gossett, "Originality in the Show," *Fort Worth Star-Telegram*, 21 May 1944.

30 Jan L. Jones, *Renegades, Showmen and Angels: A Theatrical History of Fort Worth from 1873–2001* (Fort Worth, Texas: Texas Christian University Press, 2006), 117. For brief references to the influence of vaudeville on the artist, see Hicks, "Bror Utter's 1-Man Show," 30 November 1941, and "Bror Utter Thinks Southwest Ready to Form New School of Painting," *Fort Worth Star-Telegram*, 3 February 1946.

31 Vogel, *Memories and Images*, 57. Vogel, who became an art dealer in Dallas, provided the Circle with custom frames and exhibition opportunities.

32 Other theatrical paintings Reeder executed between 1943 and 1945 include *Resting Circus Performers*, *Before the Performance*, *The Clown*, and at least two prints: *Carnival Machinery* (engraving) and *Two Clowns and a Lady* (soft-ground etching).

33 In 1944 Reeder executed a print of Scaramouche, or Scaramuccia, a stock figure in commedia dell'arte. See Reeder Papers, Special Collections, The University of Texas at Arlington Library, Arlington, Texas, and *Fort Worth Star-Telegram*, 3 March 1945. Reeder's depiction of Scaramouche is similar to that of the figure in the lower left corner of *Masquerade*. The impetus for these subjects may also have been related to the work of Alexandra Exter, who used the commedia dell'arte theme and with whom Reeder studied in Paris. He exhibited a painting, *Scaramouch*, in 1945 in *Exhibition of the Work of Dickson Reeder*, The Gallery of the Fort Worth Art Association, Public Library, Fort Worth, Texas, May 21–June 15, 1945.

34 A theater program in the Reeder Papers suggests that one or both of them attended Jean Cocteau's masked *Oedipus Rex* while they lived in Paris in 1937. Reeder Papers, Special Collections, The University of Texas at Arlington Library, Arlington, Texas.

35 Louise Tythacott, *Surrealism and the Exotic* (London and New York: Routledge, 2003), 74.

36 Fearing interview, 2002, p. 5.

37 "Large Audiences See Ballet Group in Other Cities," *Dallas Morning News*, 19 February 1935.

38 Utter interview, 1979, p. 23.

39 Fearing interview, 2002, p. 8.

40 Flora Reeder revived the school during the 1980s. See Jones, *Renegades*, 251–55, and Carol Roark, "The Reeder School," in Judy Alter and James Ward Lee, eds., *Literary Fort Worth* (Fort Worth: Texas Christian University Press, 2002), 338–40.

41 Ellen Rodman, "Edith King and Dorothy Coit and the King-Coit School and Children's Theatre," in Roger L. Bedard and C. John Tolch, eds., *Spotlight on the Child: Studies in the History of American Children's Theatre* (New York: Greenwood Press, 1989), 51–67; and the King-Coit School and Children's Theatre Papers, Library of the Performing Arts, New York Public Library. Information on Flora's teaching style was also provided by Jeff Reeder, Dickson Reeder's nephew, who collaborated with Flora Reeder during the school's later incarnation. Jeff Reeder, interview with the author, 4 August 2006, Amon Carter Museum Archives.

42 Flora Reeder, "The Reeder School, Inc.," Reeder Papers, Special Collections, The University of Texas at Arlington Library, Arlington, Texas.

43 Roger L. Bedard, "Junior League Children's Theatre: Debutantes Take the Stage," in Bedard and Tolch, *Spotlight on the Child*, 47.

44 Exter taught theatrical design in Paris at Fernand Léger's Académie d'Art Moderne in the 1920s and later at her own Paris atelier. Andréi B. Nakov, "Painting and Stage Design: A Creative Dialogue," in *Artist of the Theatre: Alexandra Exter* (New York: The New York Public Library, 1974), 8. John E. Bowlt and Matthew Drutt, eds., *Amazons of the Avant-Garde: Alexandra Exter, Natalia Goncharova, Liubov Popova, Olga Rozanova, Varvara Stepanova, and Nadezhda Udaltsova* (Berlin: Deutsche Guggenheim, 2000), 137.

45 *The Rose and the Ring* was performed by the Reeder School in 1946 and again in 1953; *A Midsummer Night's Dream* was performed in 1948 and 1954.

46 Vogel, *Memories and Images*, 58.

47 In addition to oil paintings, the exhibition included three casein drawings, one watercolor, and one gouache drawing. Flora Reeder described her mother's involvement. Panel discussion, symposium, Modern Art Museum of Fort Worth, 14 April 1992, Amon Carter Museum Archives.

48 New York and Fort Worth reviews for the Weyhe exhibition include: Eleanor Morehead, unidentified clipping, Amon Carter Museum Archives; Edith Alderman Guedry, *Fort Worth Press*, 15 September 1944; E. A. Jewell, *New York Times*, 24 September 1944; Melville Upton, *New York Sun*, 23 September 1944; *New York Tribune*, 24 September 1944; *Art News*, 1–14 October 1944; Ida Belle Hicks, *Fort Worth Star-Telegram*, 10 September 1944 and 17 September 1944; and Maude Riley, "Six Texans," *Art Digest* 19:1, 1 October 1944.

MODERN PORTRAITS

EPIGRAPH Dickson Reeder, undated lecture, Reeder Papers, Special Collections, The University of Texas at Arlington Library. He paraphrased Monroe Wheeler's exhibition catalogue *Twentieth Century Portraits* (New York: Museum of Modern Art, 1942), 10.

49 Peggy Louise Jones, "Texas General Exhibit Opens at Museum," *Dallas Morning News*, 11 November 1945. The seventh *Texas*

General was on view in San Antonio, Dallas, Houston, and Austin from October 1945 through February 1946.

50 Reeder, undated lecture, Reeder Papers, The University of Texas at Arlington Library. See also Sam Cantey: "He never compromised on the most important element of art, the artist's view of the subject. He knew that his view was unique and the most important thing he had to offer." Manuscript, Samuel Benton Cantey Papers, Archives of American Art, Reel 1691.

51 Charles McCally was a student at Fort Worth's McLean Junior High School when his portrait was painted. He later founded the Globe Theater in Odessa, Texas.

52 I am grateful to Scott Barker for this observation.

53 I thank Howard Ross for providing this information.

54 Reilly Nail, *Per Stirpes: The John M. Nail Family in Texas, 1839–1995* (Texas: Reilly Nail, 1995), 249.

PRINTS: A HOTBED OF INNOVATION

EPIGRAPH Kelly Fearing, in Jeff Prince, "Wanna See my Etchings?," *Fort Worth Weekly*, 11 April 2007.

55 "Hayter and Studio 17," in *The Museum of Modern Art Bulletin*, 12:1, August 1944 (New York: The Museum of Modern Art).

56 Ida Belle Hicks, "Two New Shows Are of Contrasting Interest," *Fort Worth Star-Telegram*, 25 February 1945.

57 Marynell Sharp, "Fort Worth Group in Exhibition at the Telenews," *Dallas Morning News*, 19 May 1945. The Telenews Theater showed news clips of current events. See also Vogel, *Memories and Images*, 67.

58 One of the earliest references to their collaboration as printmakers appears in a letter from Dickson to Flora, 25 September 1944. Dickson reported that he was teaching Helfensteller "soft ground etching...but the results were poor." Reeder Papers, Special Collections, The University of Texas at Arlington Library. The primary source on the Circle's prints is *Prints of the Fort Worth Circle, 1940–1960* (Austin, Texas: Archer M. Huntington Art Gallery, 1992).

59 Kelly Fearing letter to Donald Vogel, undated. Collection of Kevin and Cheryl Vogel. See also Utter interview, 1979, p. 39, and Fearing interview, 2002, p. 13.

60 The identifiable figures from left to right include Flora Reeder, Utter, Lia Cuilty, and Dickson Reeder.

61 Patricia Peck, "Texas Takes to Lithography for Annual Print Exhibition," *Dallas Morning News*, 12 December 1943.

62 Peter Black, *The Prints of Stanley William Hayter: A Complete Catalogue* (Mount Kisco, New York: Moyer Bell Ltd., 1992), 35.

63 As a young man, Bill Bomar undertook analysis with Portia Hamilton, a Jungian psychologist in Fort Worth. She later became his father's second wife. Pat Steel, interview with the author, 15 June 2007, n.p., Amon Carter Museum Archives.

64 Hicks, "Two New Shows," 25 February 1945. Works featured in the Amon Carter Museum exhibition, which were also included in the 1945 presentation: Helfensteller's *Rock Formation* and *Bottles of the Sea*; Dickson Reeder's *The Keyhole Extraordinary* and *Fish*; Kelly Fearing's *Floating Objects* and *Tribulation*; and Bror Utter's *Cells* and *Cacti*.

65 Kelly Fearing, interview with the author, 5 July 2006, Amon Carter Museum Archives.

66 See Scott Barker, *The Etchings of Blanche McVeigh: Forty Years of Printmaking* (Fort Worth: privately printed, 2003), and Lyle Williams, "Blanche McVeigh," *Paths to the Press: Printmaking and American Women Artists, 1910–1960*, Elizabeth G. Seaton, ed. (Manhattan, Kansas: Marianne Kistler Beach Museum of Art, 2006), 192–93.

67 Flora Reeder letter to Dickson Reeder, 26 September 1944, Reeder Papers, Special Collections, The University of Texas at Arlington Library, Arlington, Texas.

68 Although the Carter's impression is dated 1941, this inscription was probably added by the artist at a later date. The print actually dates to 1945. The Carter's impression is also inscribed with the title *Tree of Life*. However, in the etching's first exhibition in the fifth annual *Texas Print Exhibition* at the Dallas Museum of Fine Arts (November 25, 1945 – January 6, 1946), it was entitled *Tree of Knowledge*. Other known impressions of the print are also inscribed *Tree of Knowledge*.

69 Utter interview, 1979, p. 27. Hayter began experimenting with soft ground in the 1930s. "He was endeavoring to create an illusion of space, in the same way as is often done on the stage by the use of backdrops. This illusion is created on the stage by the use of translucent curtains hung between the actors at different distances from the footlights." Hacker, ed., *Renaissance of Gravure*, 76.

70 Multiple states of these and other prints by Fearing are located at the Blanton Museum of Art, University of Texas at Austin.

71 "I remember my first Paul Klee that I adored so was called *Around the Fish* (1926, Museum of Modern Art).... It had a profound influence on me." Fearing interview, 2002, p. 13. Bill Bomar purchased all his works by Klee at Nierendorf's Gallery (Fearing interview, 2002, p. 29). One of Bomar's Klees, *Der Weg Ins Blaue* (Old Jail Art Center, 1934), is reproduced in *Klee and America* (Houston: The Menil Collection, 2006), 209. See this resource also for reception of Klee in America during midcentury.

REASONABLE UNREALITY

EPIGRAPH Vogel, *Memories and Images*, 60.

72 Patricia Peck, "Fact and Fancy in Fort Worth," *Dallas Morning News*, 17 May 1944.

73 The inspiration was the yard of Lorraine Sherley, English professor at Texas Christian University. Steel interview, 2007.

74 Melville Upton, "Art of Soviet Children," *New York Sun*, 23 September 1944. The title of the article refers to the principal exhibition addressed in Upton's review; he reviewed several concurrent shows, including *Six Texas Painters*.

75 Weyhe Gallery held regular solo exhibitions of Bomar's work into the 1960s.

76 One autobiographical element centered on the thorns, said to be related to his family's heraldic crest. Steel interview, 2007.

77 "Exhibition, Weyhe Gallery," *Art News*, 45:8 (October 1946): 69.

78 See *Art of Tomorrow: Fifth Catalogue of the Solomon R. Guggenheim Collection of Non-Objective Paintings* (New York: Solomon R. Guggenheim Foundation, 1939) and Vivian Barnett, Robert Rosenblum, et al., *Art of Tomorrow: Hilla Rebay and Solomon R. Guggenheim* (New York: Guggenheim Museum, 2005).

79 There were thirty-eight paintings in the exhibition. See Ida Belle Hicks, "Prizes Announced for West Texas Art Show," *Fort Worth Star-Telegram*, 21 January 1945, and "Nonobjective Paintings Go on Exhibit Monday," 28 January 1945.

80 Rosenblum, "The Music of the Spheres," *Art of Tomorrow* (2005), 222.

81 Hilla Rebay, "The Power of Spiritual Rhythm," *Art of Tomorrow* (1939), 5.

82 Another of his 1949 paintings was entitled *Spanish Requiem (Bill Bomar Exhibition*, Weyhe Gallery, New York, October 3–November 3, 1949, no. 17).

83 Peggy Louise Jones, "Fine Painting in Exhibition at McLean's," *Dallas Morning News*, 12 October 1951.

84 "They were all cryptographers, and they were under high secrecy." Fearing interview, 2002, p. 6.

85 The foreground figure is a self-portrait. Fearing later recognized an artistic affinity in the work of French-Polish artist Balthus: "It has only been in recent years that I've looked at [*The Lifters*] and discovered that, for me, it has such a Balthus feeling. But I never knew Balthus until many years later…it has some of that kind of emotional quality." Fearing interview, 2002, p. 21.

86 Fearing interview, 2002, p. 10.

87 Her niece, Sharon Conger, recalled that her aunt always had animals around. Sharon Conger, interview with the author, 17 October 2006, n.p., Amon Carter Museum Archives.

88 From 1940 to 1944 alone, Helfensteller made frequent appearances in many prestigious national exhibitions. Helfensteller letter to McNeir, 1944, curatorial files, Museum of Fine Arts, Houston.

89 Ibid.

90 Ibid.

91 Helfensteller's letters to Sam and Betsy Cantey document her trip to Mexico in the summer of 1948 and her move to New Mexico the same year. Samuel Benton Cantey Papers, Archives of American Art, Reel 1687).

92 *Selected Works of Art from the Private Collection of Mr. & Mrs. Sam B. Cantey III of Fort Worth*, Department of Art, Texas State College for Women, Denton, Texas (Feb. 17–March 2, 1952). Lyle Saxon, "The Centaur Plays Croquet," appeared in the anthology *The American Caravan: A Yearbook of American Literature* (New York: Literary Guild of America, 1927), 344–69.

93 The same year Helfensteller exhibited illustrations for poems by T. S. Eliot and two stories by Edgar Allan Poe. *Exhibition of Paintings, Prints and Drawings by Veronica Helfensteller*, Fort Worth Art Association, May 2–May 21, 1944.

94 Hicks, "Bror Utter Thinks Southwest," 3 February 1946.

95 Utter interview, 1979, p. 38.

96 Patricia Peck, "Abstractions, Good and Bad, in Fort Worth," *Dallas Morning News*, 16 February 1947.

97 Patricia Peck, "New Gouaches by Bror Utter," *Dallas Morning News*, 1 January 1947.

98 The Roman arches he employed in his embellished forms continued to grow in importance. He later recalled: "I, for some reason, was very interested in the shape of the Roman arch. And I introduced architectural elements that looked somewhat like Roman aqueducts." Utter interview, 1979, p. 28.

99 Utter interview, 1979, p. 25.

100 *Texas Contemporary Artists*, Knoedler Galleries, June 10–September 28, 1952.

101 See Howard Devree, "National Round Up, Exhibition at the Metropolitan Reveals Growth and Strength in Our Art," *New York Times*, 10 December 1950, and *American Painting Today – 1950: A National Competitive Exhibition* (New York: The Metropolitan Museum of Art, 1950).

102 For an assessment of Brants' career, see Margaret Blagg, *Cynthia Brants: Beyond the Circle* (Albany, Texas: Old Jail Art Center, 2007).

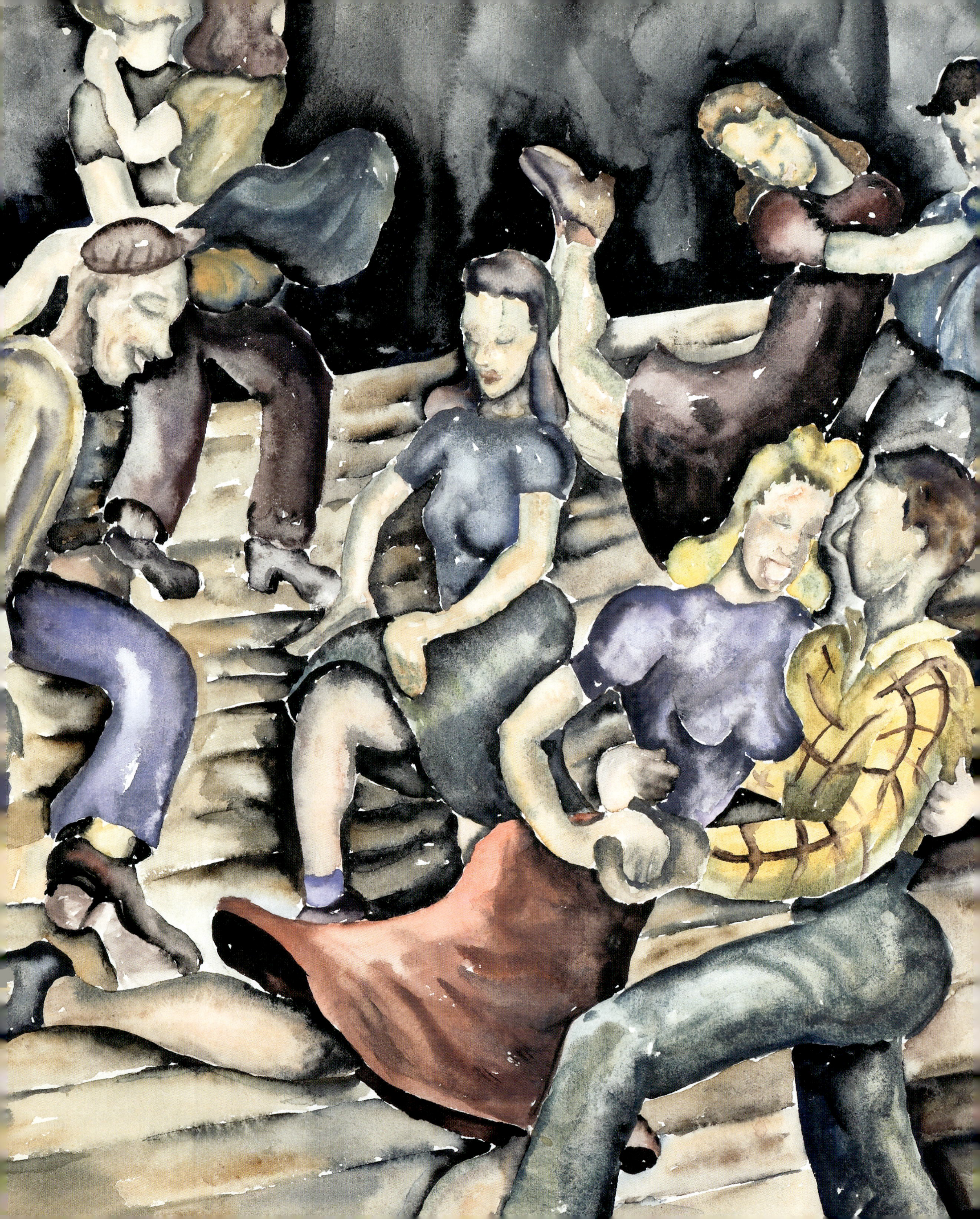

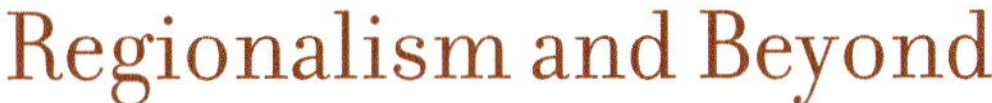

Regionalism and Beyond

PLATE **1** Bill Bomar, *Santa Fe View*, 1942

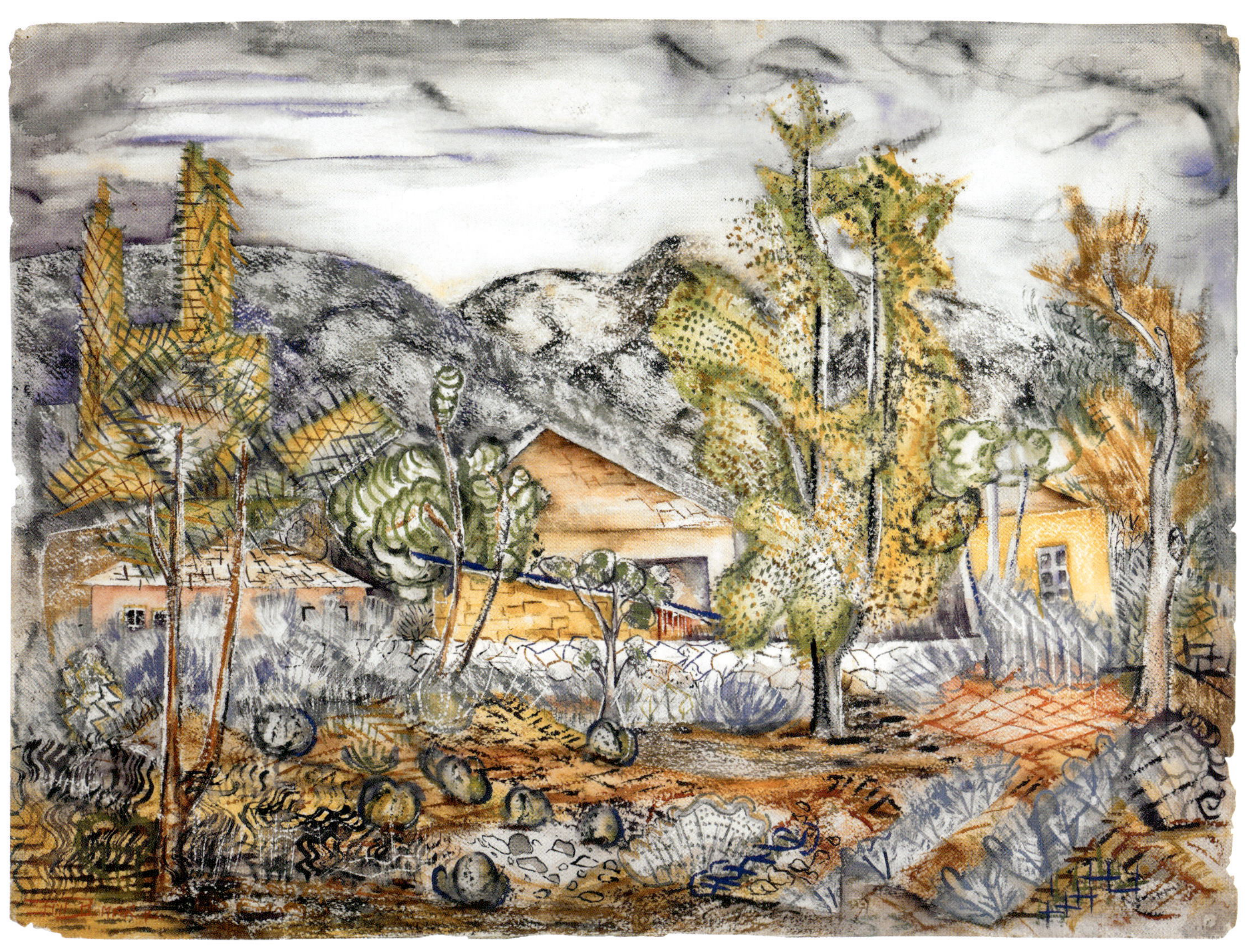

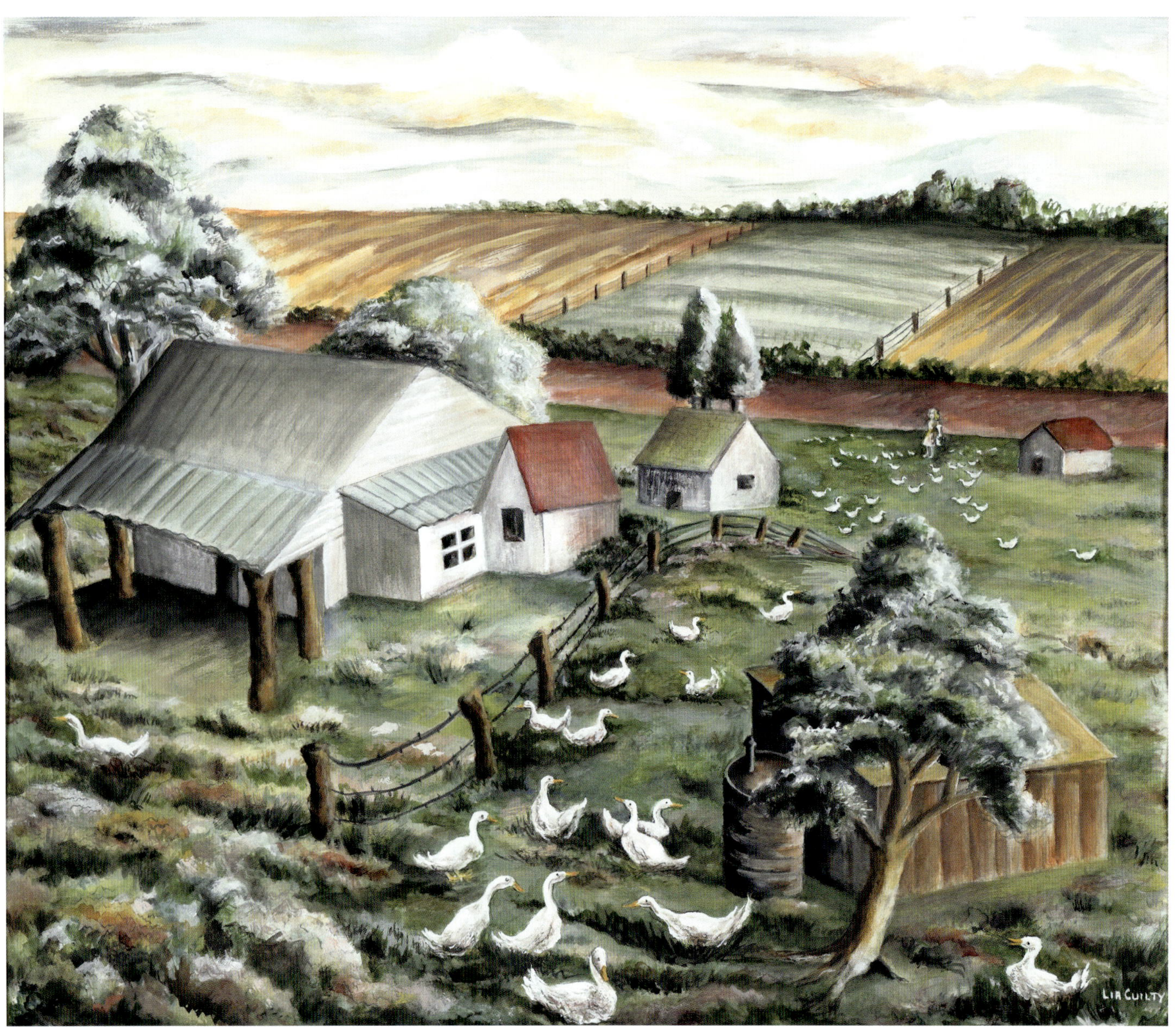

PLATE **2** Lia Cuilty, *The Day's at Morn*, 1944

PLATE **3** Kelly Fearing, *Jitterbuggers*, 1939

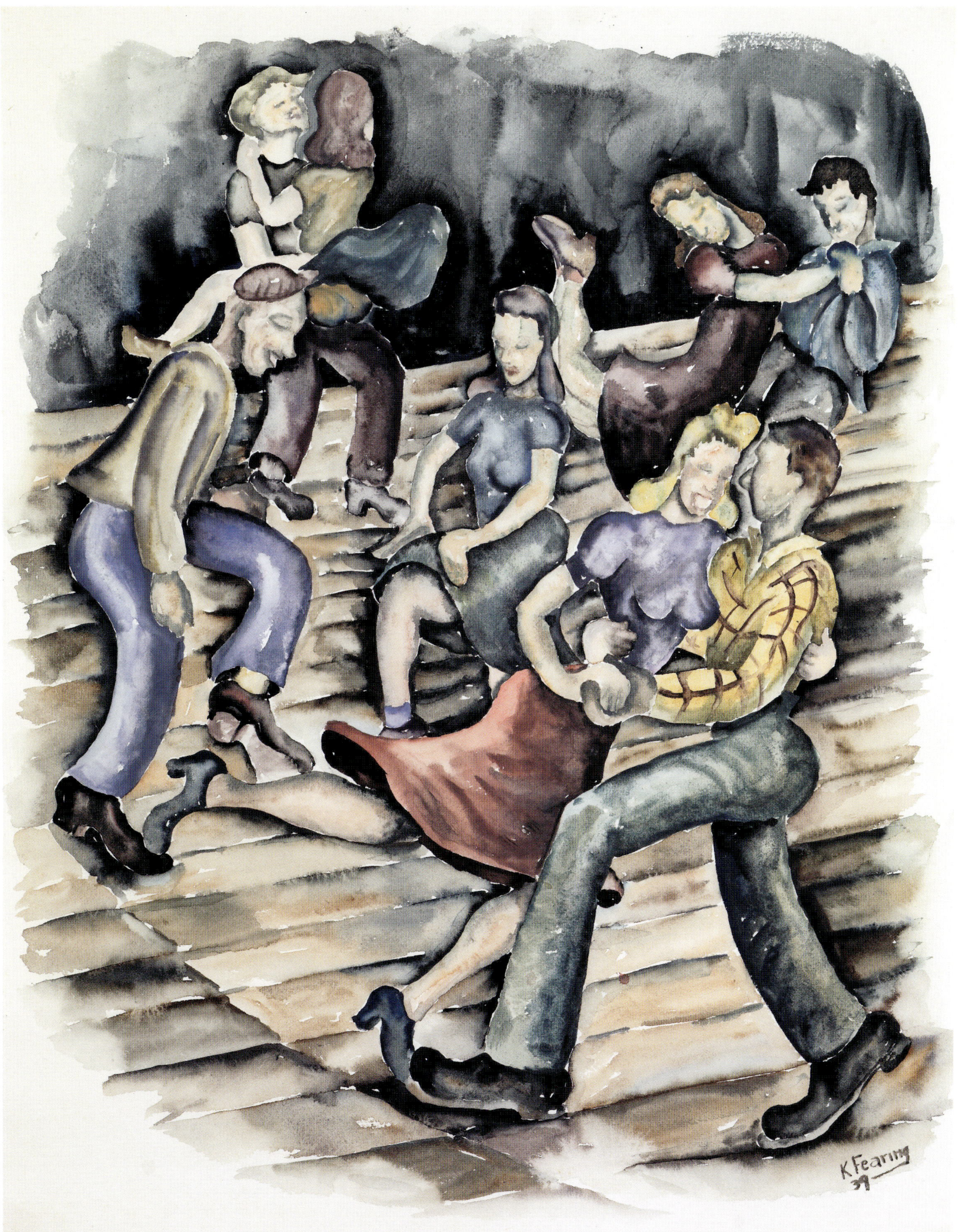
K Fearing
39

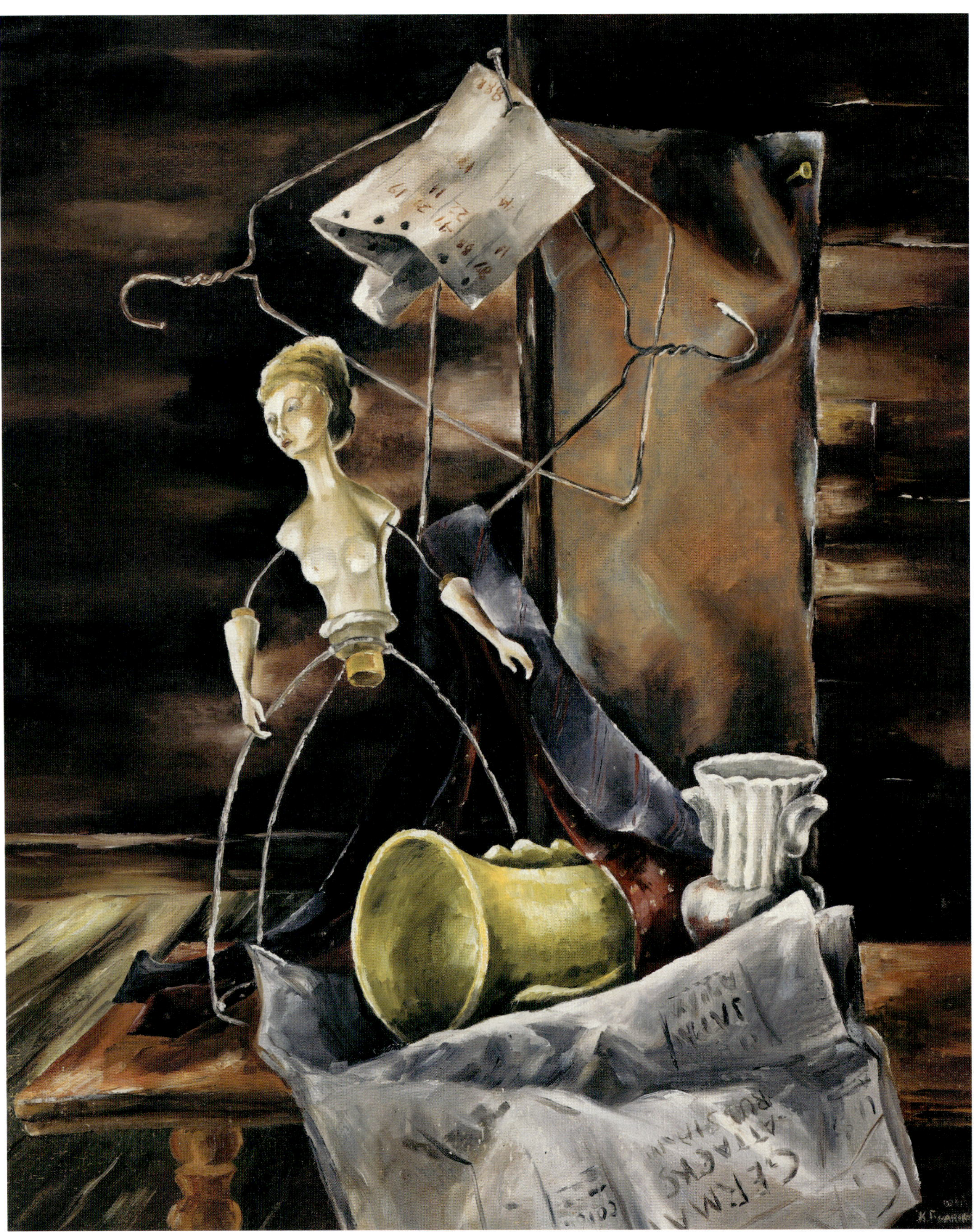

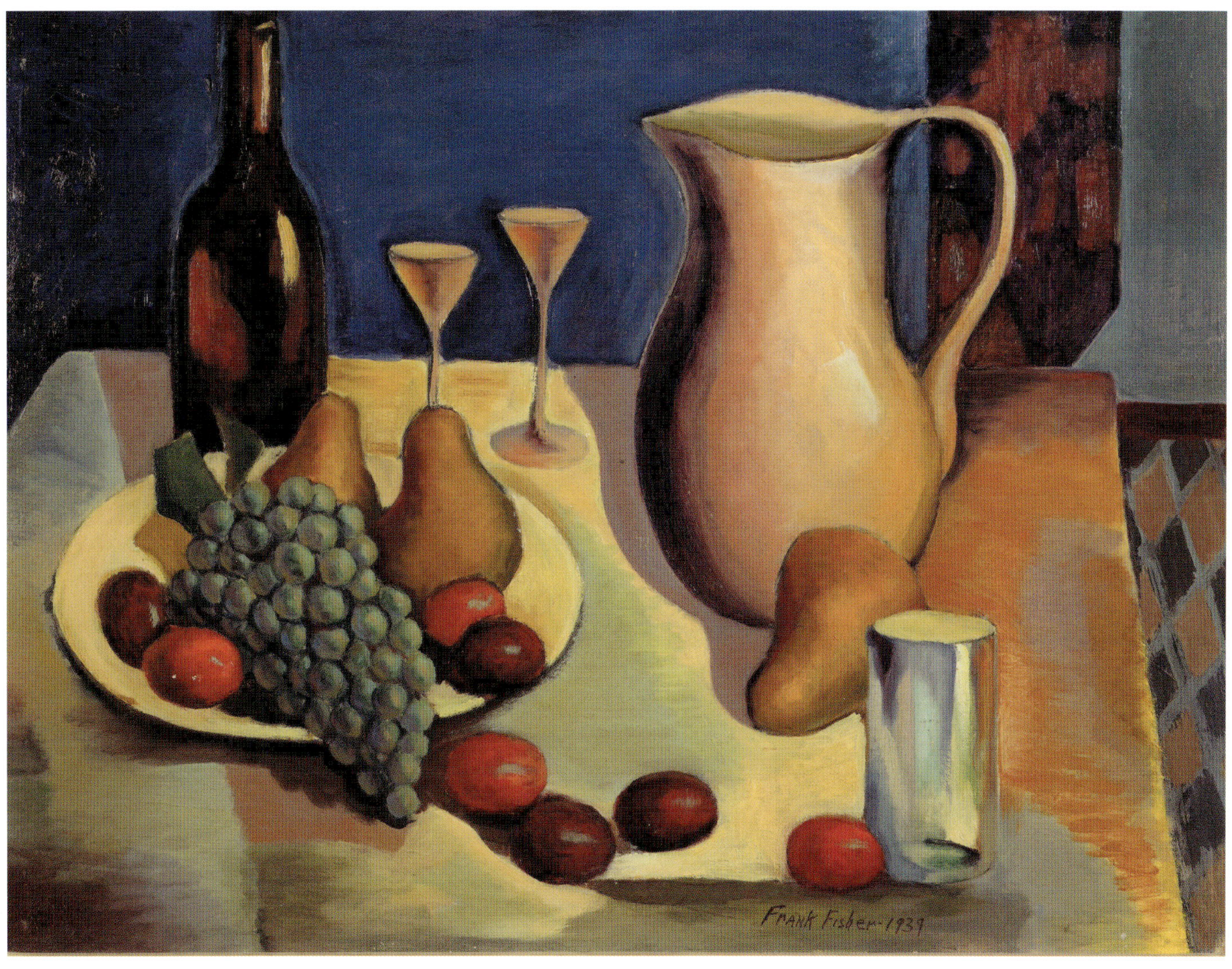

PLATE **4** Kelly Fearing, *Attic Piece*, 1941

PLATE **5** Frank Fisher, *Still Life*, 1939

PLATE **6** Veronica Helfensteller, *Untitled [St. Louis Apartment House]*, ca. 1935–37

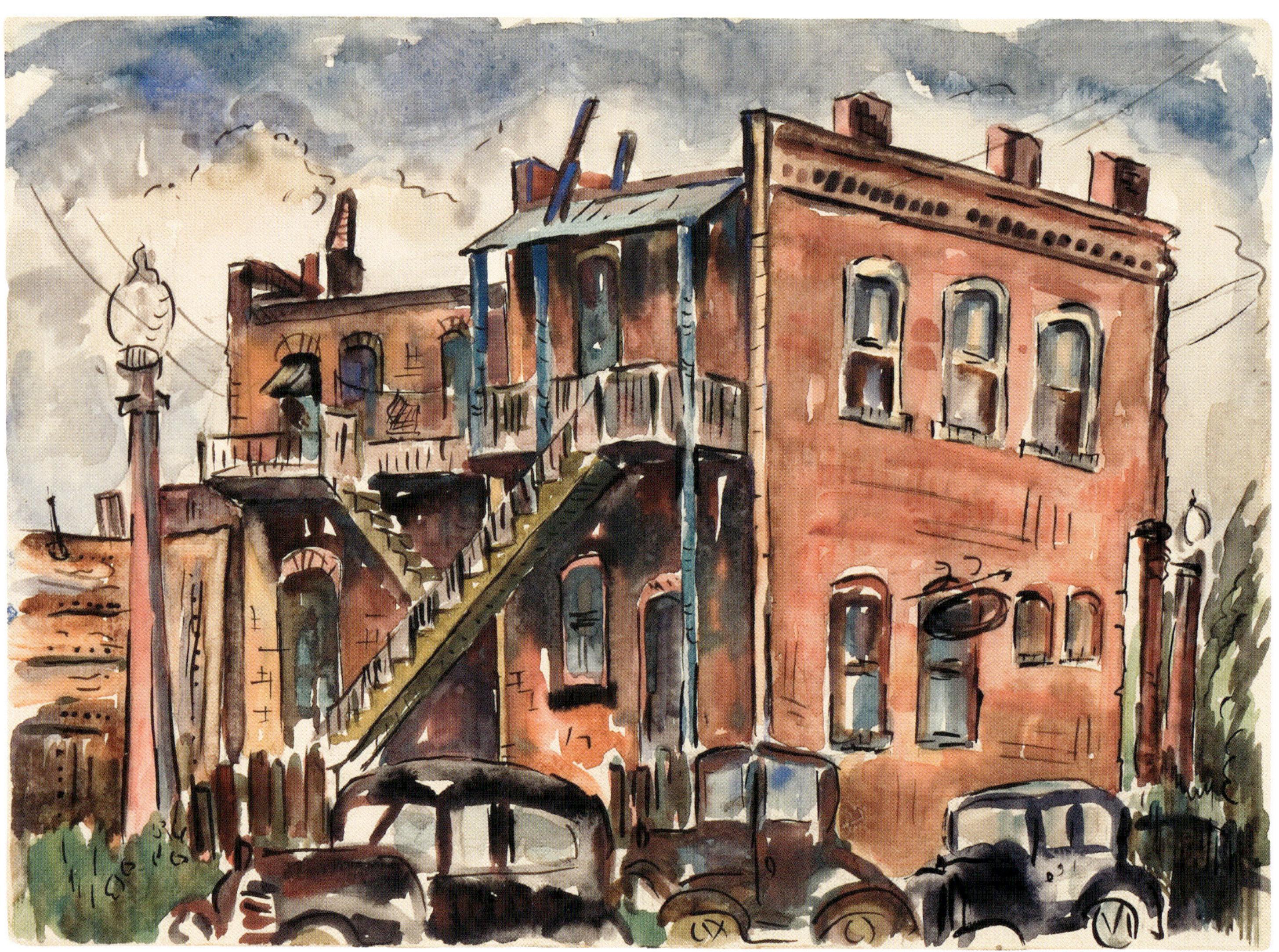

PLATE **7** Veronica Helfensteller, *Untitled [Eads Bridge, St. Louis]*, ca. 1935–37

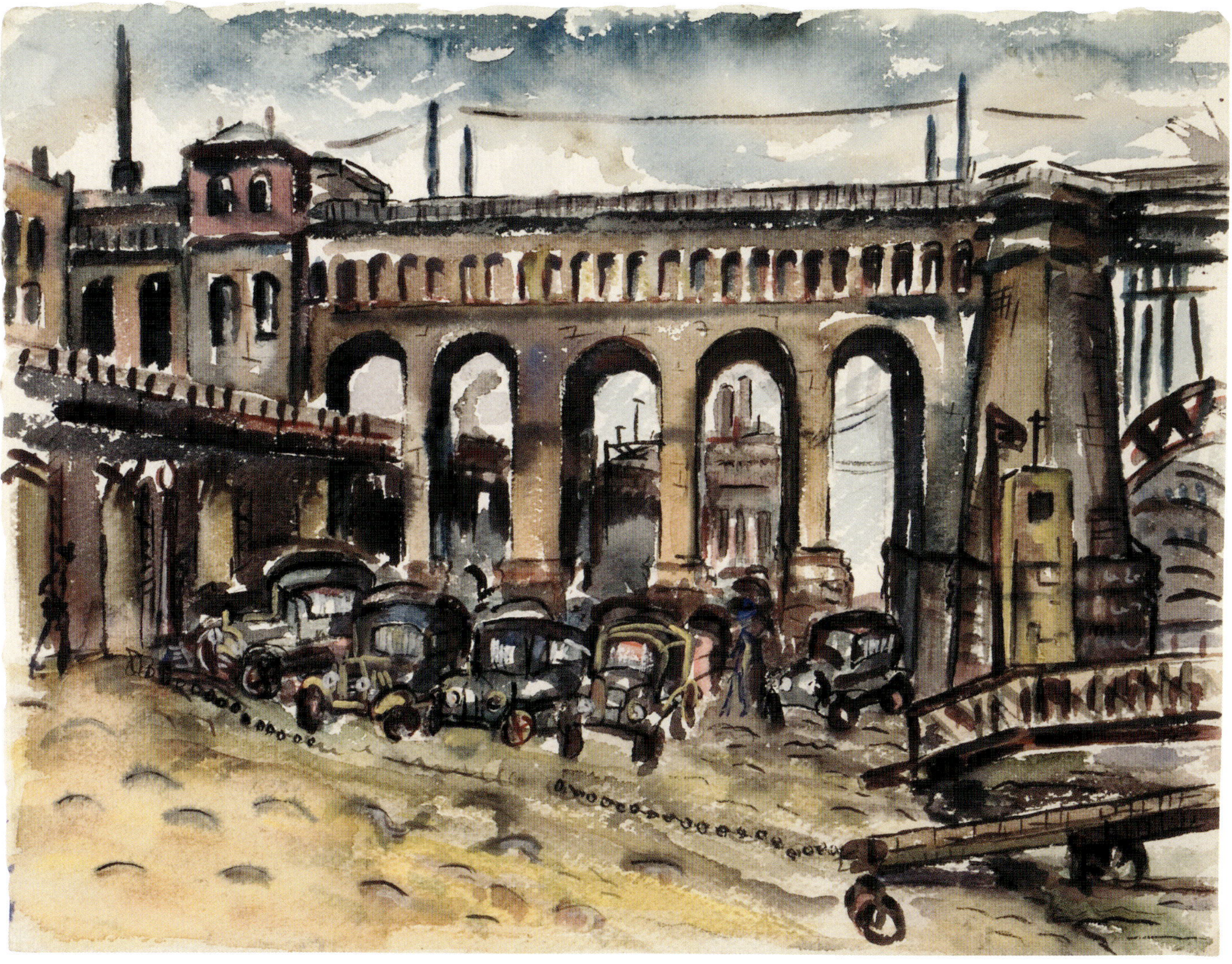

PLATE **8** Dickson Reeder, *Mazy*, 1937, i/ii (object reproduced at actual size)

PLATE **9** Dickson Reeder, *Mazy*, 1937, ii/ii (object reproduced at actual size)

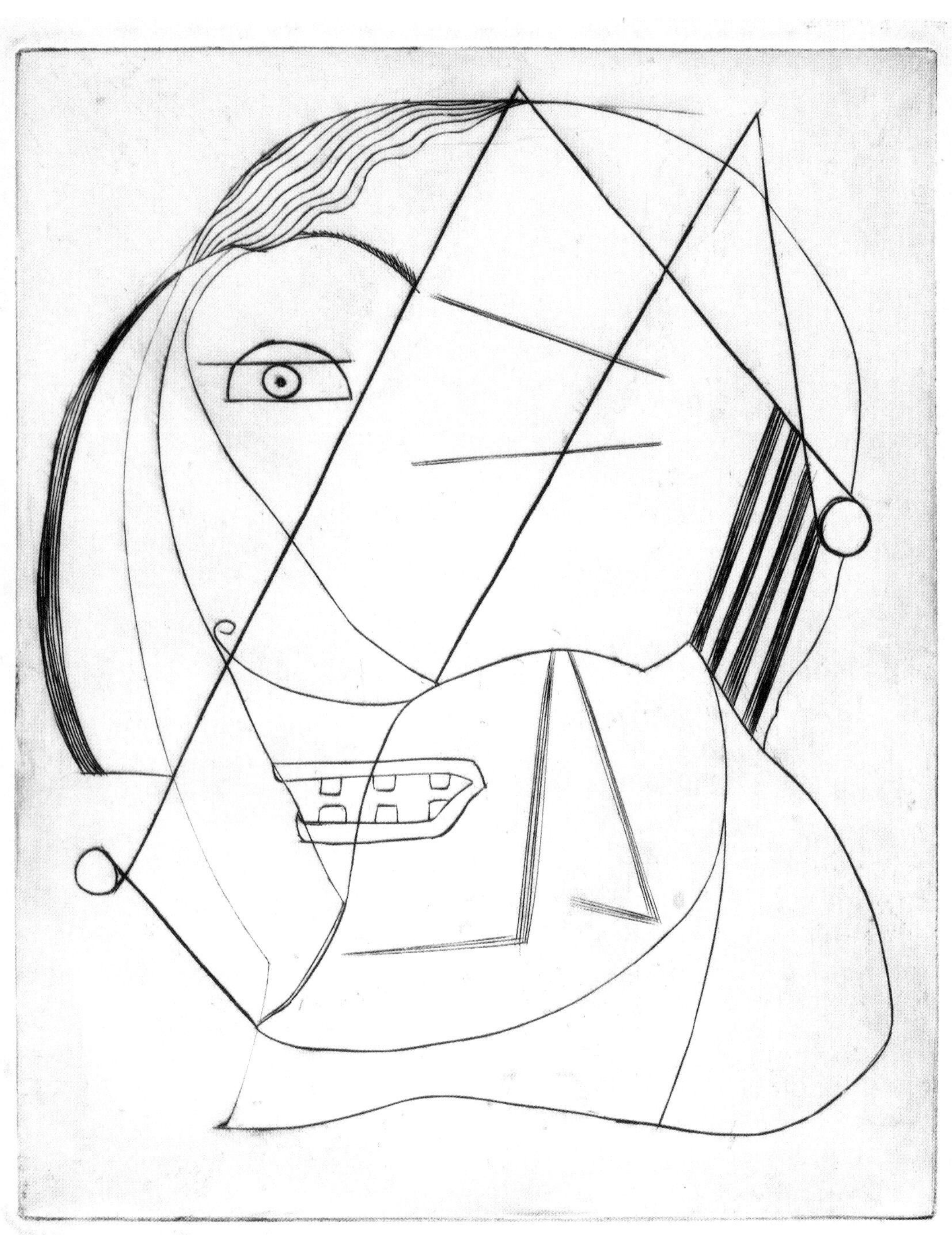

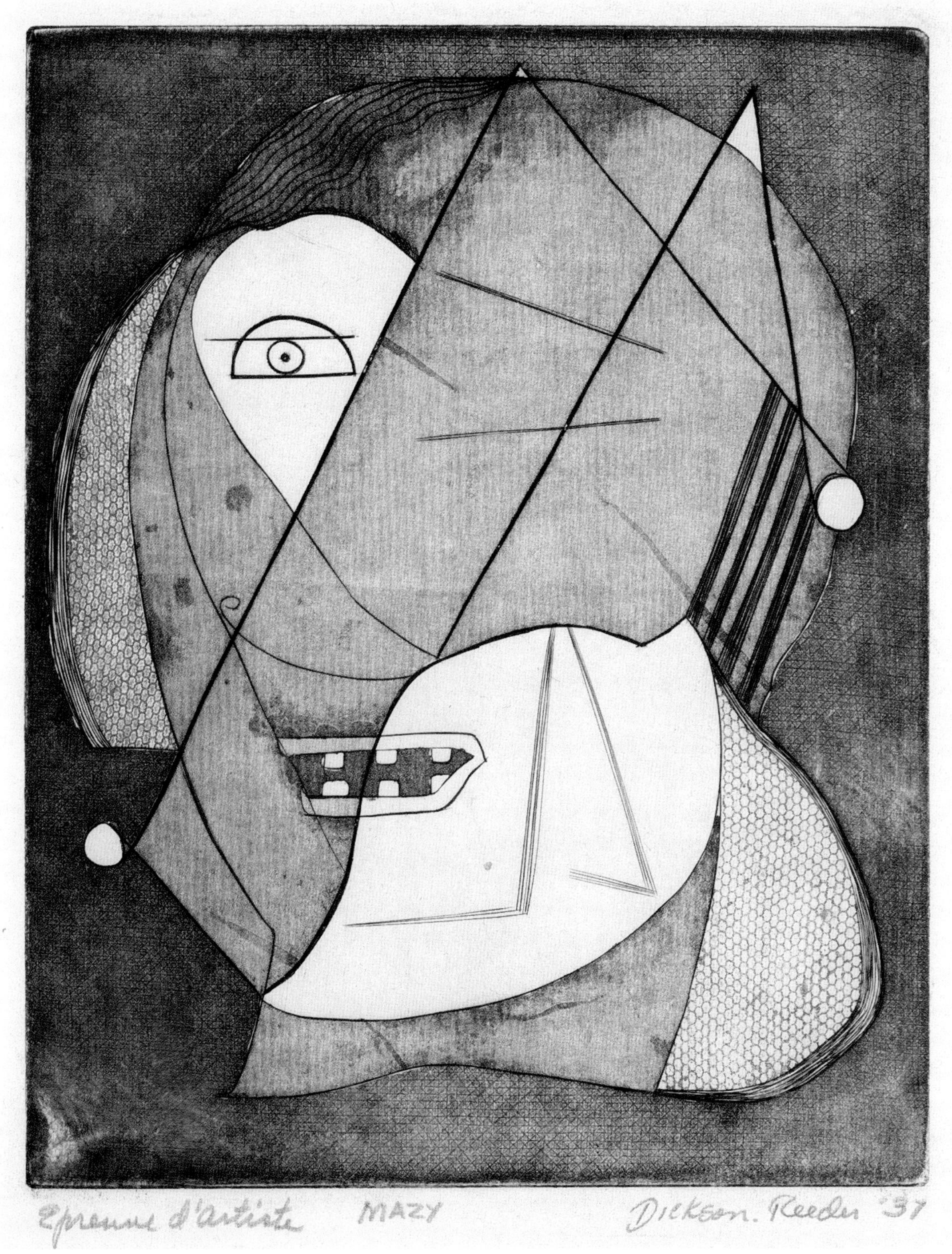
Epreuve d'artiste
MAZY
Dickson. Reeder '37

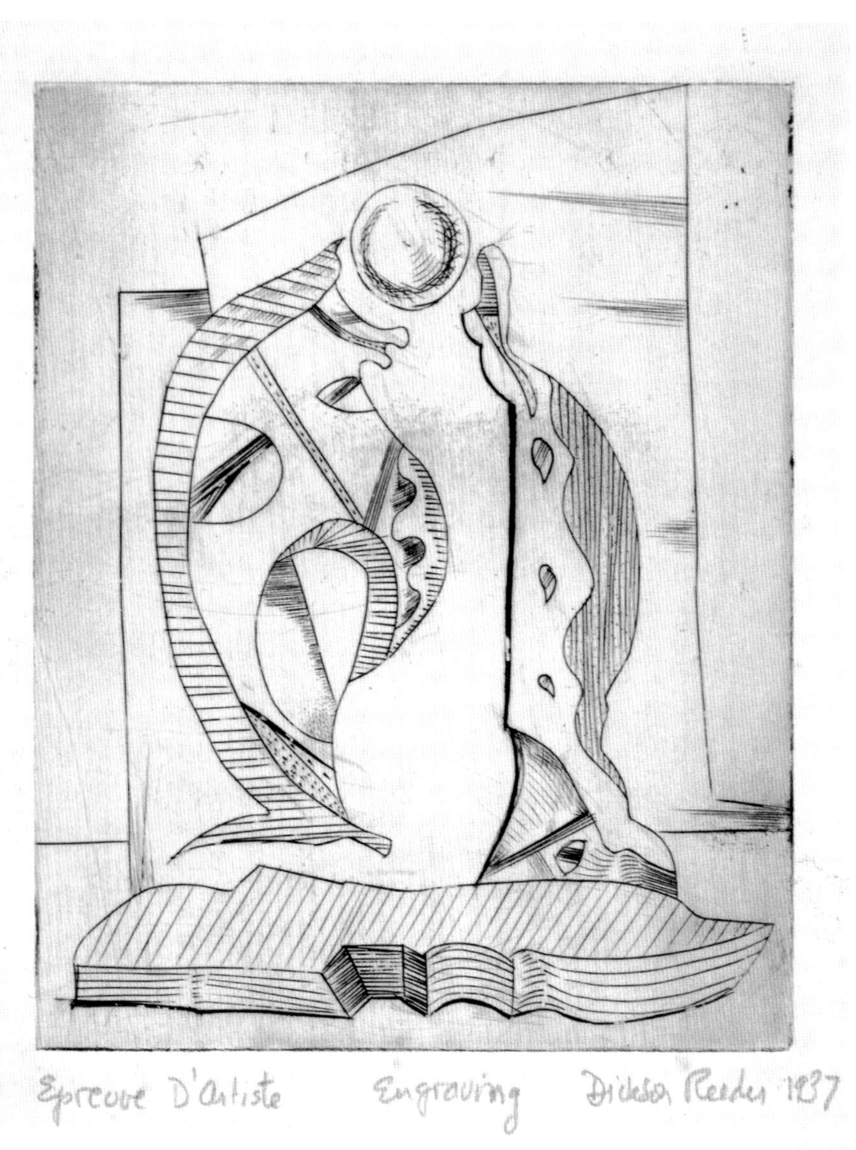

PLATE **10** Dickson Reeder, *Untitled*, 1937 (object reproduced at actual size)

PLATE **11** Dickson Reeder, Sketchbook, 1937

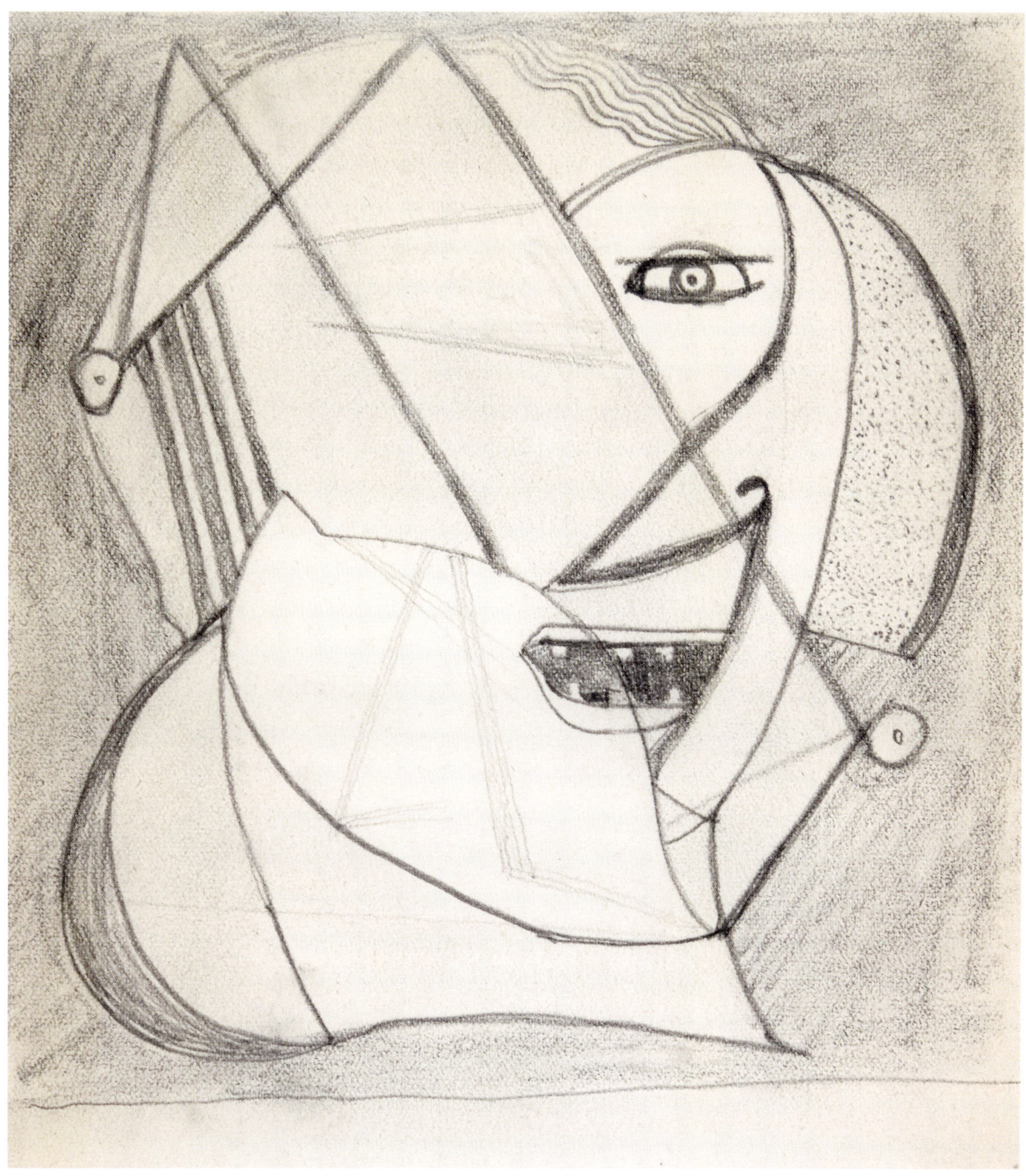

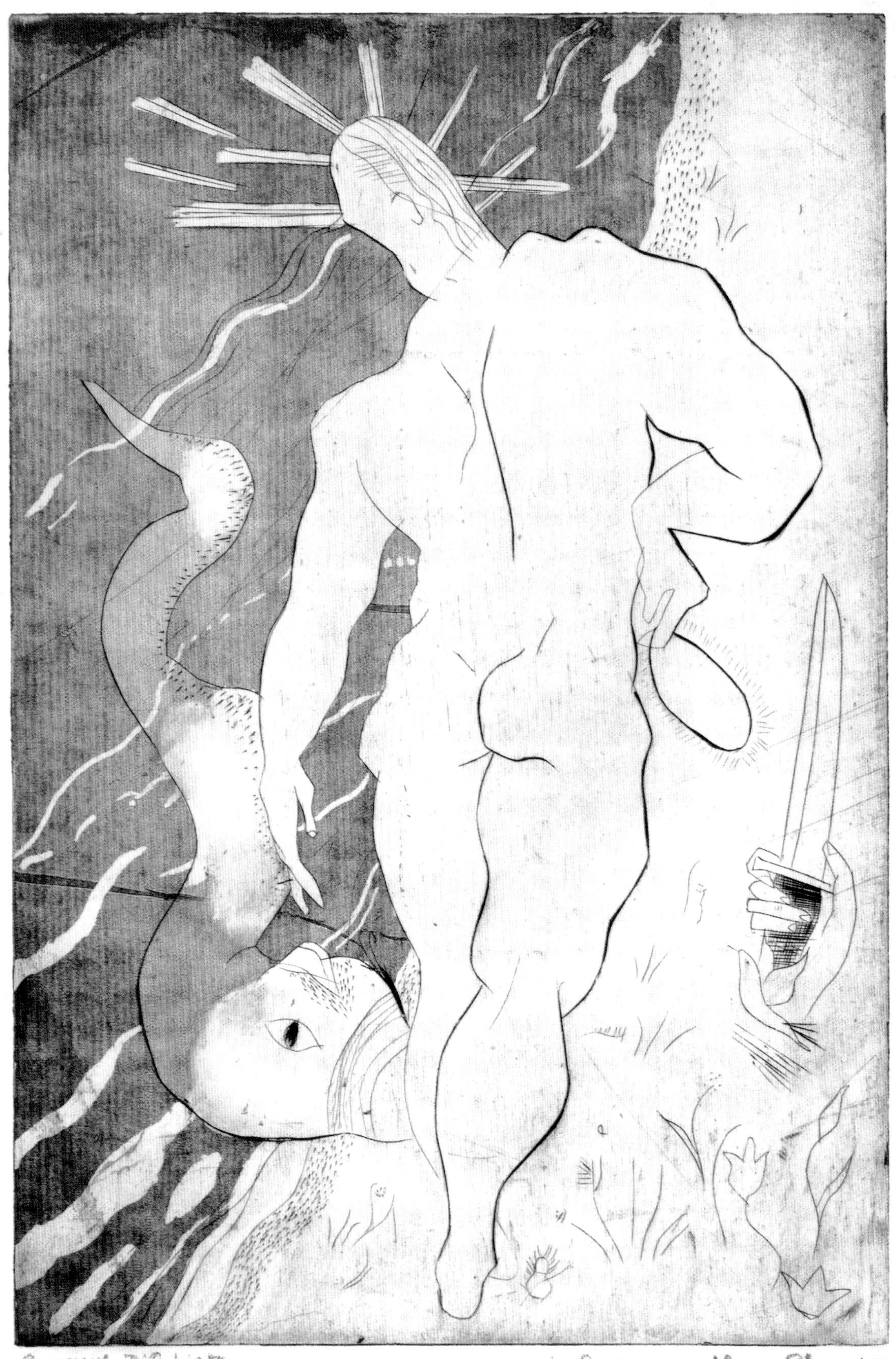
Epreuve D'Artiste
"The Dragon and Saint George
Flora Blanc '37

PLATE **12** Flora Blanc Reeder, *The Dragon and Saint George*, 1937

PLATE **13** Bror Utter, *Going Home*, 1944

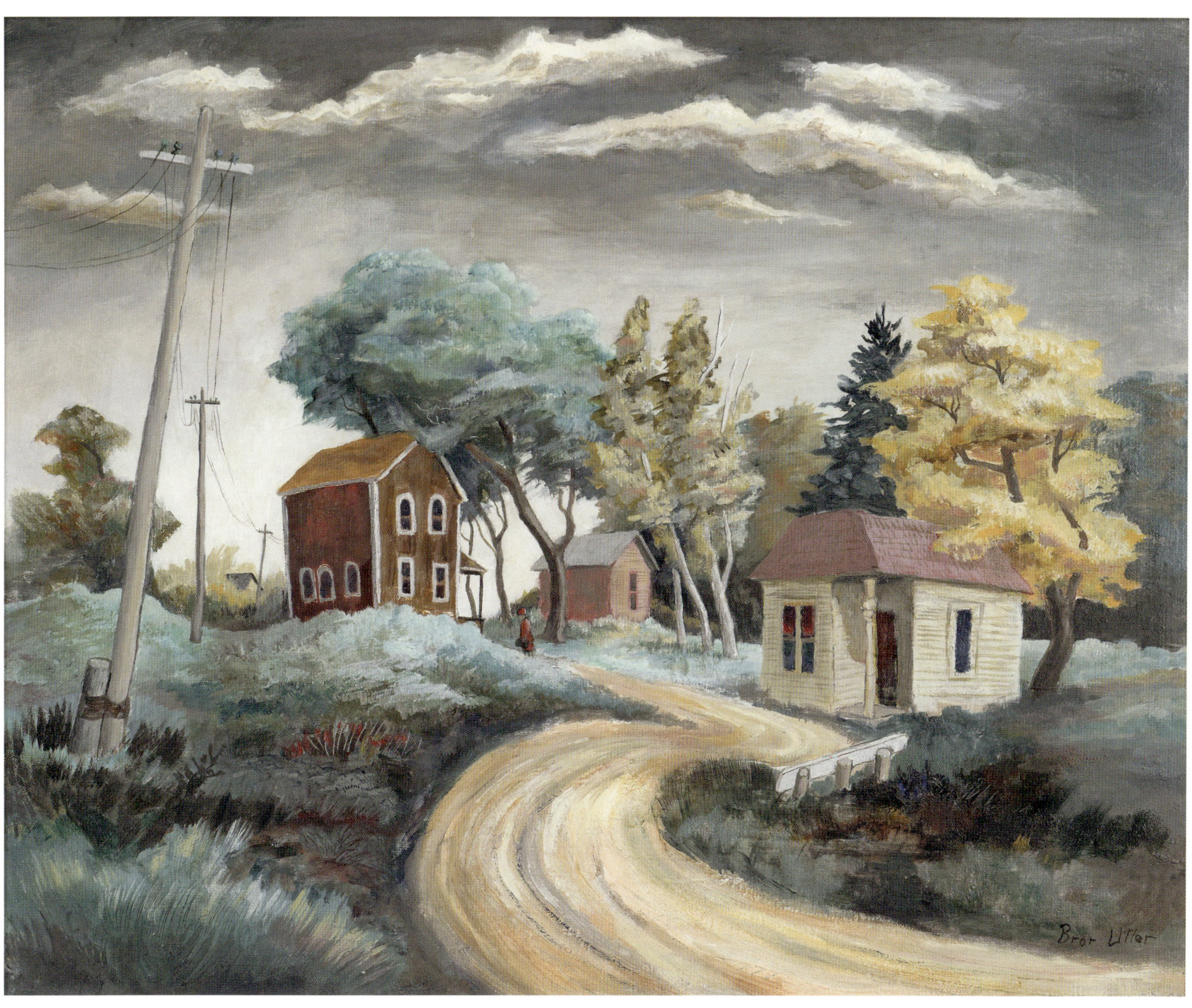

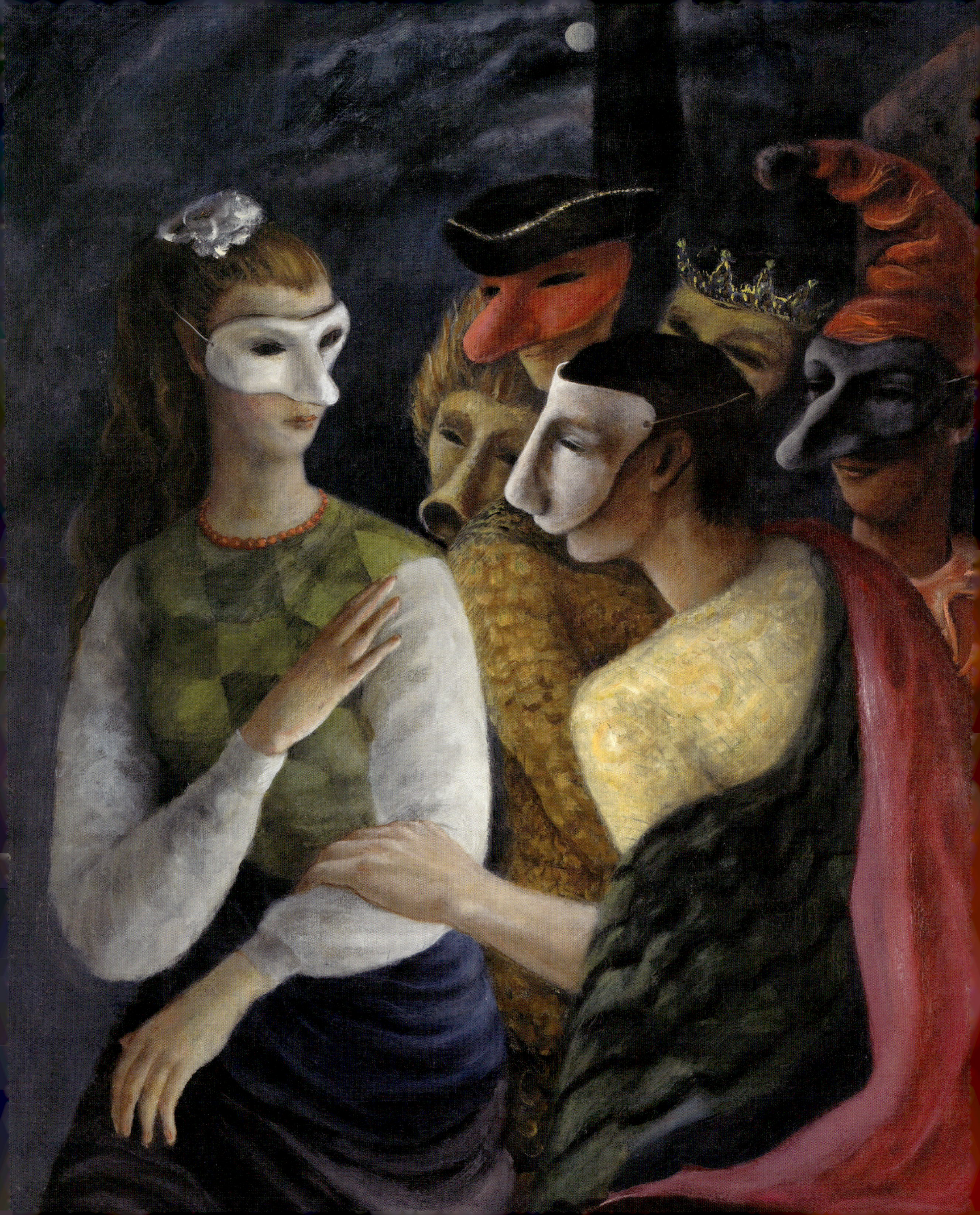

The Energy of Escape: Art, Theater, and Dance

PLATE **14** Veronica Helfensteller, *The Host in the Coffin*, 1943

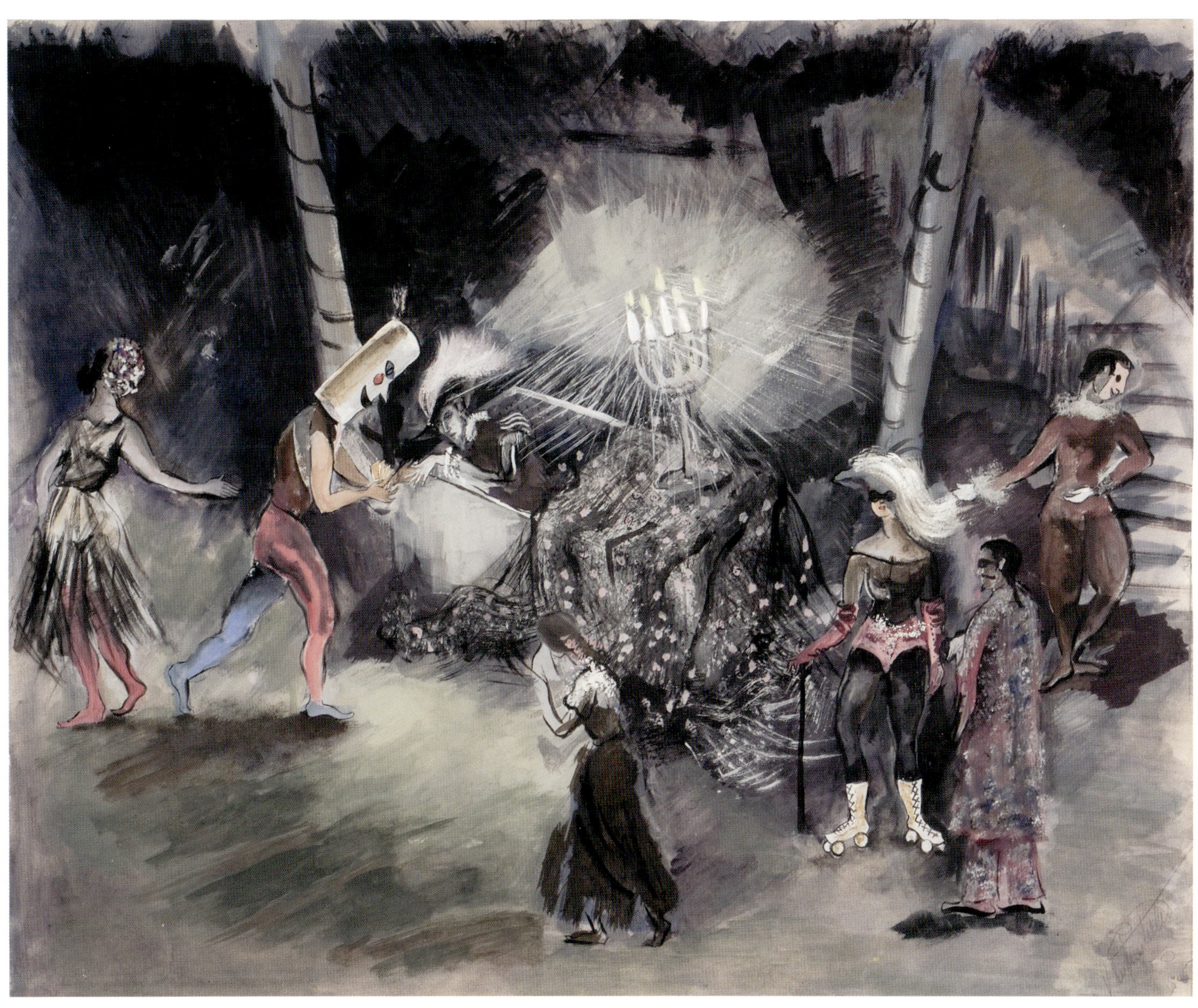

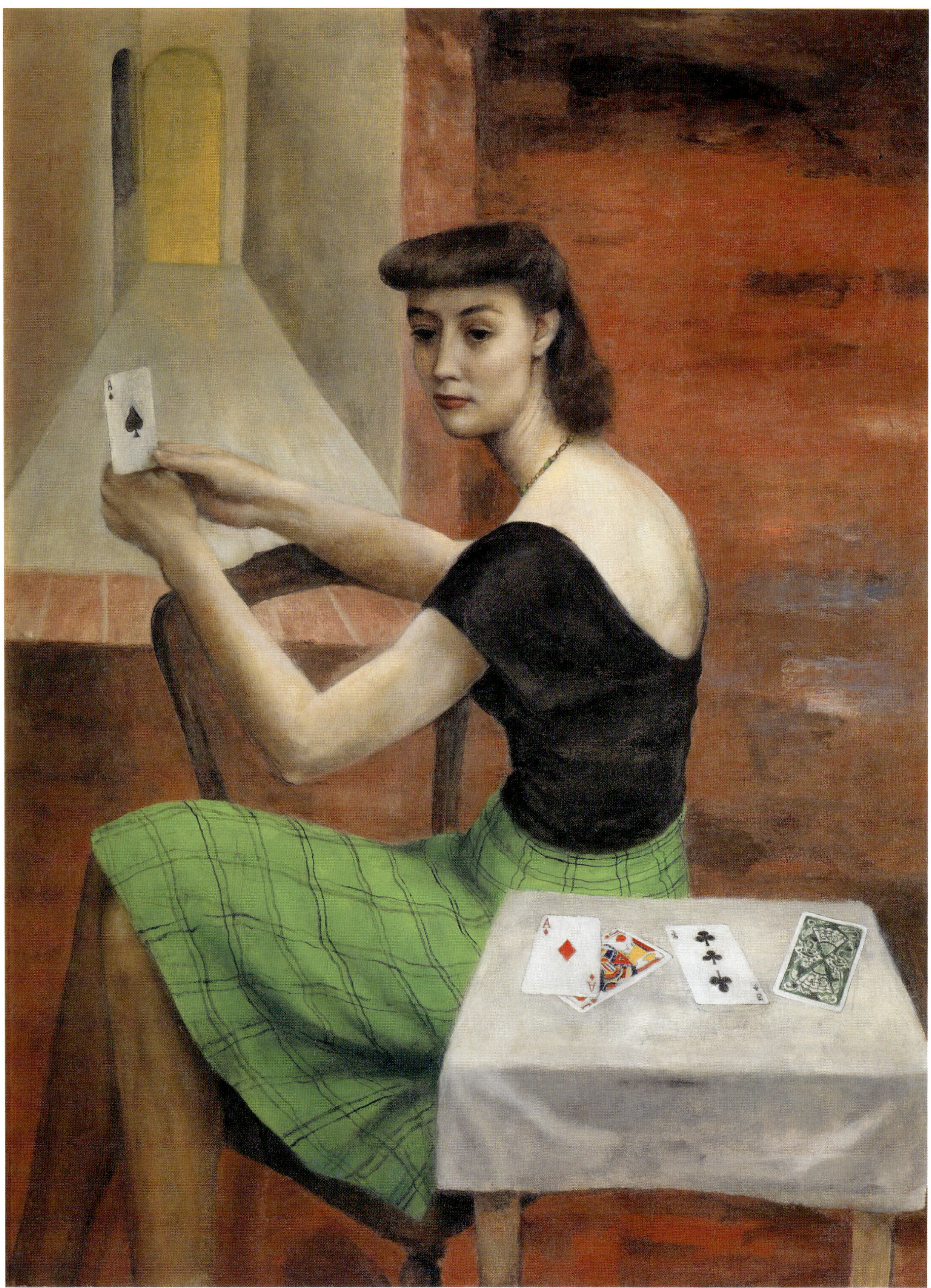

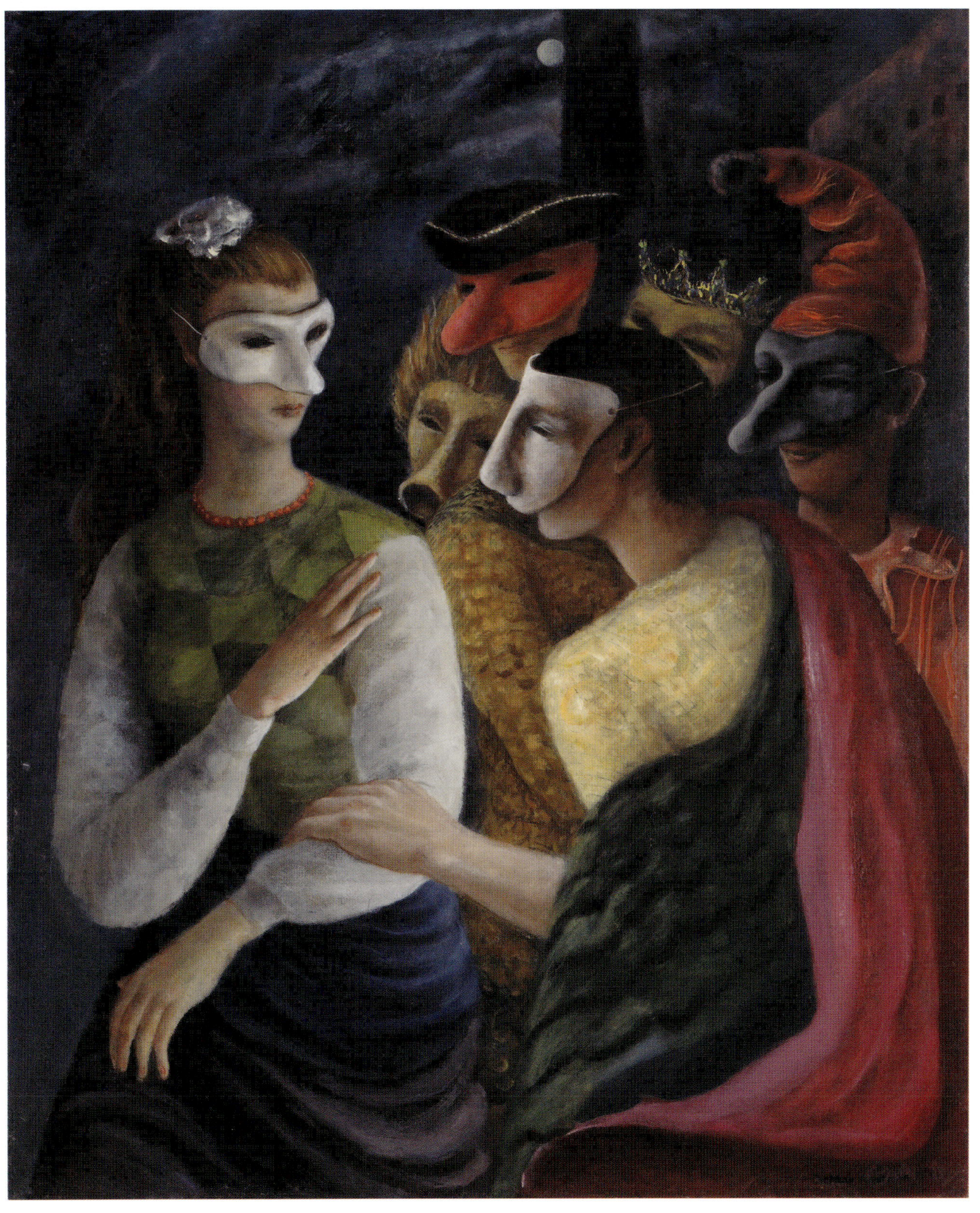

PLATE **15** Dickson Reeder, *Untitled [Sara with the Ace of Spades]*, ca. 1942

PLATE **16** Dickson Reeder, *All Hallow's Eve*, 1945

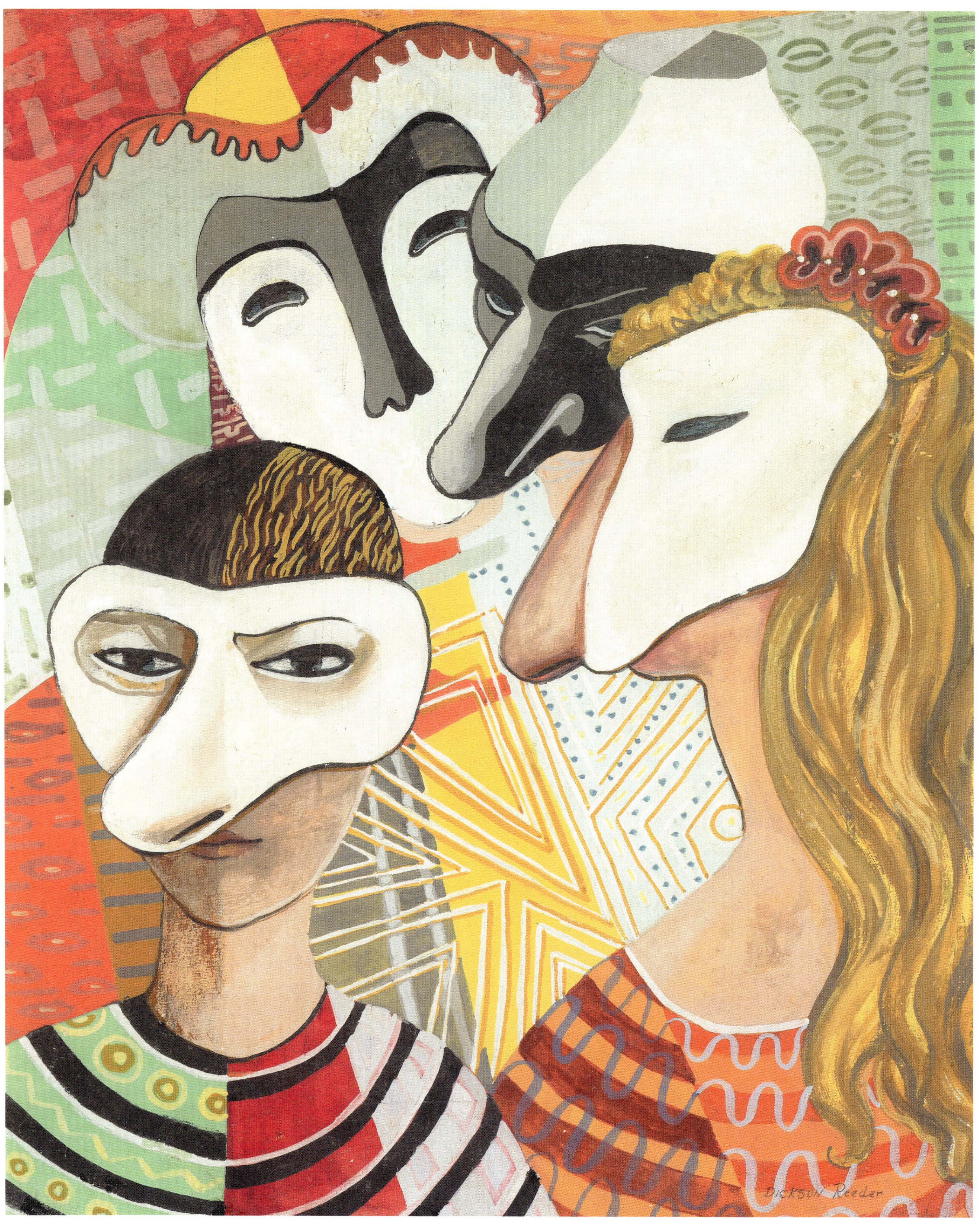
DICKSON Reeder

PLATE **17** Dickson Reeder, *Masquerade*, 1945

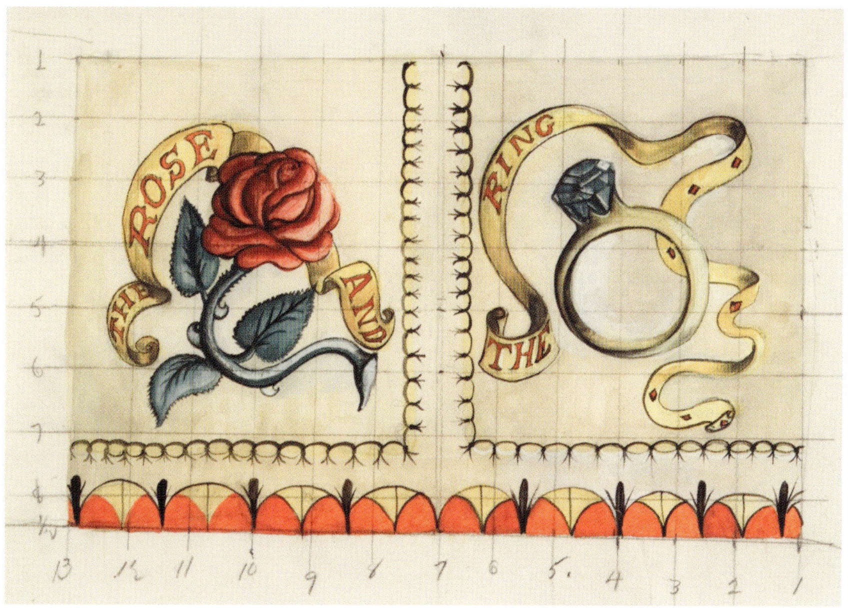

PLATE **18** Dickson Reeder, Study for stage curtain, *The Rose and the Ring*, ca. 1946–53

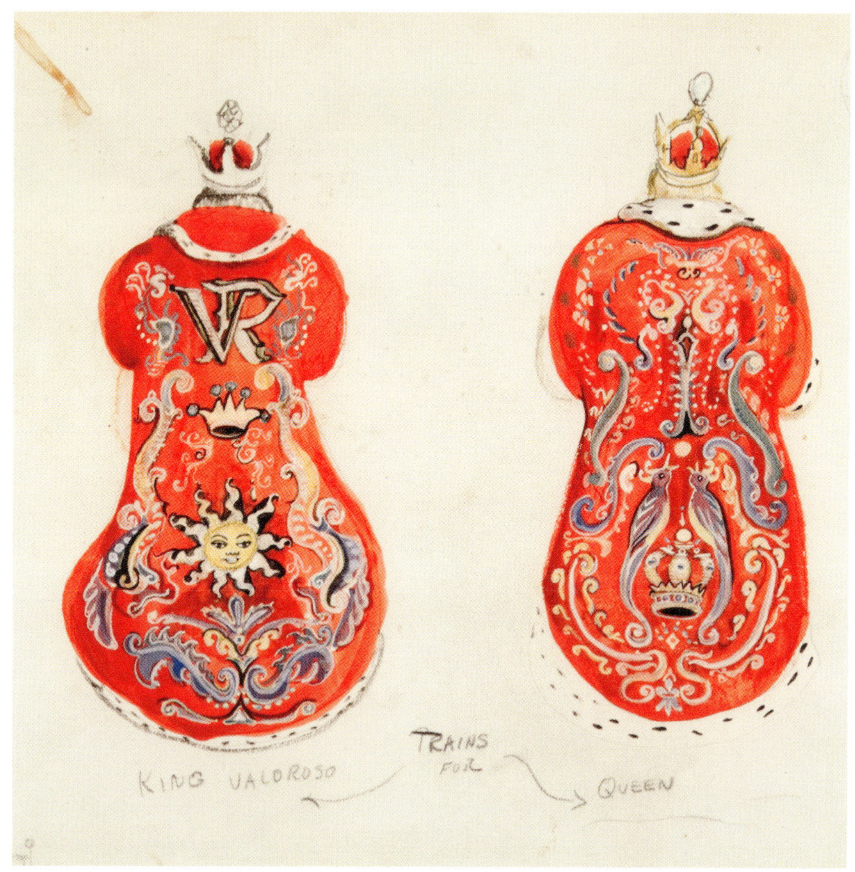

PLATE **19** Dickson Reeder, Costume study for *The Rose and the Ring*, ca. 1946–53

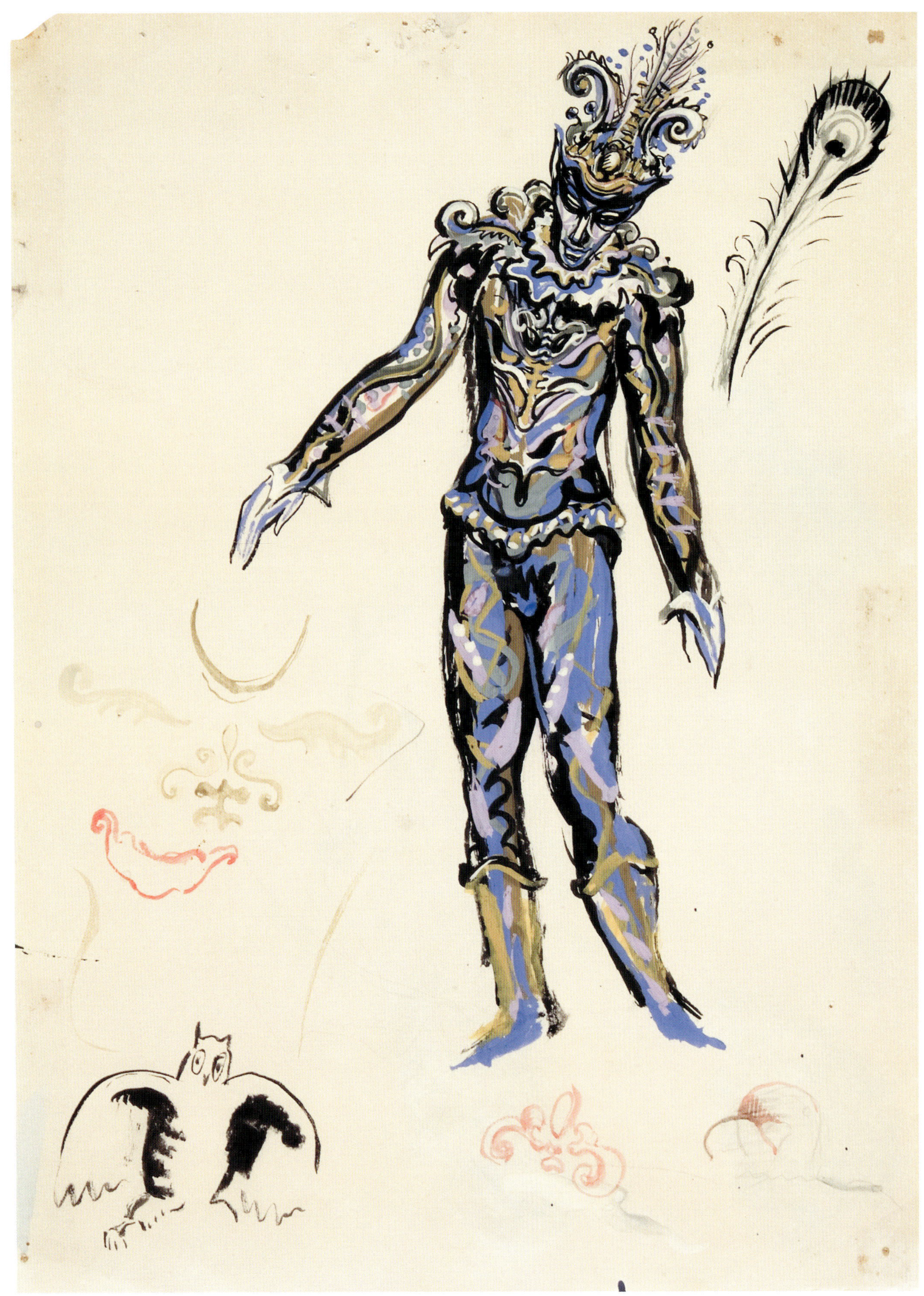

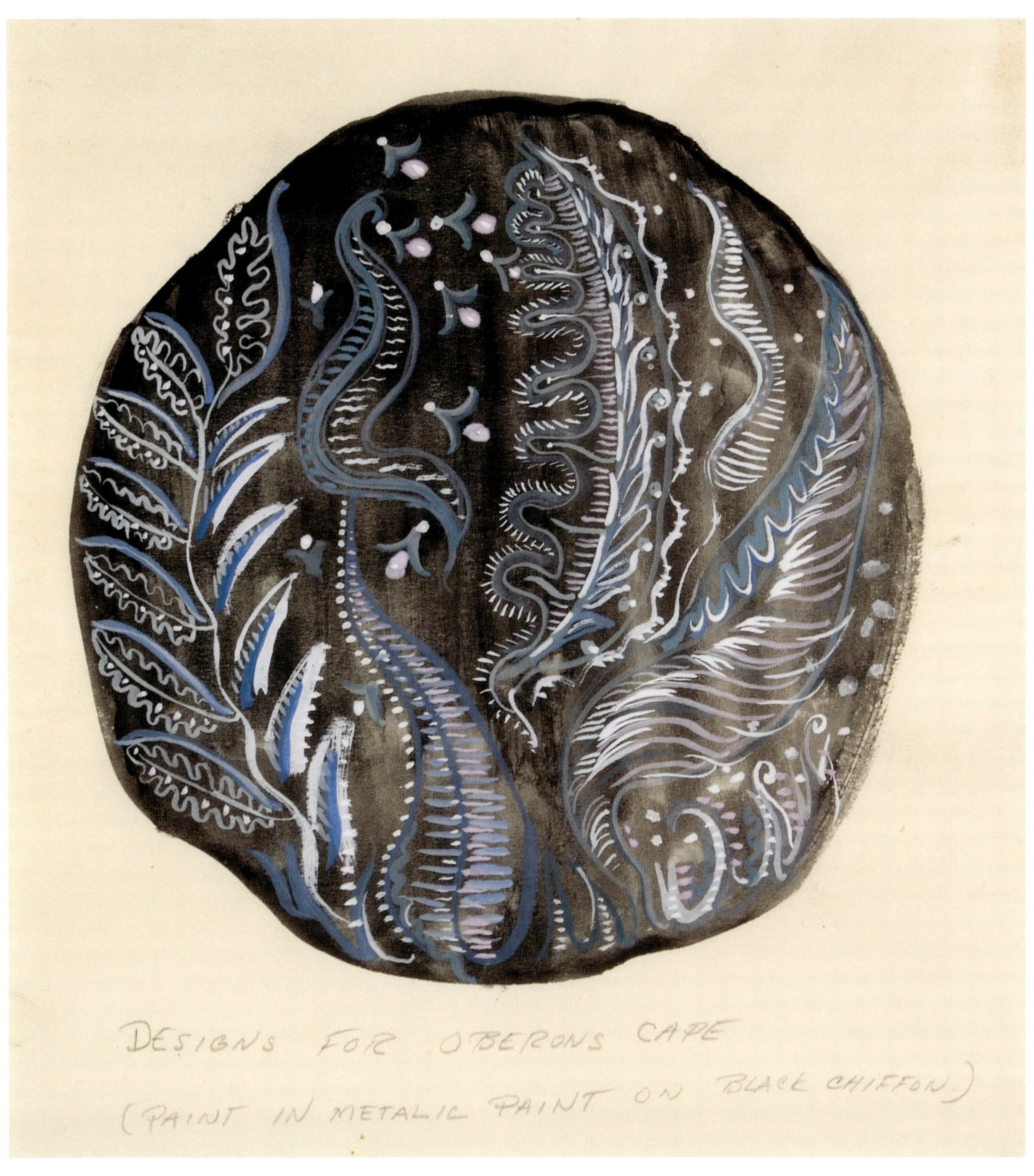

PLATE **20** Dickson Reeder, Costume study for *A Midsummer Night's Dream*, ca. 1948–54

PLATE **21** Dickson Reeder, Costume study for *A Midsummer Night's Dream*, ca. 1948–54

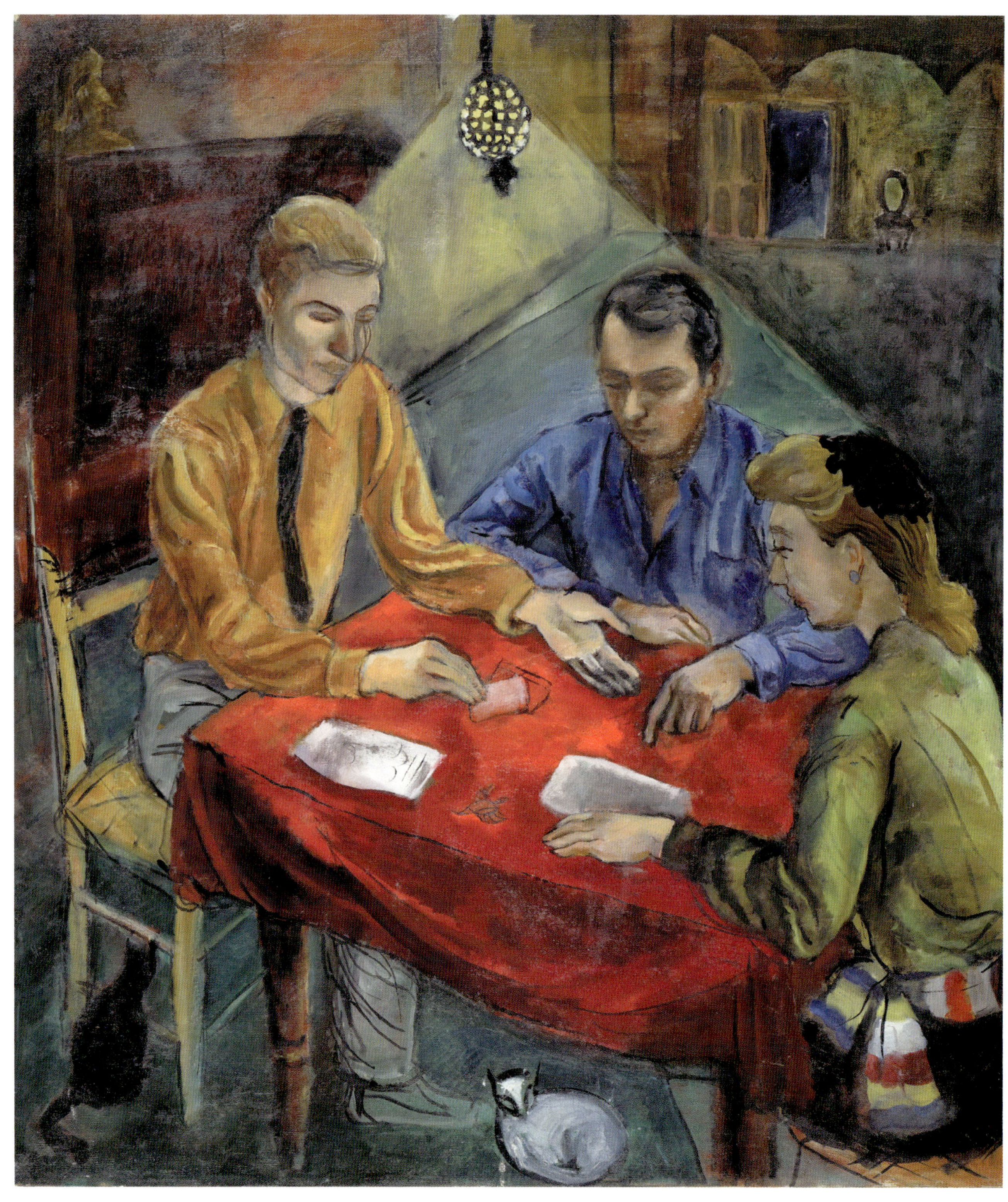

PLATE **22** Flora Blanc Reeder, *Reading the Cards*, ca. 1943

PLATE **23** Sara Shannon, *Ballet on the Stairs*, 1943

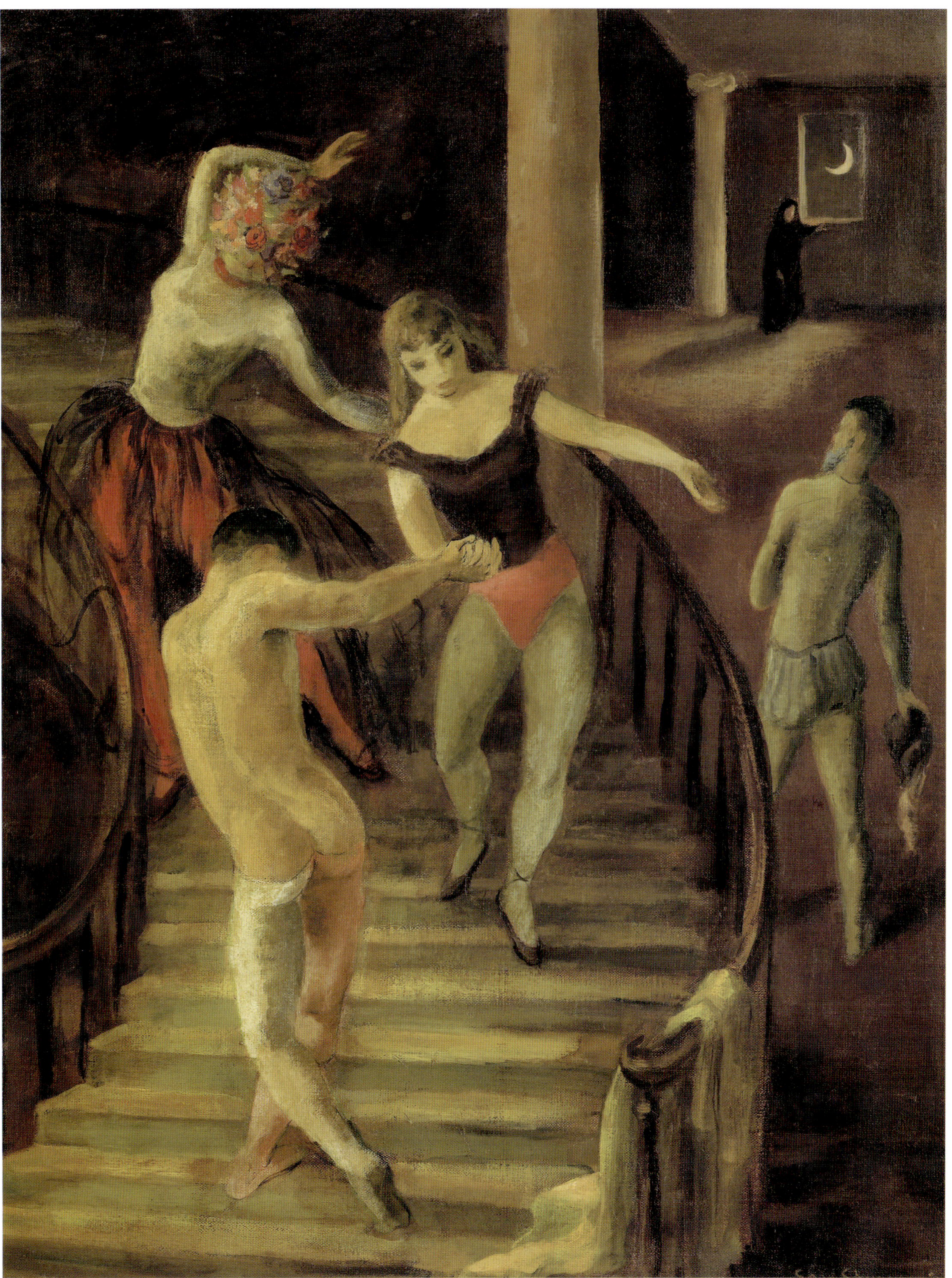

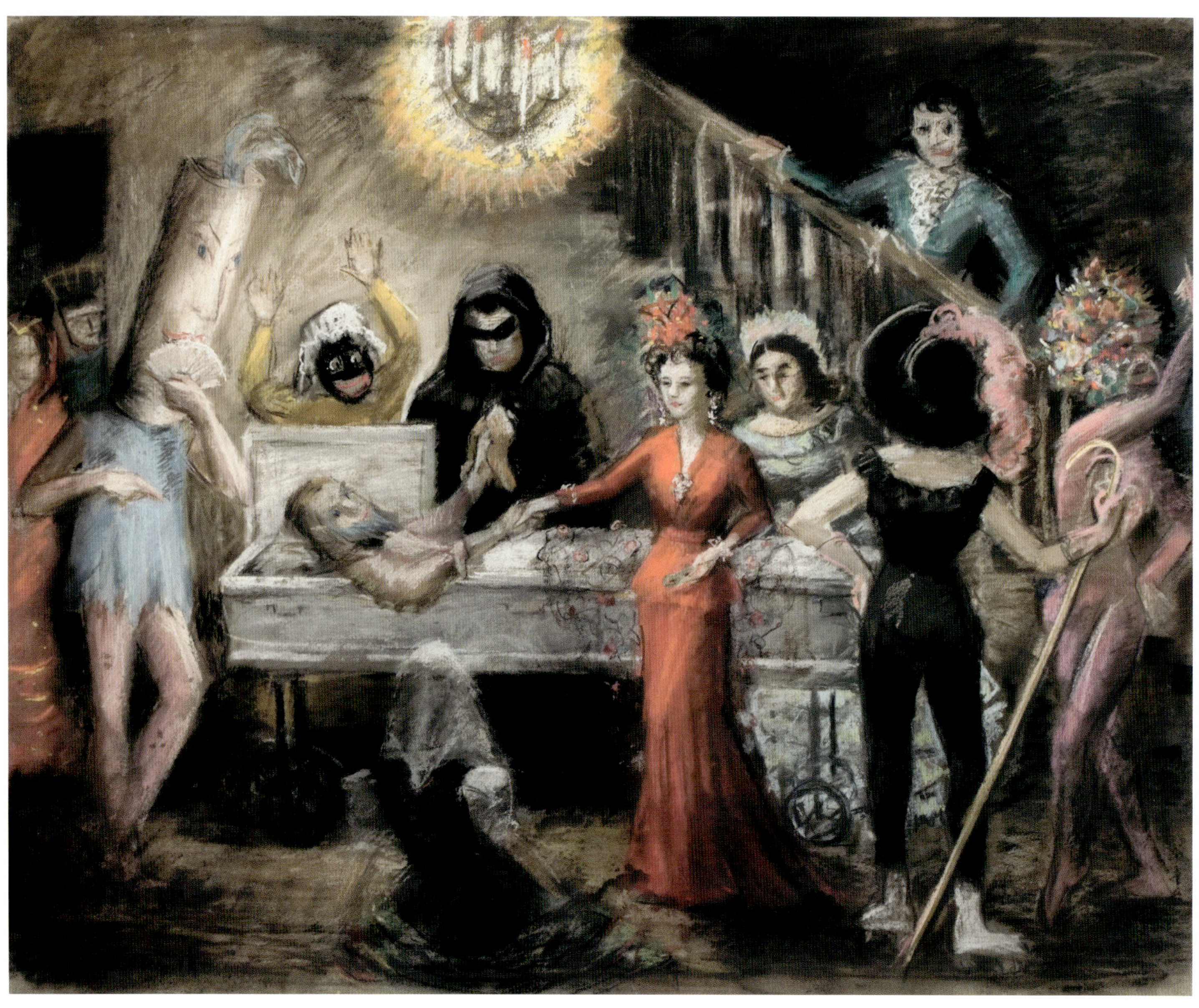

PLATE **24** Emily Guthrie Smith, *The Halloween Party*, 1943

PLATE **25** Bror Utter, *Lady with a Box*, 1941

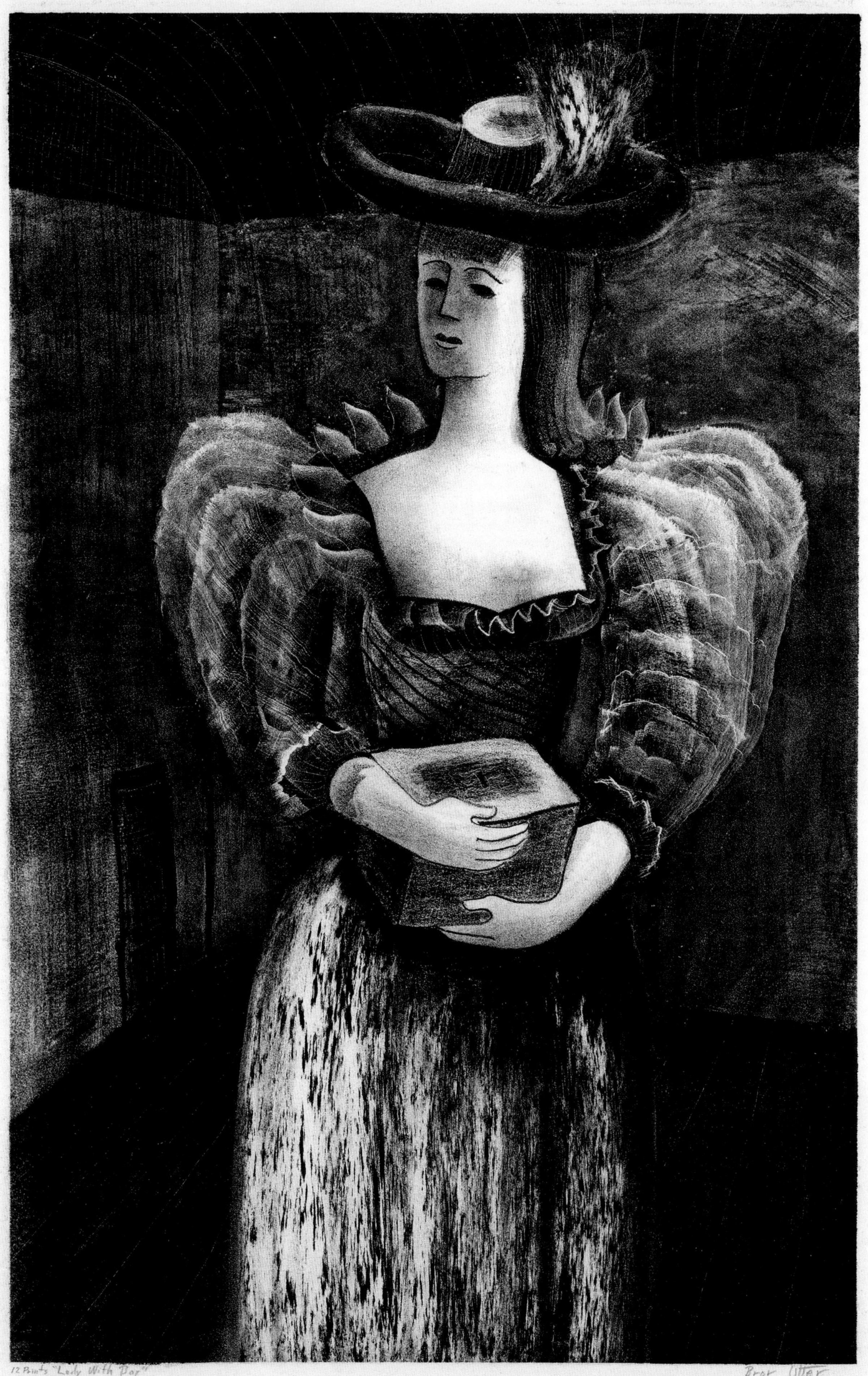
12 Prints "Lady With Box"
Bror Utter

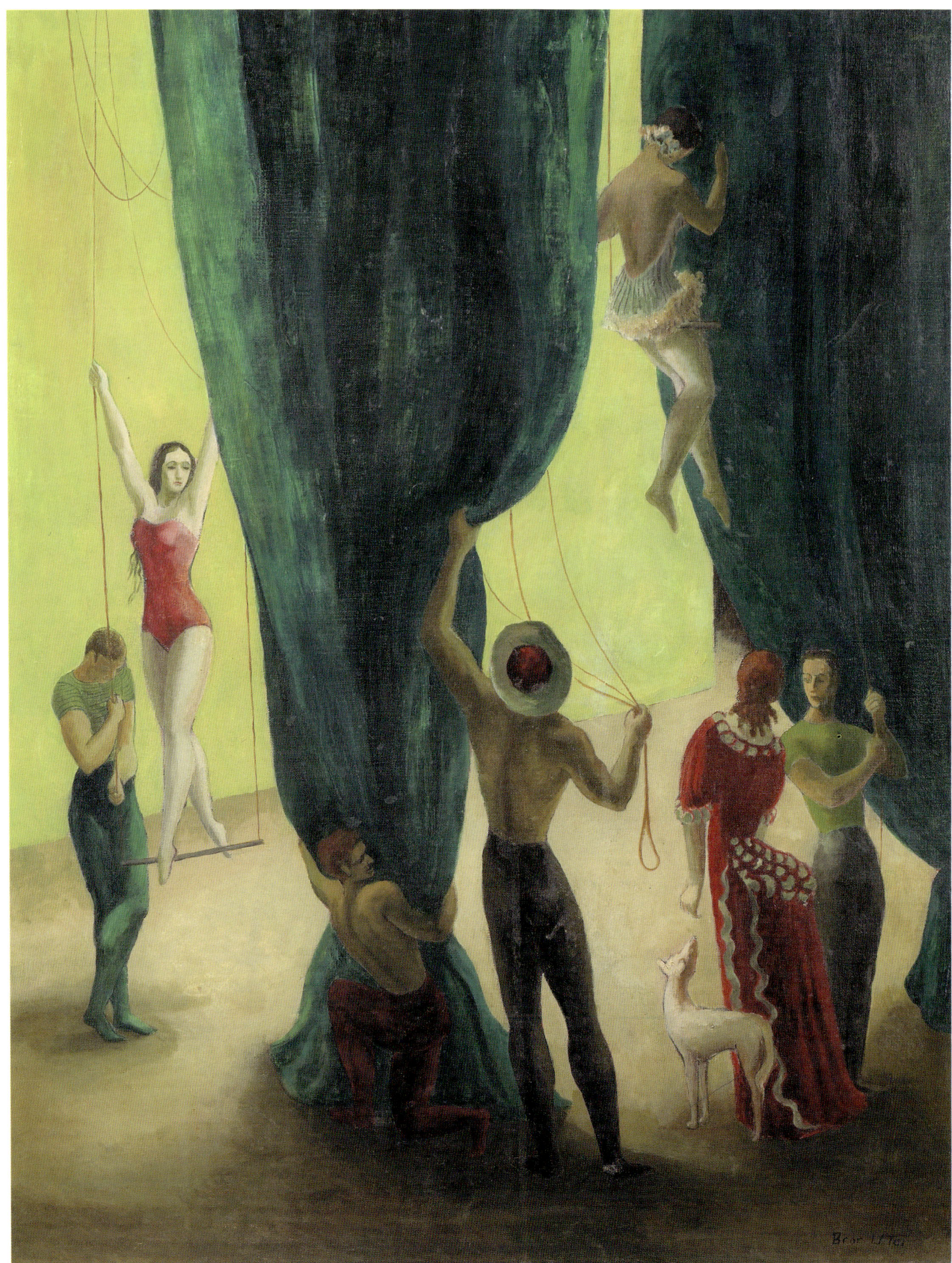

PLATE **27** Bror Utter, *Party*, 1946

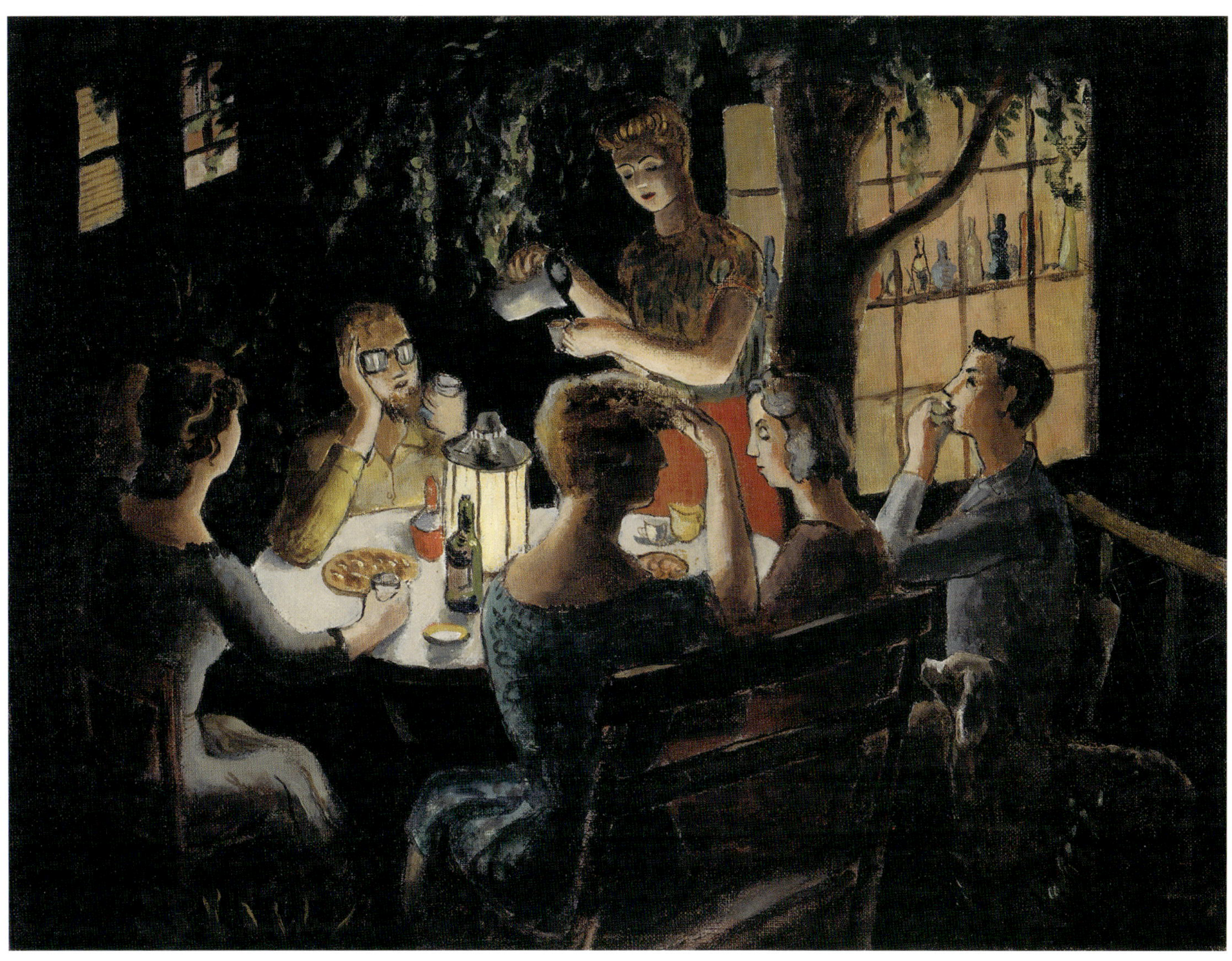

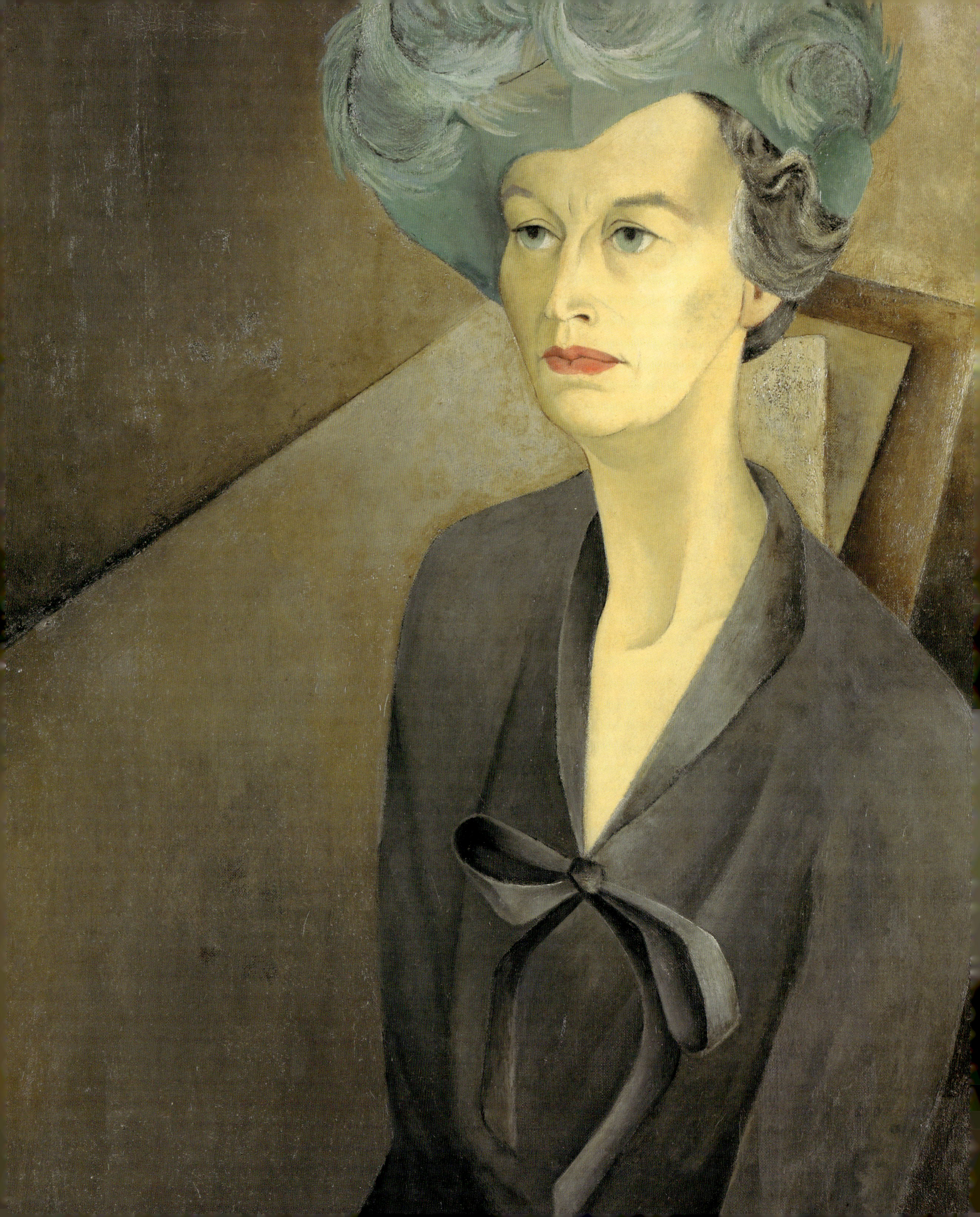

Modern Portraits

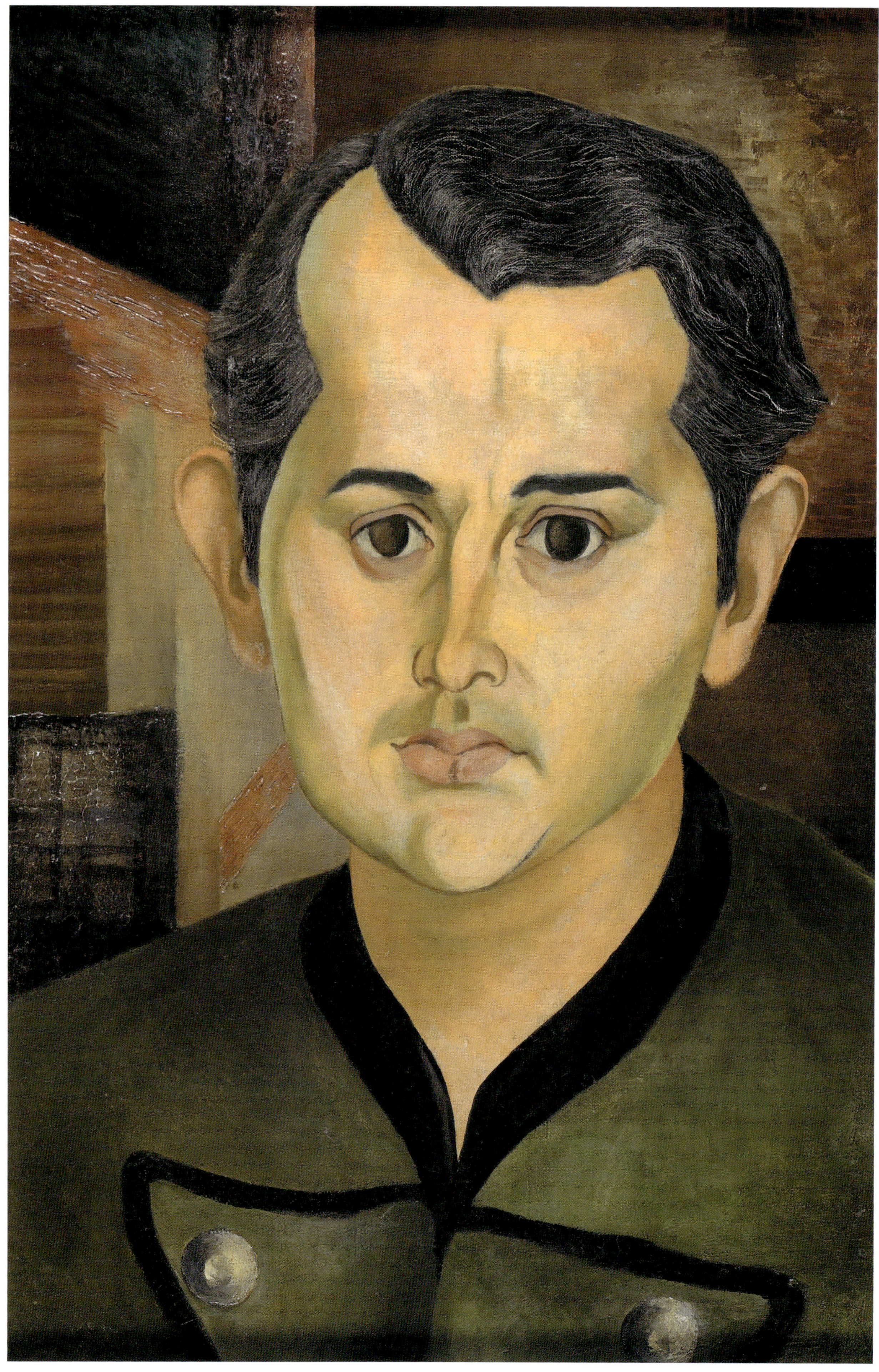

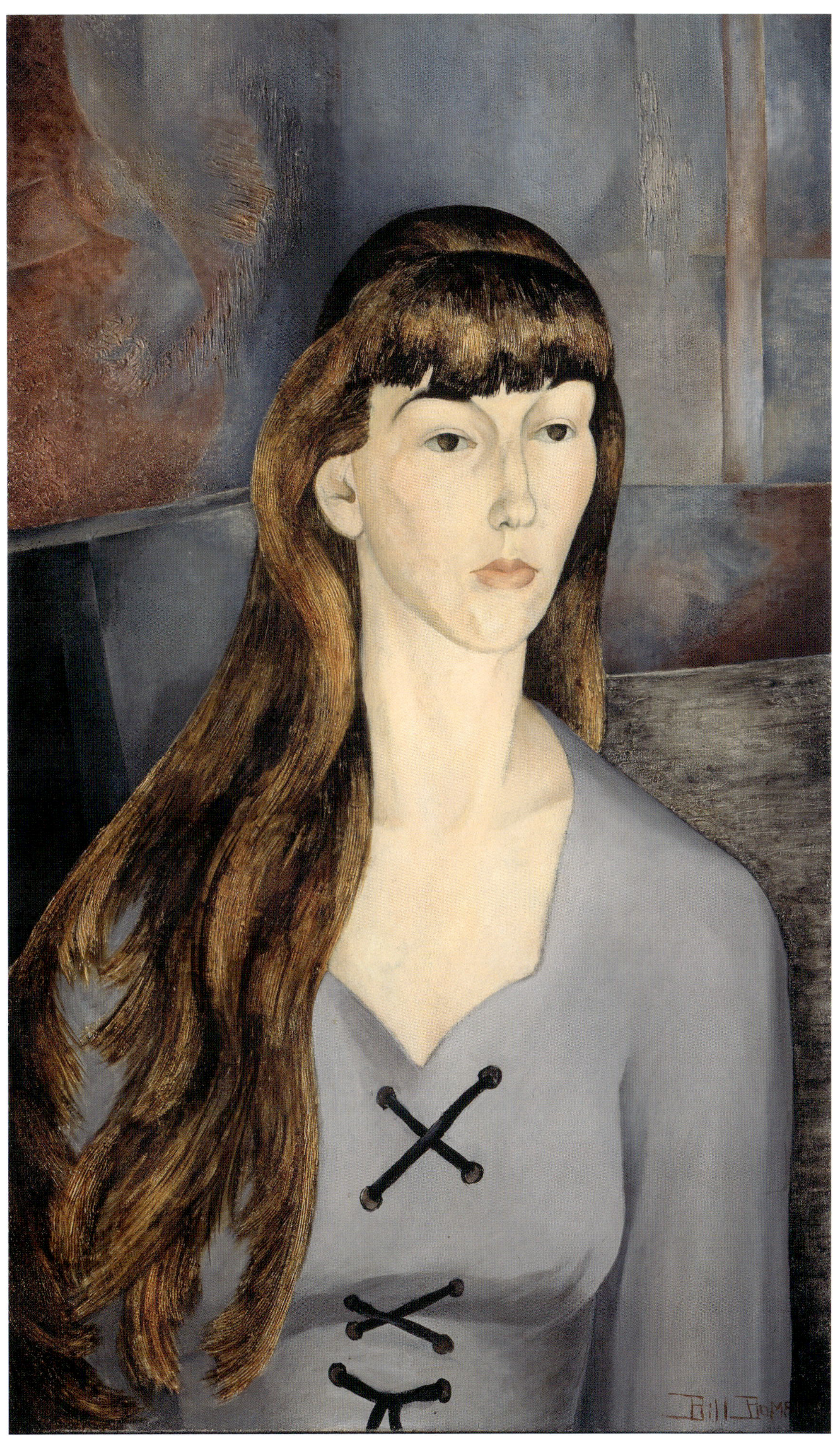

PLATE **28** Bill Bomar, *Head of an Artist*, 1944

PLATE **29** Bill Bomar, *Flora*, 1944

PLATE **30** Bill Bomar,
Sara, 1946

PLATE **31** Bill Bomar,
Jewel's Feathered Hat, 1947

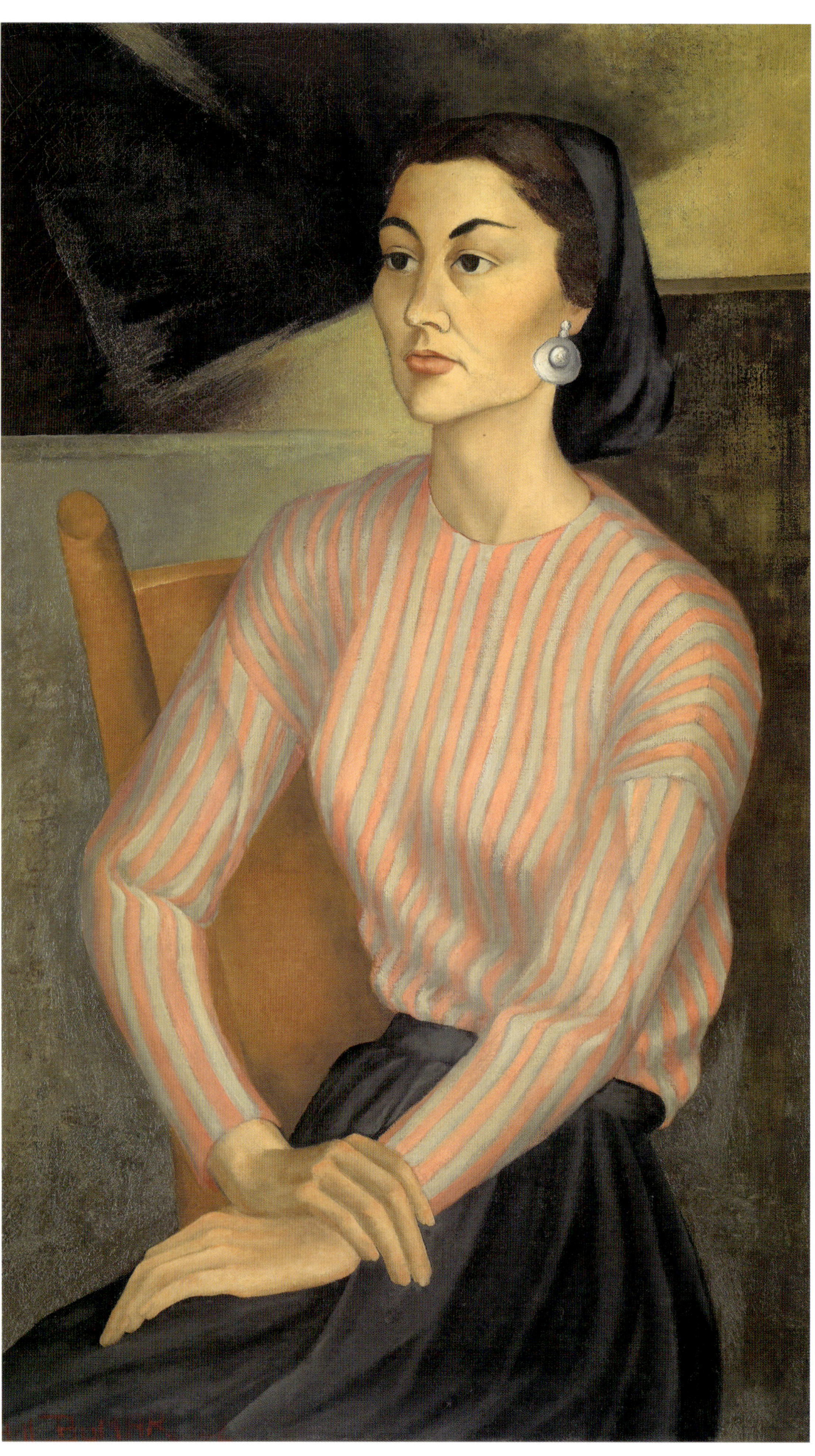

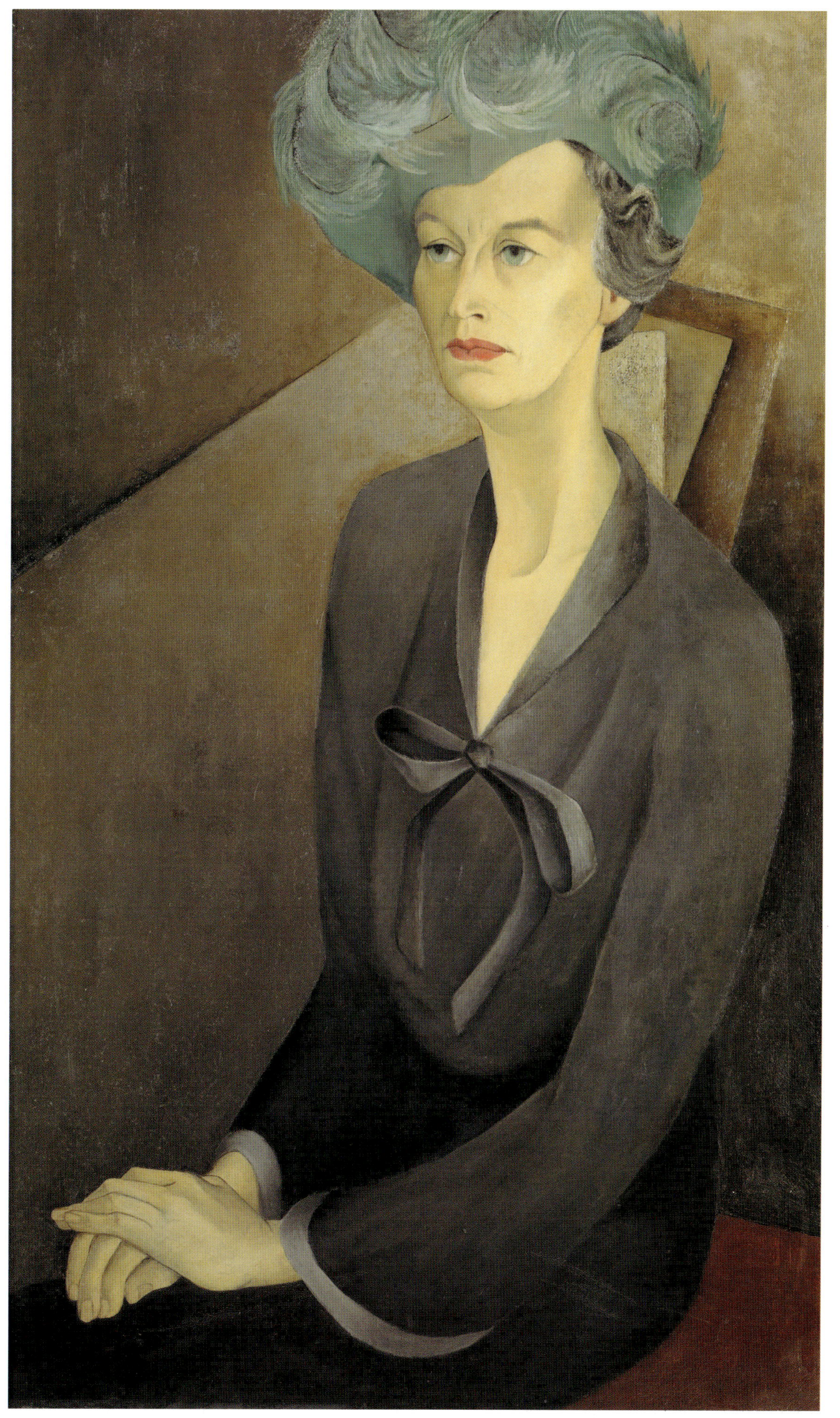

PLATE **32** Bill Bomar, *Lia*, 1953

PLATE **33** Dickson Reeder, *The Shannon Children*, 1941

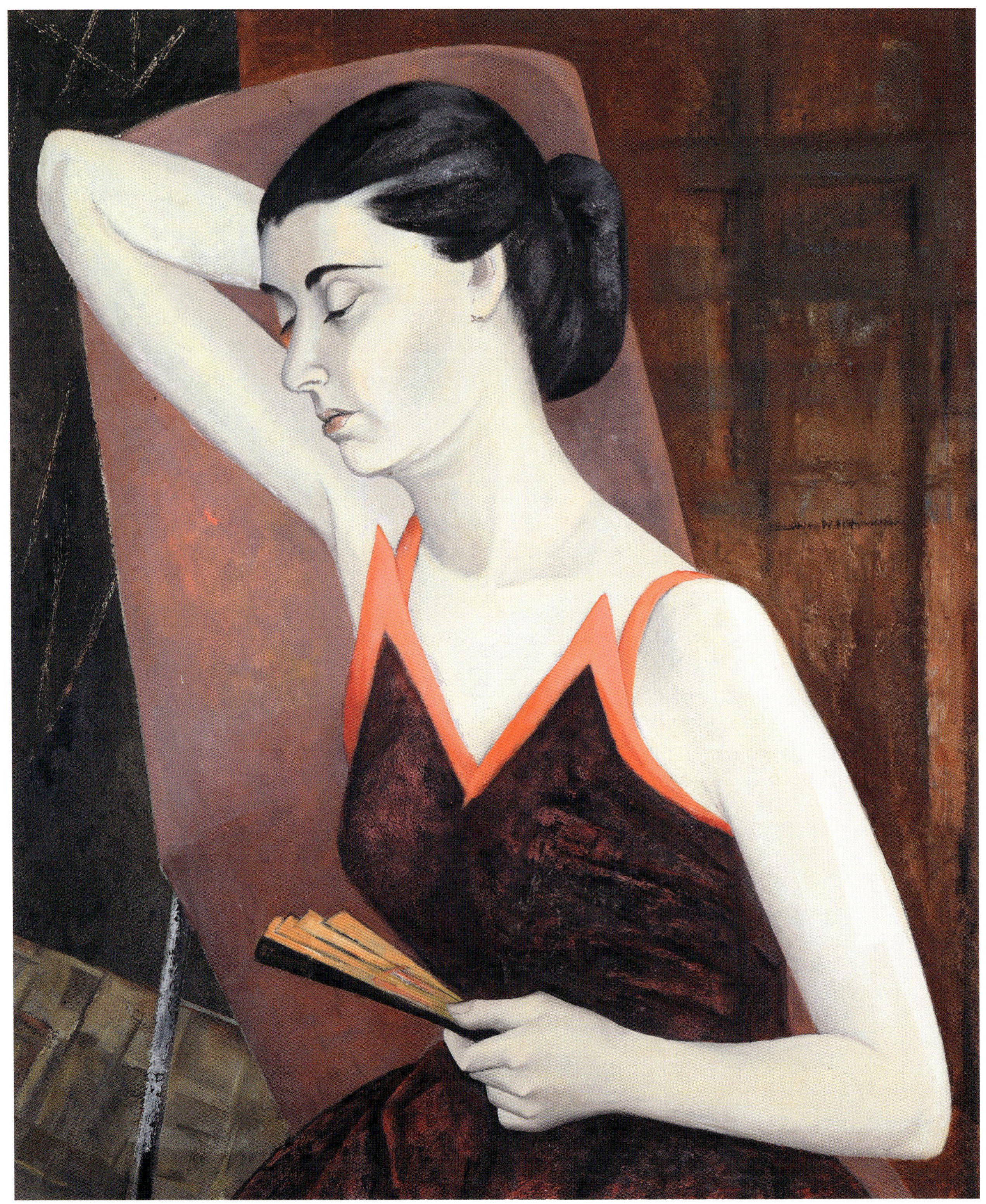

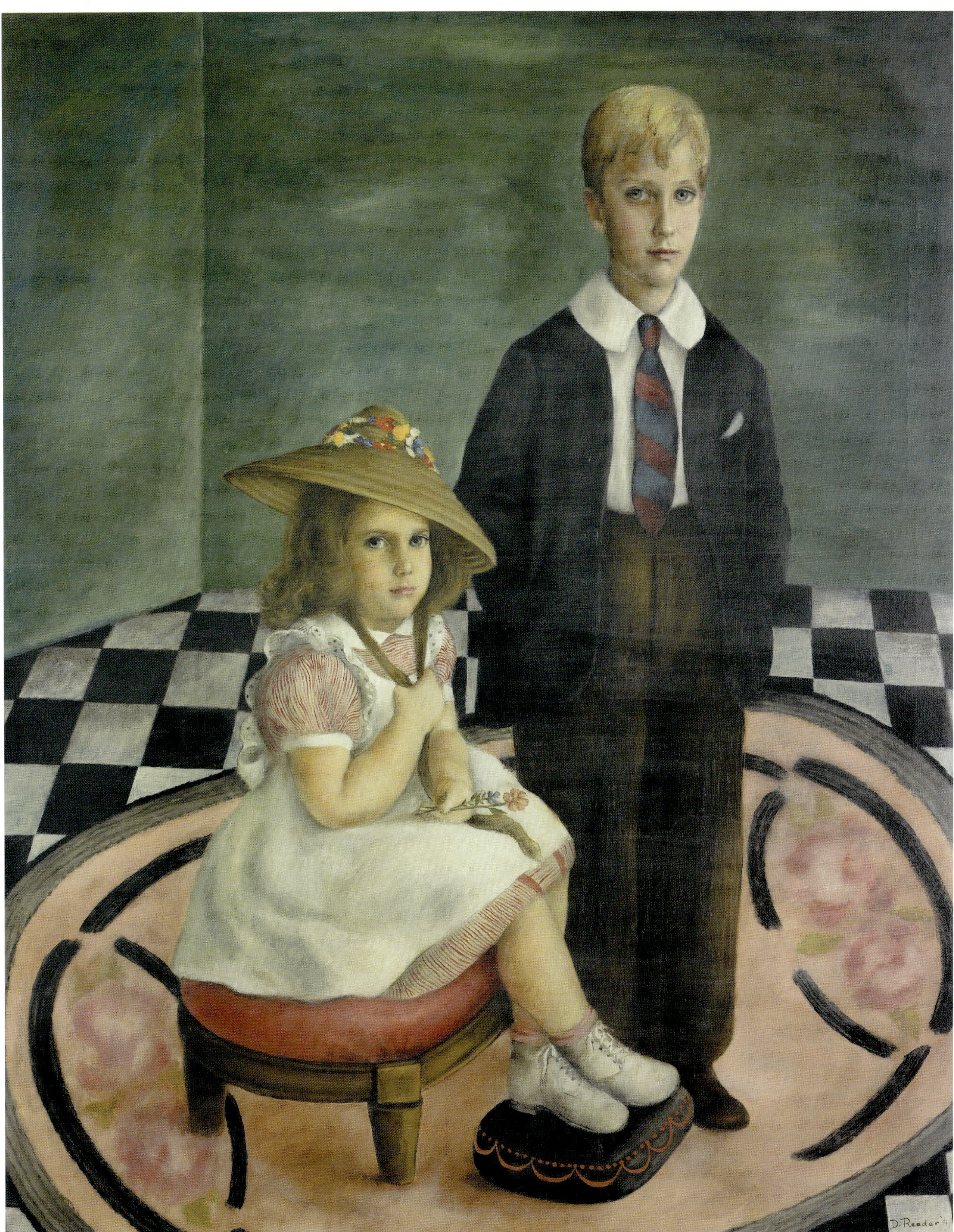

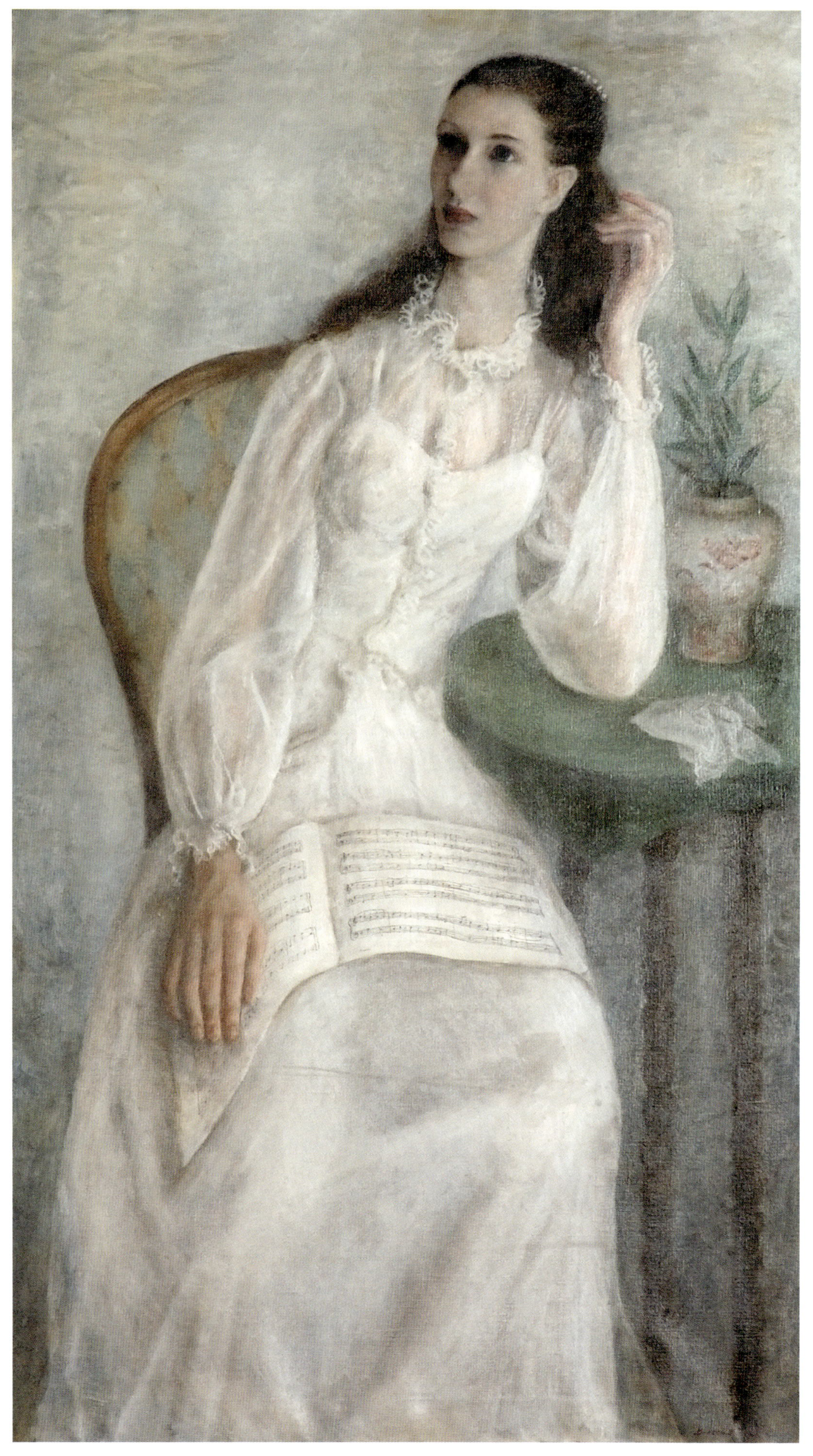

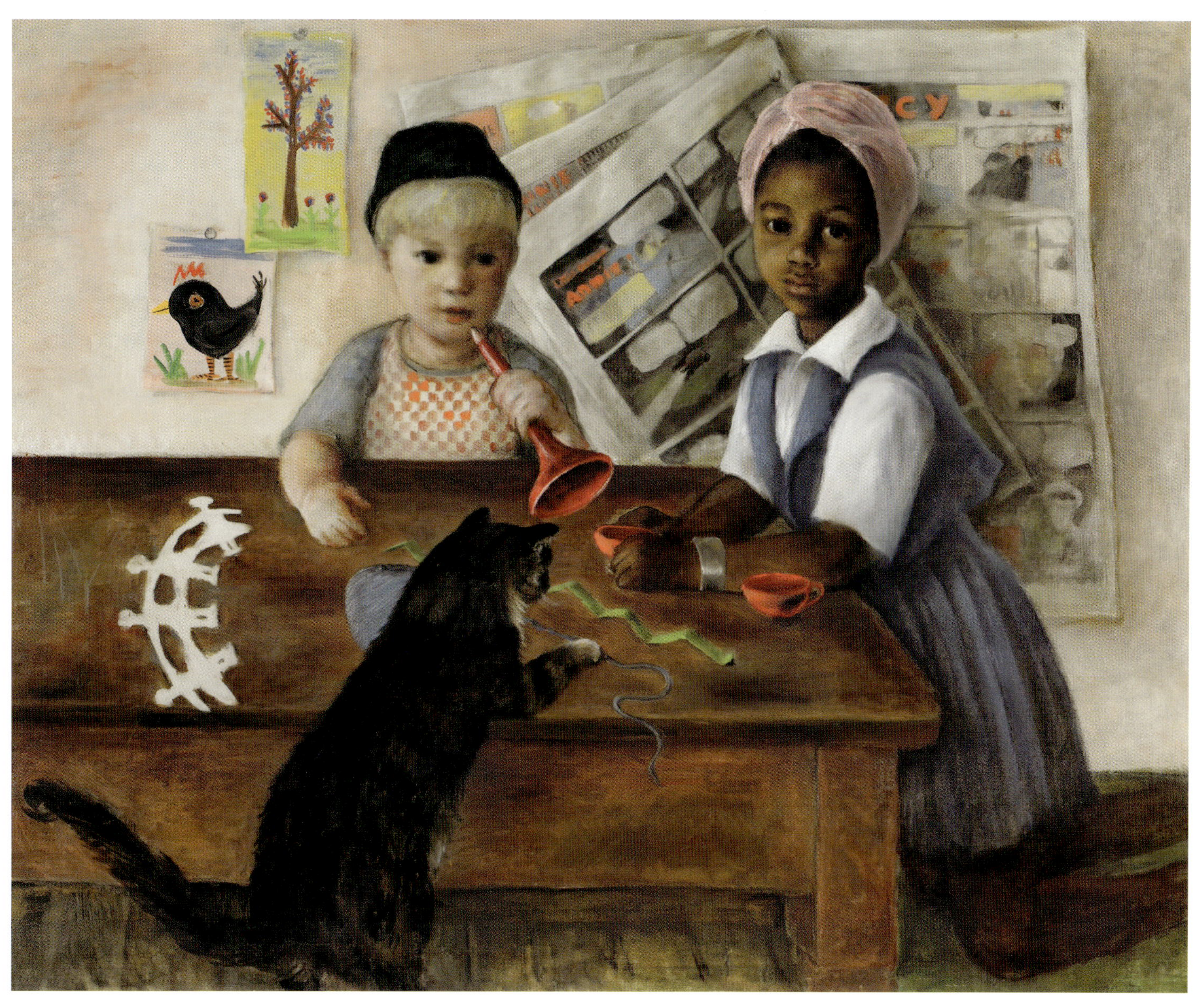

PLATE **34** Dickson Reeder, *Ellaraye*, 1945

PLATE **35** Dickson Reeder, *Conversation Piece*, 1945

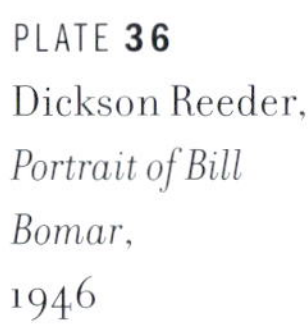

PLATE **36**
Dickson Reeder,
Portrait of Bill Bomar,
1946

PLATE **37**
Dickson Reeder,
Portrait of Veronica Helfensteller,
ca. 1947

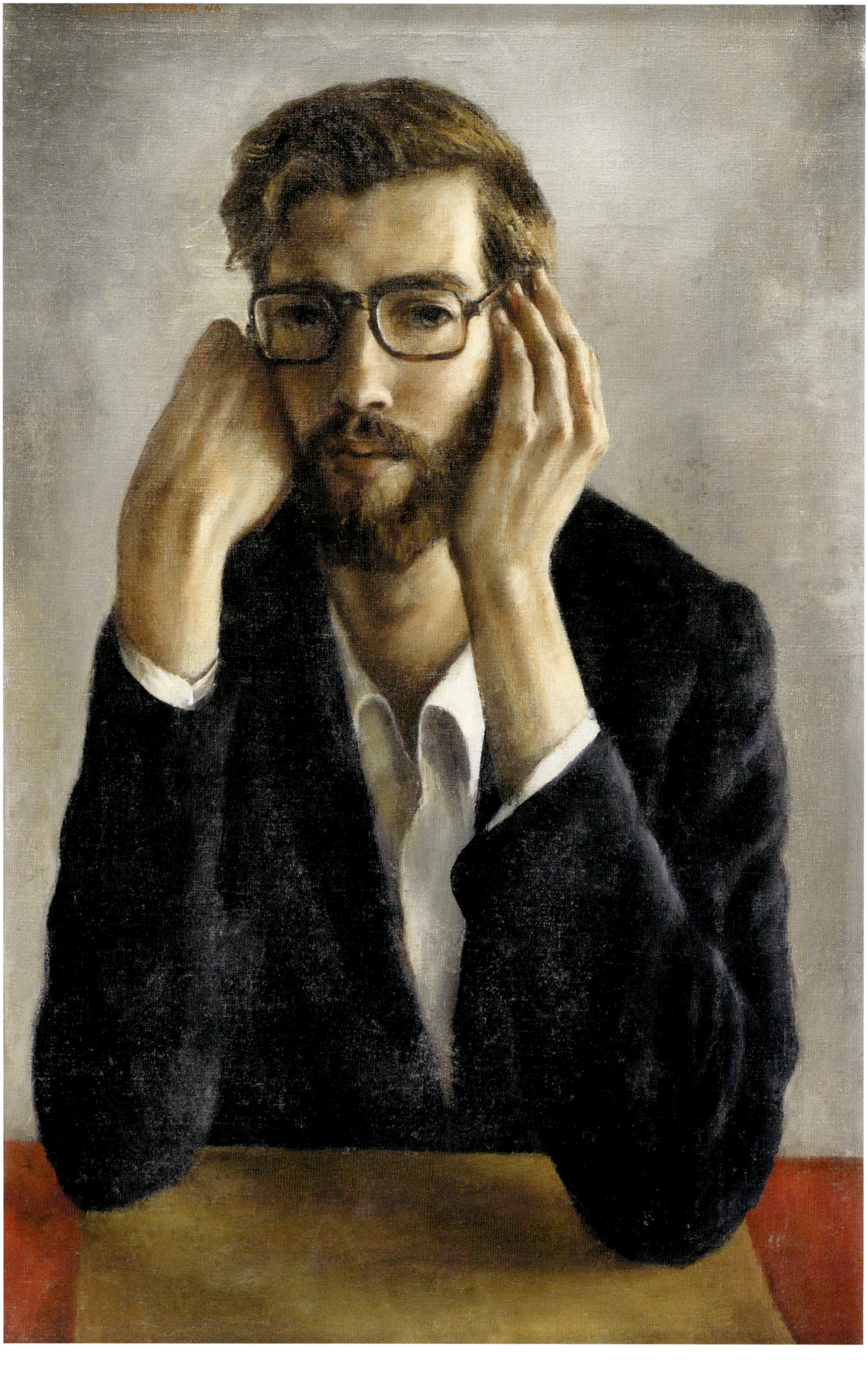

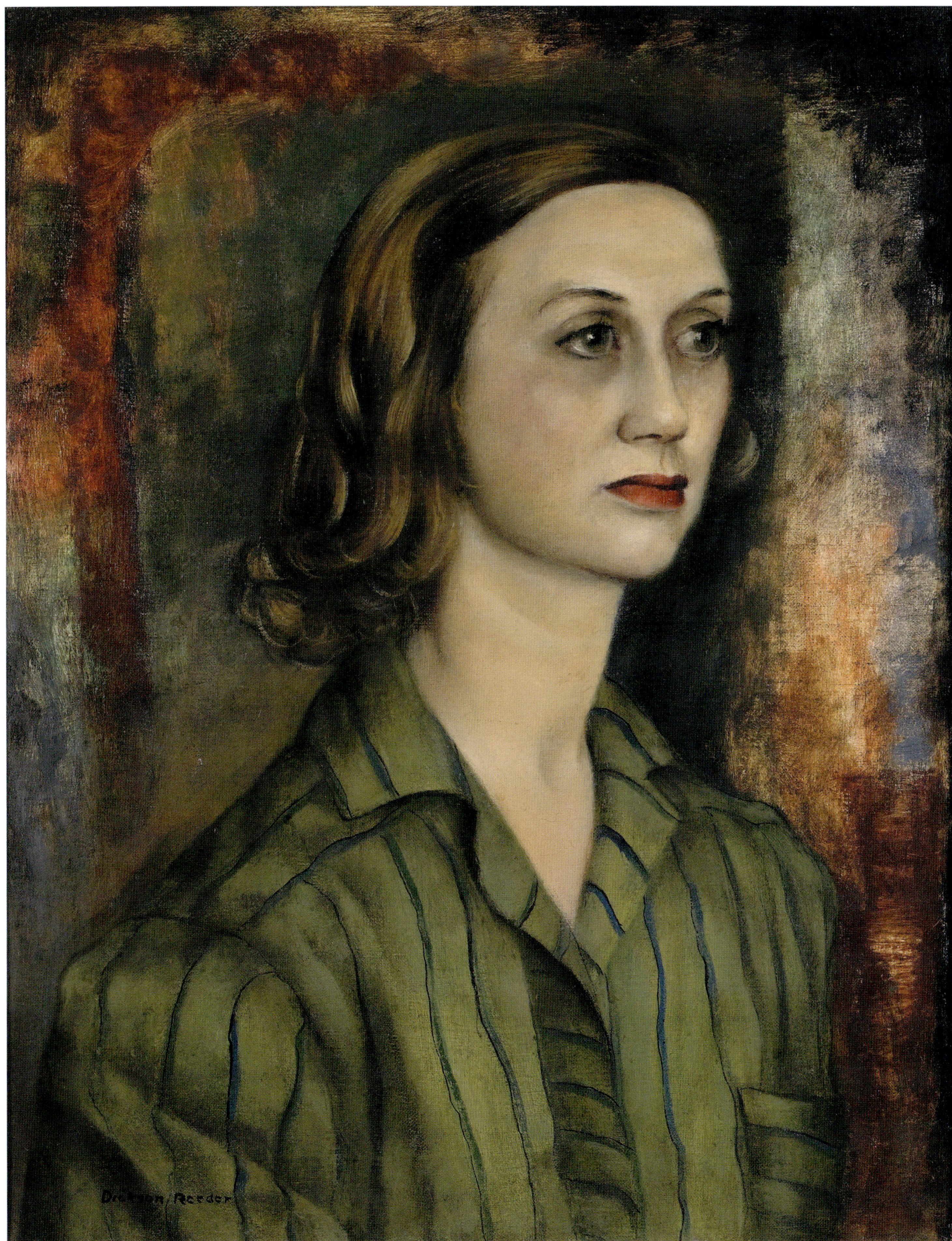

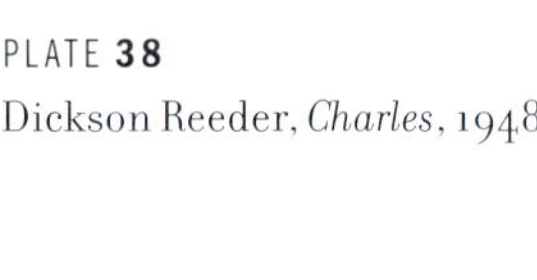

PLATE **38**
Dickson Reeder, *Charles*, 1948

PLATE **39**
Dickson Reeder, *Joe Harris*, ca. 1947–48

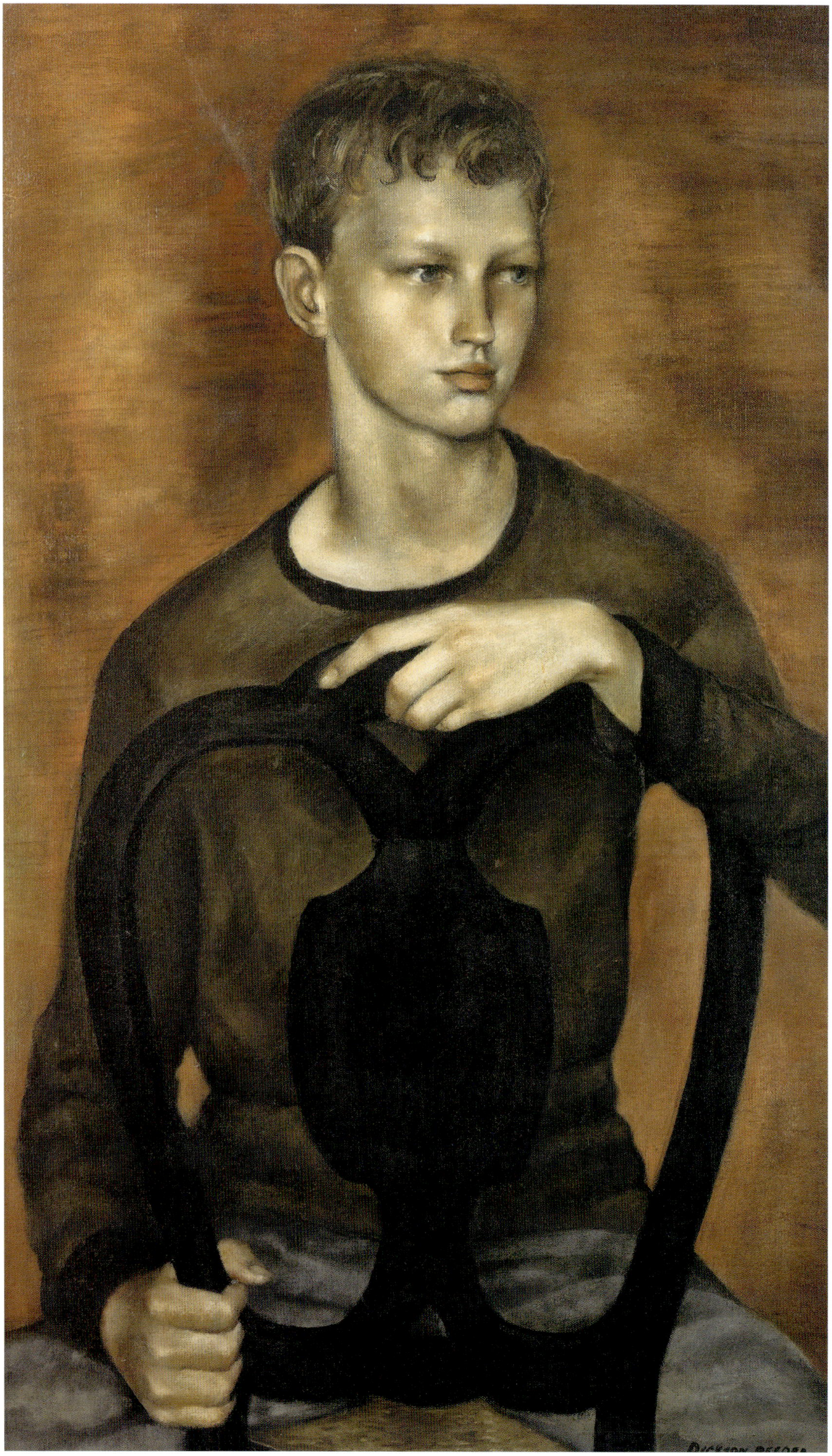

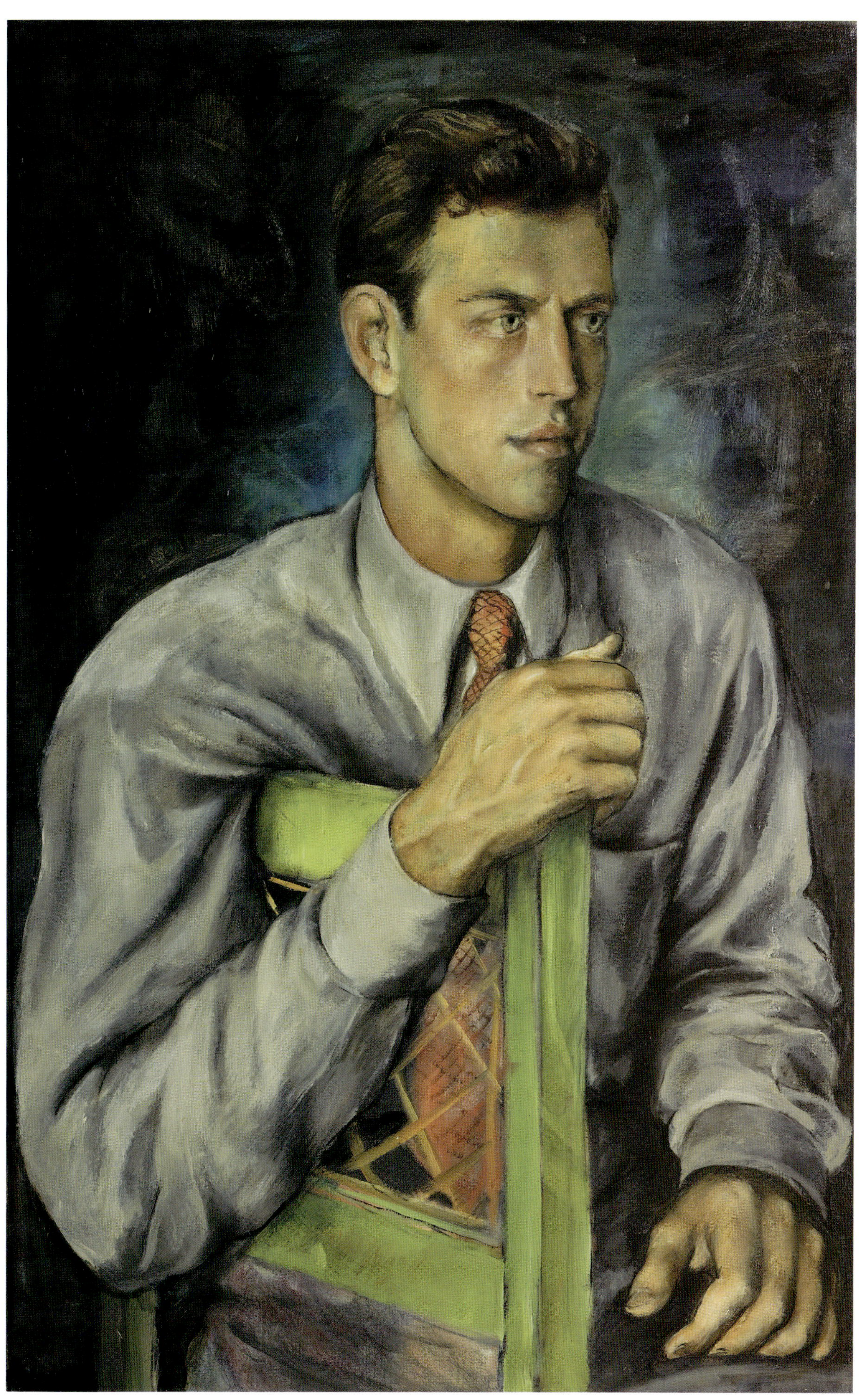

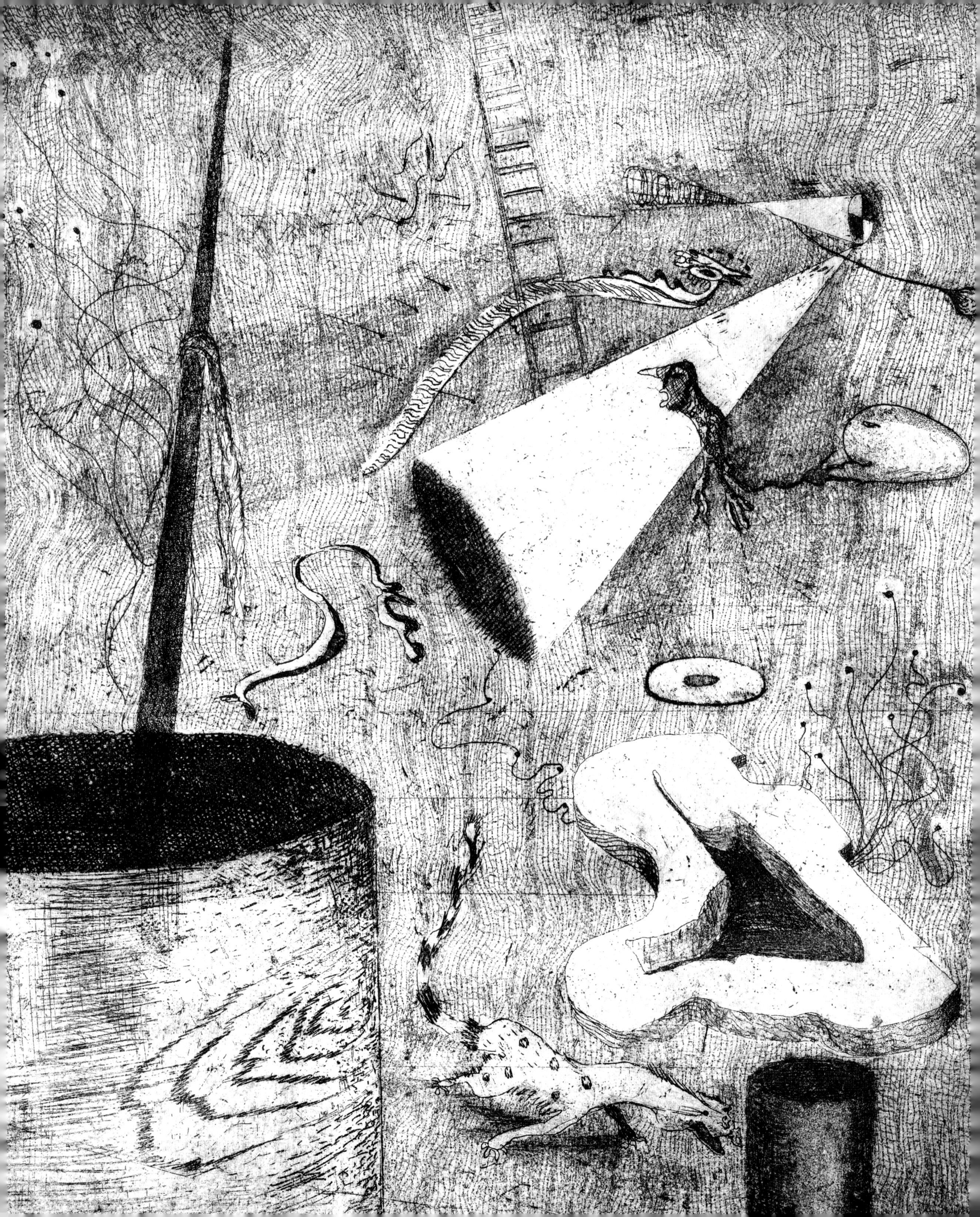

Prints: A Hotbed of Innovation

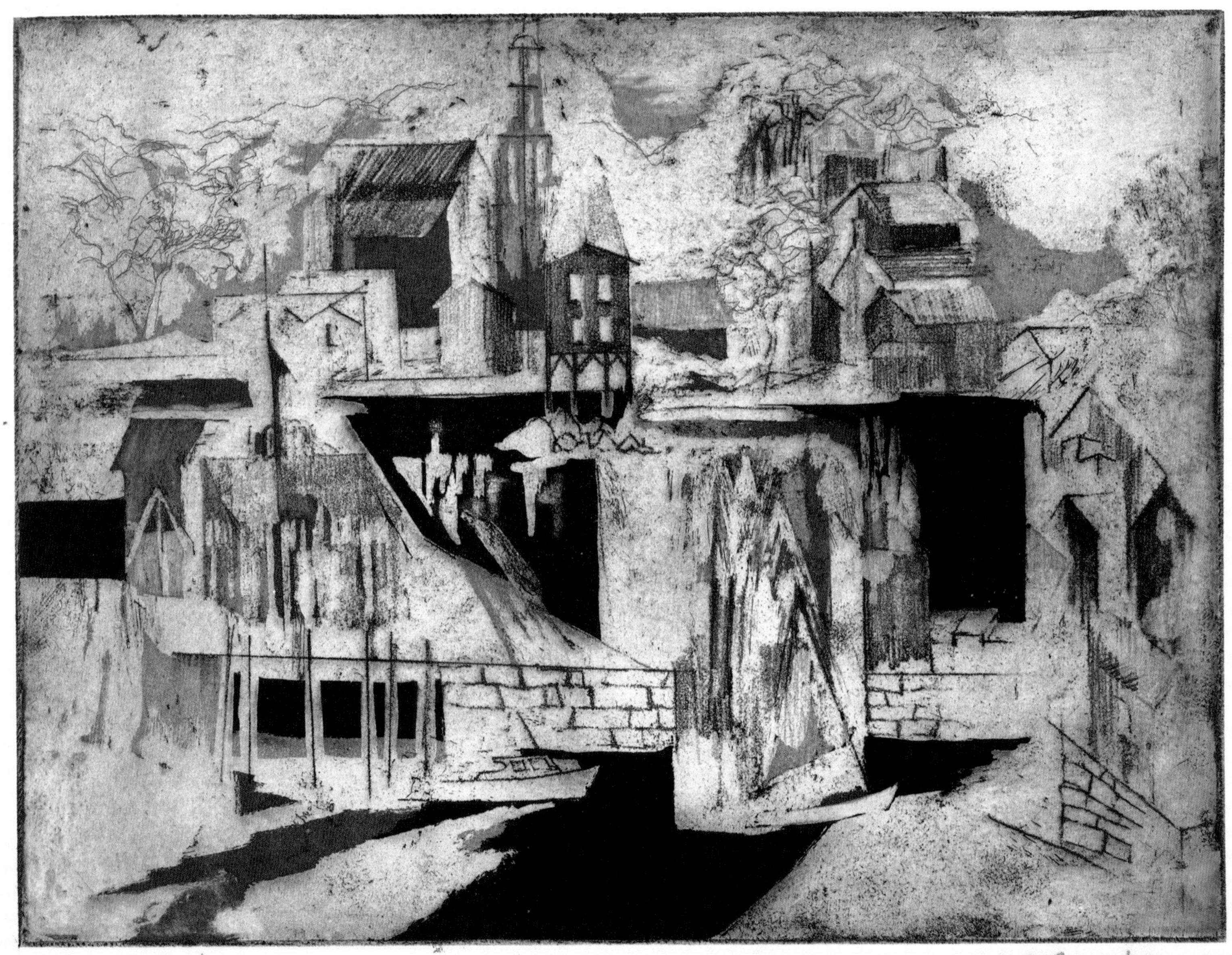

PLATE **40** Cynthia Brants, *New England Harbor*, ca. 1951–52

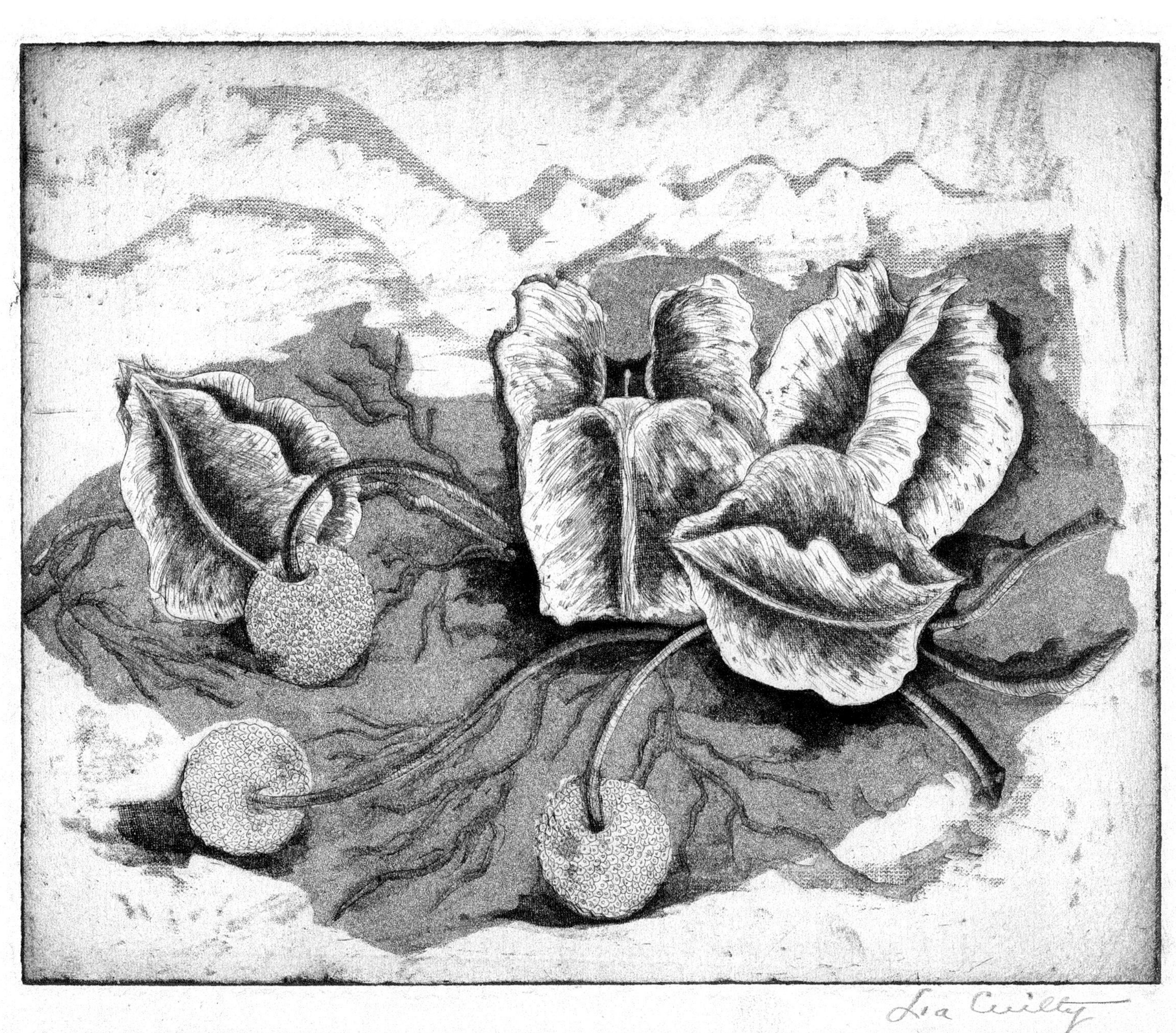

PLATE **41** Lia Cuilty, *Seed Pods*, 1947 (object reproduced at actual size)

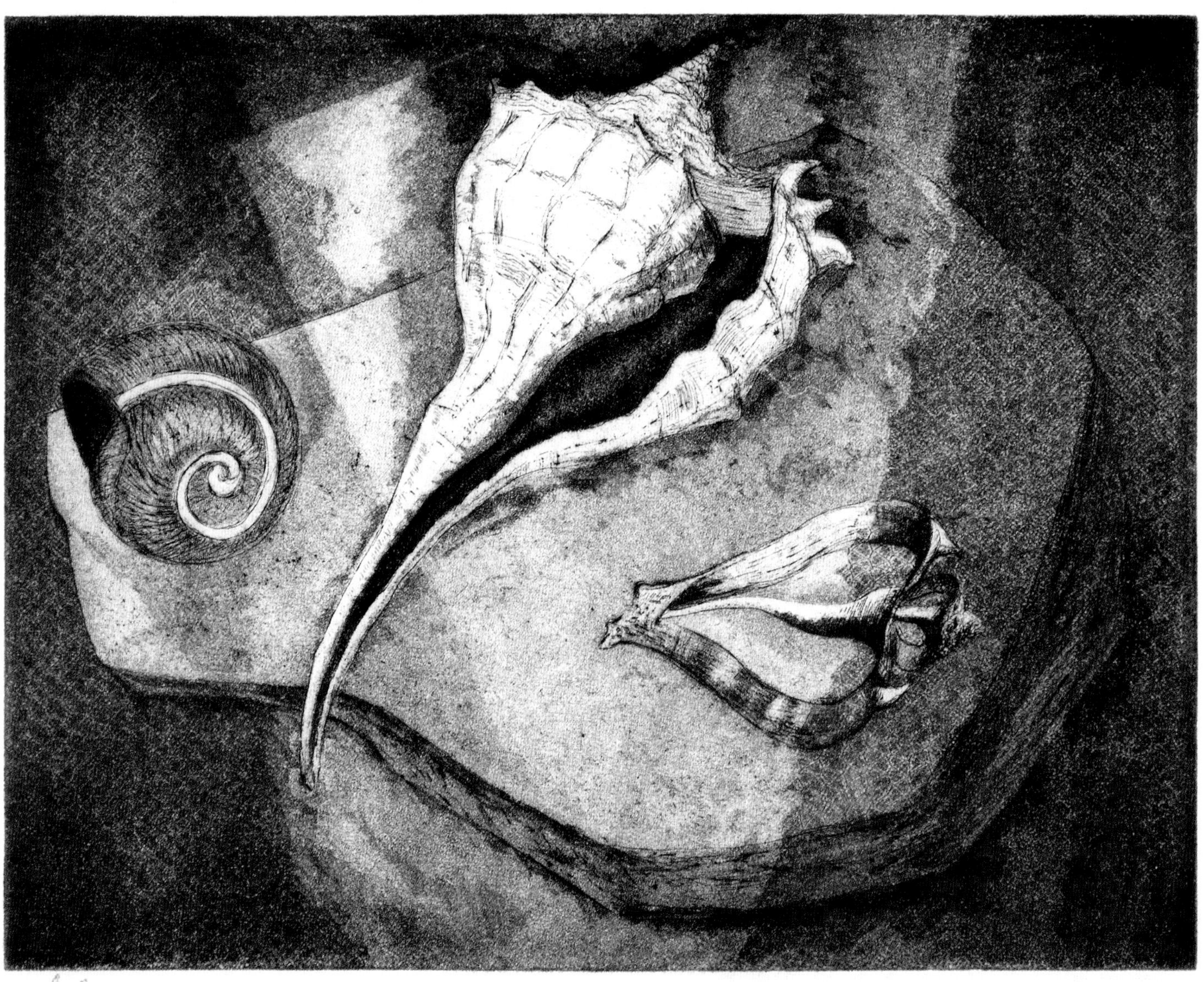

PLATE **42** Lia Cuilty, *Shells*, 1950 (object reproduced at actual size)

PLATE **45** Kelly Fearing, *Floating Objects (Floating Above)*, 1945
(object reproduced at actual size)

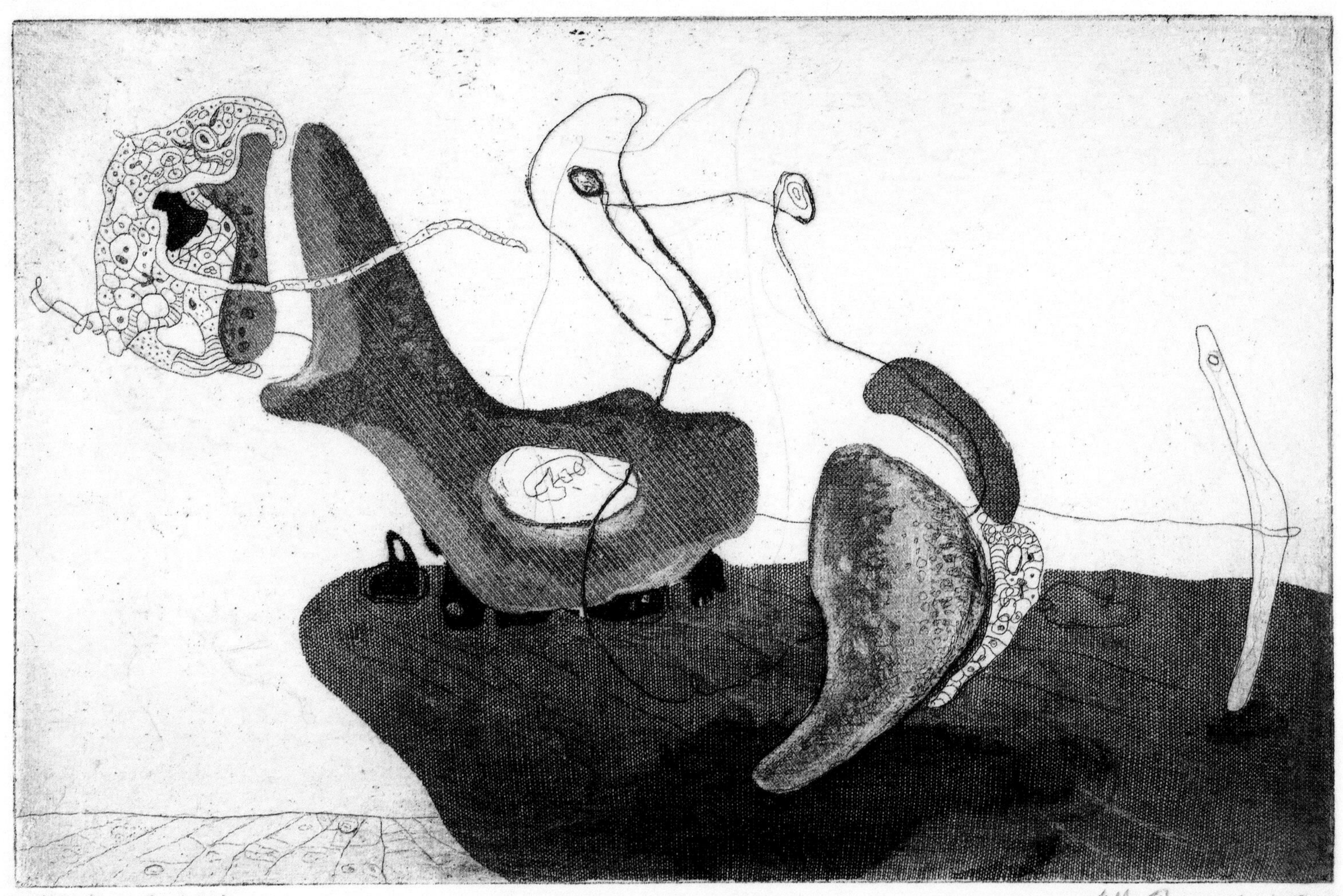

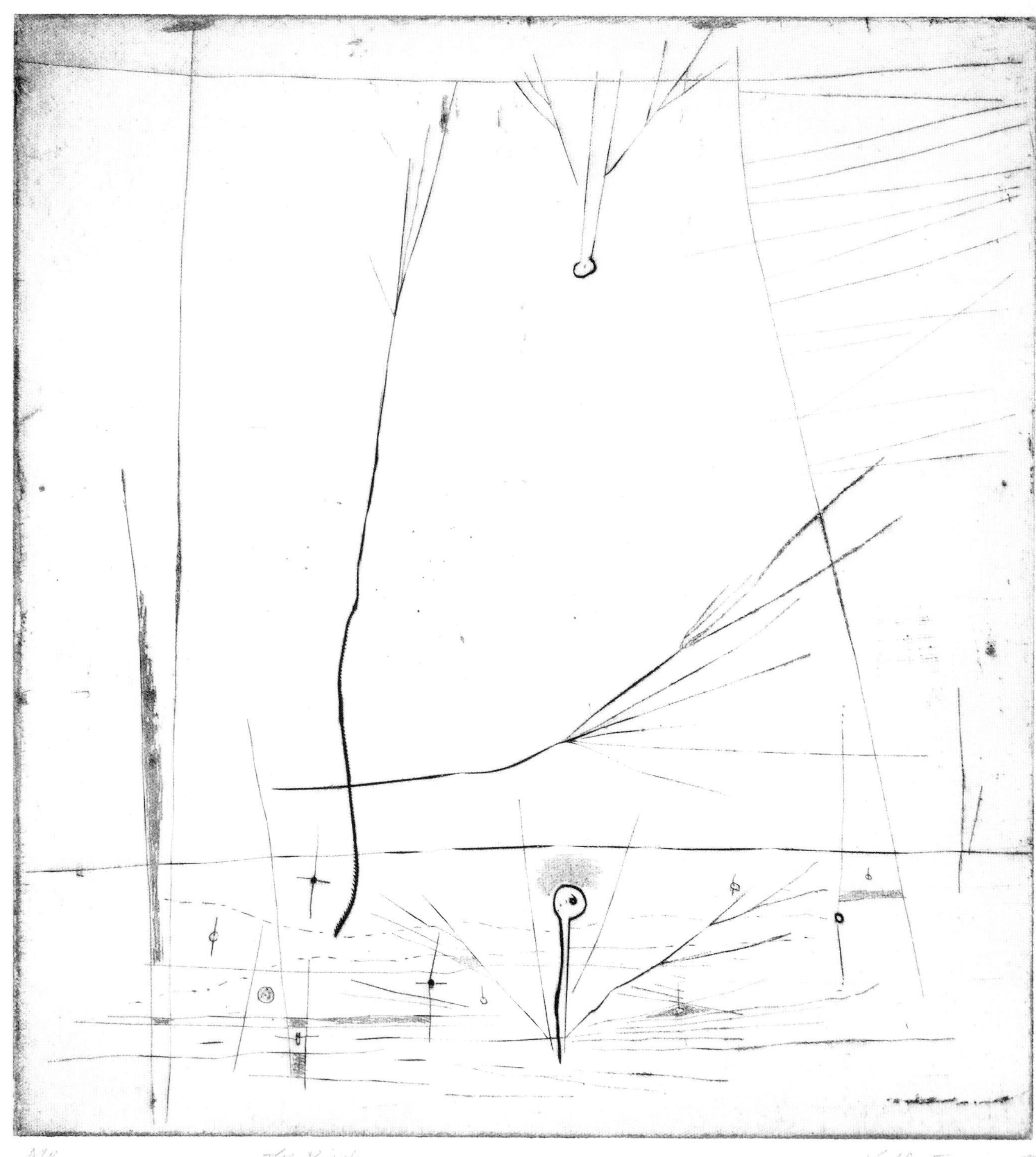
A/P
The Birds
Kelly Fearing

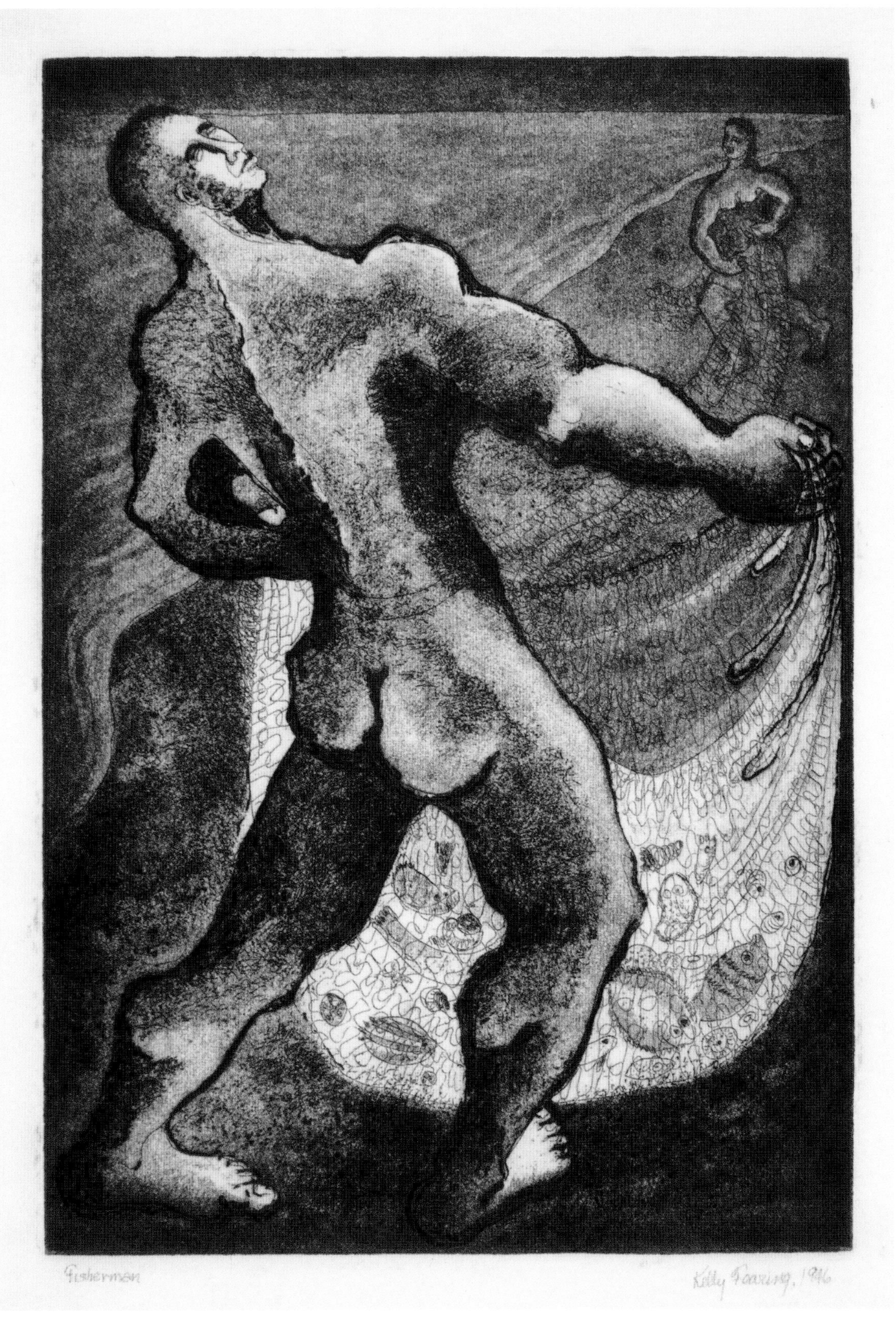

PLATE **46** Kelly Fearing, *The Birds*, 1946
(object reproduced at actual size)

PLATE **47** Kelly Fearing, *Fishermen*, 1946
(object reproduced at actual size)

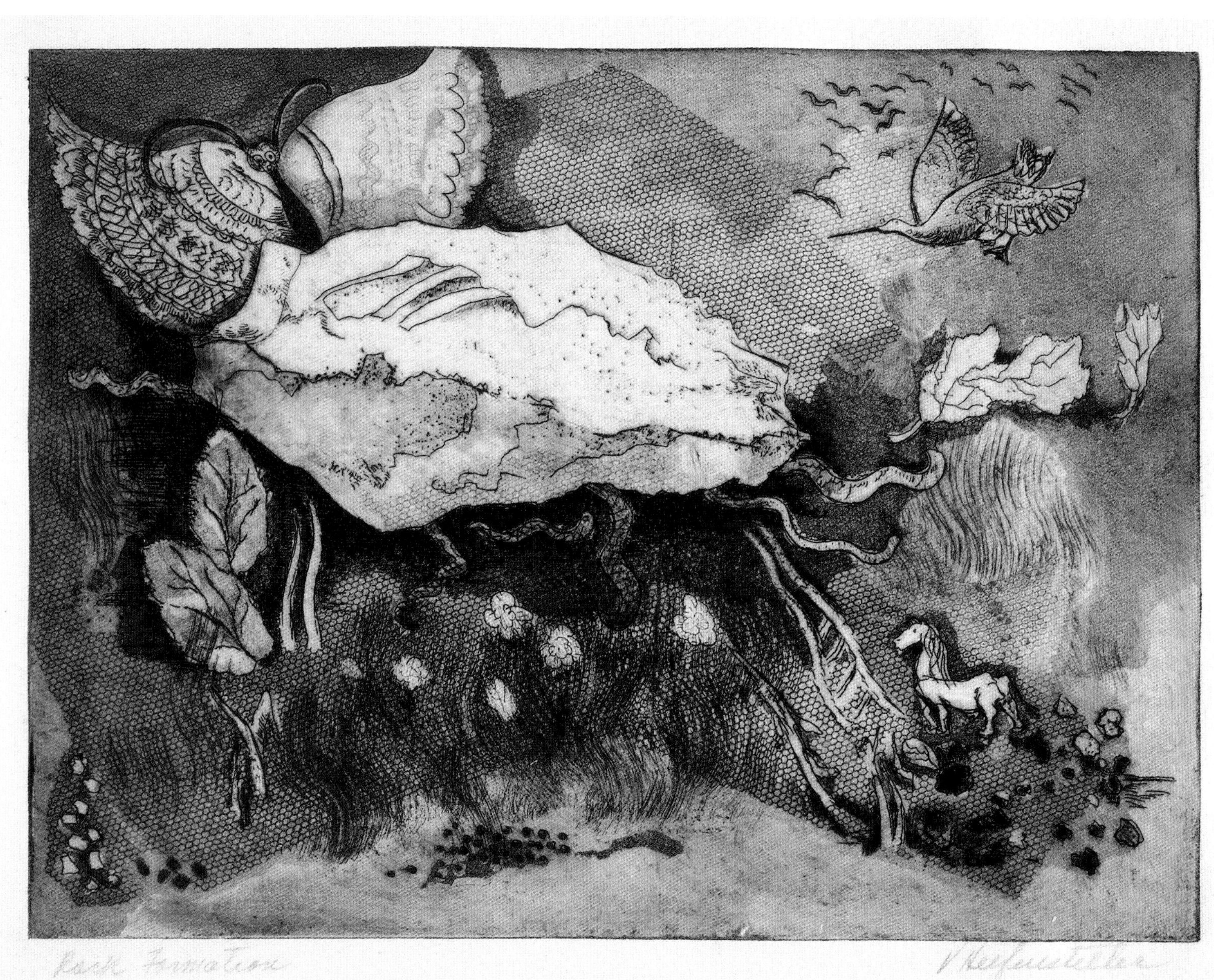

PLATE **48** Veronica Helfensteller, *Rock Formation*, 1945 (object reproduced at actual size)

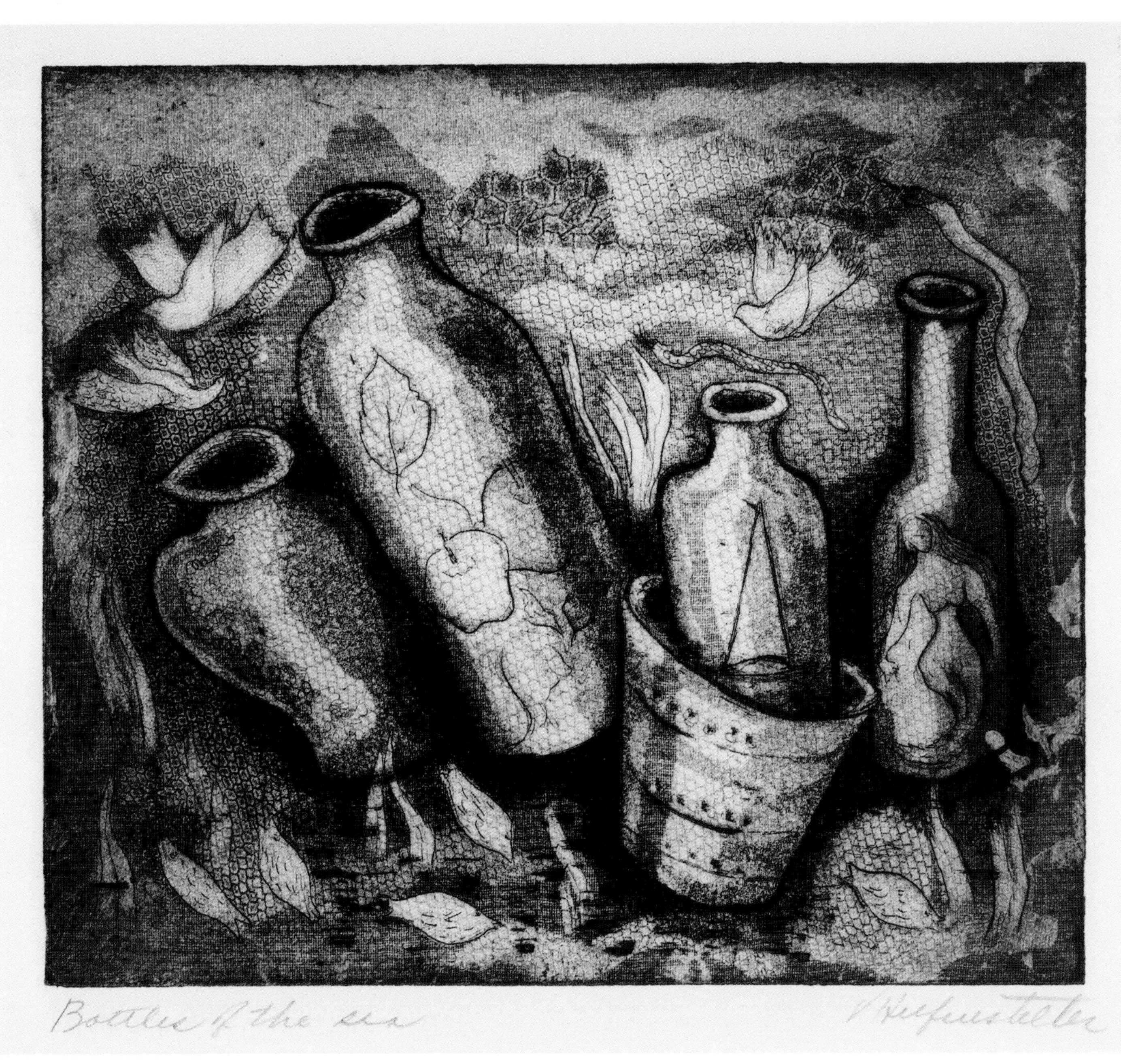

PLATE **49** Veronica Helfensteller, *Bottles of the Sea*, 1945 (object reproduced at actual size)

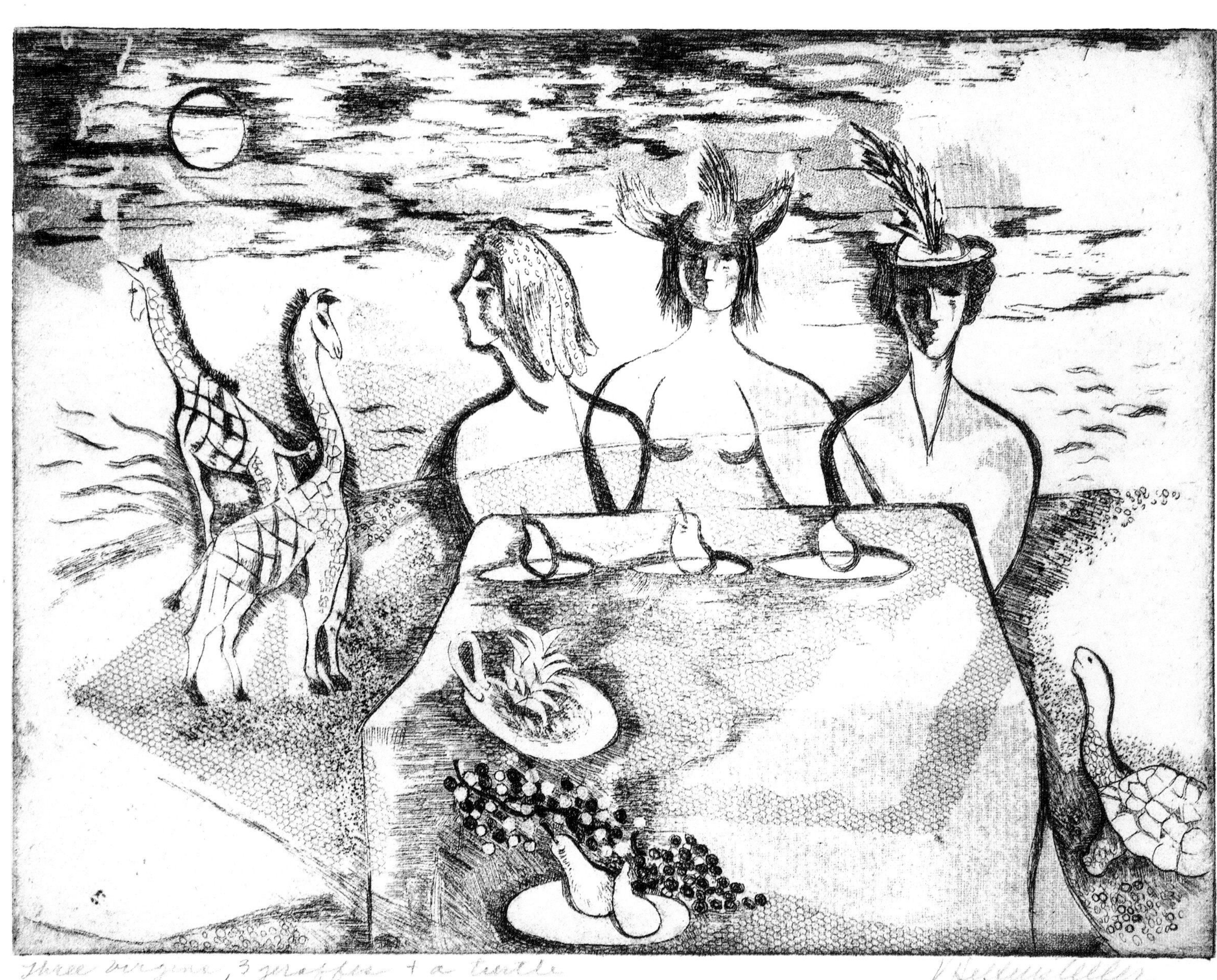

PLATE **50** Veronica Helfensteller, *Three Virgins, Three Giraffes and a Turtle*, ca. 1945
(object reproduced at actual size)

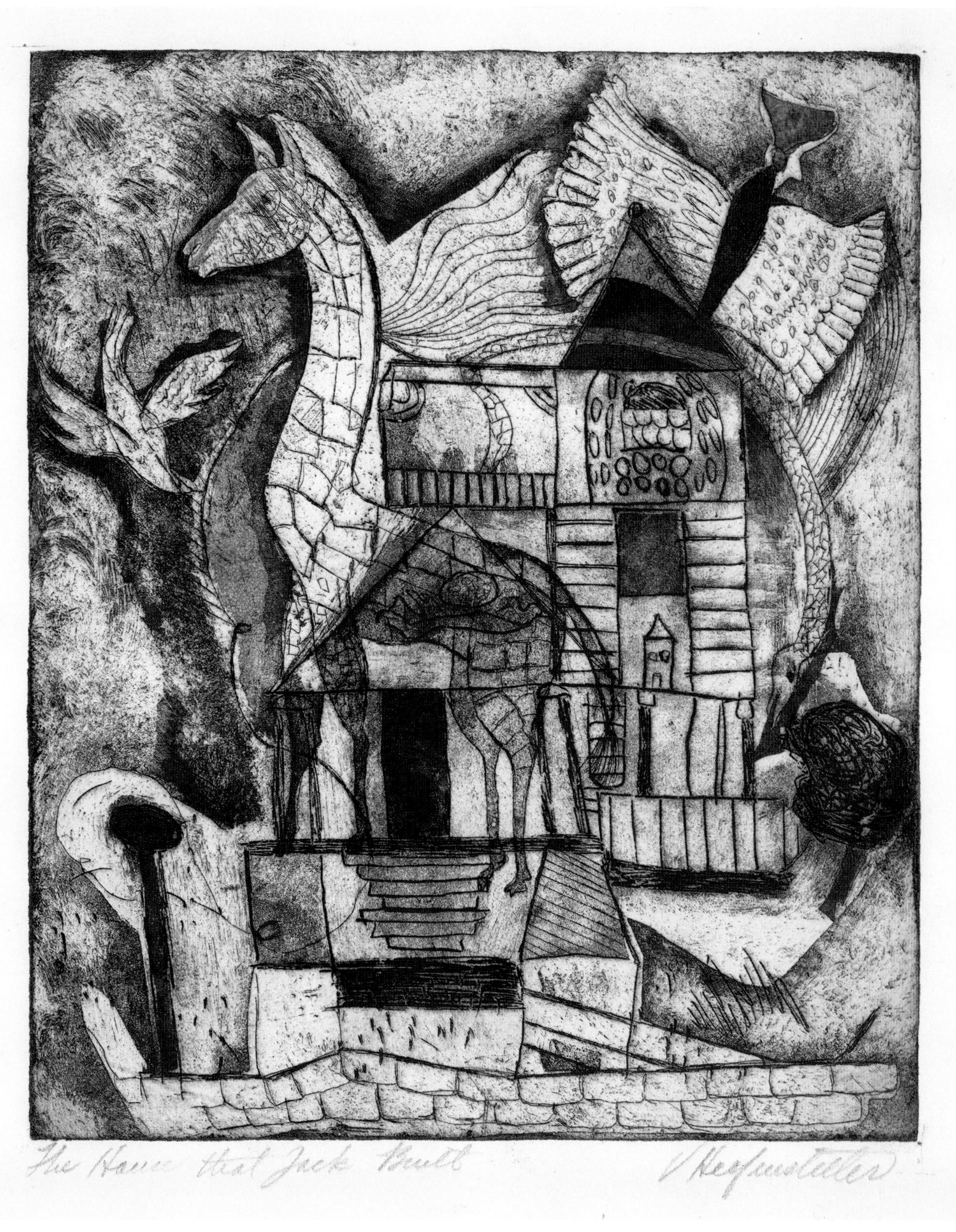

PLATE **51** Veronica Helfensteller, *The House that Jack Built*, 1947
(object reproduced at actual size)

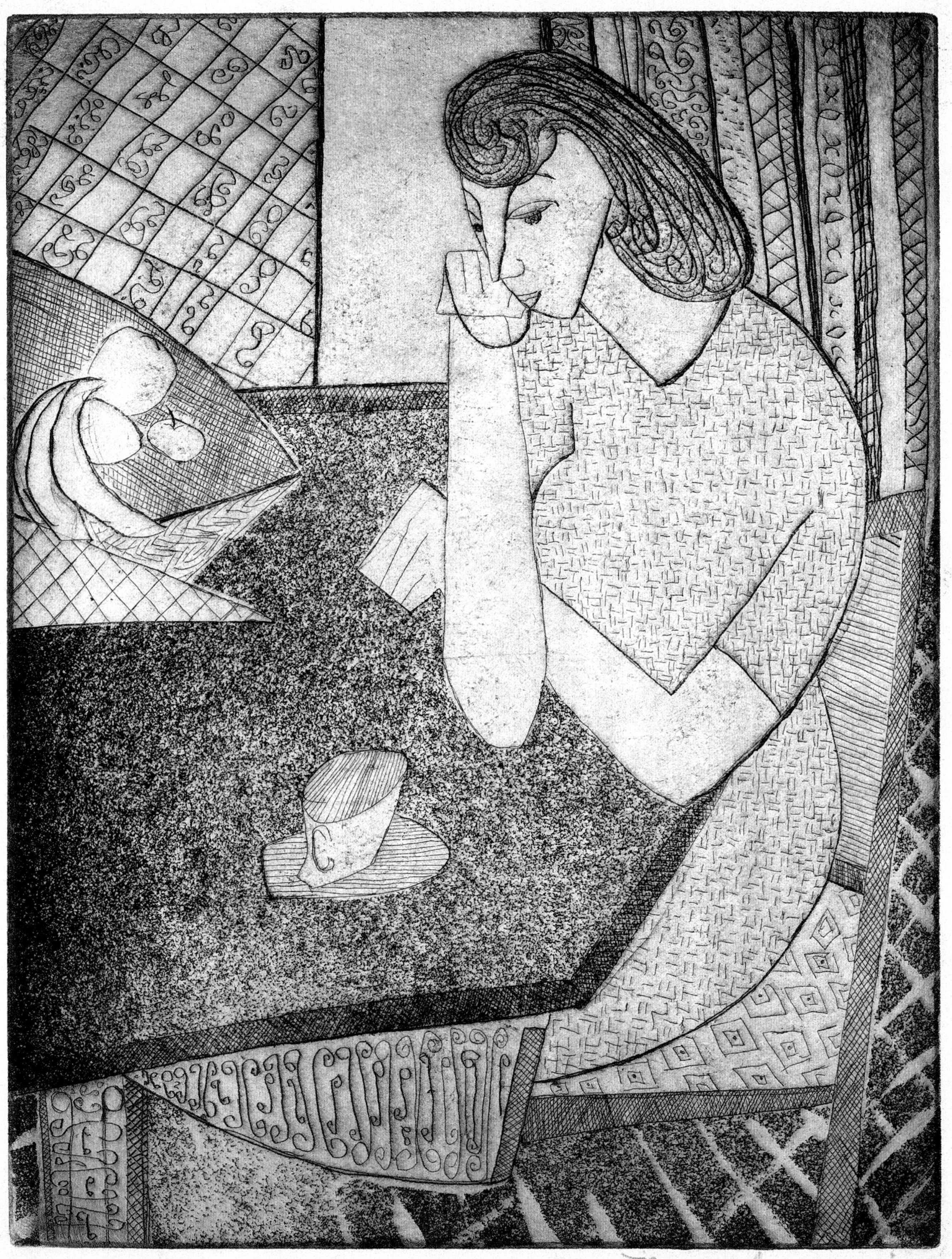

M. Johnson '46

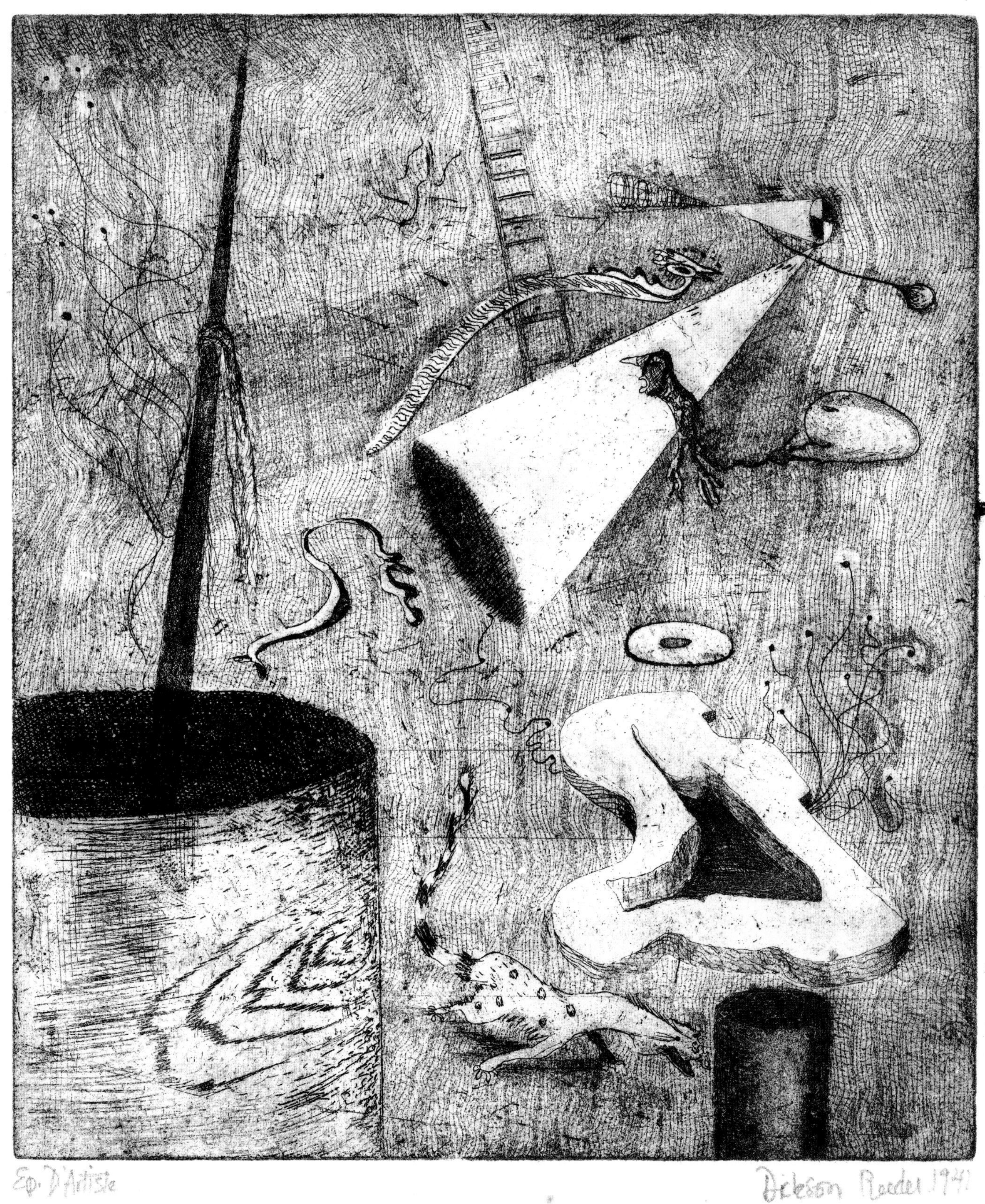

PLATE **52** Marjorie Johnson, *Untitled [Woman at Table]*, 1946
(object reproduced at actual size)

PLATE **53** Dickson Reeder,
Mysterious Pool, 1941
(object reproduced at actual size)

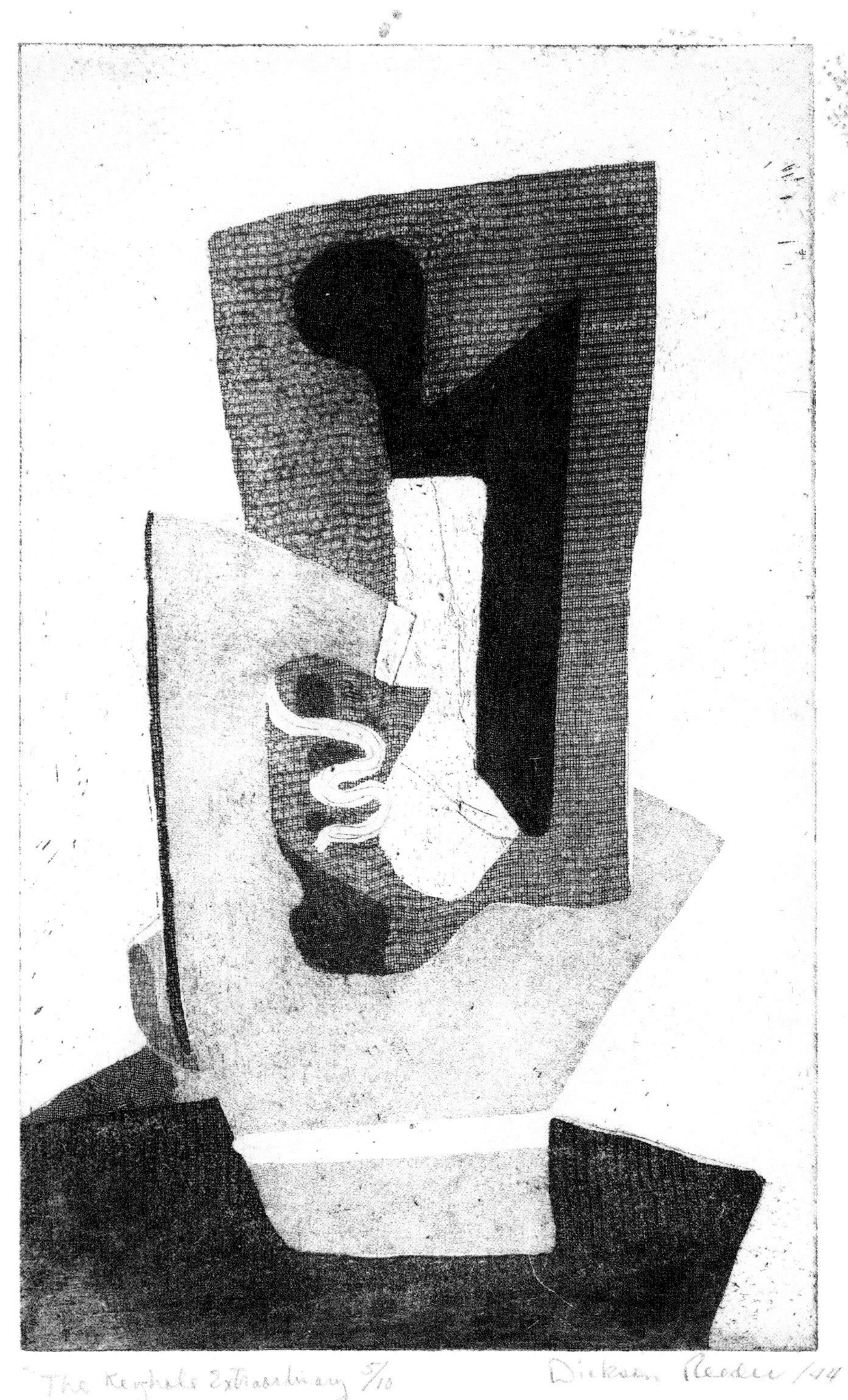

PLATE **54** Dickson Reeder, *The Keyhole Extraordinary (Extraordinary Keyhole)*, 1944
(object reproduced at actual size)

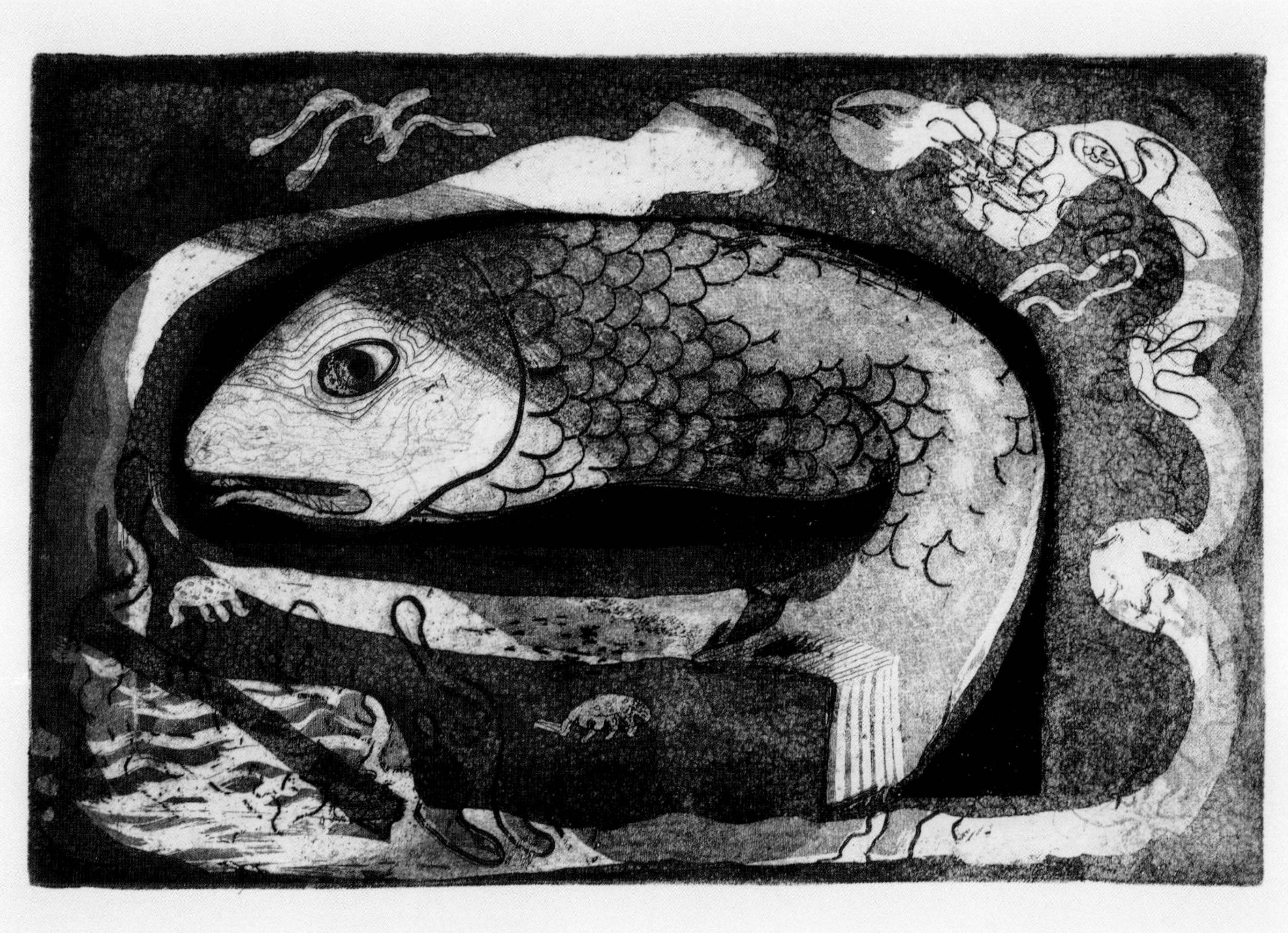

PLATE **55** Dickson Reeder, *Fish*, 1944

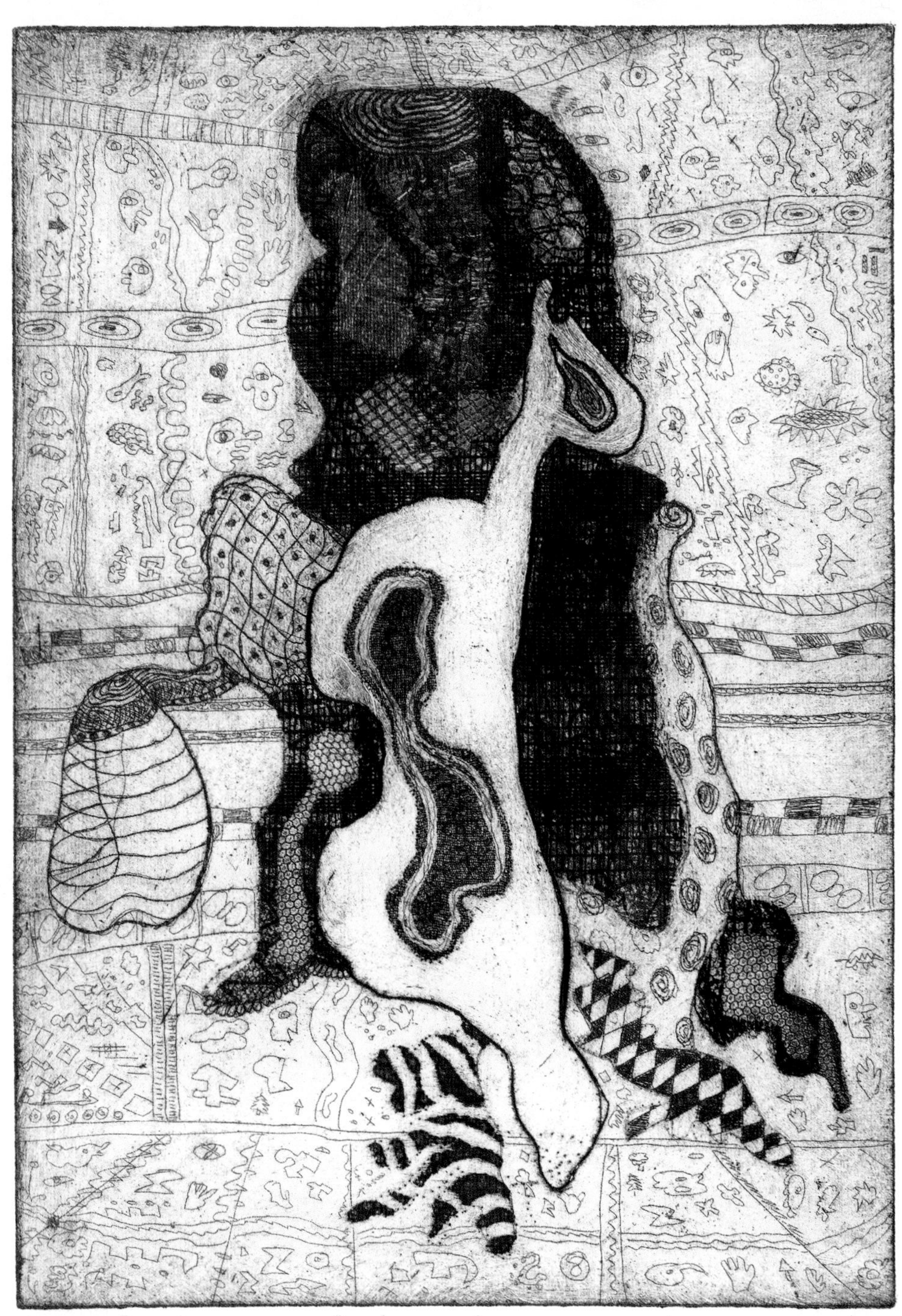

PLATE **56** Dickson Reeder, *Graffitage*, 1944 (object reproduced at actual size)

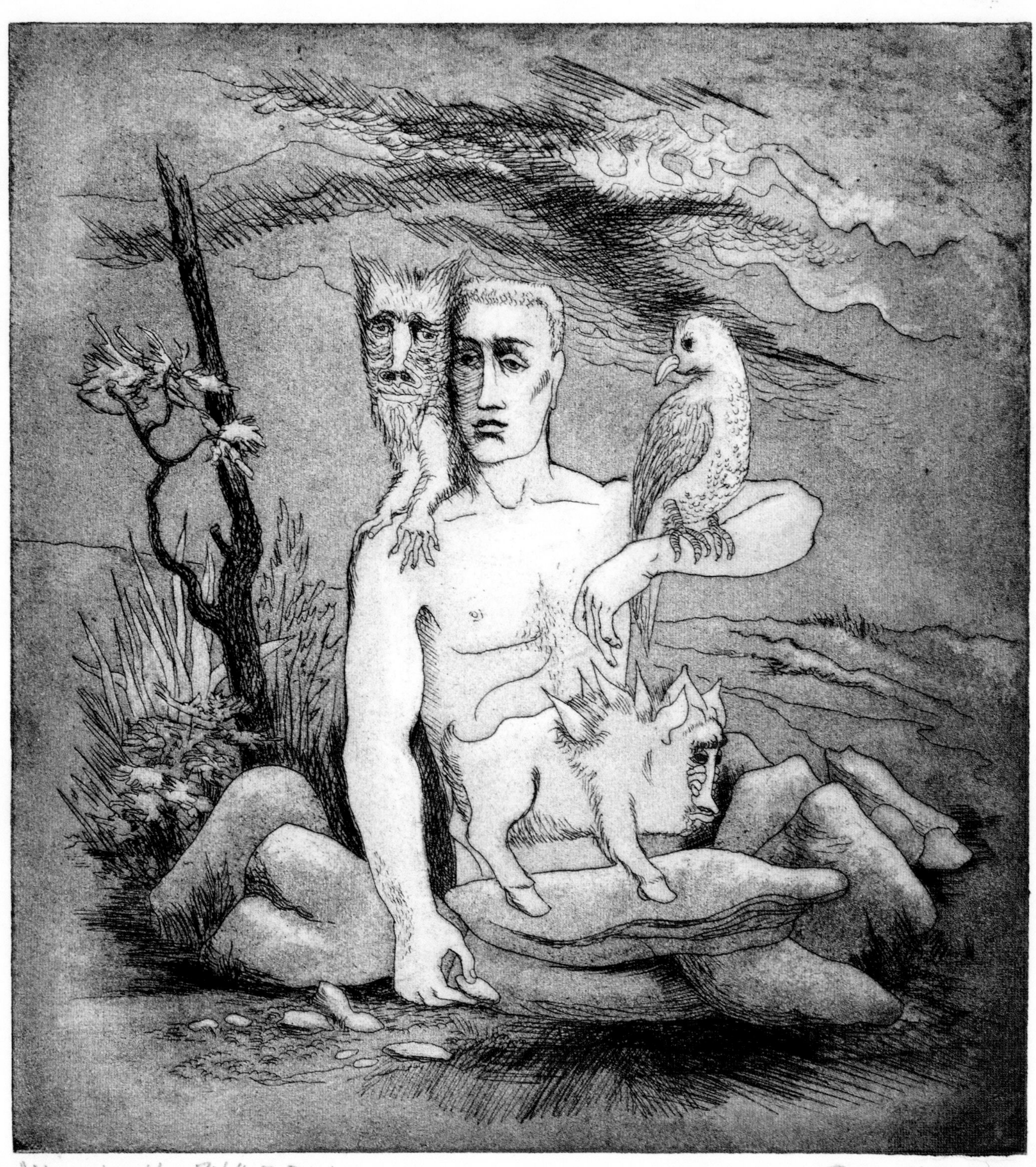

PLATE **57** Bror Utter, *Man in the Pit*, ca. 1943[27, p.69]

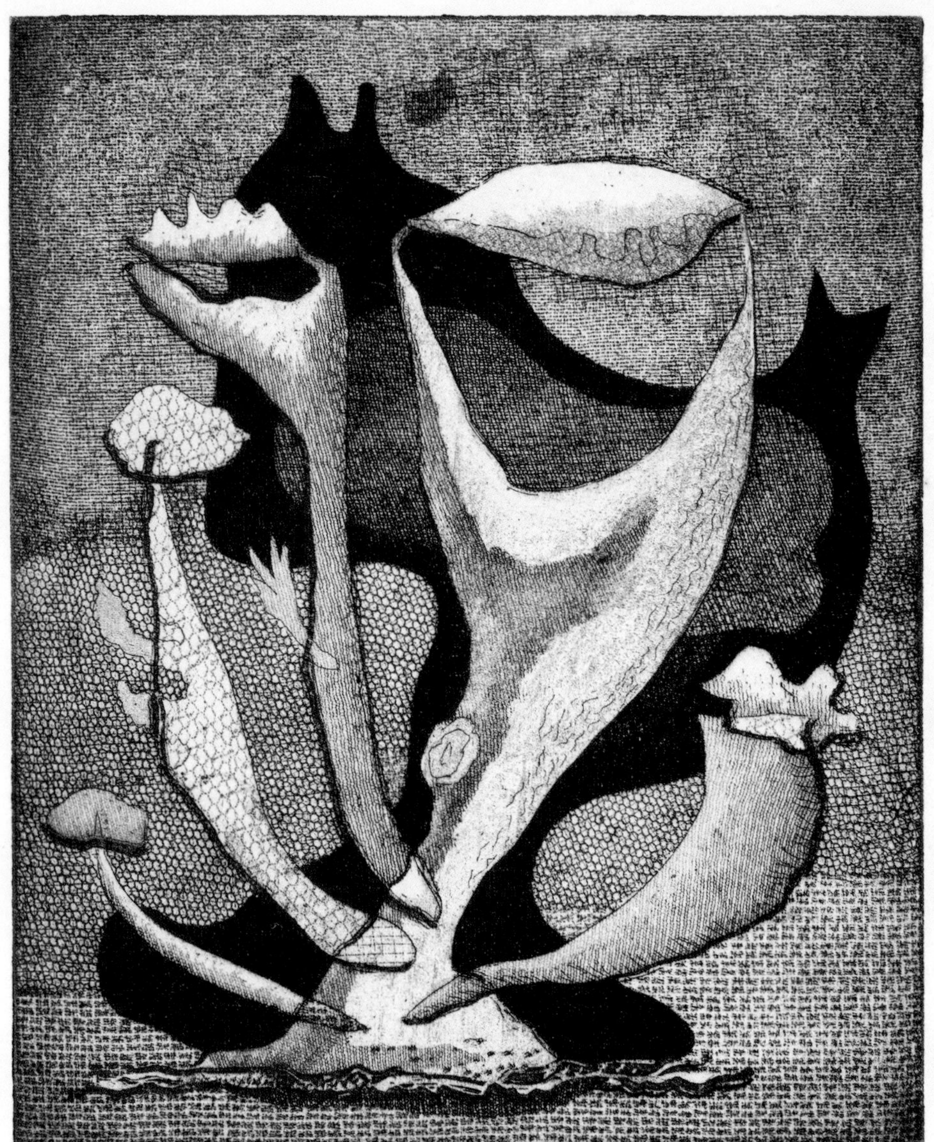

PLATE **58**
Bror Utter, *Cacti*, 1945
(object reproduced at
actual size)

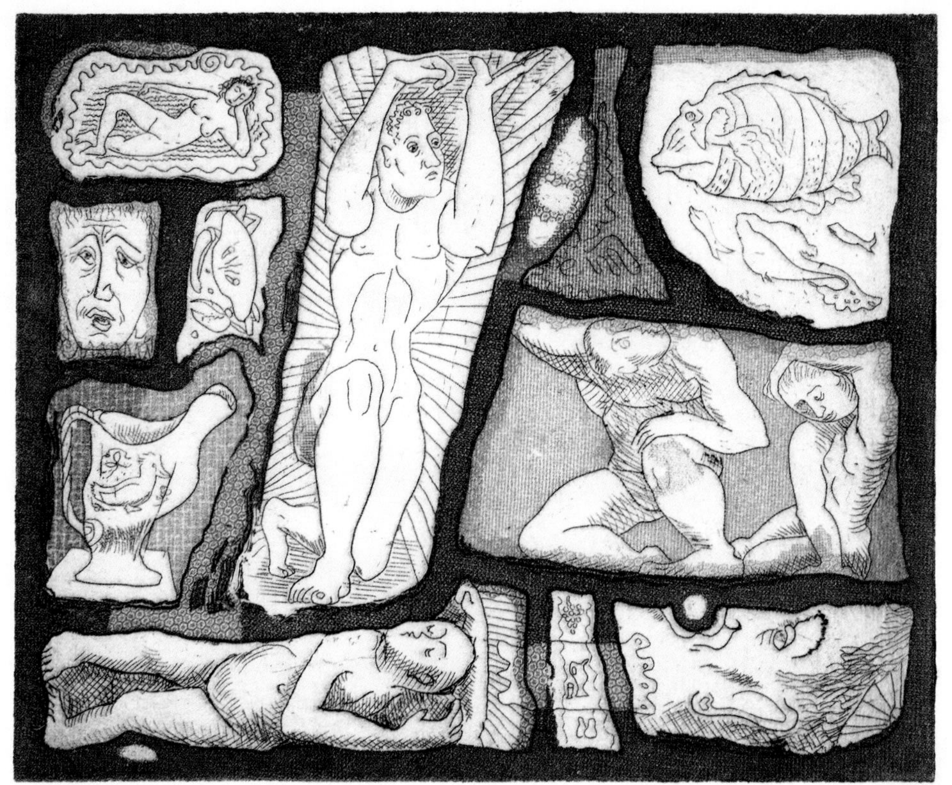

PLATE **59**
Bror Utter, *Cells*, 1945
(object reproduced at actual size)

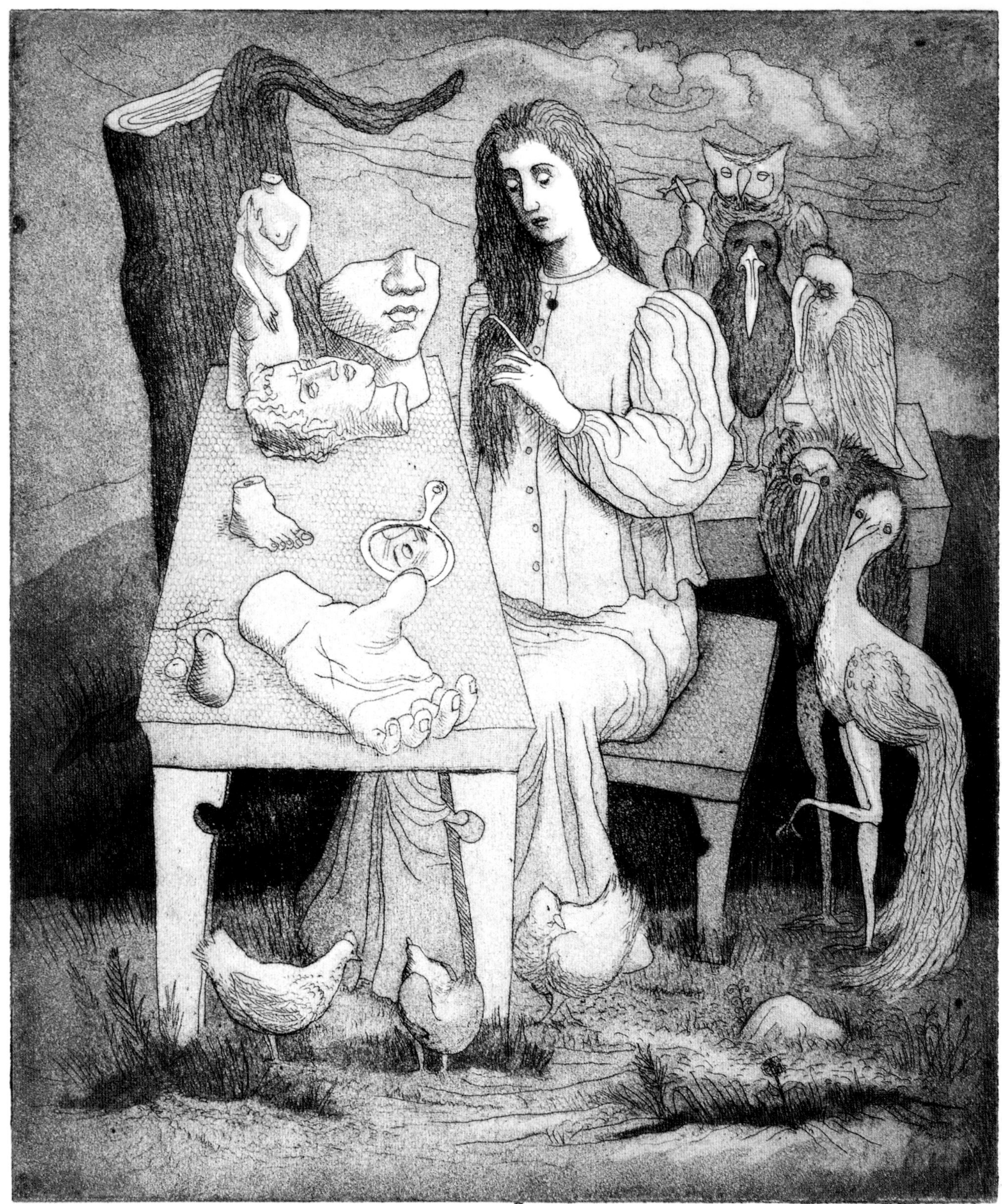

PLATE **60** Bror Utter, *Woman Combing Her Hair (Lady Combing Her Hair)*, 1945 (object reproduced at actual size)

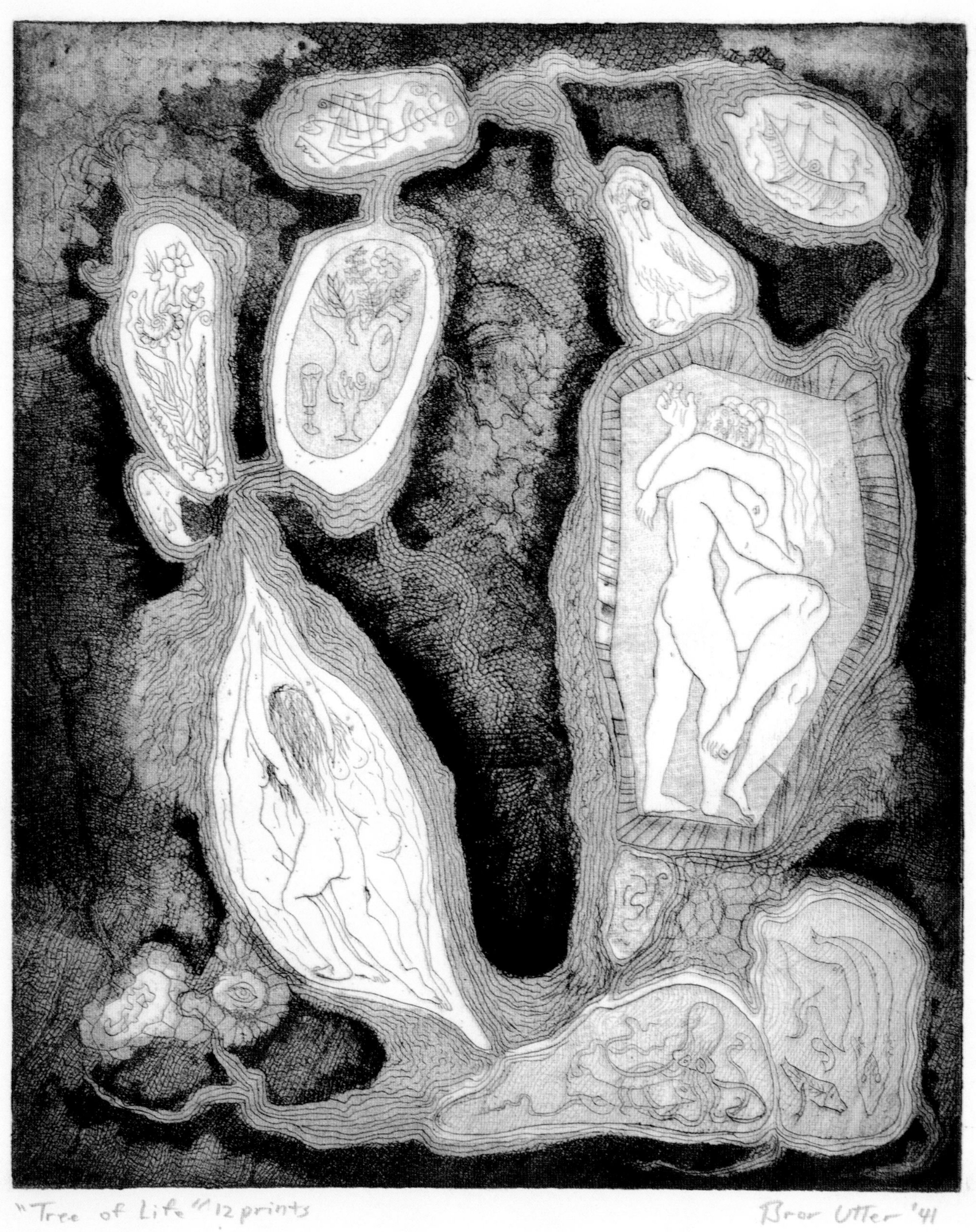

PLATE 61 Bror Utter, *Tree of Knowledge*, 1945[68, p. 72] (object reproduced at actual size)

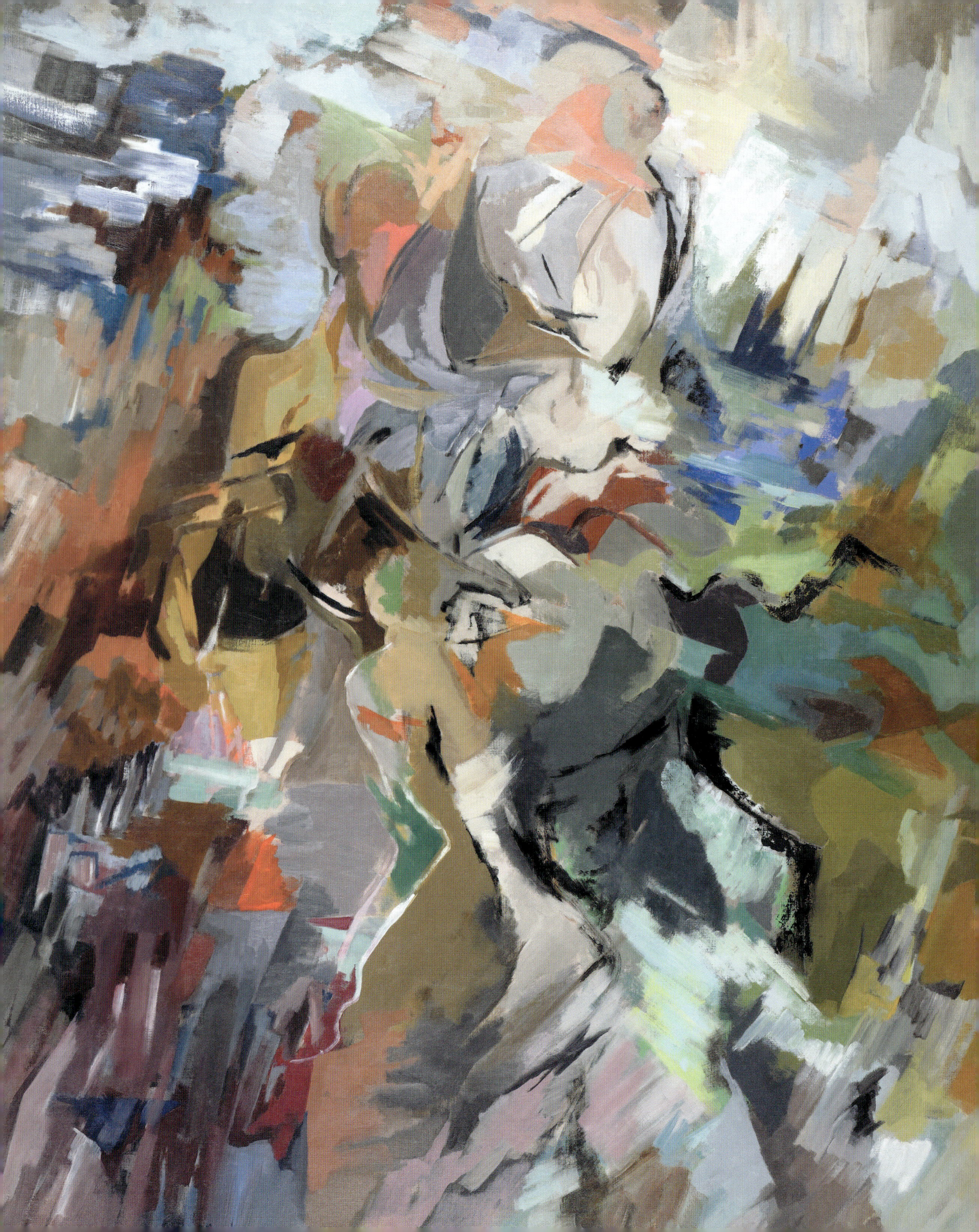

Reasonable Unreality

PLATE **62** Bill Bomar, *Jay's Pool*, 1944

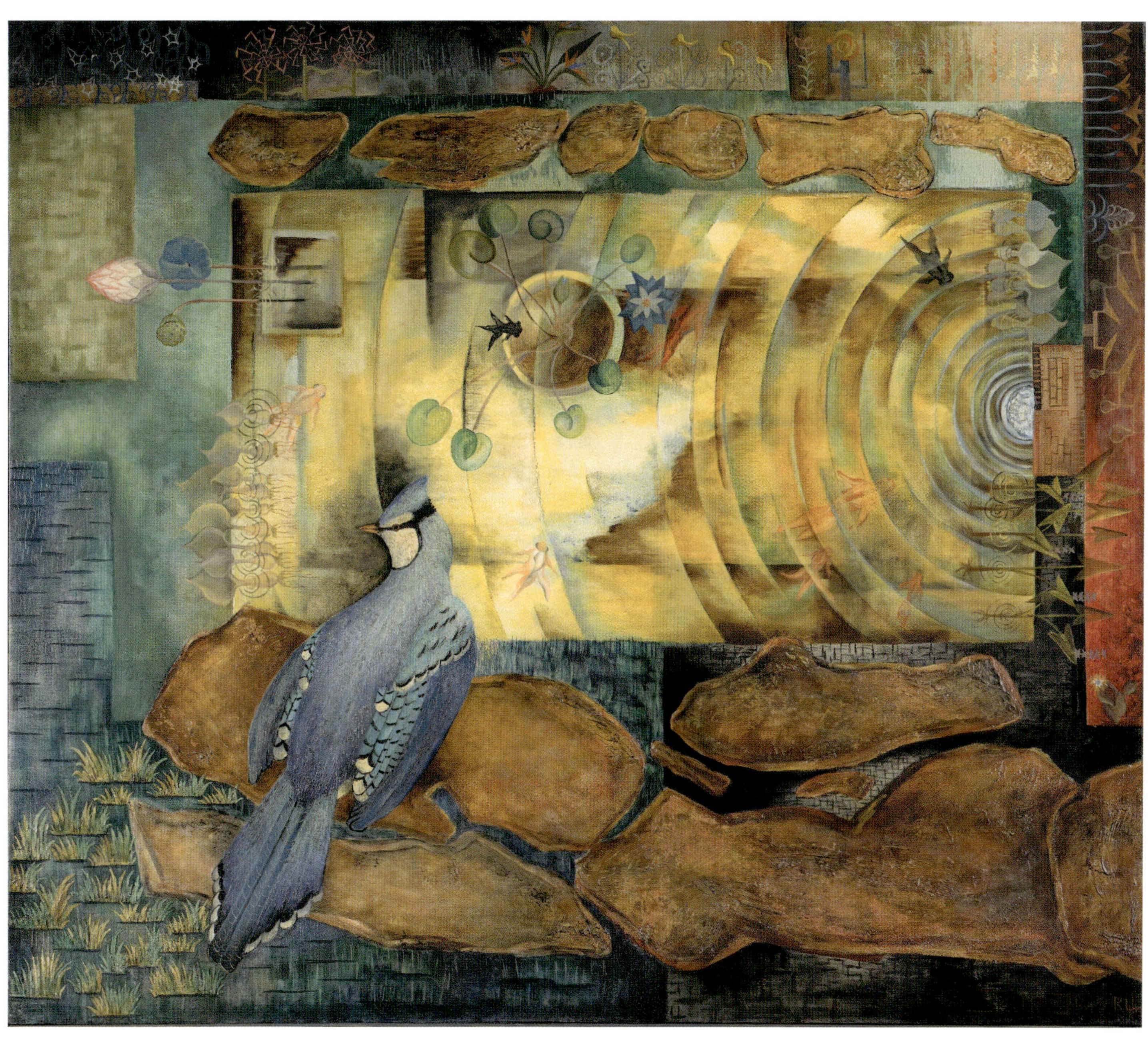

PLATE **63** Bill Bomar, *Day Observation for a Harlequin*, 1947

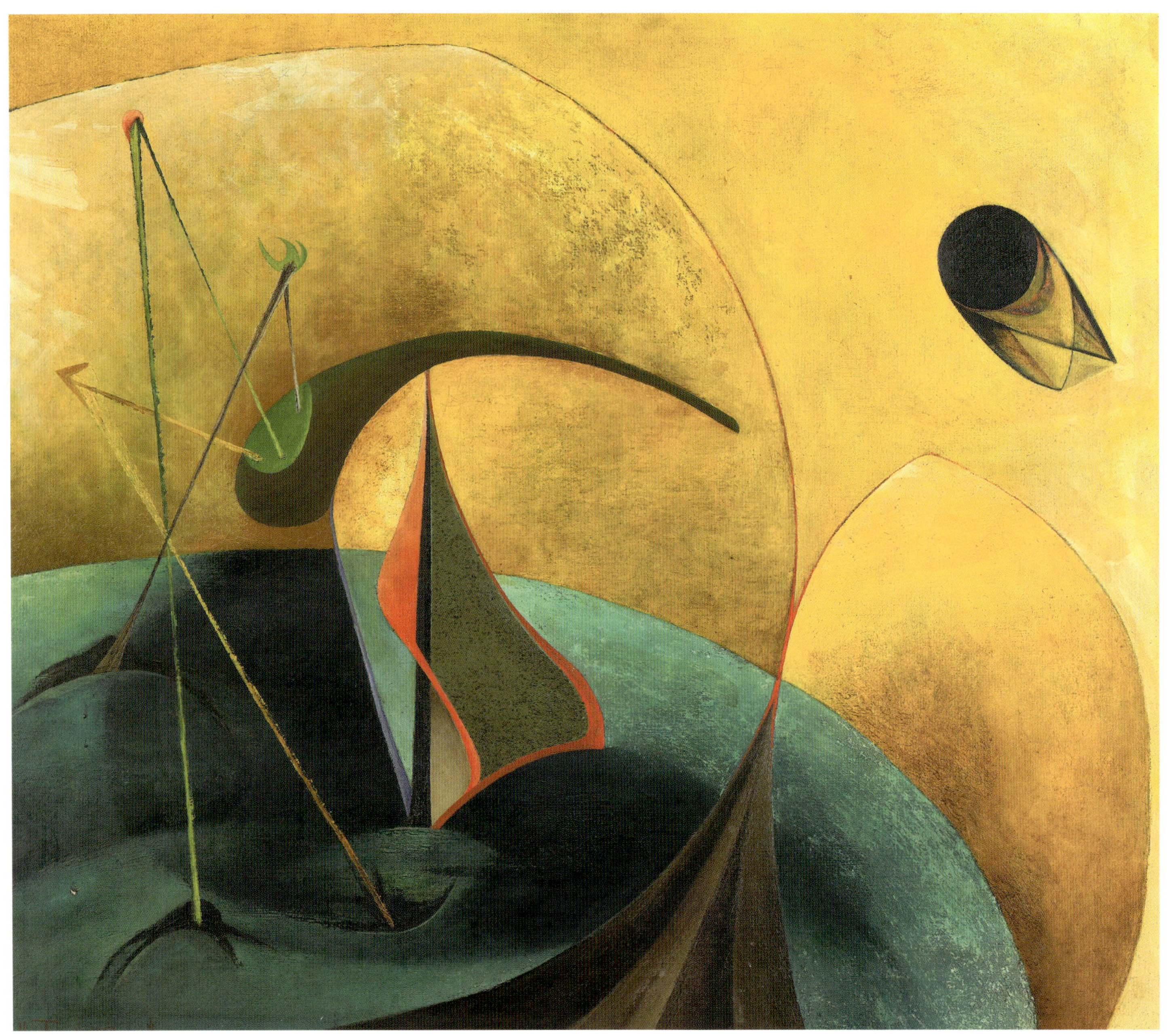

PLATE **64** Bill Bomar, *Web and Roses*, ca. 1947–48

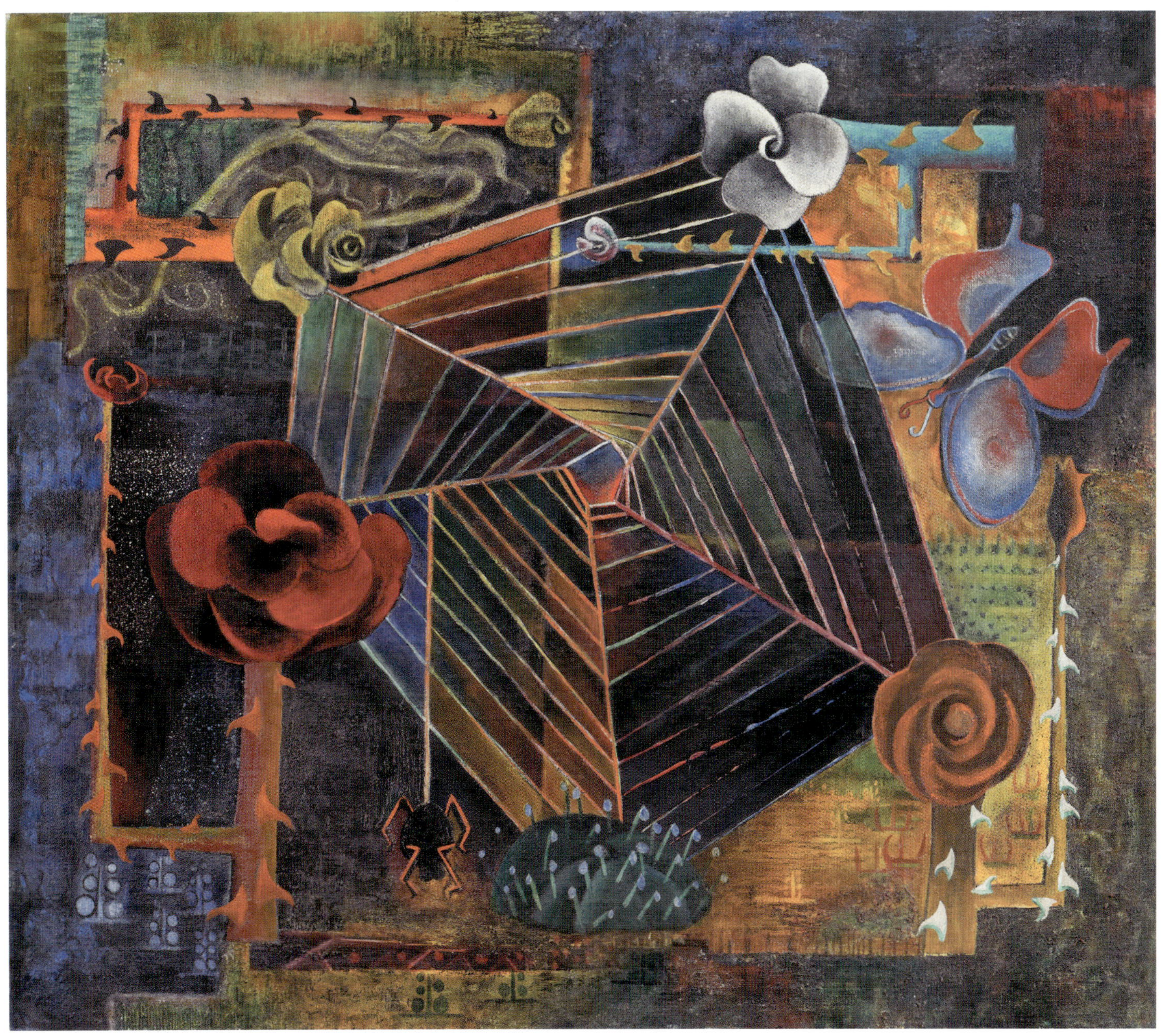

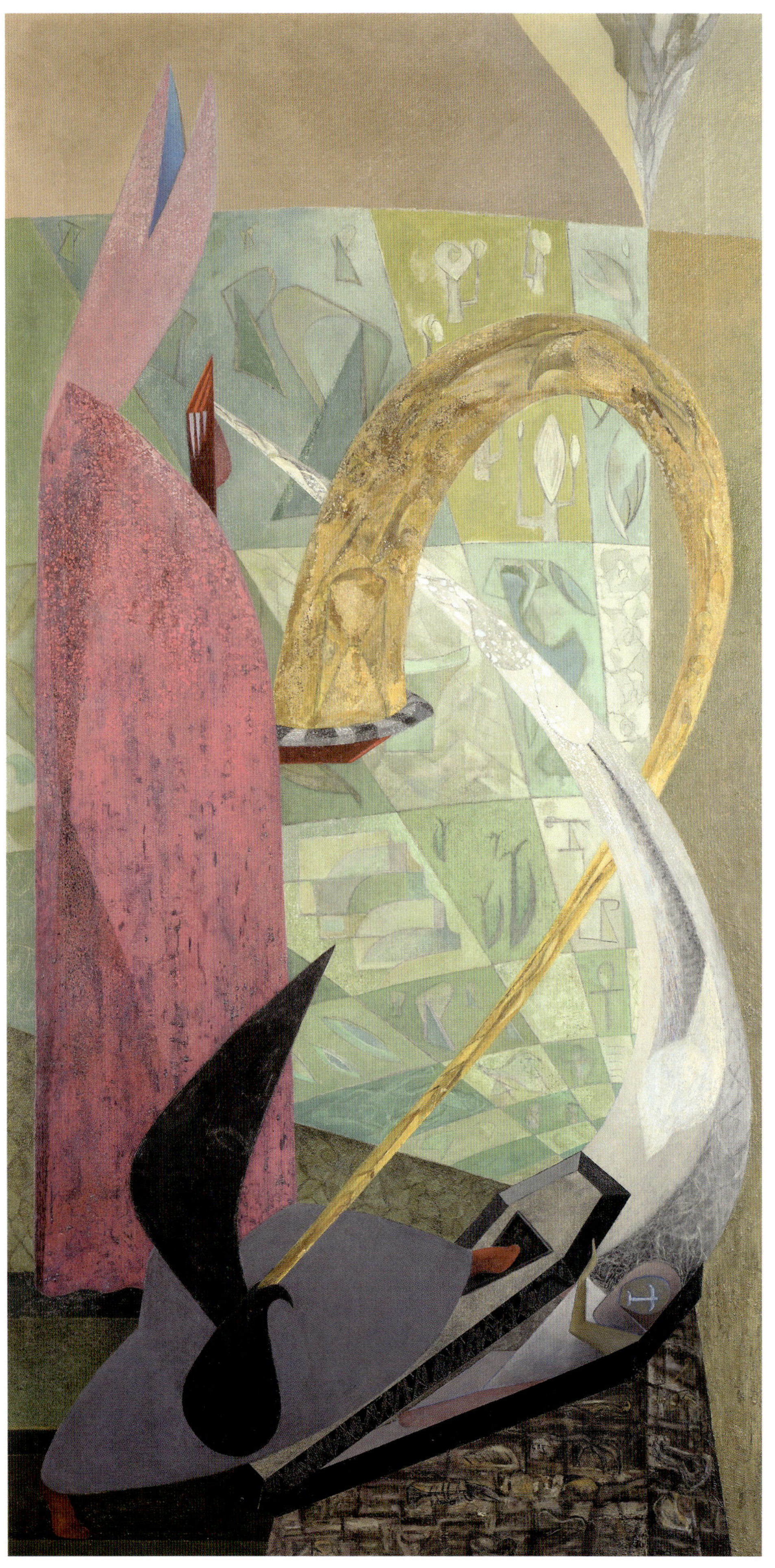

PLATE **65** Bill Bomar, *Burial in Spain*, 1949

PLATE **66** Cynthia Brants, *The Cocktail Party*, 1947

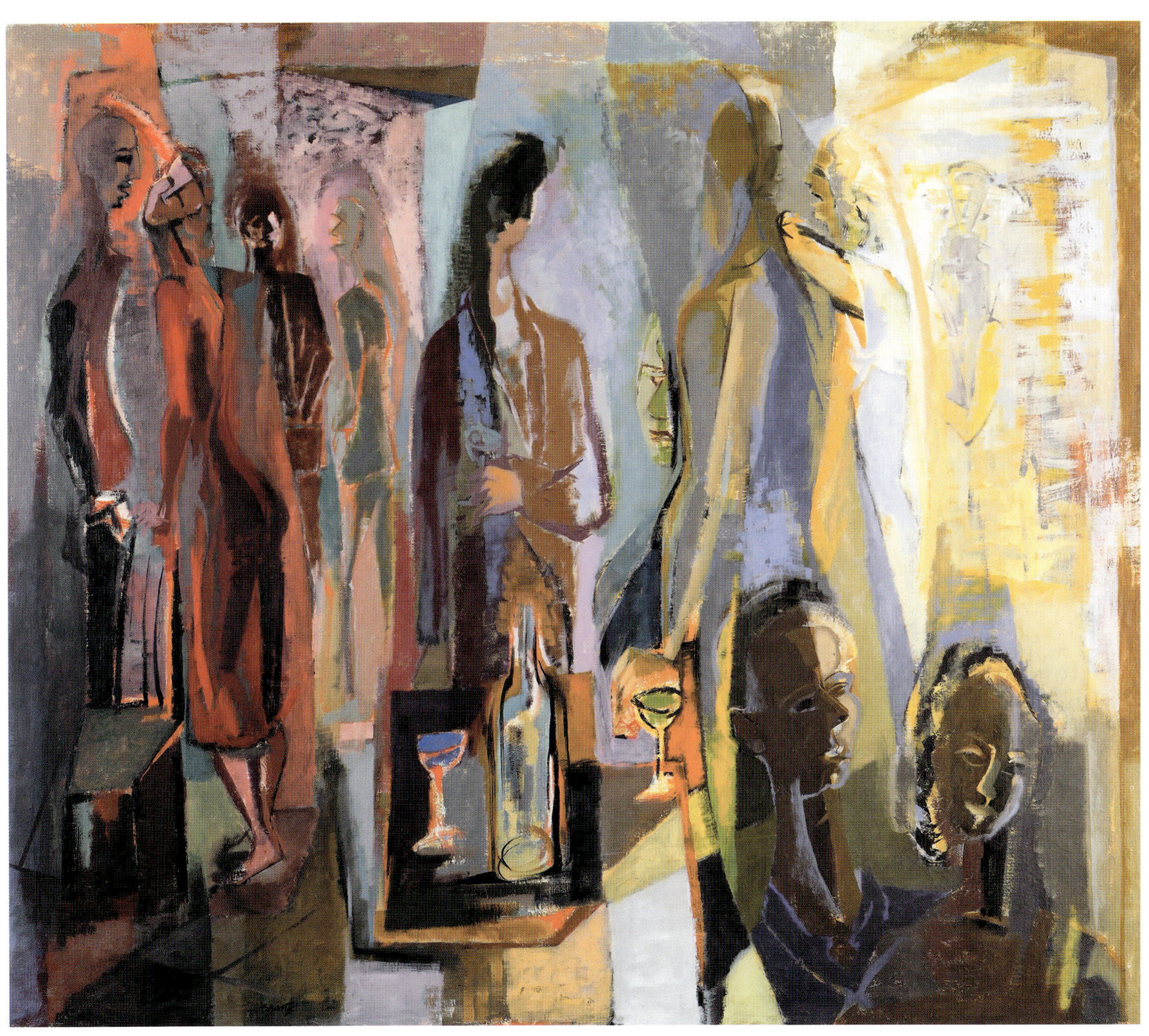

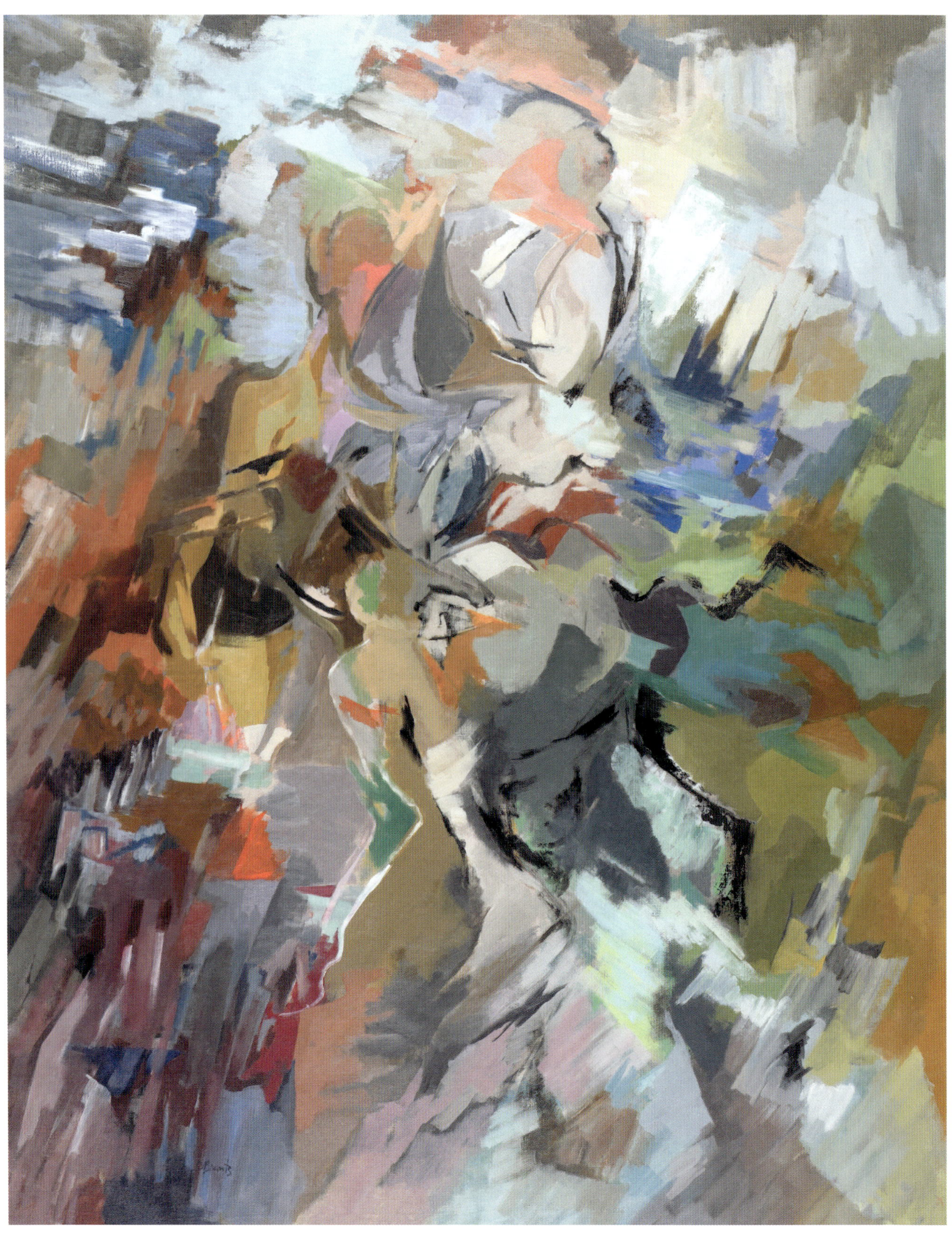

PLATE **67** Cynthia Brants, *The Centaur*, 1953

PLATE **68** Lia Cuilty, *Arrested Flight*, ca. 1943

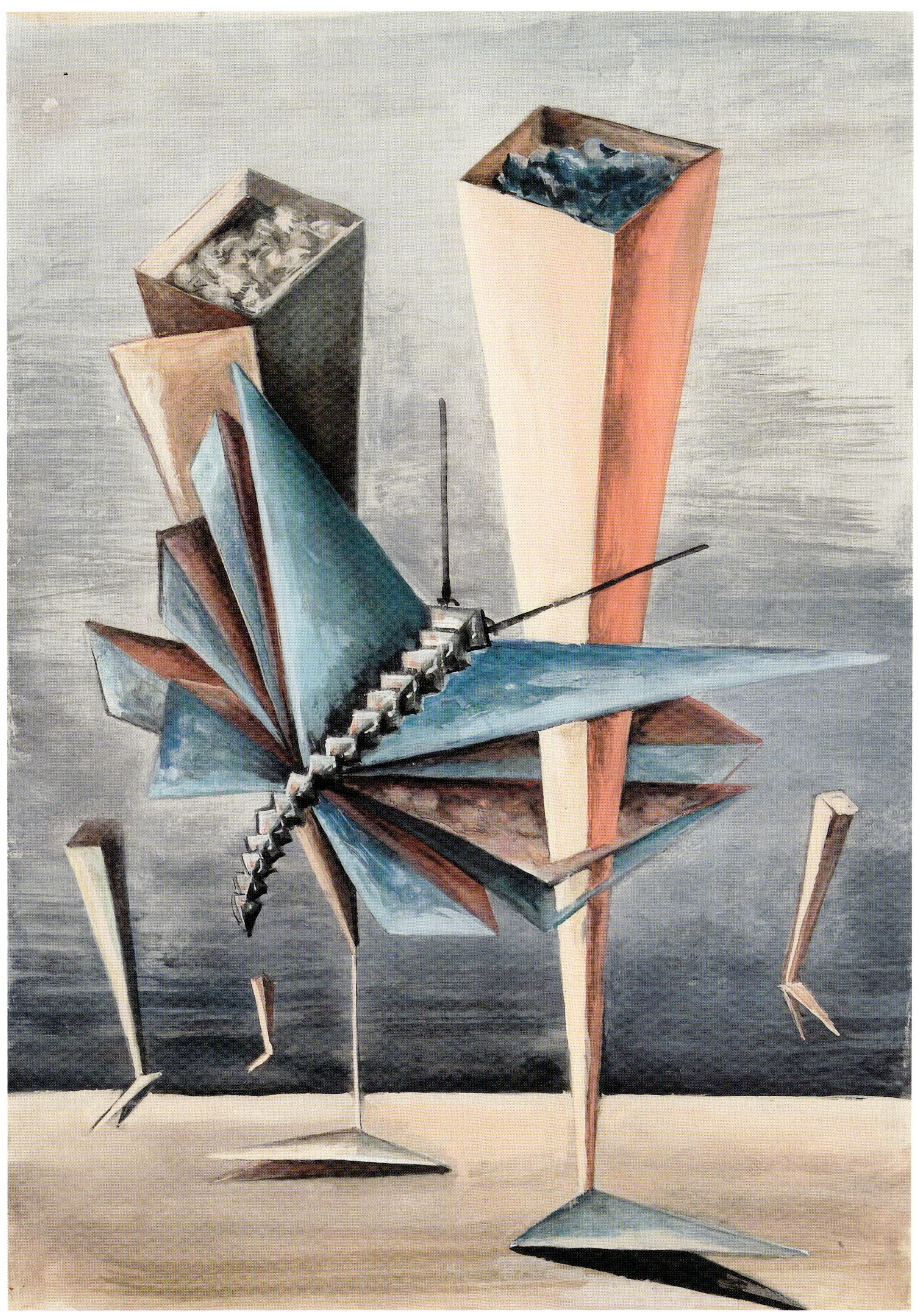

PLATE **69** Kelly Fearing, *The Kite Flyers*, 1945

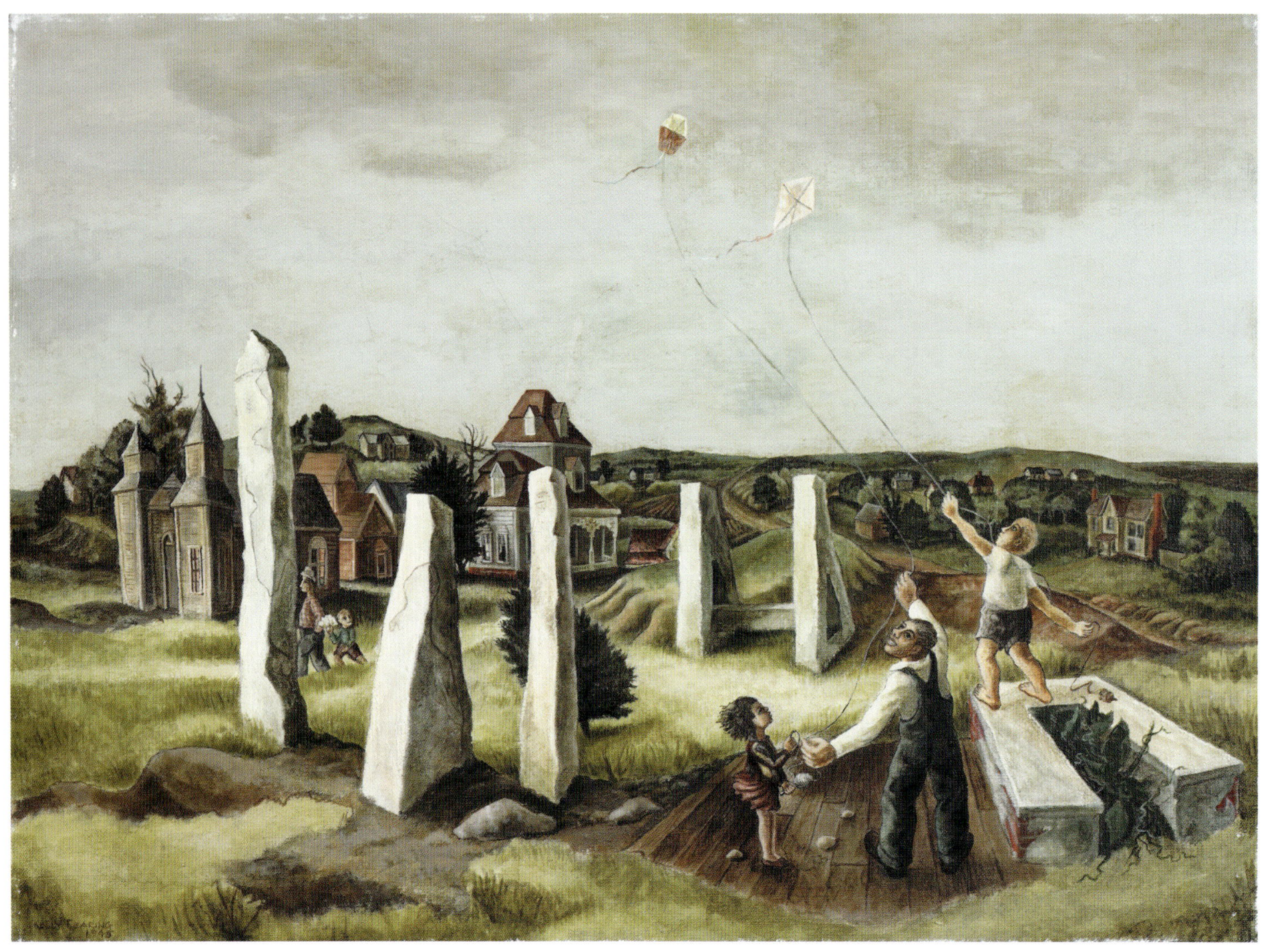

PLATE **70** Kelly Fearing, *The Lifters*, 1946

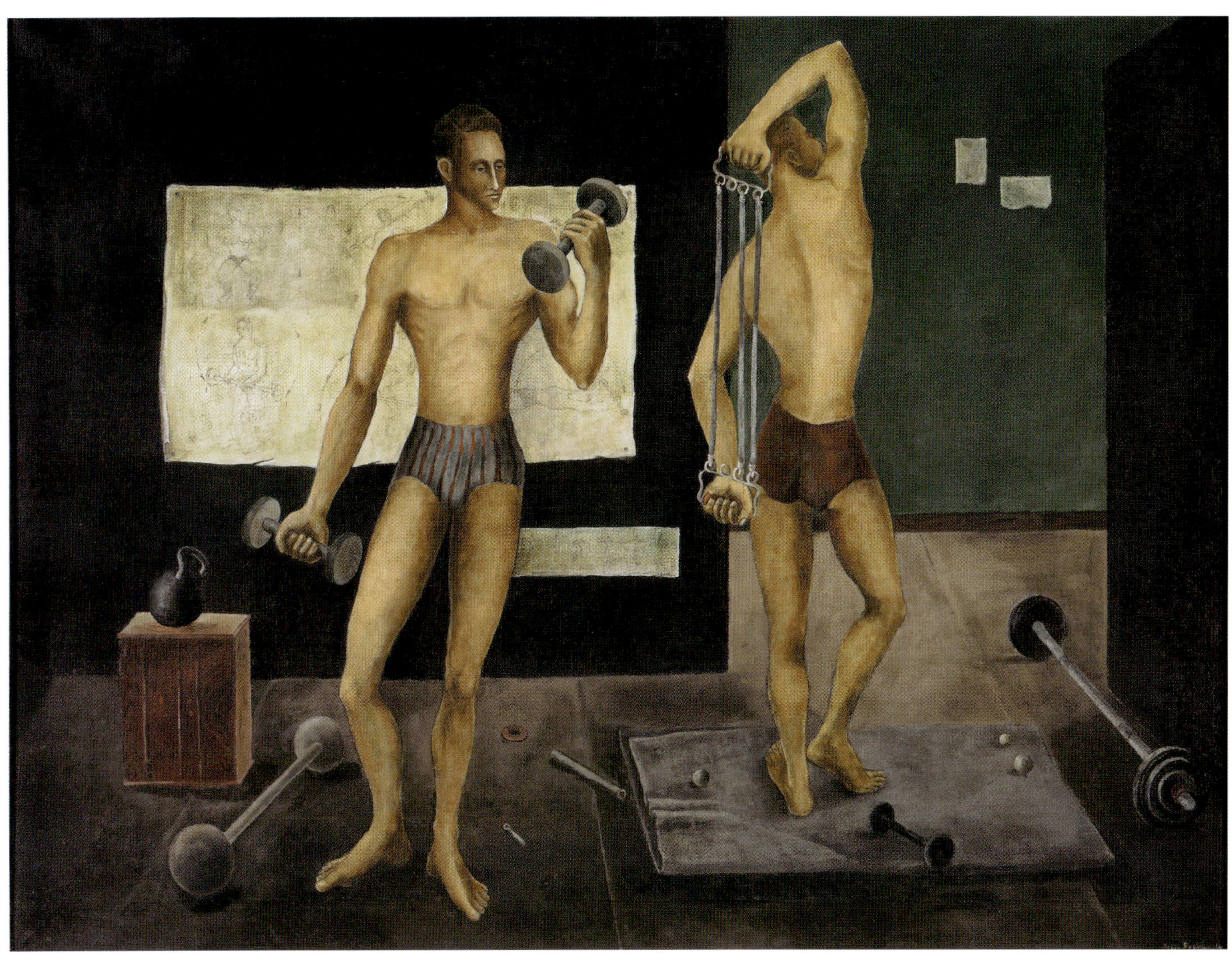

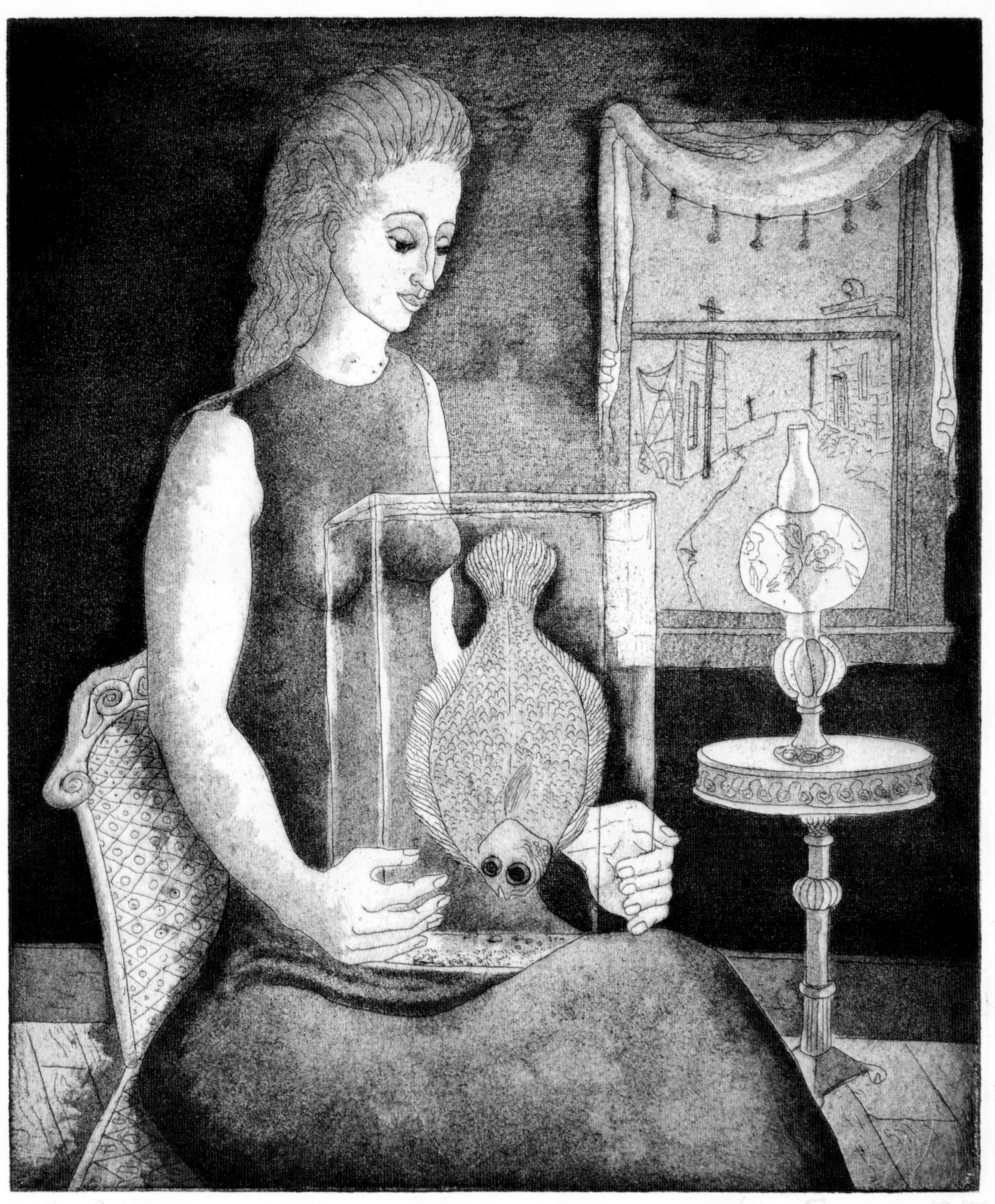
"The Collector
Kelly Fearing, 1945

PLATE **71** Kelly Fearing, *The Collector*, 1945

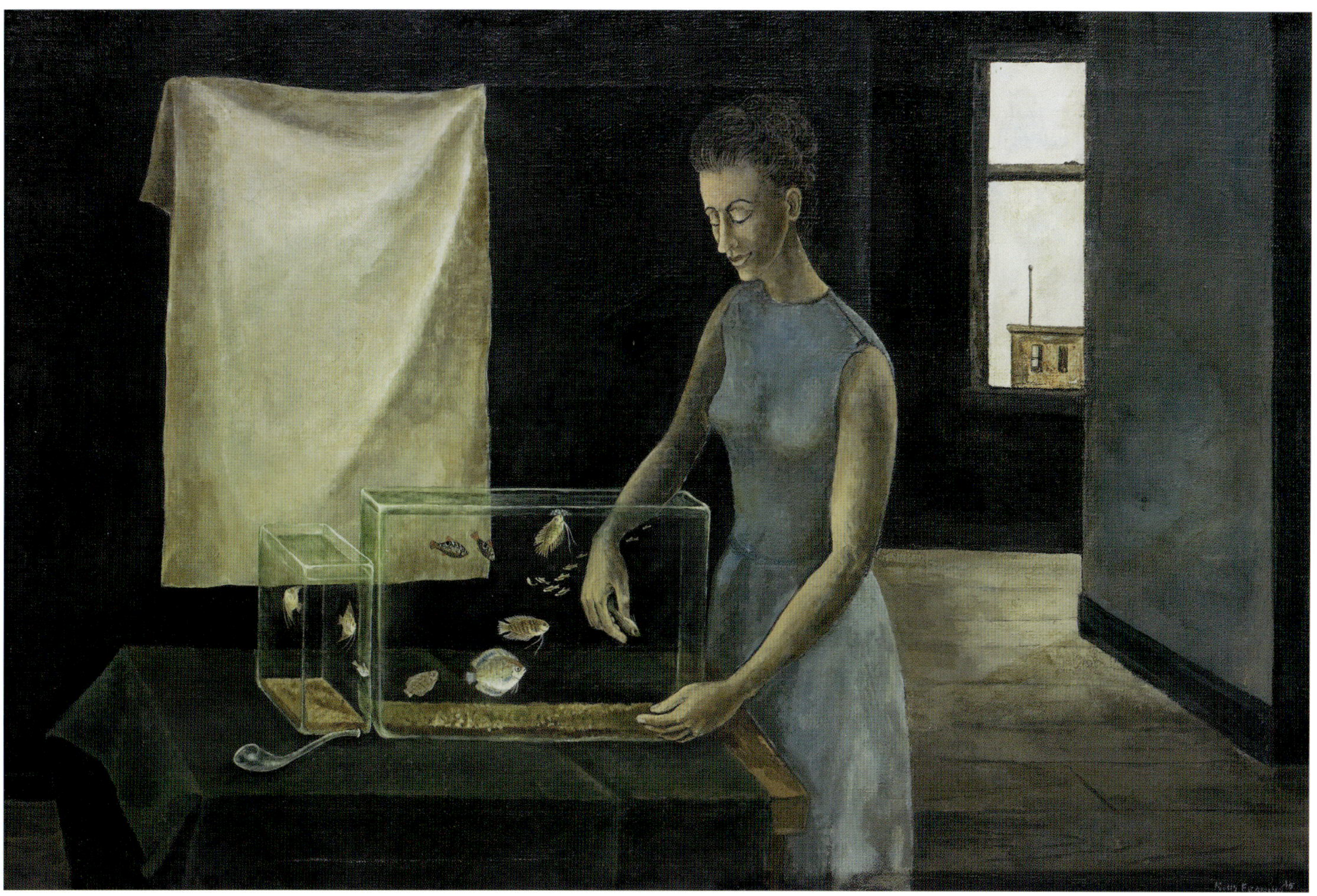

PLATE **72** Kelly Fearing, *The Aquarist*, 1945

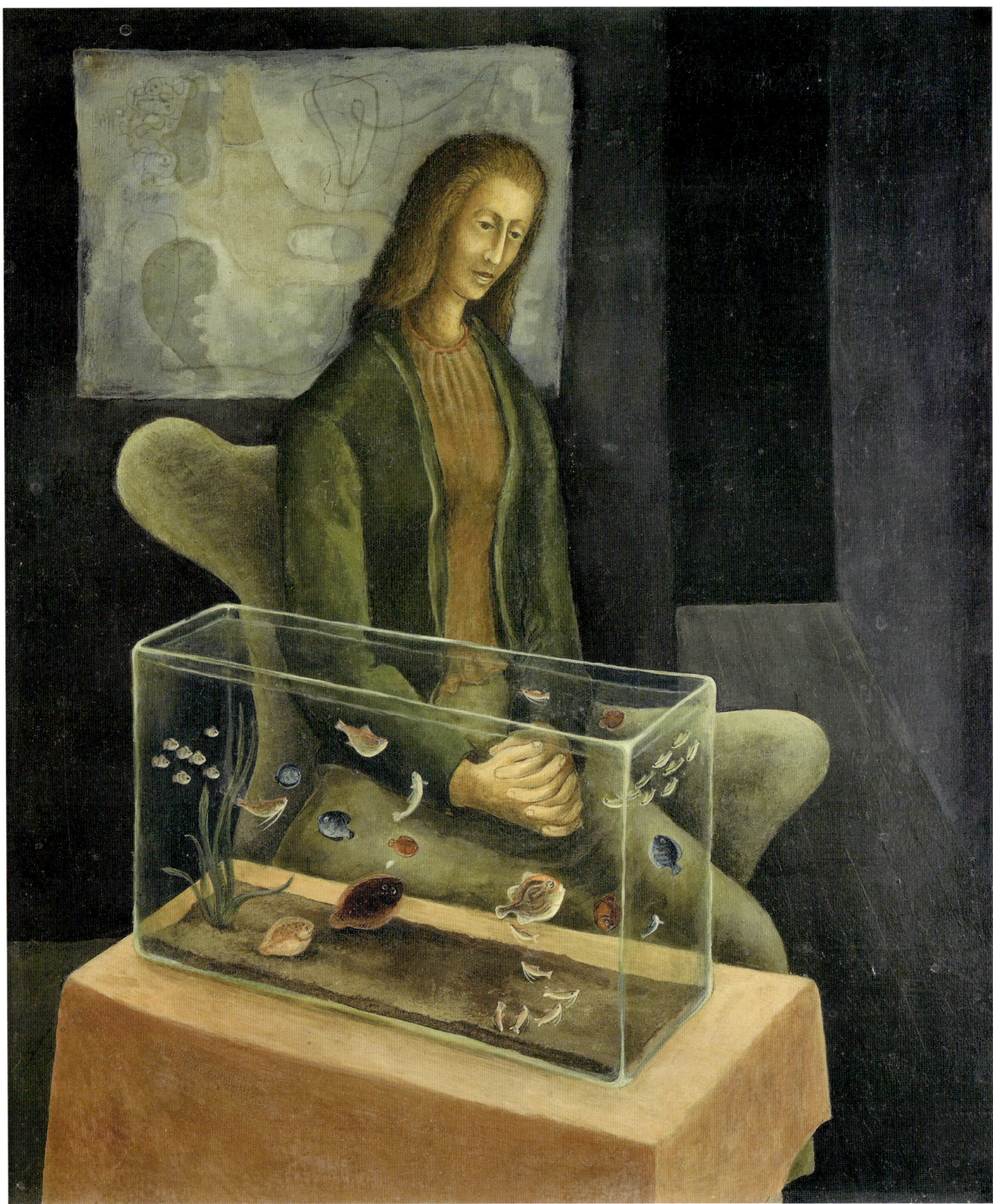

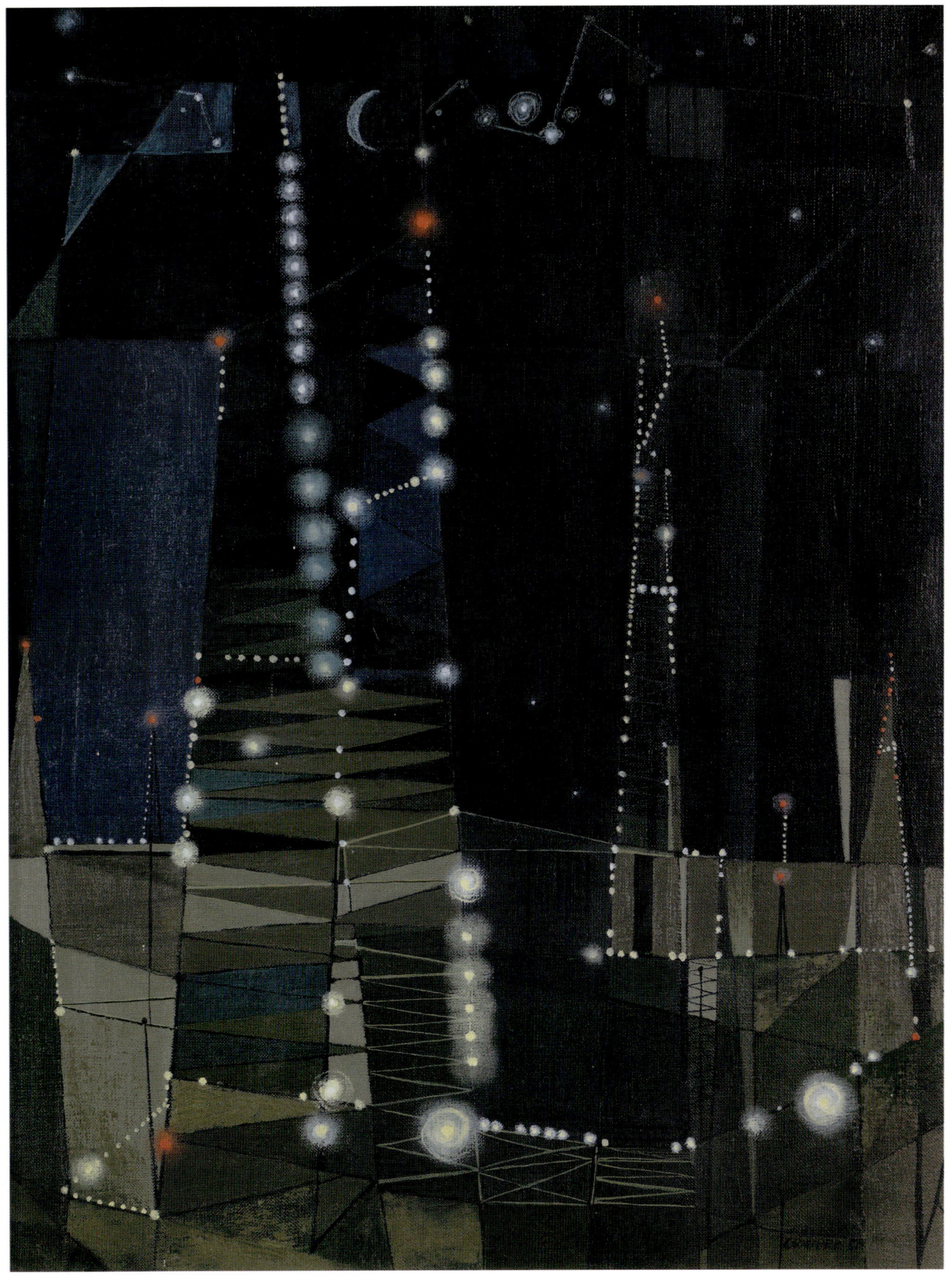

PLATE **73** Kelly Fearing, *The Collector*, 1946

PLATE **74** George Grammer, *Oil Wells at Night*, 1950

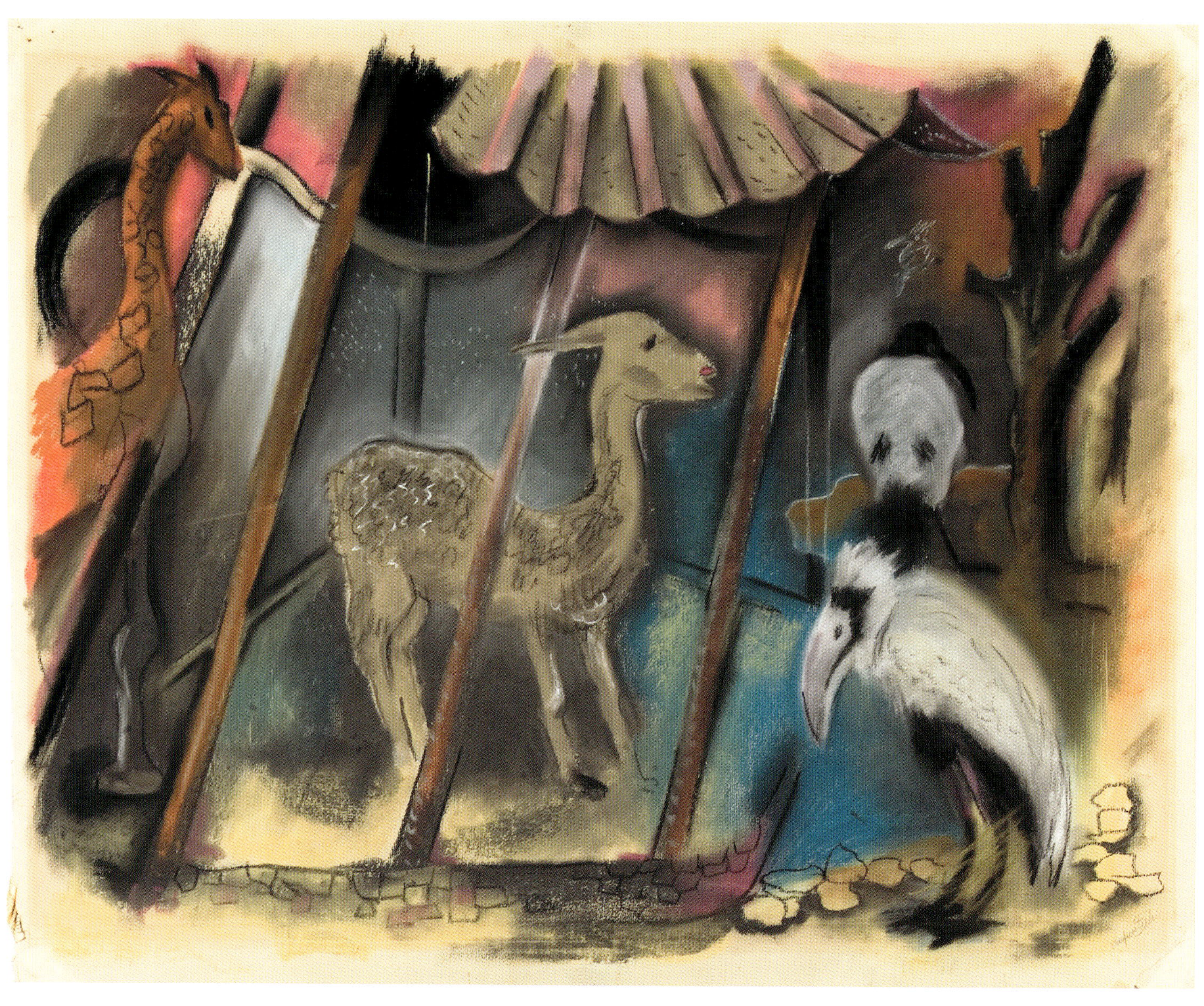

PLATE **75** Veronica Helfensteller, *Untitled [Animals at the Zoo]*, ca. 1945

PLATE **76** Veronica Helfensteller, *Animals at the Zoo*, 1946

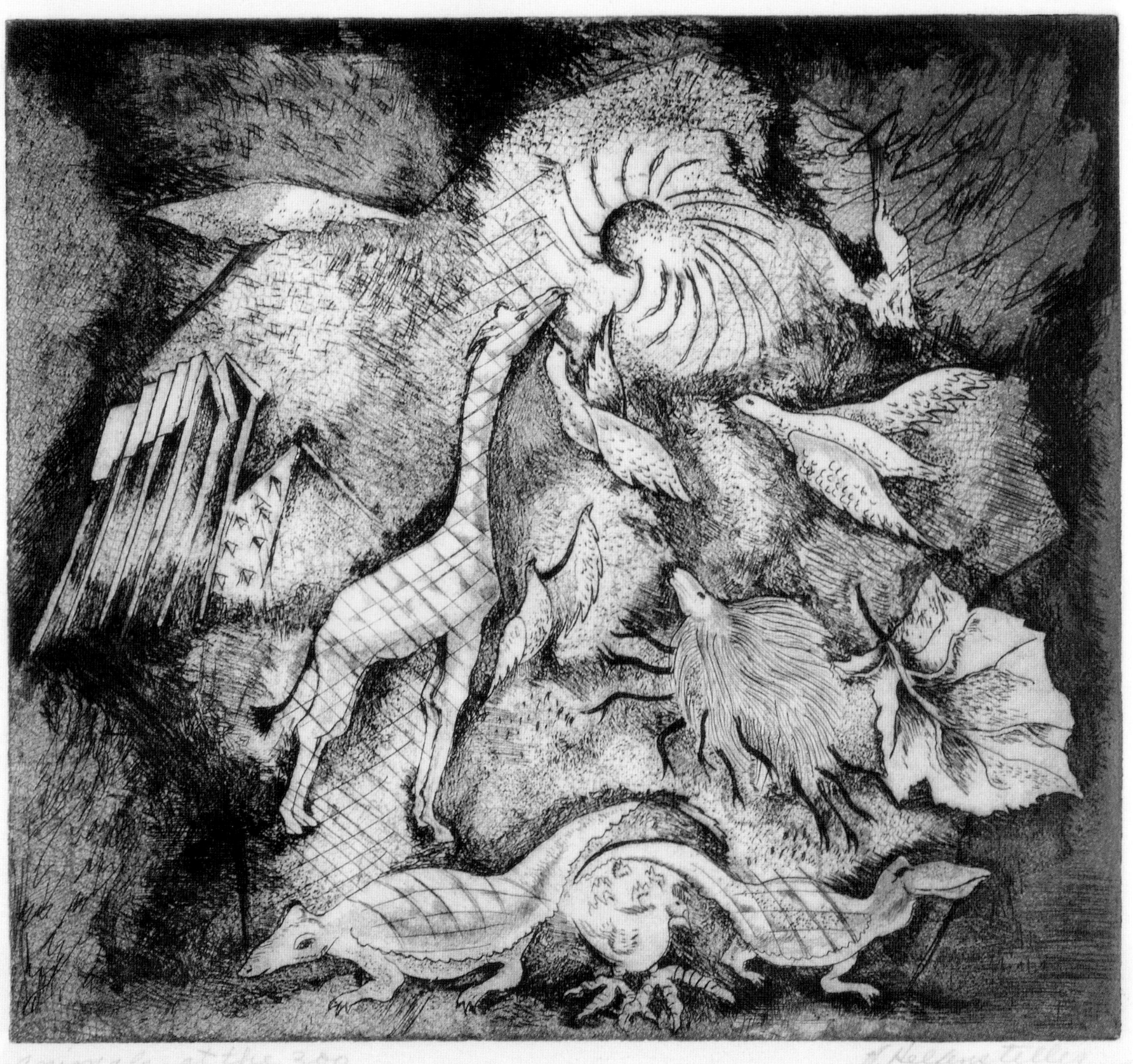
animals at the zoo

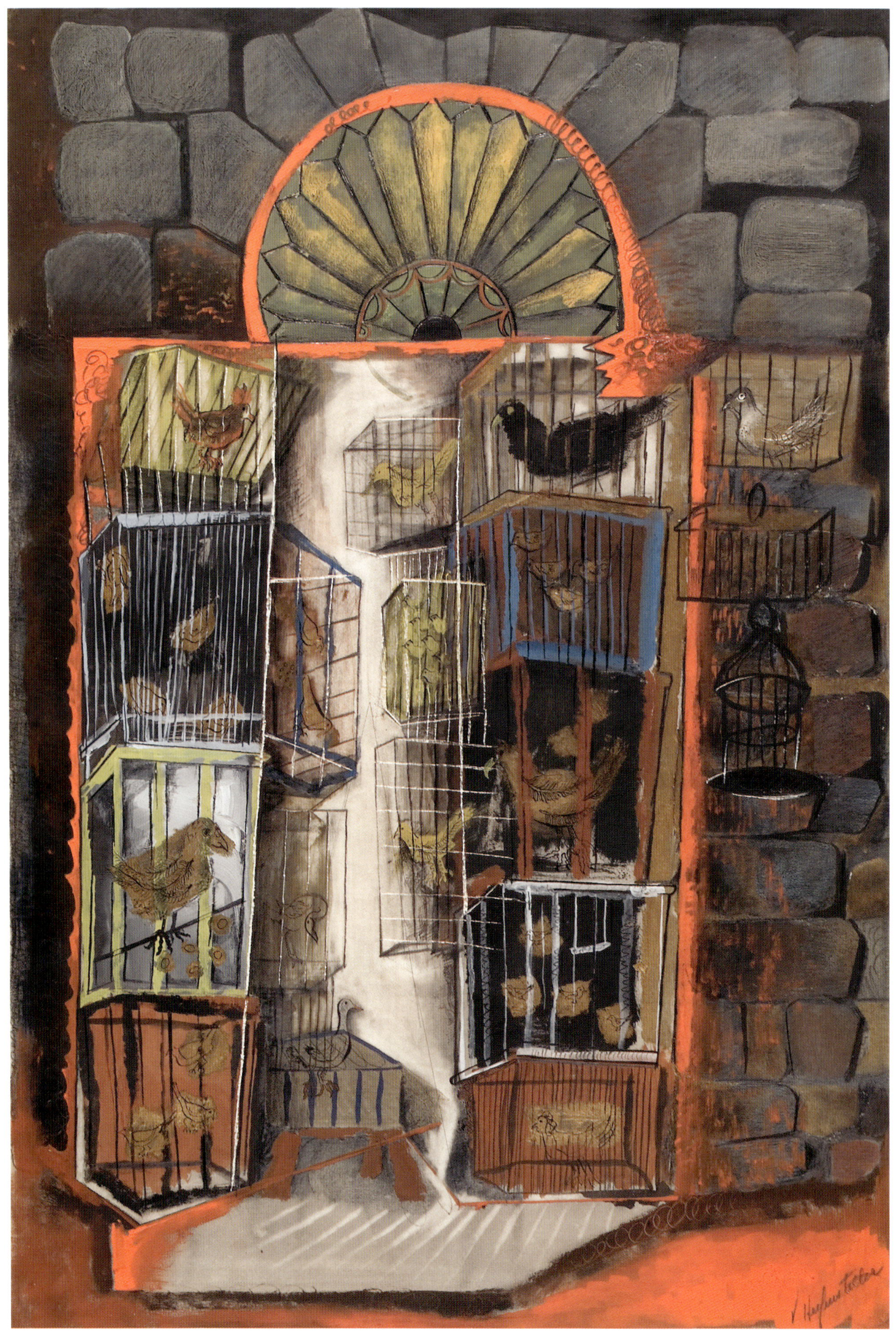

PLATE **77** Veronica Helfensteller, *Doorway Aviary*, 1948

PLATE **78** Veronica Helfensteller, *Poor Little Girl Who Swallowed the Seeds*, ca. 1947–48

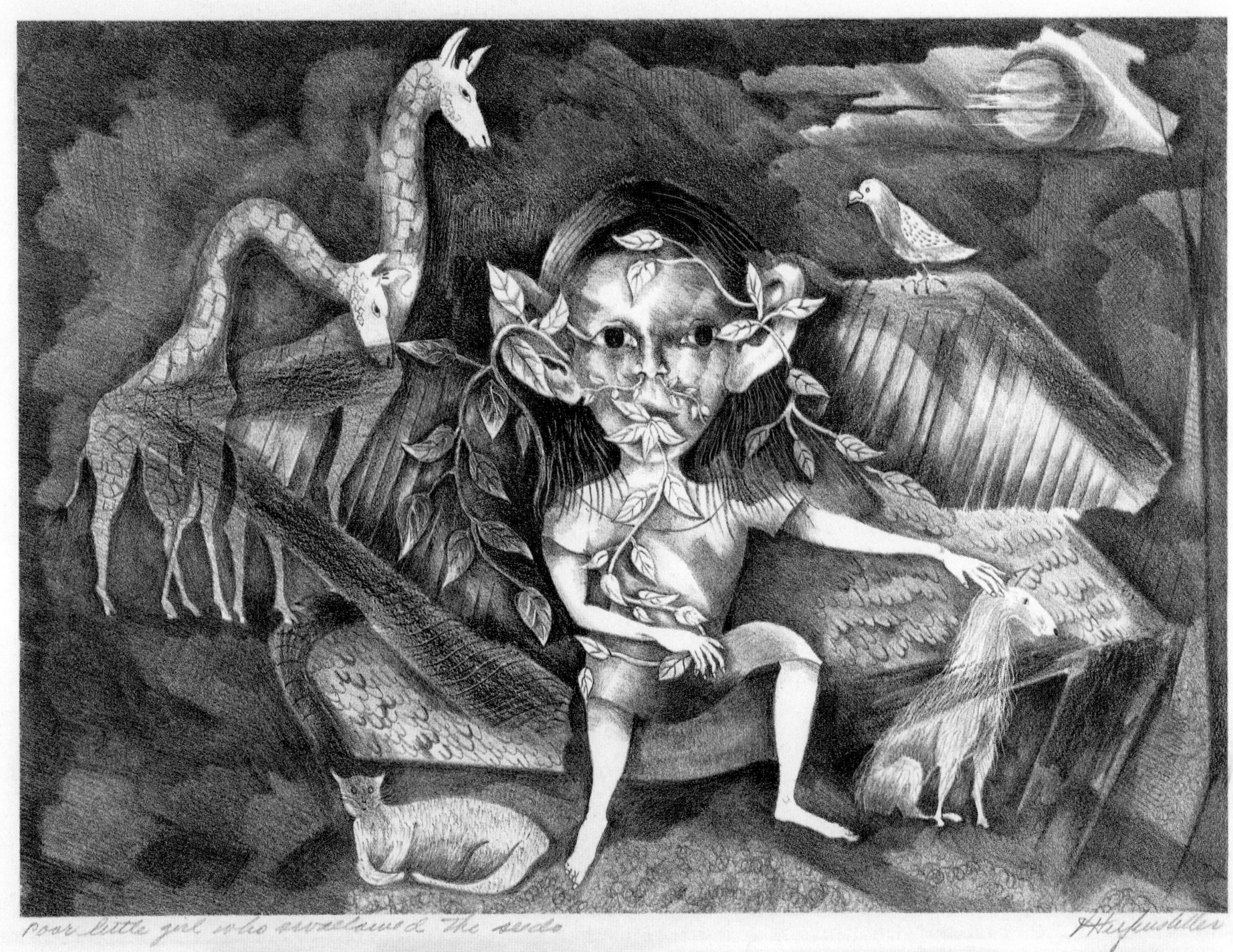

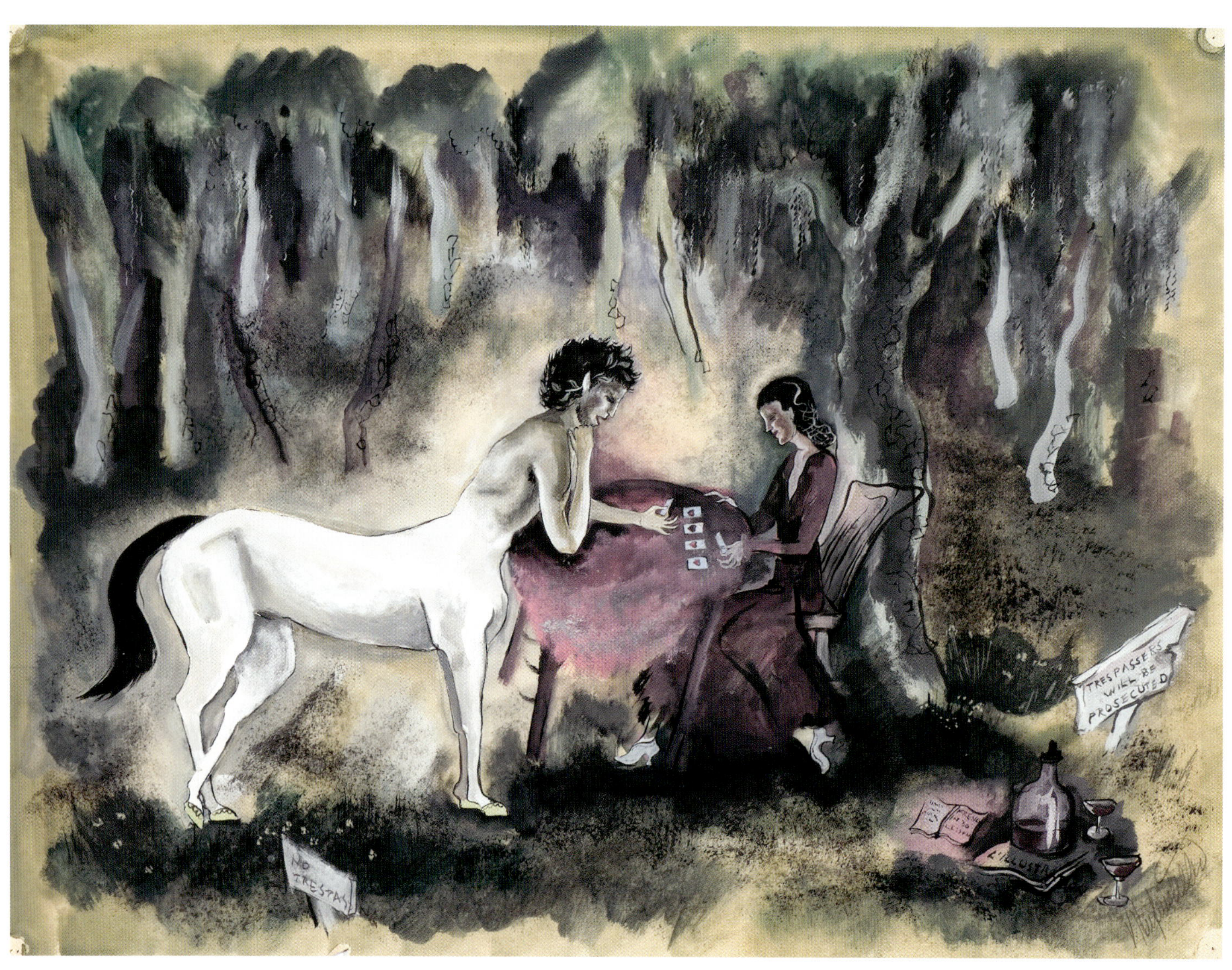

PLATE **79** Veronica Helfensteller, *"Reclining under a tree (they) played at chess and cards . . . ,"* 1944

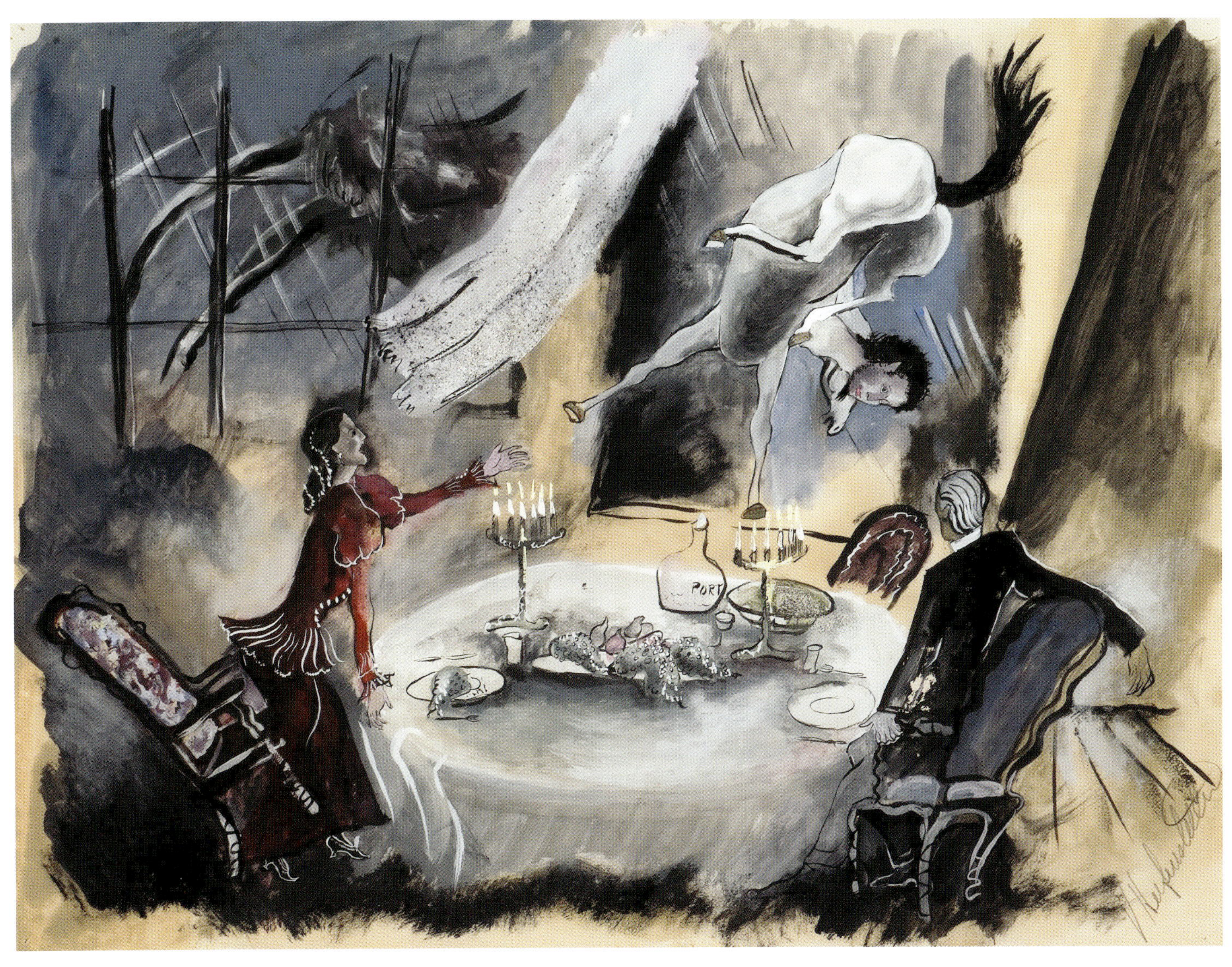

PLATE **80** Veronica Helfensteller, *"'Horace,' she cried ...,"* 1944

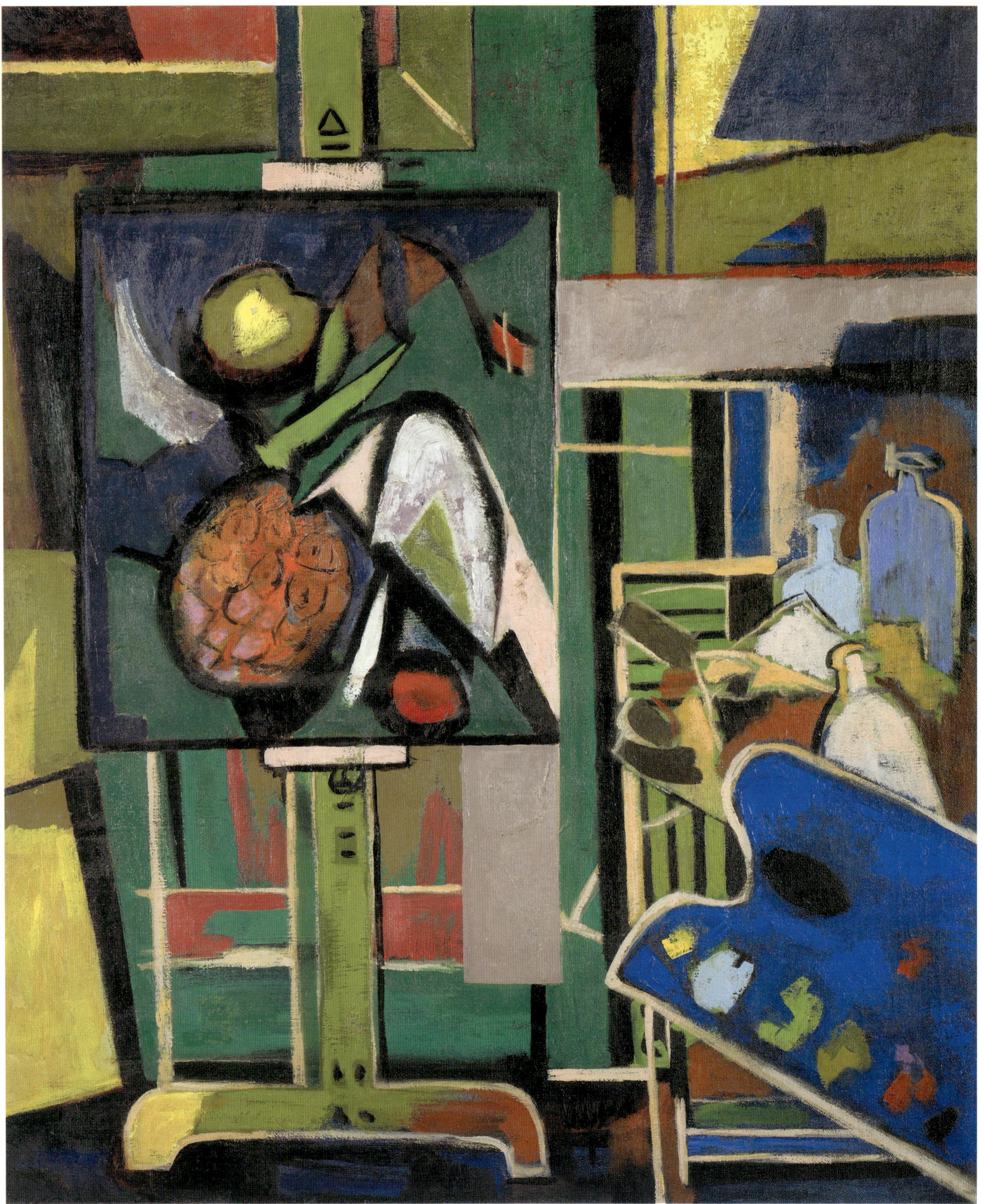

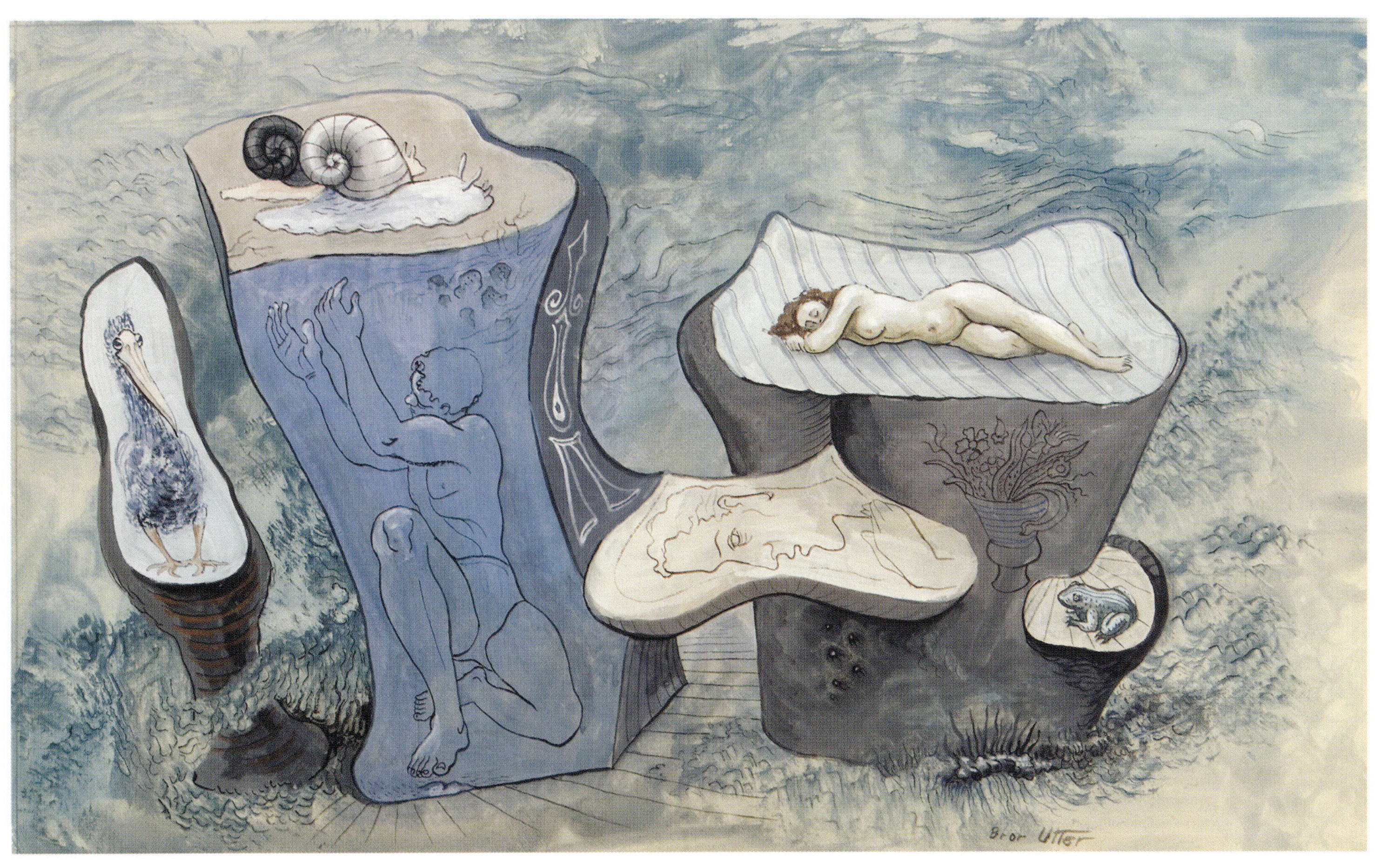

PLATE **81** Marjorie Johnson, *Studio Corner*, 1949

PLATE **82** Bror Utter, *The Dreamer (Embellished Forms No. 2)*, 1946

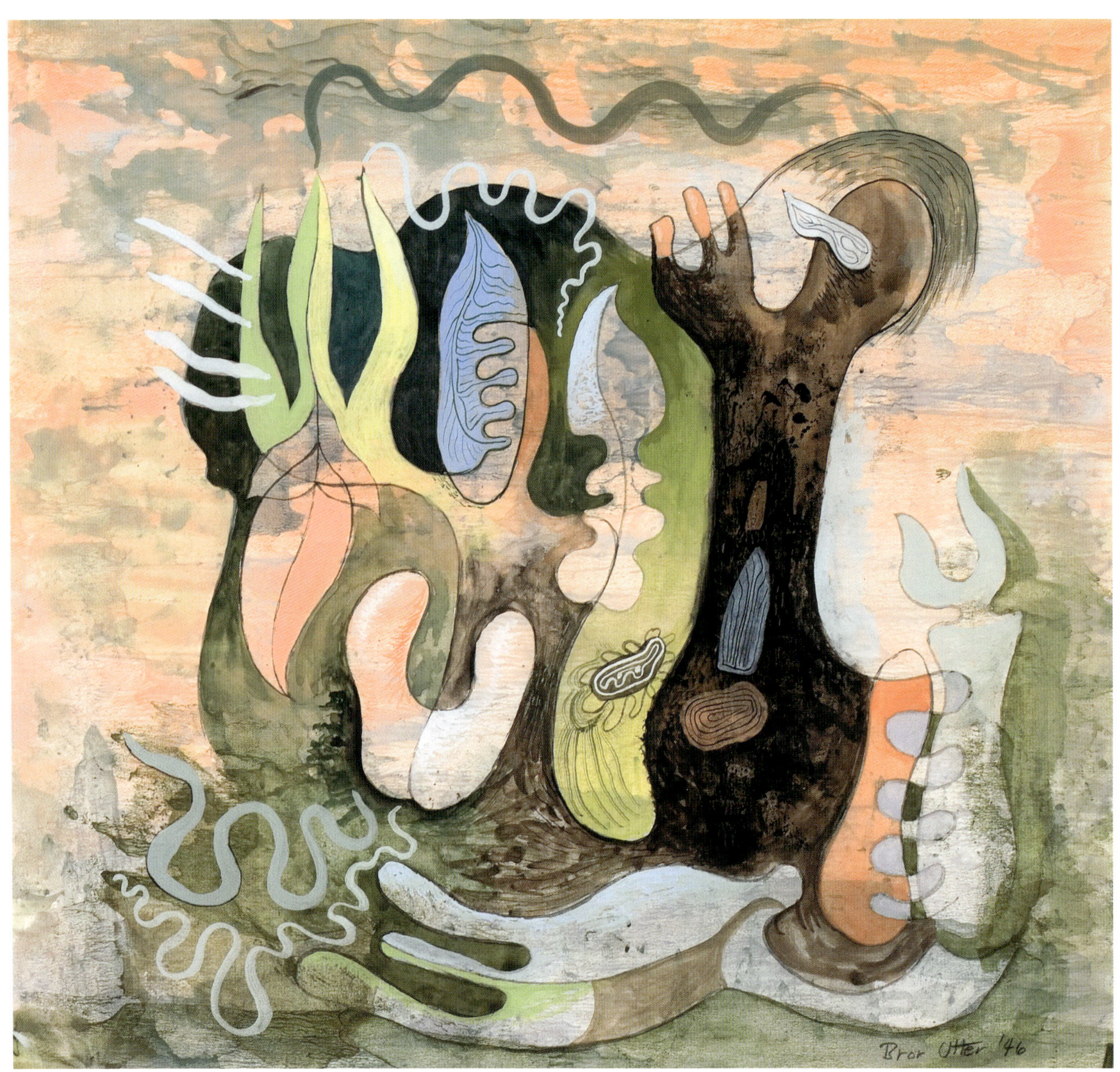

PLATE **83** Bror Utter, *Garden of Earthly Delights*, 1946

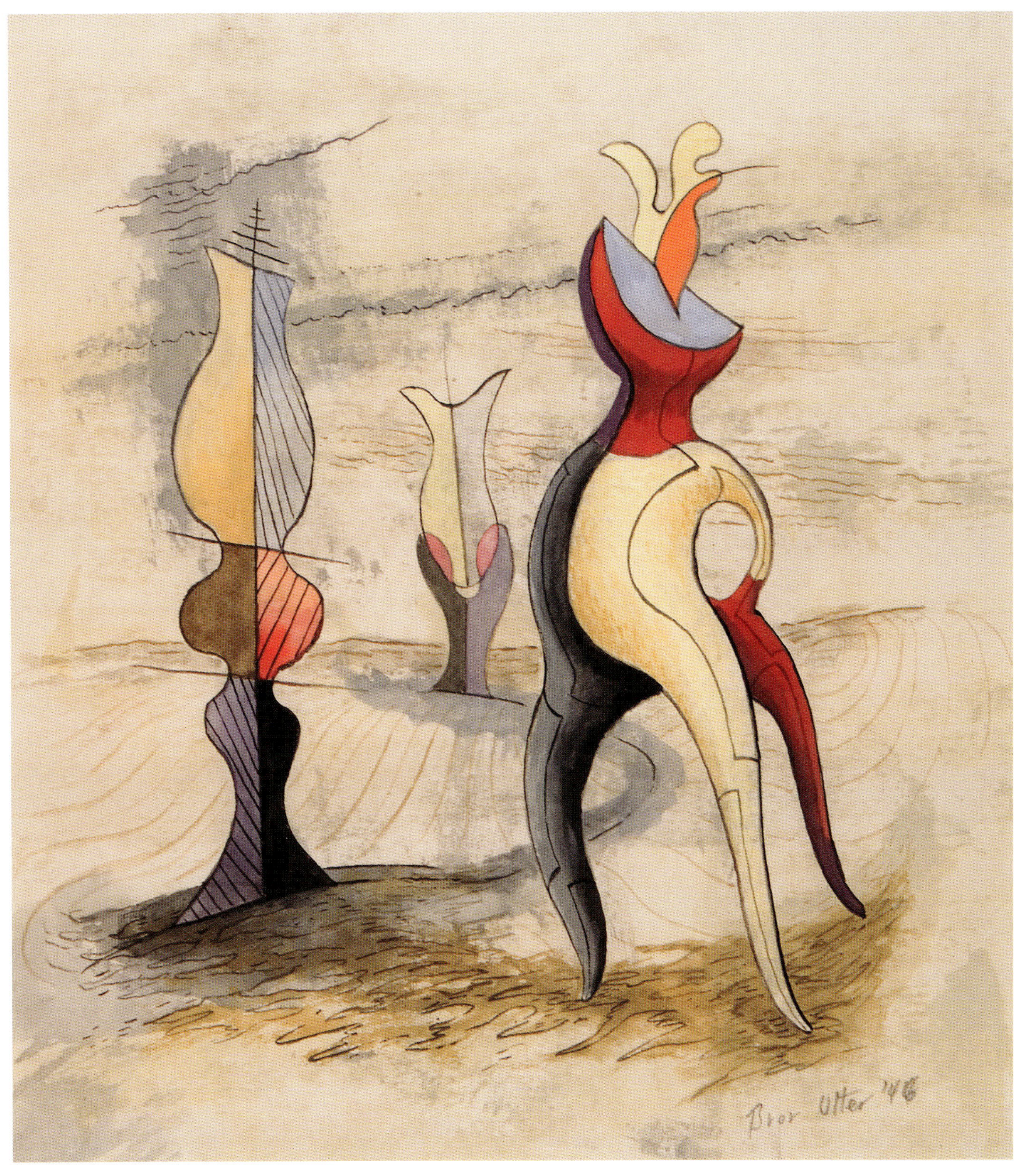

PLATE **84** Bror Utter, *Untitled*, 1946

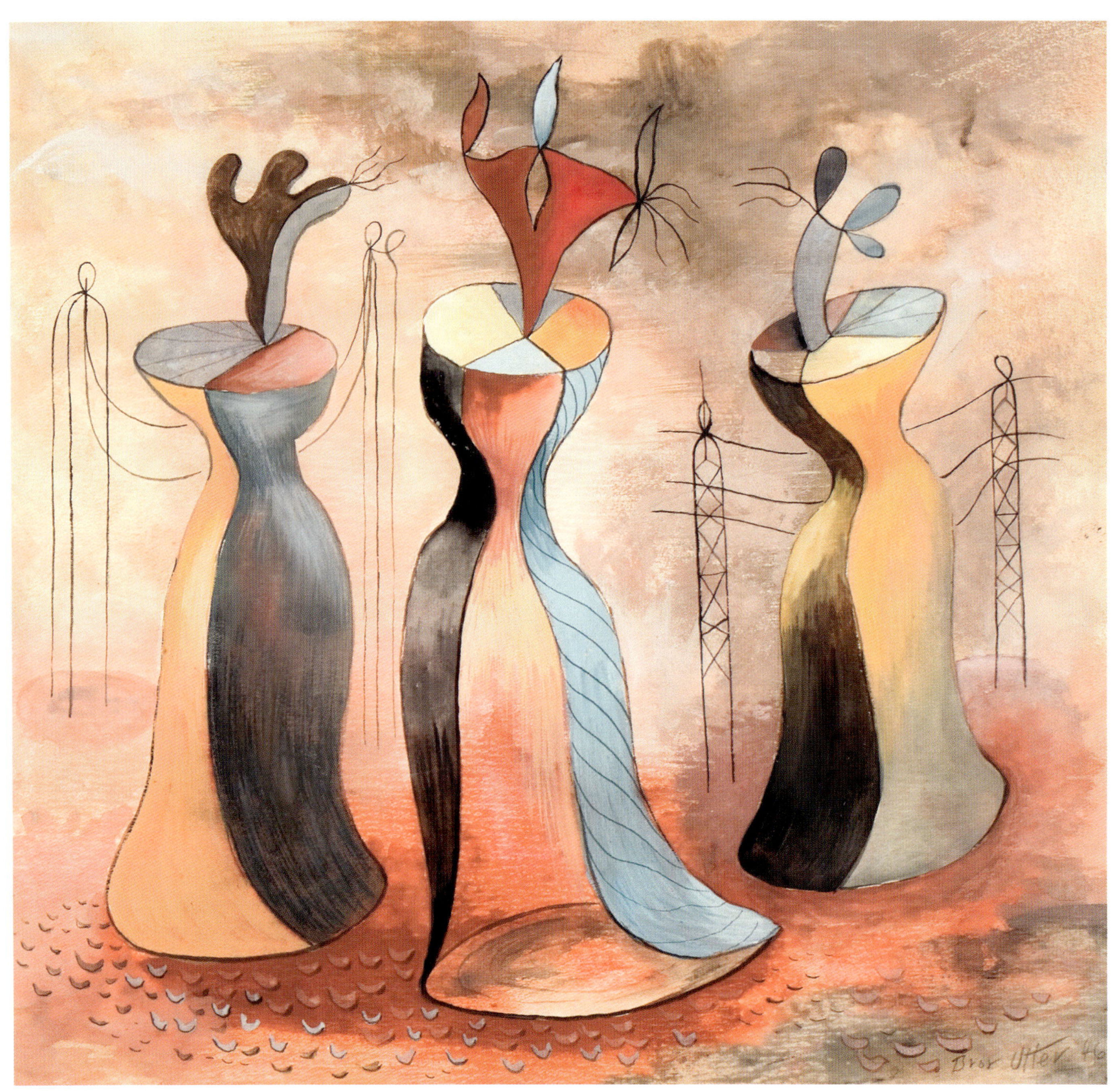

PLATE **85** Bror Utter, *Untitled*, 1946

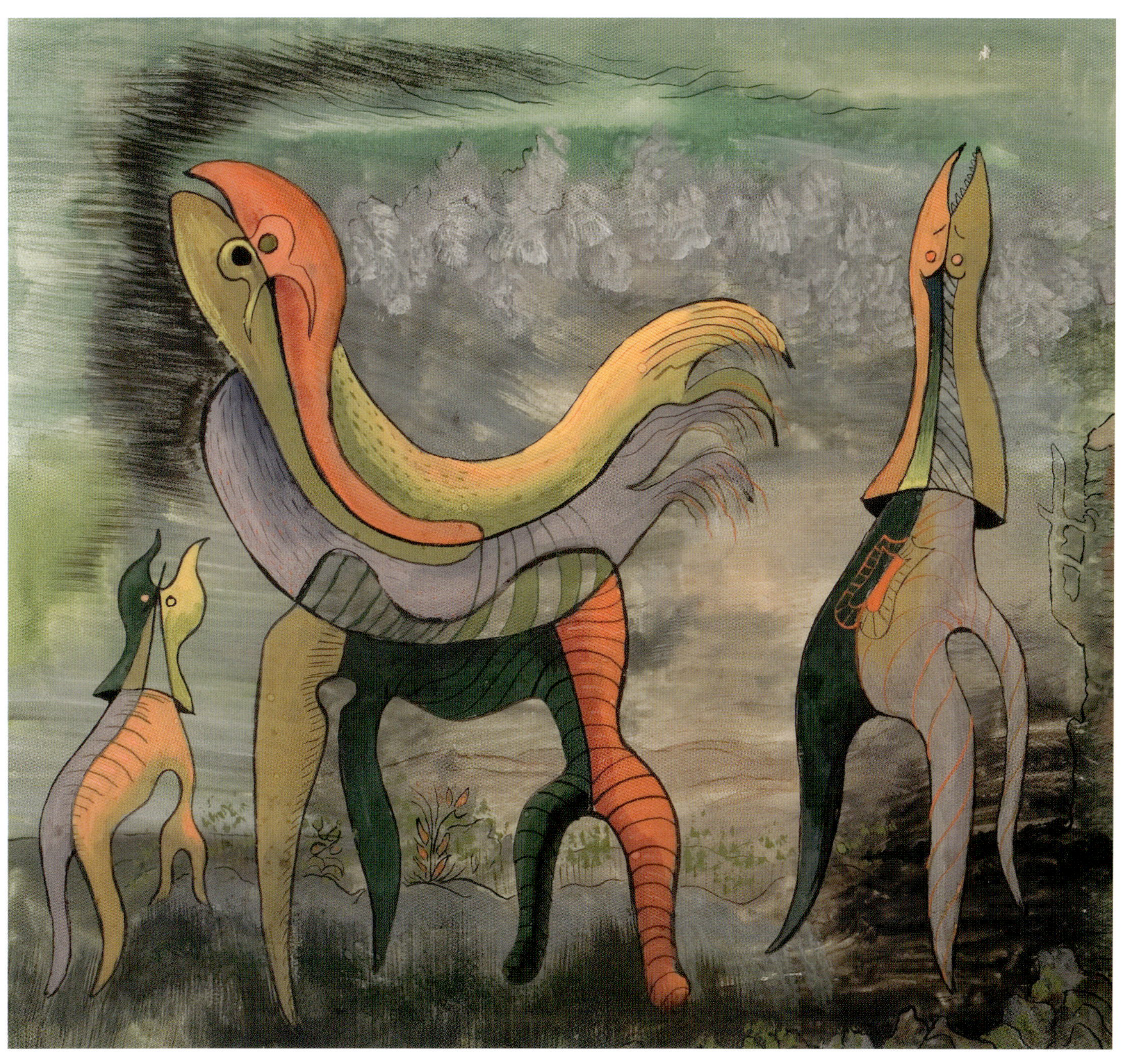

PLATE **86** Bror Utter, *Untitled*, 1946

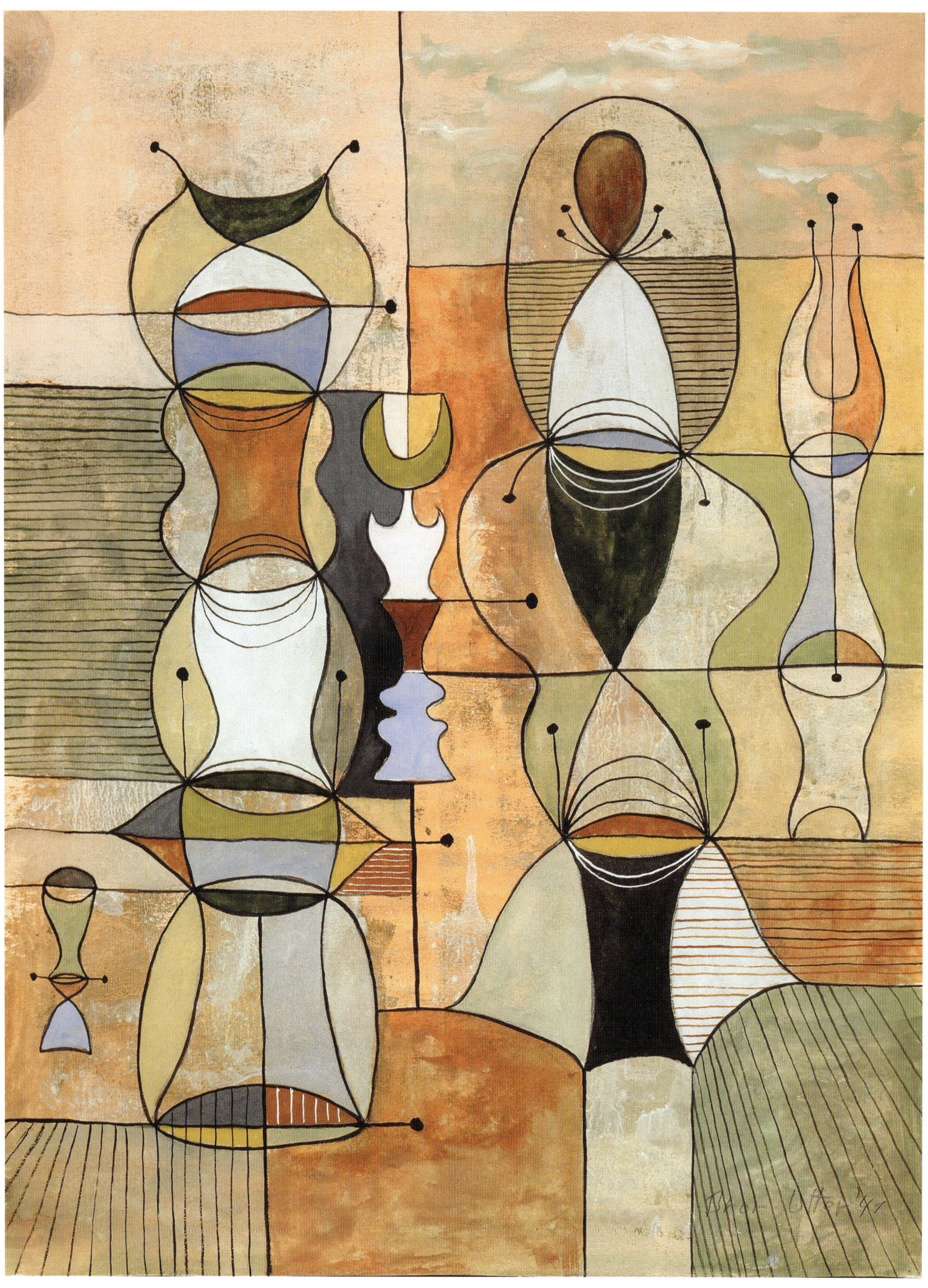

PLATE **87** Bror Utter, *Presence*, 1947

PLATE **88** Bror Utter, *Untitled*, 1947

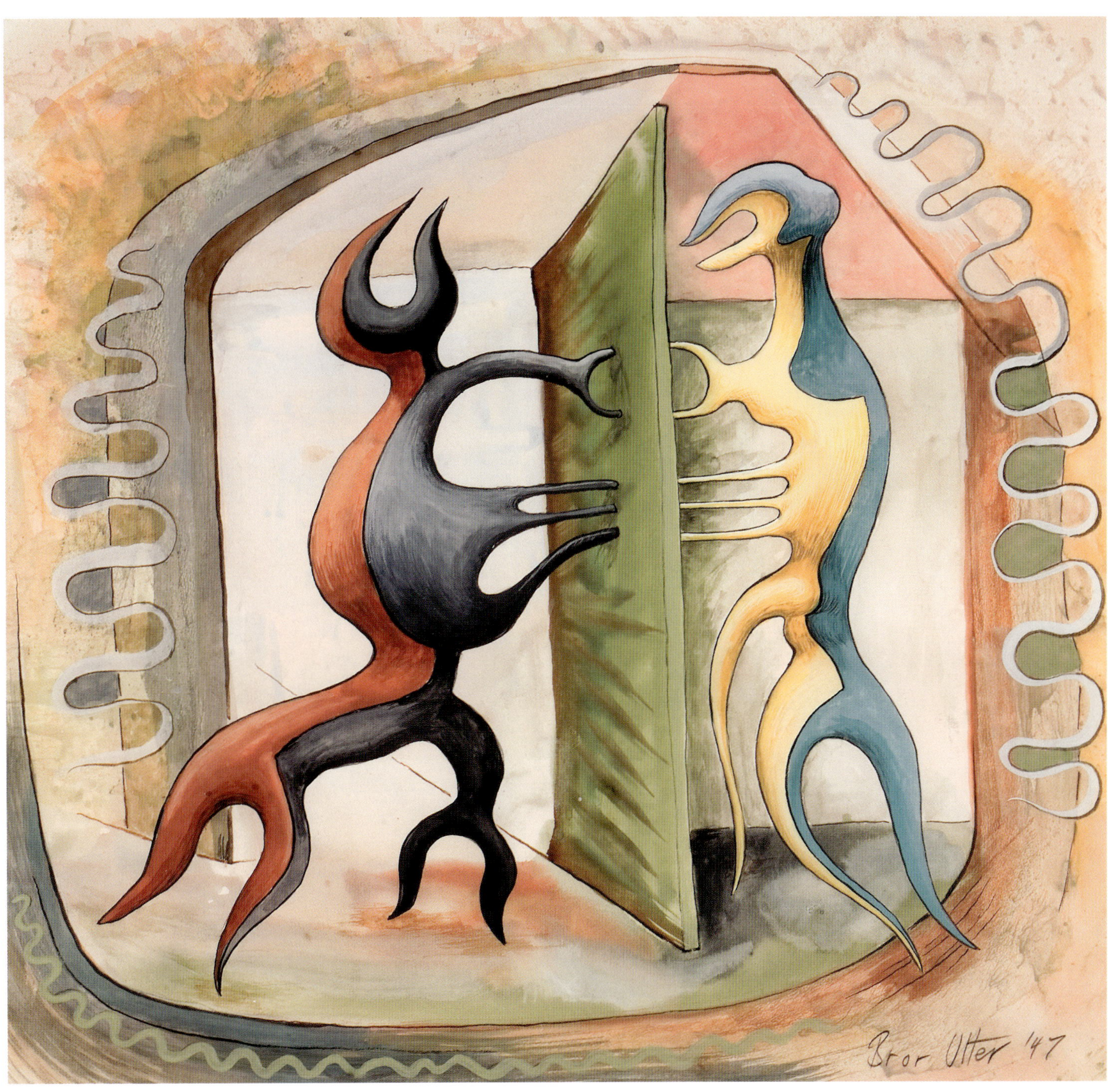

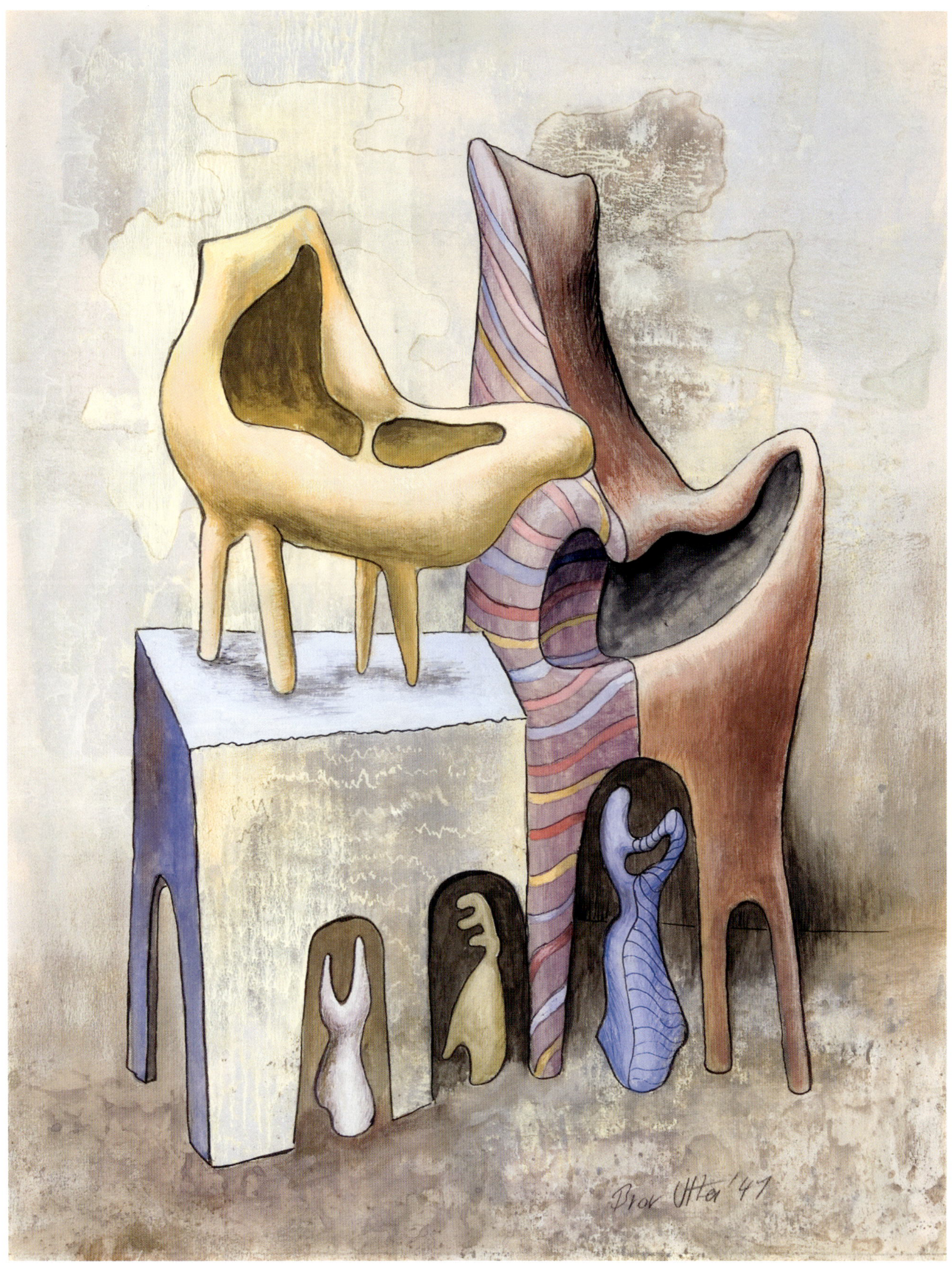

PLATE **89** Bror Utter, *Untitled*, 1947

PLATE **90** Bror Utter, *Untitled [Two Women]*, 1948

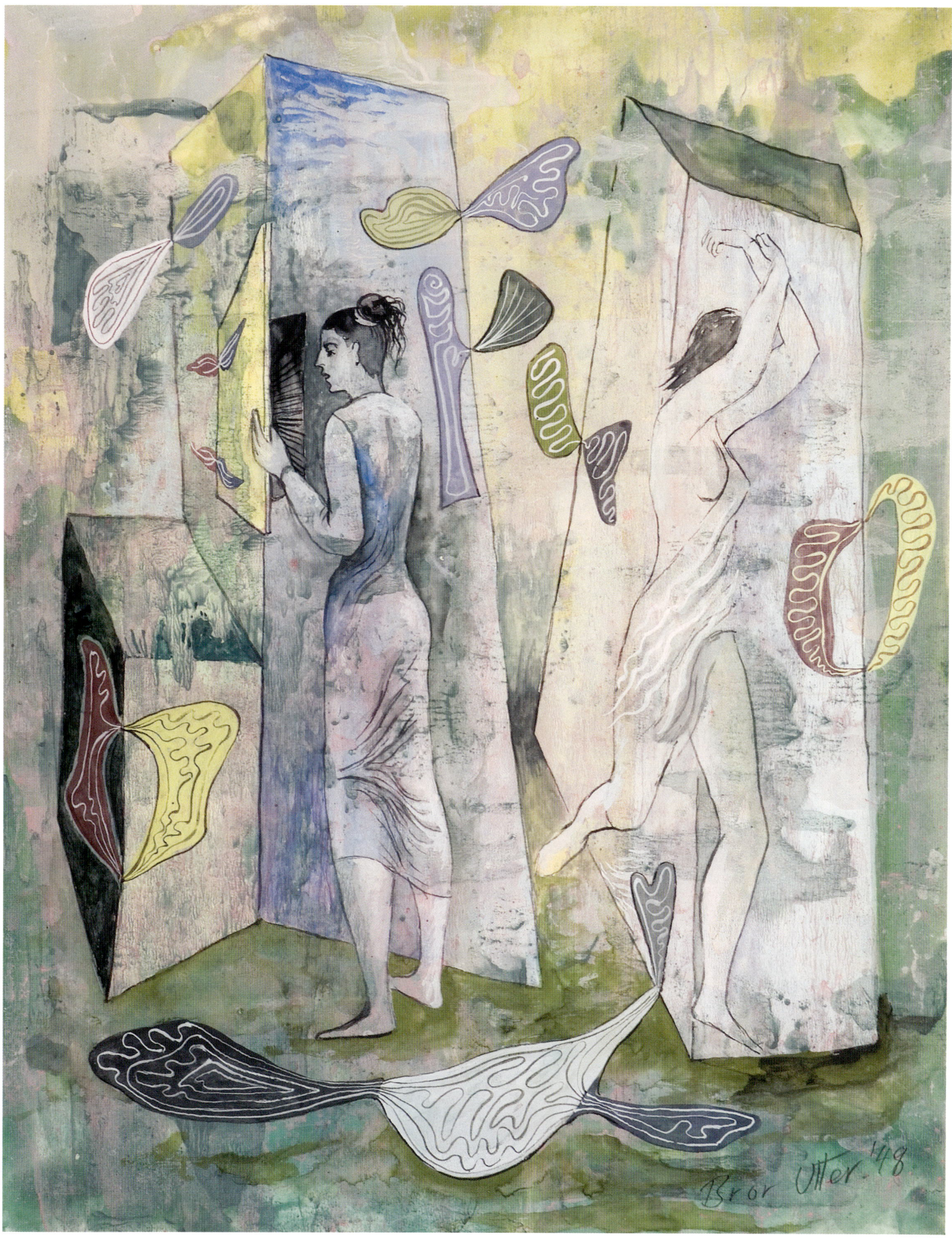
Bror Utter '48

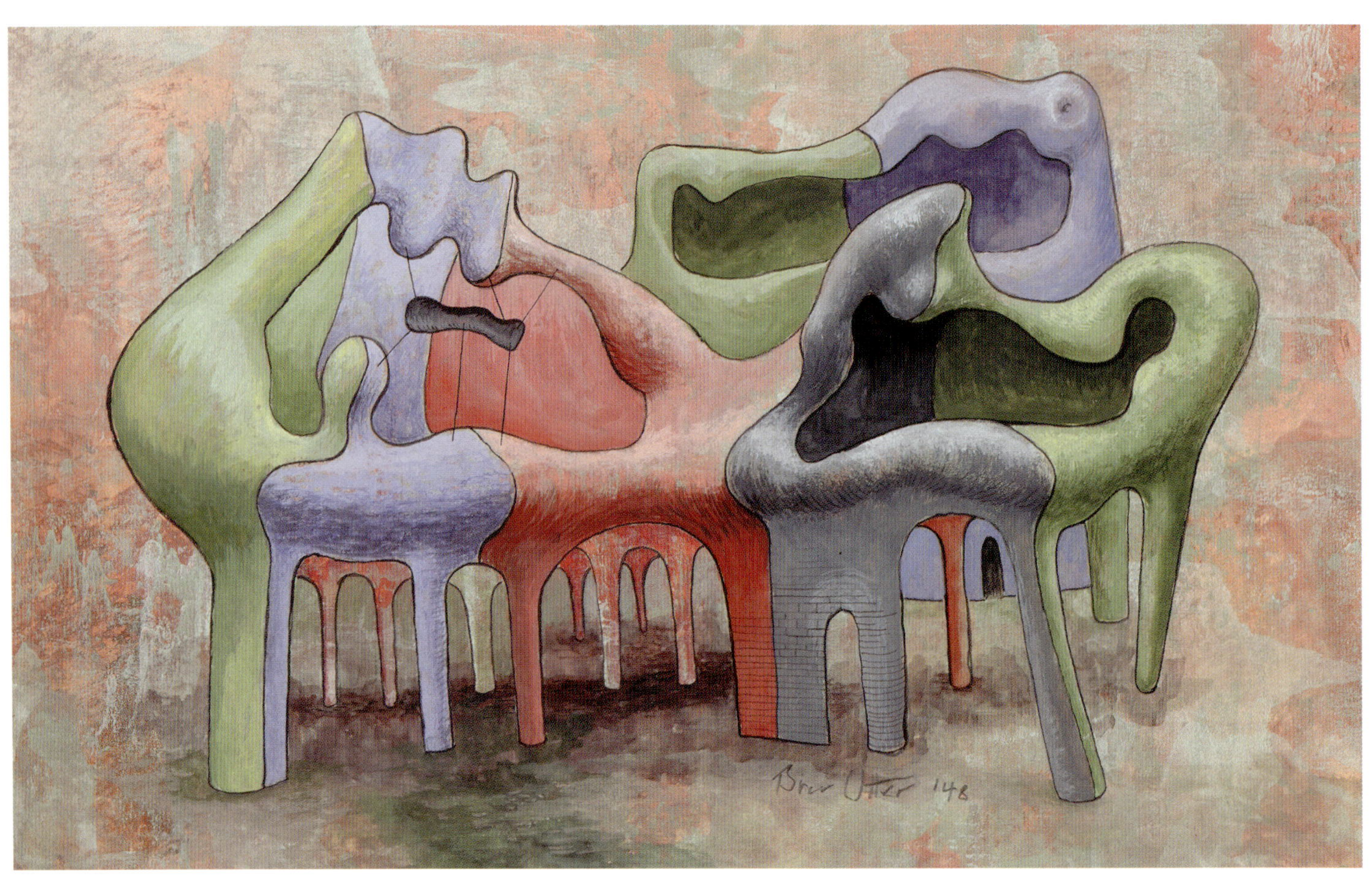

PLATE **91** Bror Utter, *Untitled*, 1948

PLATE **92** Bror Utter, *Evening Reflections*, 1949

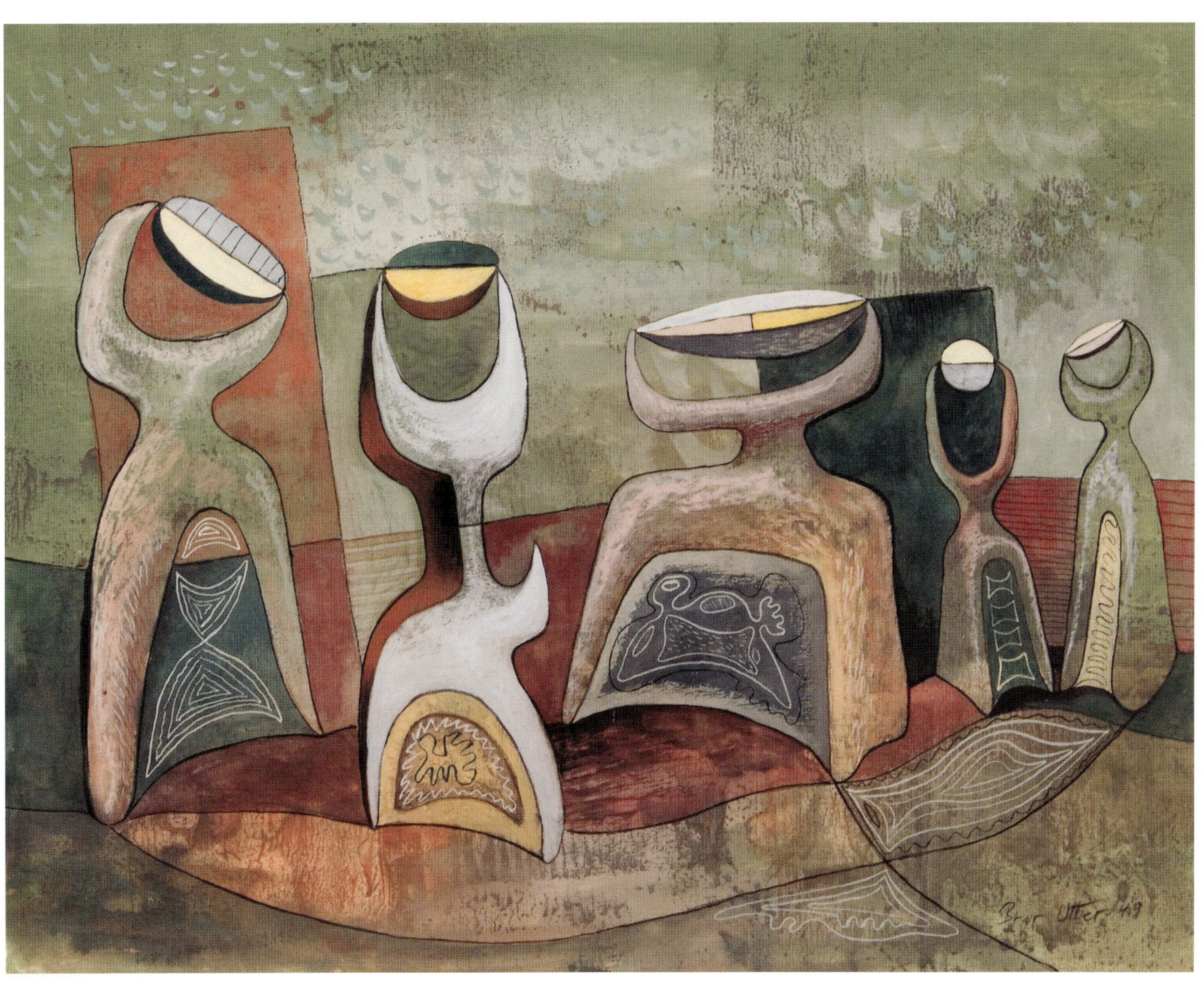
Bror Utter /49

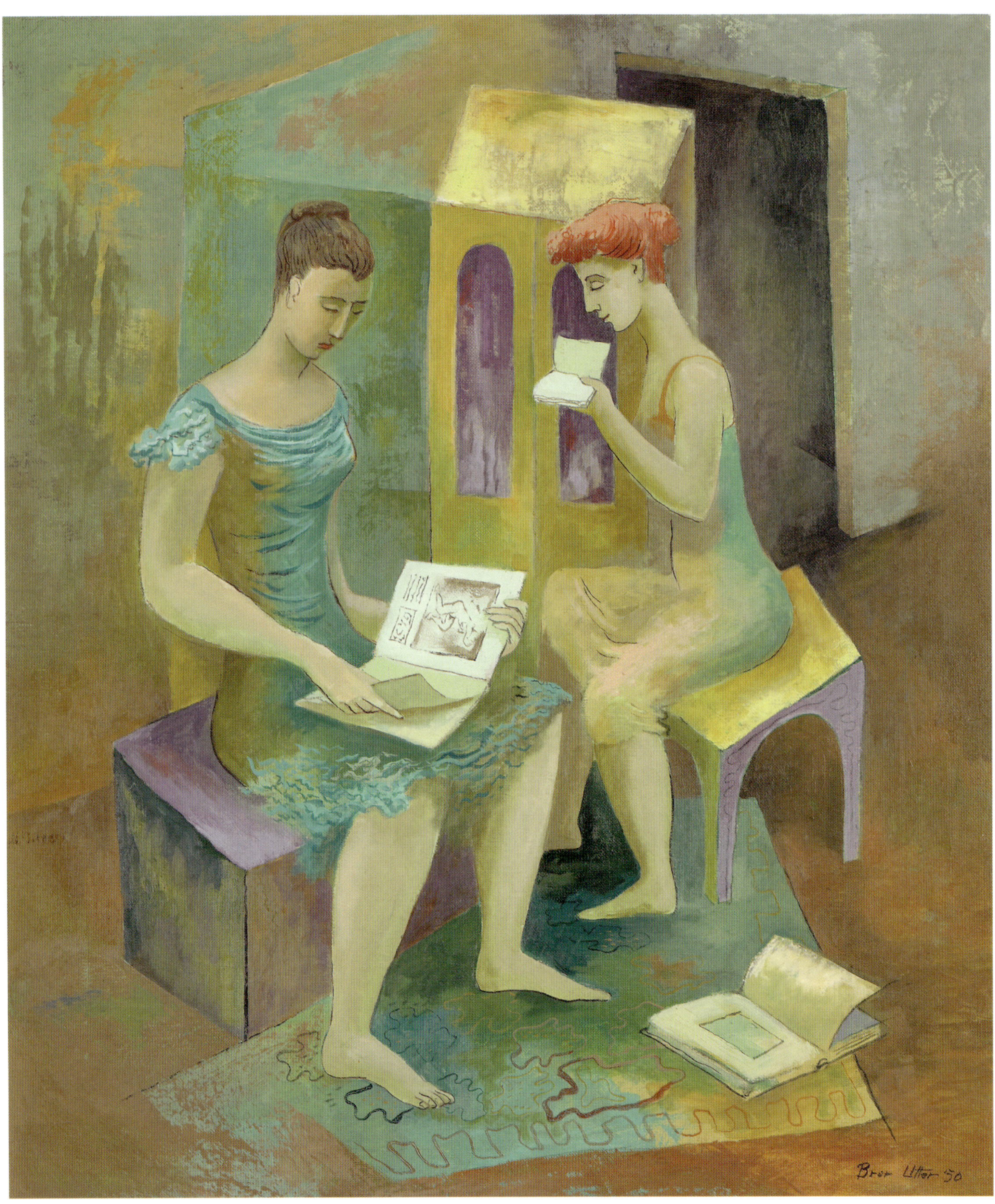
Bror Utter 50

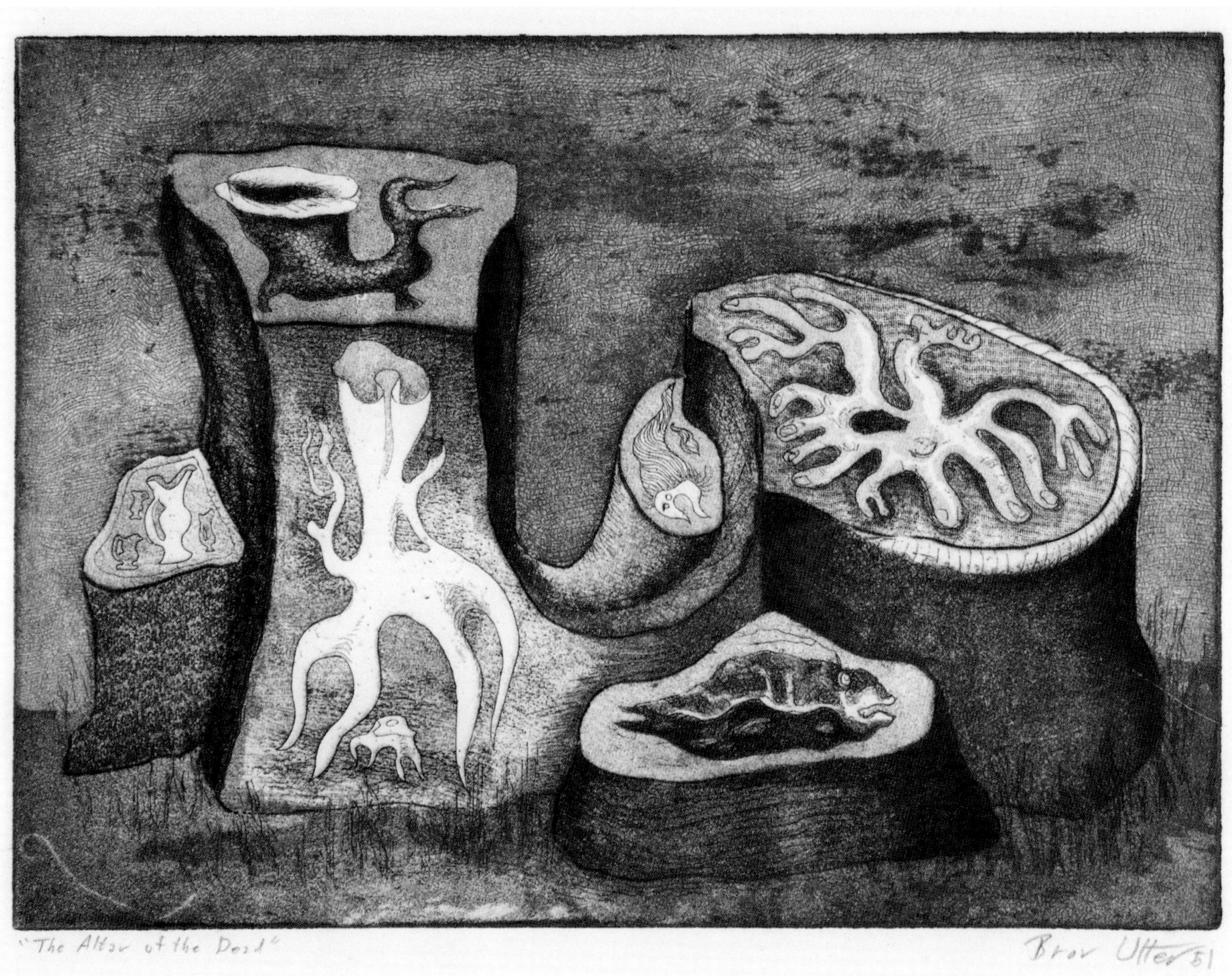

PLATE **93** Bror Utter, *Near and Farsighted Readers*, 1950

PLATE **94** Bror Utter, *The Altar of the Dead*, 1951

PLATE **95** Bror Utter, Sketchbook, 1952

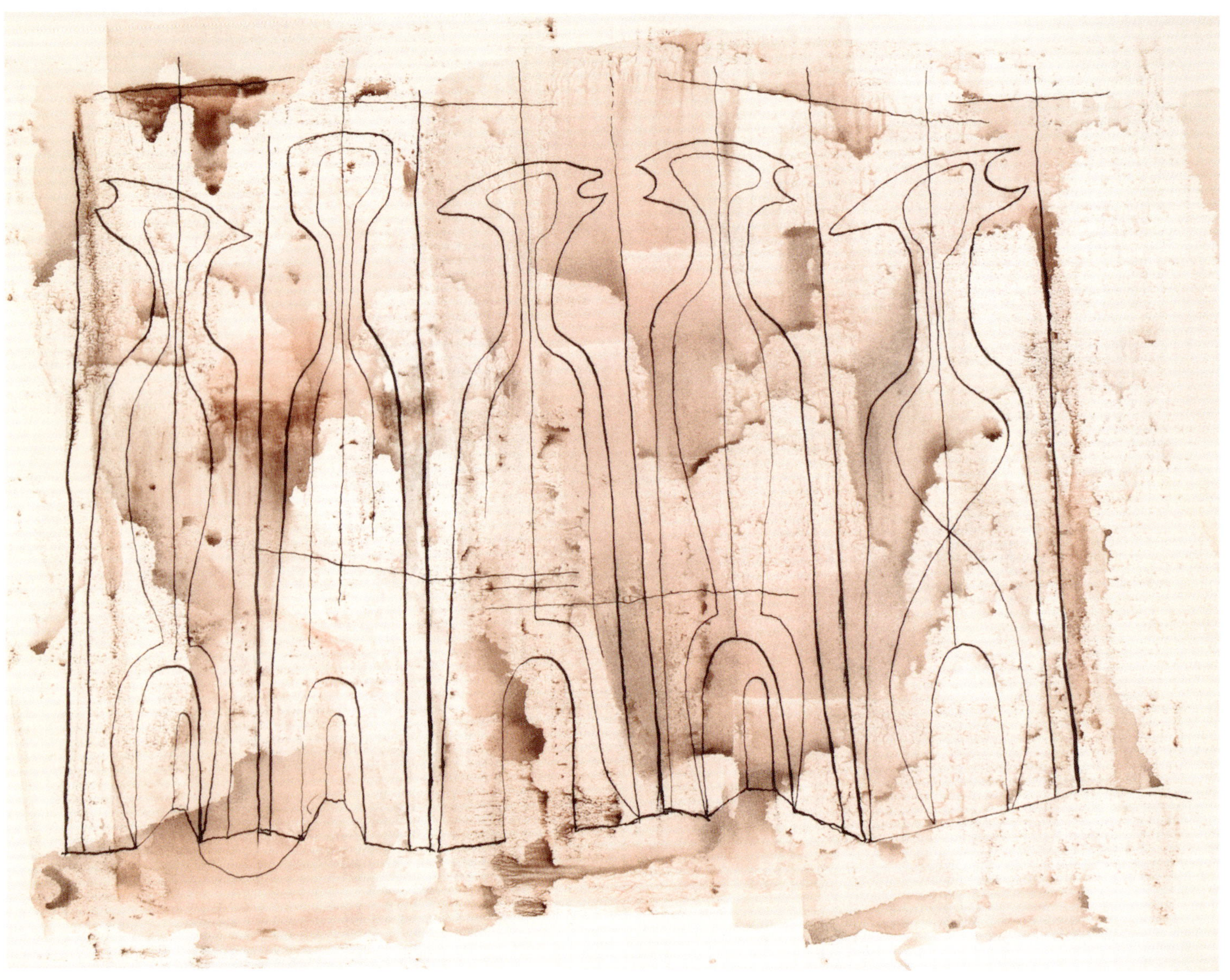

PLATE **96** Bror Utter, *Metamorphosis III (Assembly of Birds)*, 1953

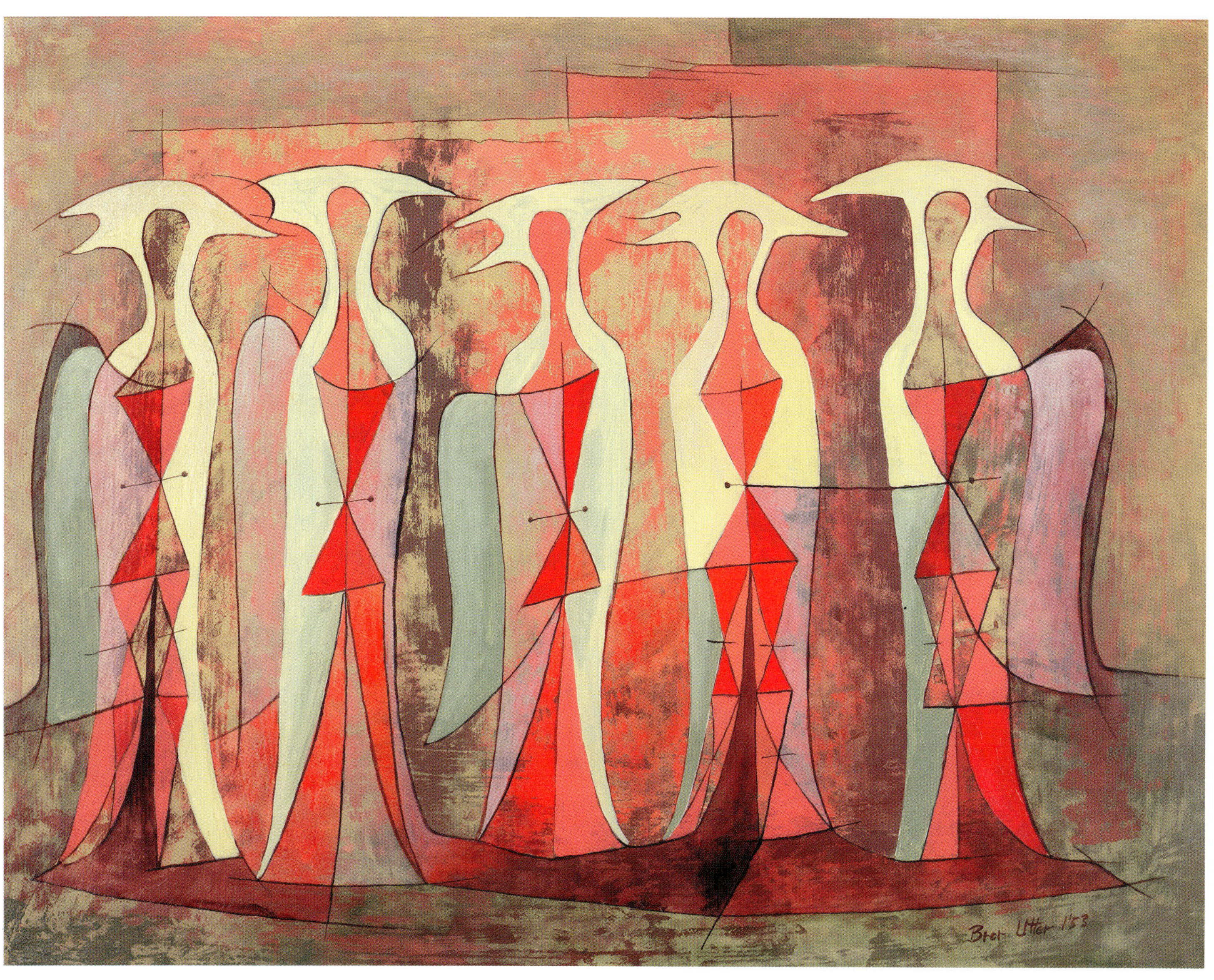

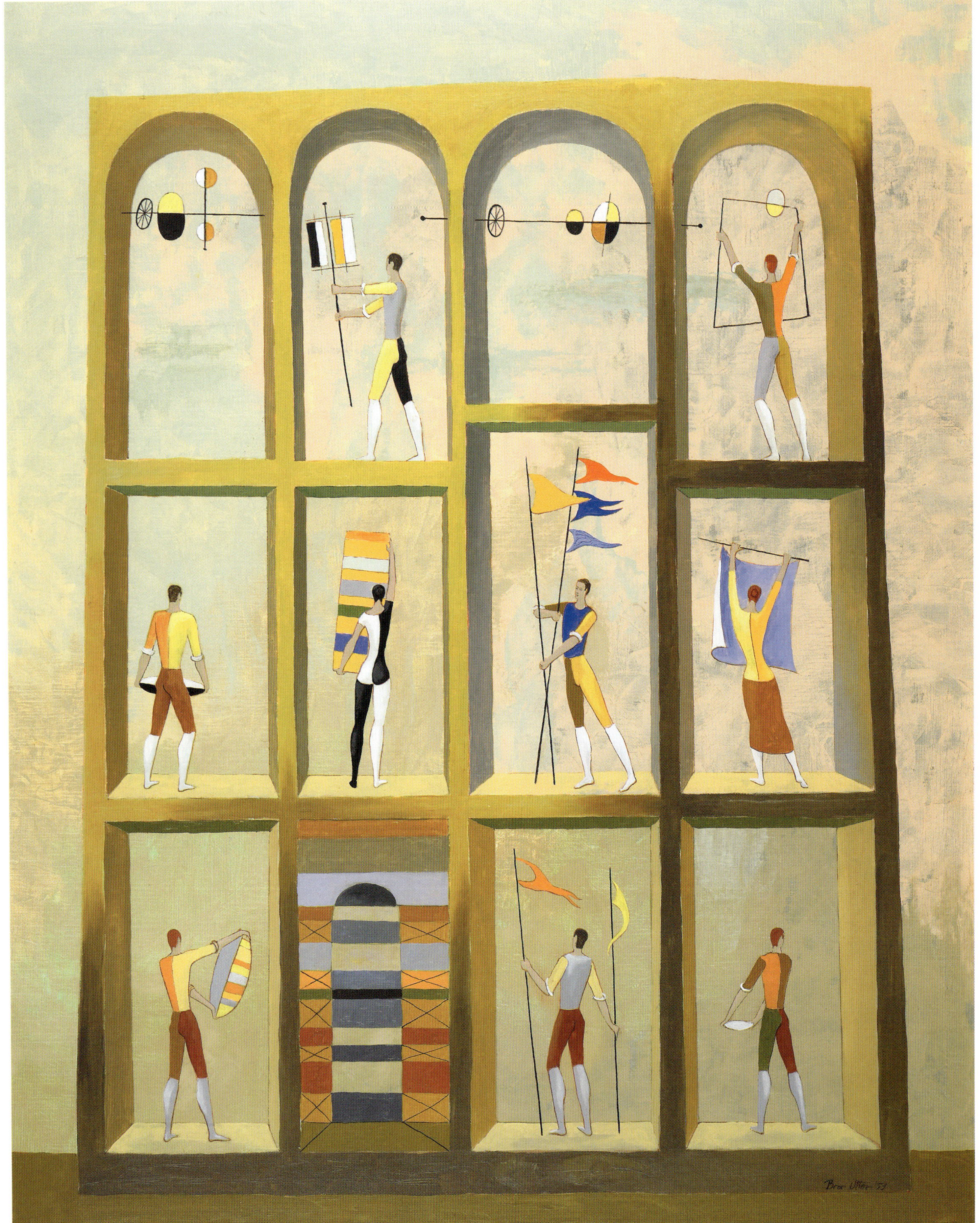

PLATE **97** Bror Utter, *Signals*, 1953

PLATE **98** Bror Utter, *Trio*, 1953

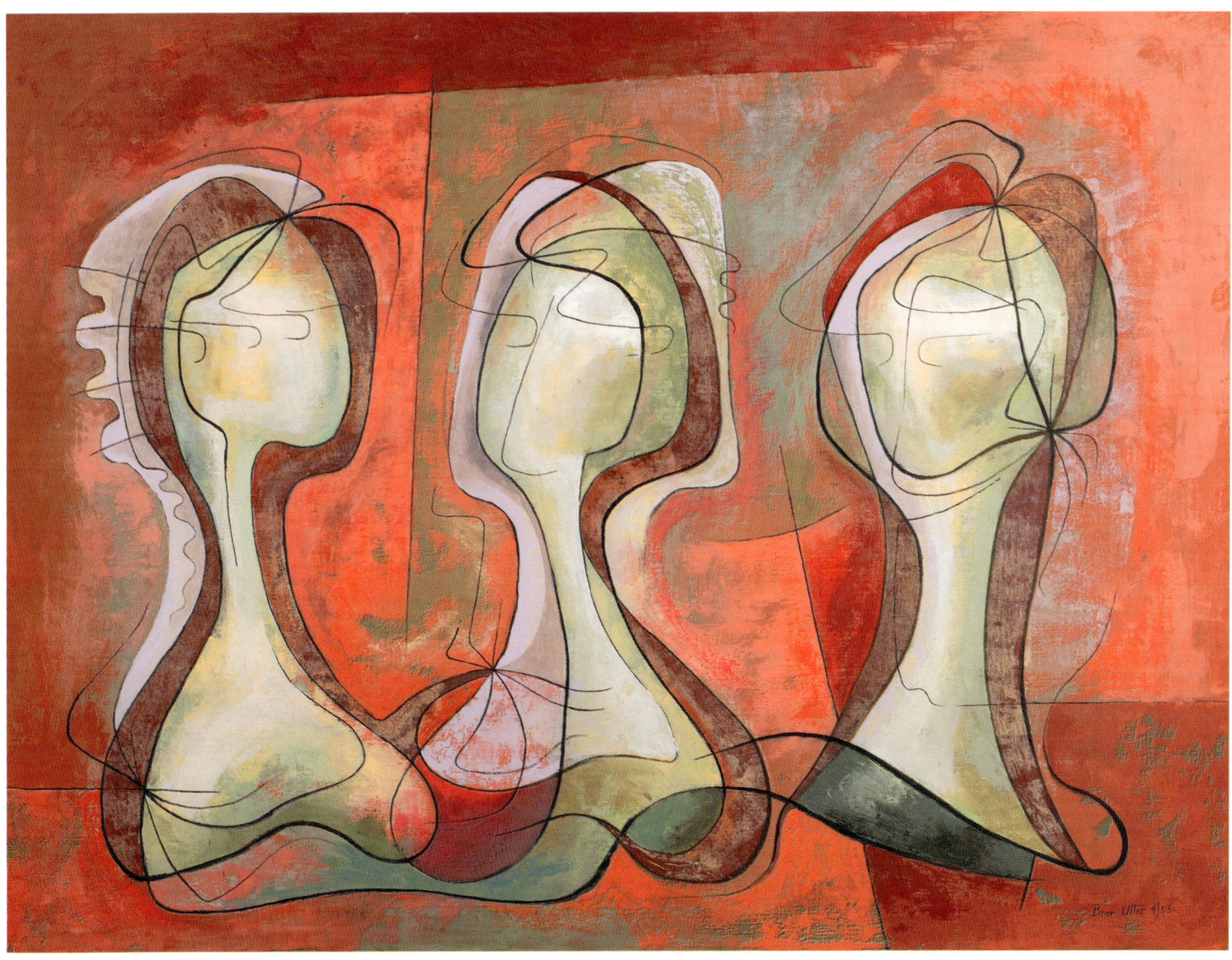

WILLIAM P. (BILL) BOMAR JR. Bill Bomar was born December 30, 1919, in Fort Worth, the only child of wealthy parents. From birth, he was afflicted with cerebral palsy, a condition which affected his walk, speech, and coordination. His right hand was malformed by the disease as well, but before the age of ten he demonstrated a gifted ability to draw with his left hand. Bomar received private schooling, along with extensive physical therapy, during his adolescent and teenage years, and he was sent to Fort Worth teacher Sallie Blyth Mummert for his first formal art training.

Bomar was introduced to watercolor painting at age sixteen by Joseph Bakos in Santa Fe, New Mexico. At twenty he enrolled at the Cranbrook Art Academy, afterward moving to New York City. Between 1941 and 1945 Bomar studied privately with John Sloan, and he received instruction from Amédée Ozenfant and Hans Hofman. An apartment in Manhattan's Chelsea Hotel, obtained with the help of Sloan, served as his residence and studio. Bomar's thirty-year stay in New York City was highlighted by a long-term association with the Erhard Weyhe Gallery, where he received several solo shows between 1946 and 1964. He twice exhibited at the Whitney Museum of American Art (1952 and 1954).

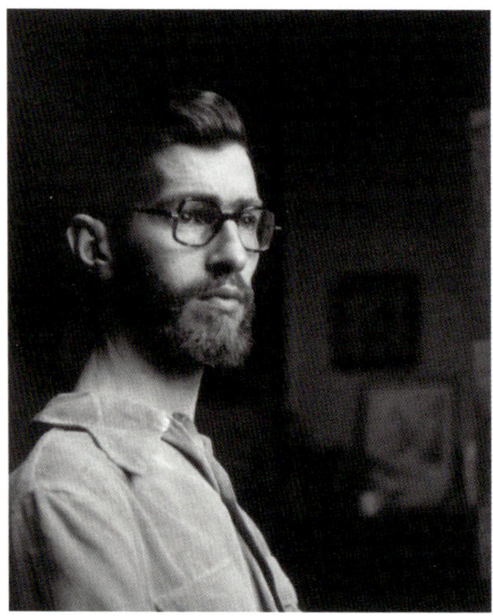

Bill Bomar, ca. 1950

Through frequent visits home, Bomar maintained a strong presence in Fort Worth and close contact with the other artists of the Circle. He exhibited in the Fort Worth *Local Artists Show* for twenty-three consecutive years beginning in 1942. Bomar was the first in the Circle to assume a serious interest in abstraction. He won First Prize in the *Local* in 1944 for *Cat in Portia's Garden*, and he repeated the win in 1948 for *Web and Roses* (pl. 64). Bomar was among the stable of Texas modernists promoted by the Betty McLean Gallery in Dallas in the early 1950s. After 1960, he was continuously represented in Texas by a succession of Fort Worth art dealers.

In 1972 Bomar relocated to Taos, New Mexico. The splendor of the northern New Mexico landscape had long attracted him, as did the Taos art community's code of individualism. There, he became an accepted and much loved figure. Bill Bomar died in Taos on November 26, 1991.

CYNTHIA BRANTS Cynthia Brants was born June 20, 1924, to a prominent Fort Worth family. At age twelve she studied etching and aquatint with Blanche McVeigh at the Fort Worth School of Fine Arts. After private schooling at the Madeira School in McLean, Virginia, she entered Sarah Lawrence College in Bronxville, New York, to major in studio art. At Sarah Lawrence, Brants' interest in cubism was nurtured by her mentor and painting teacher, Kurt Roesch.

In 1943, while still in college, Brants began advanced printmaking studies with Stanley William Hayter at the New School for Social Research in Greenwich Village. Hayter, who had moved his atelier from Paris to avoid the German occupation, accepted Brants on Roesch's recommendation. Brants' ties to Fort Worth artists Dickson and Flora Reeder, both former students of Hayter's in Paris, put her in good stead with the master of intaglio printmaking. In Hayter's Atelier 17, Brants met and worked alongside Marc Chagall, Mauricio Lasansky, Jacques Lipchitz, and Abraham Rattner. Brants concluded studies with Hayter upon graduation from Sarah Lawrence in 1945.

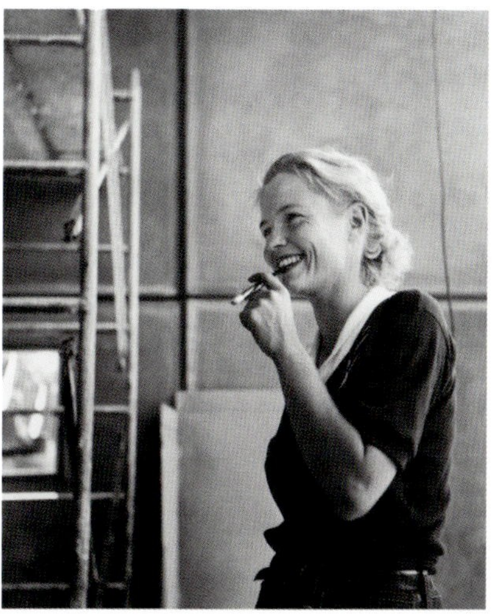

Cynthia Brants, ca. 1955

Returning to Fort Worth, Brants quickly came to prominence, propelled by a combination of eye-catching beauty, biting wit, and determination to paint. *The Cocktail Party* (1947) (pl. 66), an image of lively revelers in a crowded room, demonstrated Brants' cerebral approach to painting, while an evolving fascination with cubism marked her as a unique figure in the Fort Worth Circle. By 1950, her use of small fields of color to create complex images matured into a signature style. Using this concept, Brants won First Prize for painting in the *Local Artists Show* in 1950 for *Rooftops of Florence*; in 1952, she won for *Fort Worth in Winter*; and in 1956, she again took First Prize for *River Town*. She was given large solo exhibitions by the Fort Worth Art Association in 1950 and 1964.

Brants returned to Sarah Lawrence College to teach from 1958 to 1962, and she later taught at Texas Woman's University in Denton. In the 1970s she moved to Granbury, Texas, where she maintained separate studios for painting and printmaking. She remained a working artist and gallery owner up to the time of her death on January 11, 2006.

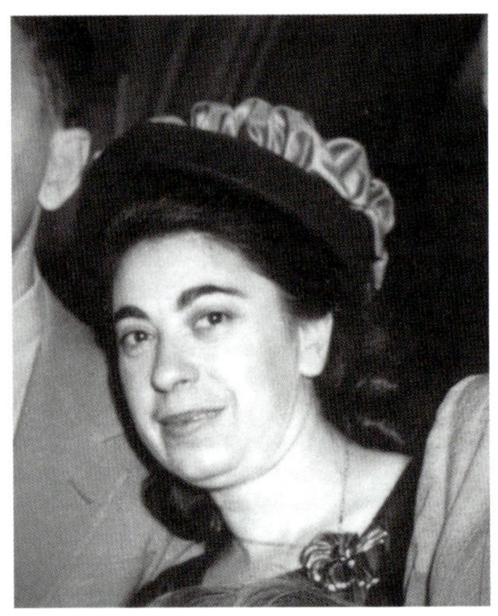

Lia Cuilty, 1947

LIA ALEXANDRA MANUELA CUILTY Lia Cuilty was born June 30, 1908, in Ciudad Chihuahua, the capital of the Mexican state of Chihuahua. The Mexican Revolution forced Cuilty and her family to evacuate to El Paso, Texas, about 1913. Her father, a pharmacist, later opened a drugstore in Fort Worth, and in 1916 Cuilty joined him there.

In public school Cuilty was a cerebral student, excelling in art, Latin, and physics. She graduated from North Side High School in 1925. In the early 1930s she studied at the Dallas Art Institute under Olin Travis, and by 1935 she was enrolled at the Fort Worth School of Fine Arts, joining Marjorie Johnson and Bror Utter. As the Fort Worth Circle emerged, Cuilty kept a low profile, a stance that mirrored her subtle and experimental approach to art.

Between 1943 and 1945, Cuilty worked primarily in gouache. She gained public notice in the 1944 *Local Artists Show* with *Merry Go Round Sleeps* (1944), a stark painting depicting a merry-go-round shrouded in winter weather. Cuilty won Third Prize in the 1945 *Local* for *The Grapevine Swing*, a painting of a young girl at play in a bizarre landscape. *The Day's at Morn* (pl. 2), another gouache, was shown in the sixth *Texas General Exhibition* in 1944–45.

Cuilty's ability to produce etchings of extraordinary sensitivity was rooted in the printmaking sessions held in Veronica Helfensteller's studio. There, in 1944 and 1945, Cuilty acquired the technical proficiency that allowed her to produce prints ranging from the abstract *False Flags* (1947) to the beautiful *Shells* (1950) (pl. 42). Between 1947 and 1957, Cuilty's etchings were regularly shown in the *Local* and in a number of other Texas venues. Along with Helfensteller and Blanche McVeigh, Cuilty was active in the Dallas-based Texas Printmakers, a cooperative group that included, and vigorously promoted, most of Texas' best-known women printmakers.

True to the cohesive nature of the Fort Worth Circle, Cuilty remained close to the other artists of the group throughout her life. She died in Fort Worth on November 4, 1978, at the age of seventy.

WILLIAM KELLY FEARING Kelly Fearing was born October 18, 1918, in Fordyce, Arkansas. In the late 1930s he enrolled in the Louisiana Polytechnic Institute. Under Louisiana Tech instructors Elizabeth Bethea and Mary Moffett, he integrated his love of painting with an intense interest in symphony and ballet. He received a BA from Louisiana Tech in 1941.

In 1943, Fearing left a middle-school teaching position to volunteer for defense industry training in Texas. He arrived in Fort Worth as a draftsman in training for Consolidated Vultee Aircraft. Duties as a production illustrator soon brought him into contact with fellow illustrator Dickson Reeder, and within a short time Fearing became a close friend of Reeder's and a member of the Fort Worth Circle.

Fearing emerged in 1944 as a rising figure in the Fort Worth art world. His depiction of a USO street dance won the popular vote prize in the 1944 *Local Artists Show*, and his enigmatic figural work *The Kite Flyers* (pl. 69) earned First Prize in the 1945 show. *The Aquarist* (1945) (pl. 72), an oil that features a serenely isolated woman placing her hand into an aquarium, was a prizewinner in the seventh *Texas General Exhibition* and foreshadowed Fearing's lifelong interest in themes of human spirituality.

Fearing was named head of the Texas Wesleyan College art department in July 1945, succeeding Sallie Gillespie. Among his most noted students was George Grammer, who joined the Circle in 1946. Fearing taught at Texas Wesleyan until the summer of 1947, when he applied to the masters program at Columbia University in New York. His plans abruptly changed, however, when he was offered a position on the art faculty at the University of Texas at Austin. On the advice of Flora Blanc Reeder's mother, he accepted.

Following his move to Austin, Fearing remained in close contact with his Fort Worth Circle peers and with Fort Worth collectors. He retired as Ashbel Smith Professor of Art at the University of Texas at Austin in 1987. An iconic figure in Texas art history, Fearing continues to produce art in his Austin studio.

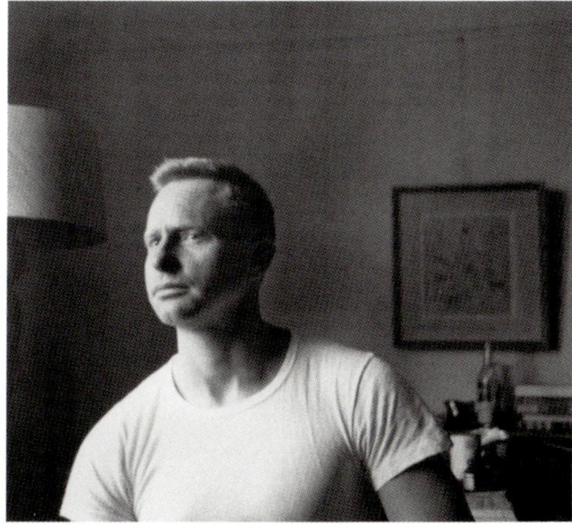

Kelly Fearing, 1948

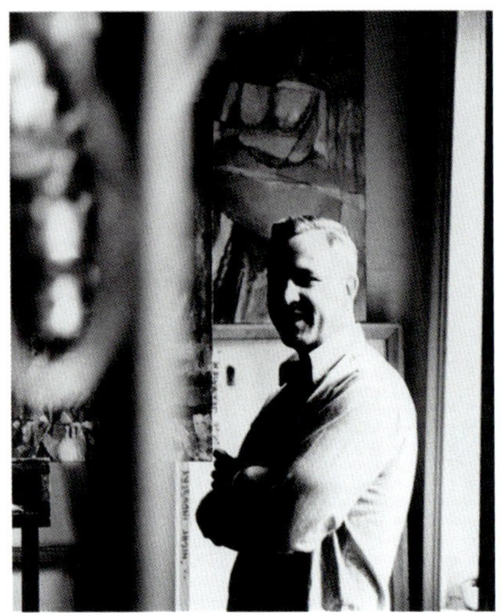

George Grammer, ca. 1955

GEORGE GRAMMER George Grammer was born October 2, 1928, in Fort Worth. As a student at Paschal High School, he studied art with Creola Searcy and won prizes for printmaking and painting in a national competition sponsored by Scholastic. Upon graduating, he received a scholarship to Texas Wesleyan College, where he trained under Kelly Fearing and, through Fearing, met Dickson Reeder and the other artists of the Fort Worth Circle.

Between 1945 and 1950, Grammer exhibited a broad range of talents and abilities. He designed sets for the Fort Worth Civic Opera, produced numerous architectural drawings for local developer Howard Kittel, and was commissioned to paint large-scale murals for the Harbor Club and Trinity State Bank. After a three-month visit to New York City, Grammer produced the first of his trademark paintings of the city, *Rain: Broadway*, and entered it in the 1949 Fort Worth *Local Artists Show*. He worked closely with Evaline Sellors in creating elaborate masks and headdresses used in the 1950 Reeder Children's School of Theater and Design production of *Lady Precious Stream*.

A chance nighttime bus trip from Jacksboro to Fort Worth provided the inspiration for Grammer's best-known works. While gazing through the bus window into the darkness, he was suddenly captivated by the patterns of light emanating from a distant oil-drilling rig. The image of the illuminated rig became the basis for a series of abstract paintings of nighttime industrial scenes. Grammer exhibited the first of them, *Derricks by Night*, in 1950. A later image, *Oil Derricks at Night*, was purchased by the Dallas Museum of Fine Arts in 1952. In 1951, on the strength of his abstractions, Grammer became one of six Fort Worth Circle artists represented by Dallas contemporary art dealer Betty McLean.

Grammer traveled to Mexico in 1952 and studied painting at Instituto Allende in San Miguel de Allende. Afterward, he studied at the Art Students League in New York. He married and settled permanently in New York City in 1954, where he won that year's Emily Lowe Award Competition. Remaining close to his roots, he was featured by the Fort Worth Art Association in solo exhibitions in 1956 and 1963. George Grammer remains a working artist and New York City resident.

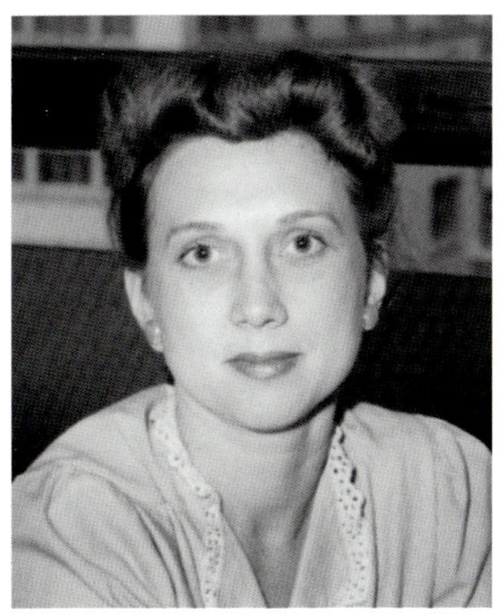

Veronica Helfensteller, n.d.

VERONICA HELFENSTELLER Veronica Helfensteller was born in Fort Worth on February 7, 1910. She was an exceptionally artistic child and thrived in a private world of imagination. Following high school, she took courses in commercial art at the St. Louis School of Fine Arts, but soon became dissatisfied and returned home. She did not study art again until she enrolled in the Fort Worth School of Fine Arts in 1936.

From that time forward, Helfensteller pursued art zealously. She traveled to Budapest, Hungary, in 1937 to study, and between 1939 and 1941 she entered many competitive exhibitions, including those organized by the American Watercolor Society in New York City and the Washington Watercolor Club in Washington, D.C. She was active in the Fort Worth Artists Guild and became a regular exhibitor in the Fort Worth *Local Artists Show*. For her somber gouache *One Autumn Day*, she received First Prize in the watercolor category in the 1943 *Texas General Exhibition*.

Among the artists of the Fort Worth Circle, Helfensteller, Marjorie Johnson, and Bror Utter were the sole members to actively study lithography; of these three, only Helfensteller embraced the medium long-term. In lithographs dating to 1942, the year she attended summer classes at the Colorado Springs Fine Arts Center, Helfensteller first created images of animal life placidly interacting with the viewer. She was a three-time prizewinner in the *Annual Texas Print Exhibition* in Dallas.

Helfensteller's signature contribution to Texas art history occurred in 1944, when she initiated weekly etching sessions in her studio. She was joined in these sessions by Lia Cuilty, Kelly Fearing, Dickson and Flora Reeder, and Bror Utter. The weekly workshop offered a seminal environment in which Dickson Reeder, who had studied with Stanley William Hayter, freely shared his expertise in soft-ground etching. Helfensteller soon began creating complex, experimental plates that placed her on the cutting edge of Texas printmaking.

In the years following World War II, Helfensteller remained a noted artist who worked as a private art teacher in Fort Worth. In 1948, after spending the summer in Guatemala, she moved to Santa Fe, New Mexico, where she married and continued to paint. After a long illness, she died at age fifty-four in Tucson, Arizona, on September 30, 1964.

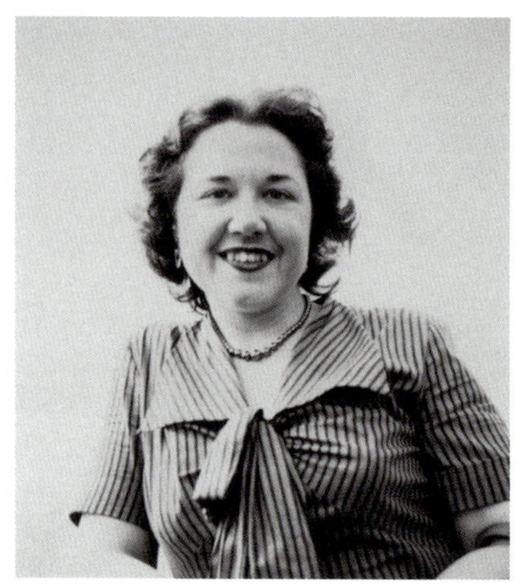

Marjorie Johnson, ca. 1953

MARJORIE JOHNSON Marjorie Johnson was born on May 31, 1911, in Upland, Texas, the daughter of a country doctor. Her family migrated eastward, arriving in Fort Worth in 1925, where Johnson began private art studies with Mrs. G. W. Greathouse. She completed high school in 1928 and took undergraduate courses in art education at Texas Christian University for the next two years.

In 1933, Johnson was recruited by Blanche McVeigh to attend the Fort Worth School of Fine Arts, where, under the tutelage of instructor Wade Jolly, she developed into a fluid watercolorist who specialized in still lifes and regionalist subjects. In 1938, she received her first solo show at the school, which she followed with a summer of study at the School of the Art Institute of Chicago under Constantine Pougialis. She exhibited with Veronica Helfensteller and Bror Utter in 1939 and 1940, and in 1942 she studied landscape painting and lithography at the Colorado Springs Fine Arts Center under Arnold Blanch and Adolph Dehn.

Johnson was a regular exhibitor in the Fort Worth *Local Artists Show*, winning Honorable Mention in 1943 for *Hillside After Rain*. Her art career halted in 1943 when she enlisted with the U.S. Navy WAVES, or Women Accepted for Volunteer Emergency Service. In 1946, she enrolled at the Art Students League in New York, where, under Vaclav Vytlacil and Cameron Booth, her approach to painting was radically transformed by an emphasis on color and hard-edged simplification of subject matter. Johnson remained in New York City but resumed exhibiting in the Fort Worth *Local Artists Show* in 1947. In 1949, at the invitation of the Fort Worth Art Association, she mounted a solo show at the Fort Worth Public Library. The thirty-two canvases in the exhibition, which included *Studio Corner* (1949) (pl. 81), confirmed her transformation into a painter with a distinctly modern view.

Johnson maintained close ties to her Fort Worth Circle compatriots, particularly Bill Bomar and Sara Shannon, who lived in New York City as well. She married New York filmmaker Francis Lee in 1960, but separated in 1974 and returned to Texas, where she actively continued to paint. Marjorie Johnson Lee died in Fort Worth on February 1, 1997.

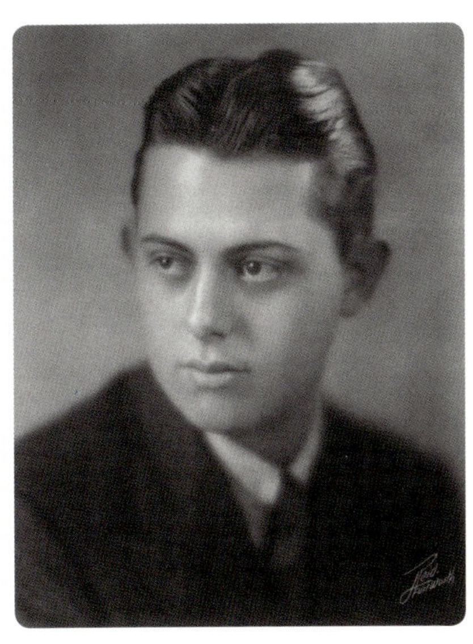

Dickson Reeder, ca. 1940

EDWARD DICKSON REEDER Dickson Reeder was born February 6, 1912, in Fort Worth. As a boy, he studied privately with Sallie Blyth Mummert; in high school, where he was known for sketching the likenesses of his friends and classmates, he studied with Sallie Gillespie. Reeder graduated from Fort Worth Central High School in 1930.

In 1931, Reeder began training with portraitist Wayman Adams in New York. He opened a portrait studio in Fort Worth in 1934 but continued to work with Adams as time allowed. His portrait of Sallie Gillespie was selected for the 1936 *Texas Centennial Exposition*. In the summer of 1936, at Gillespie's urging, Reeder went to Europe, eventually settling in Paris. There, he worked with Russian theatrical designer Alexandra Exter and met his future wife, Flora Blanc, who introduced him to printmaker Stanley William Hayter. As a student of Hayter's, Reeder discovered a flair for experimentation that remained with him for the rest of his life.

In 1940, Dickson and Flora Blanc Reeder settled in Fort Worth, where he aggressively sought portrait commissions. His portrait of *The Shannon Children* (pl. 33) won First Prize in the 1941 *Local Artists Show* and established Reeder as the most visible and progressive of the emerging Fort Worth Circle artists. *After Rehearsal*, his painting of Fort Worth ballet dancer Kitty Scales, was exhibited by the Art Institute of Chicago in 1943. In the seventh *Texas General Exhibition* (1945–46), his portrait *Ellaraye* (pl. 34) was recommended for a purchase prize by a jury that included Otis Dozier and Jerry Bywaters. Earlier that year, he was awarded a solo exhibition by the Fort Worth Art Association.

The Reeder Children's School of Theater and Design became the principal focus of Reeder and his wife after World War II. Annually, the Reeders recruited artists and musicians from Fort Worth and elsewhere, along with large numbers of volunteers, to assist in producing the school's signature plays. In the school's twelve-year history, Dickson Reeder designed all the stage sets, as well as hundreds of elaborate costumes, masks, headdresses, and properties.

Reeder again traveled to Paris in 1959 to resume studies with Stanley William Hayter and to prepare for a retrospective, held in Fort Worth in 1960. The exhibition included new work that pointed up his increasing interest in abstraction. In the 1960s, even as his health declined, Reeder and his wife continued their famously social ways and remained the glue that bound the artists of the Fort Worth Circle together. Dickson Reeder died in Fort Worth on May 8, 1970, at age fifty-eight.

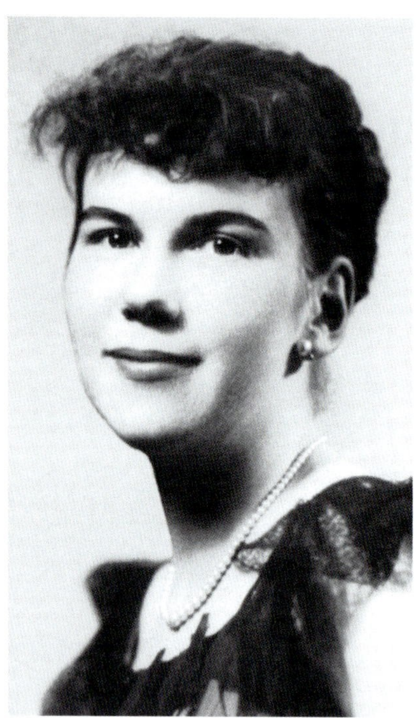

Flora Blanc Reeder, ca. 1940

FLORA BLANC REEDER Flora Blanc Reeder was a native of New York City, born November 14, 1916. From her mother, Elliot Blanc, who was deeply supportive of the arts, Flora acquired a passion for music, painting, and theater. She studied drawing with George Grosz, painting with Yasuo Kuniyoshi, and acting with Dorothy Coit at the King-Coit School and Children's Theatre.

At age nineteen, with her mother's assent, Blanc enrolled in an exclusive women's boarding school in Paris, but she soon took an apartment in the city and sought private art instruction. She studied painting with Fernand Léger and modeled for Chaim Soutine. In 1937 she was accepted for study in the atelier of Stanley William Hayter, and it was later that year that she met and married Texas painter Dickson Reeder, who was also in Paris studying at the time.

Flora Blanc and Dickson Reeder settled in Fort Worth in 1940, bringing with them a vibrant mixture of artistic interests. During the war years and afterward, the Reeders were the social epicenter of the Fort Worth Circle. Flora Blanc became a regular exhibitor in the *Local Artists Show* and was accepted into the *Texas General Exhibition* four times between 1941 and 1945.

In 1945, Flora Blanc was invited to direct a play for Dr. Lorraine Sherley of Texas Christian University, and she agreed on the condition that the cast be made up entirely of children. Six weeks later, in the backyard of Dr. Sherley's home, Blanc and her cast of Fort Worth youngsters presented the medieval romance *Aucassin and Nicolette* before an audience of disbelieving parents and onlookers. Reaction to the performance was so strong and positive that Blanc was persuaded to continue her efforts in a more formal venue. That same year, she and her husband founded the Reeder Children's School of Theater and Design, patterned after the King-Coit School in New York. By annually challenging her students, ages four to fourteen, with a single script drawn from classic literature or the Shakespearean repertoire, Blanc demanded and received their finest efforts. The consistently impressive performances of her students, delivered in the glare of high public expectations, represented her crowning achievement.

Flora Blanc Reeder remained active in theater circles for the remainder of her life. She died in Fort Worth on September 26, 1995, at the age of seventy-eight.

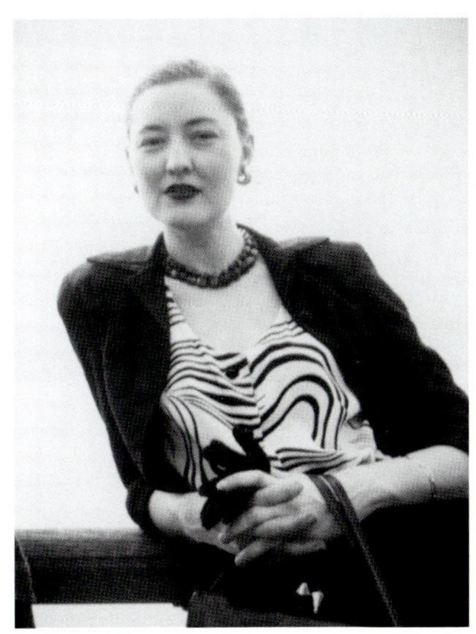

Sara Shannon, ca. 1949

SARA SHANNON Sara Shannon was born on January 13, 1920, in Burleson, Texas. During the Depression she moved to Fort Worth, where she lived with an aunt and attended Paschal High School. In the summer of 1939, Shannon met the core artists of the Fort Worth Circle when she enrolled in a life-drawing class at The Studios, the successor institution to the Fort Worth School of Fine Arts. Other members of the class included Lia Cuilty, Veronica Helfensteller, Marjorie Johnson, and Bror Utter. Shannon's work from these sessions was exhibited in a group show in the fall of 1939.

During the war years, Shannon's art was regularly accepted into the Fort Worth *Local Artists Show*. Three of her paintings were shown in the *Local* in 1943, and she won Honorable Mention in the *Local* the following year for her softly focused oil *Country House*. Her best known Texas work, *Ballet on the Stairs* (1943) (pl. 23), was exhibited in both the 1945 *Local* and the 1945 *Texas General Exhibition*. A rollicking depiction of a gathering of members of the Fort Worth Circle, the painting is a compelling rendering of the group's social cohesion.

A slender figure with classic features, Shannon served as both muse and subject to her fellow painters. Over a span of two or three years, images of her were produced by Flora Blanc Reeder (1942), Dickson Reeder (ca. 1942), and Bill Bomar (1944). Bror Utter depicted her in Grecian fashion in a series of gouaches he executed after the war.

Shannon married Pat Steel in 1946, and the couple lived briefly in Paris, Texas, before moving to New York City. There, she maintained close ties to other Fort Worth Circle artists living in New York and Texas. In the 1970s, she and her family moved to Dallas, where she excelled as a textile artist and volunteer textile conservator at the Dallas Museum of Art. Sara Shannon Steel died in Dallas on March 12, 1996. She was seventy-six.

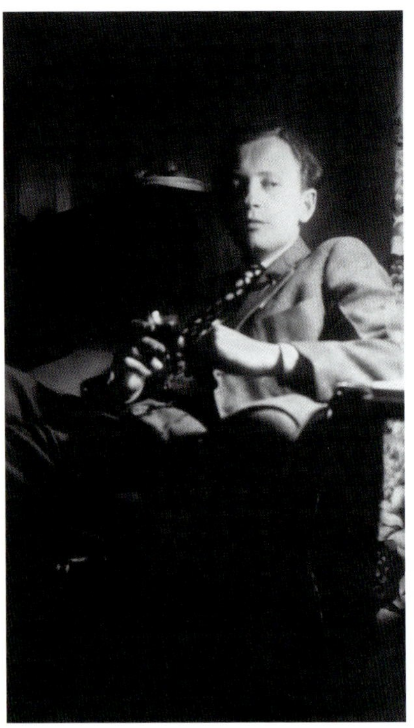

Bror Utter, ca. 1950

BROR ALEXANDER UTTER Bror Utter was born on August 21, 1913, in Fort Worth. He was the grandson of Finnish painter Nikolai Utter. Utter was educated in public schools, taking art classes from Ella Ray Ledgerwood and Sallie Gillespie at Central High School before graduating in 1931. About 1933, he enrolled in the Fort Worth School of Fine Arts, where at night he studied figure drawing with Blanche McVeigh and painting with Wade Jolly. Utter was considered one of the school's most promising painters.

Utter's early art encompassed landscapes and still lifes, as well as figural compositions inspired by a fascination with theater and vaudeville. His work was first shown publicly in a solo show in 1936, followed by solo exhibitions at Texas Christian University in 1939 and North Texas Agricultural College (which would become the University of Texas at Arlington) in 1941. That same year, his industrial scene *Texas Oil Refinery* was purchased for the IBM corporate collection of American watercolors.

During the 1940s, Utter was a three-time winner of the Fort Worth *Local Artists Show*, winning First Prize for *Waiting Lady* in 1942, *The Dreamer* in 1946 (pl. 82), and *Cloisters* (fig. 22) in 1949. As a member of the Fort Worth Circle, he created an approach to abstraction that he characterized as "embellished forms." Unique in postwar Texas, Utter's aesthetic combined vaguely recognizable human characteristics with fanciful shapes and colors. Utter's penchant for organizing abstract imagery within a grid of small compartments received national exposure in 1953 when *Nun's Distillery* was selected for the Whitney Museum of American Art's annual exhibition of contemporary American sculpture, watercolors, and drawings. He won First Prize for painting in the 1953 *Local* for *Trio* (pl. 98).

In 1953, Utter undertook the first of several trips to Italy, which revealed in him an instinctive love of architecture. Using an innovative, fractured picture plane, Utter extensively explored the complexity of Rome's ancient structures and the timeless allure of Venice. In 1956–57, in a series of commissioned watercolors, he used similar techniques to depict historic Fort Worth buildings. Utter's work was the subject of a large retrospective organized by the Fort Worth Art Association in 1961.

In addition to being one of Fort Worth's most widely collected painters, Bror Utter fashioned a long and substantive career as a private teacher and instructor for the Fort Worth Art Association and Woman's Club of Fort Worth. He died in Fort Worth on May 6, 1993.

SELECTED BIBLIOGRAPHY

BOOKS AND EXHIBITION CATALOGUES

Abstract and Surrealist American Art. Chicago, Illinois: The Art Institute of Chicago, 1947.

Adams, Clinton. *American Lithographers, 1900 – 1960: The Artists and Their Printers*. Albuquerque, New Mexico: University of New Mexico Press, 1983.

The Art of Bill Bomar. Taos: Harwood Foundation Museum of Taos Art, 1985.

Auping, Michael, general ed. *Modern Art Museum of Fort Worth 110*. Fort Worth, Texas: Modern Art Museum of Fort Worth, 2002.

Barker, Scott Grant. *Sallie Mummert and Her Students, 1925 – 1945*. Fort Worth, Texas: Collectors of Fort Worth Art, 2006.

Barr, Alfred H., Jr., ed. *Fantastic Art, Dada, Surrealism*. New York: Museum of Modern Art, 1936.

Beyond Regionalism: The Fort Worth School (1945 – 1955): A Texas Sesquicentennial Exhibition. Albany, Texas: The Old Jail Art Center, 1986.

Bill Bomar: Past and Present. Ranchos de Taos, New Mexico: Bill Bomar, 1983.

Black, Peter. *The Prints of Stanley William Hayter: A Complete Catalogue*. Mount Kisco, New York: Moyer Bell Limited, 1992.

Blagg, Margaret. *Cynthia Brants: Beyond the Circle*. Albany, Texas: The Old Jail Art Center, 2007.

Bror Utter. Fort Worth, Texas: Fort Worth Art Center, 1961.

Bror Utter, Fifty Years of His Art. Fort Worth, Texas: Texas Christian University, 1985.

Bywaters, Jerry. *Texas Painting and Sculpture: 20th Century*. Dallas, Texas: Broadnax Printing, 1971.

Castleman, Riva. *Prints of the 20th Century: A History*. New York: Museum of Modern Art, 1976.

Dickson Reeder. Fort Worth, Texas: Fort Worth Art Center, 1960.

Dickson Reeder: A Retrospective Exhibition. Fort Worth, Texas: Texas Christian University, 1988.

First Light: Local Art and the Fort Worth Public Library, 1901 – 1961. Fort Worth, Texas: Fort Worth Public Library Foundation, 2001.

Grauer, Paula L., and Michael R. Grauer. *Dictionary of Texas Artists, 1800 – 1945*. College Station, Texas: Texas A&M University, 1998.

Hacker, P.M.S., ed. *The Renaissance of Gravure: The Art of S. W. Hayter*. Oxford: Clarendon Press, 1988.

Harris, Paul Rogers. *The Texas Printmakers*. Dallas, Texas: The Meadows Museum, Meadows School of the Arts, Southern Methodist University, 1990.

——. *The Women Who Challenged: Interviews With Nine Artists*. Dallas, Texas: Meadows Museum, Meadows School of the Arts, Southern Methodist University, 1990.

Hayter e l'Atelier 17. Milano: Electa, 1990.

Hayter et l'Atelier 17. Gravelines: Musée du dessin et de l'estampe originale, 1993.

Hayter, Stanley William. *About Prints*. London and New York: Oxford University Press, 1962.

——. *New Ways of Gravure*. New York: Pantheon, 1949.

Janis, Sidney. *Abstract & Surrealist Art in America*. New York: Reynal & Hitchcock, 1944.

Johnson, Una E. *American Prints and Printmakers: A Chronicle of Over 400 Artists and Their Prints from 1900 to the Present*. Garden City, New York: Doubleday & Company, Inc., 1980.

Jones, Jan L. *Renegades, Showmen and Angels: A Theatrical History of Fort Worth from 1873 – 2001*. Fort Worth, Texas: Texas Christian University Press, 2006.

Knight, Oliver. *Fort Worth, Outpost on the Trinity*. Fort Worth, Texas: Texas Christian University, 1990.

Lee, Amy Freeman, and Mark L. Smith. *The Mystical World of Kelly Fearing: A Sixty-Year Retrospective*. Austin: The University of Texas at Austin, 2002.

Life Stories: Bill Bomar, Lydia Madrid, Bea Madelman, Florence Pierce. Santa Fe, New Mexico: Museum of Fine Arts Santa Fe, 1990.

The McLean Art Collection. Fort Worth, Texas: Stafford-Lowden Co., 1968.

Nail, Reilly. *Per Stirpes: The John M. Nail Family in Texas, 1839 – 1995*. Texas: Reilly Nail, 1995.

Oglesby, Resa C. *History of the Fort Worth Art Association*. MA thesis, Denton, Texas: Texas Woman's University, 1950.

Prints of the Fort Worth Circle, 1940 – 1960. Austin, Texas: Archer M. Huntington Art Gallery, 1992.

Roark, Carol. "The Reeder School." In *Literary Fort Worth*, edited by Judy Alter and James Ward Lee, 338 – 40. Fort Worth, Texas: Texas Christian University Press, 2002.

Rodman, Ellen. "Edith King and Dorothy Coit and the King-Coit School and Children's Theatre." In *Spotlight on the Child: Studies in the History of American Children's Theatre*, edited by Roger L. Bedard and C. John Tolch, 51 – 67. New York: Greenwood Press, 1989.

Seaton, Elizabeth G., ed. *Paths to the Press: Printmaking and American Women Artists, 1910 – 1960*. Manhattan, Kansas: Marianne Kistler Beach Museum of Art, 2006.

Seventeen Years: An Exhibition of the First Prize Winners in Painting, Drawing, Printmaking and Sculpture in the 17 Annual Exhibitions of Work by Fort Worth Artists held by the Fort Worth Art Association. Fort Worth, Texas: Fort Worth Art Association, 1954.

Stewart, Rick. *Lone Star Regionalism: The Dallas Nine and Their Circle, 1928 – 1945*. Dallas, Texas: Dallas Museum of Art and the Texas Monthly Press, 1985.

Texas Modern: The Rediscovery of Early Texas Abstraction (1935 – 1965). Waco, Texas:

Martin Museum of Art, Baylor University, 2007.

Vogel, Donald. *Memories and Images: The World of Donald Vogel and Valley House Gallery*. Denton, Texas: The University of North Texas Press, 2000.

Watrous, James. *American Printmaking: A Century of American Printmaking, 1880–1980*. Madison, Wisconsin: University of Wisconsin Press, 1984.

JOURNAL ARTICLES

Brach, Paul. "Veronica Helfensteller." *Art Digest* 26 (1 February 1952): 21.

Breuning, Margaret. "Bill Bomar in Second Show." *Art Digest* 24 (15 October 1949): 20–21.

——. "Veronica Helfensteller." *Art Digest* 25 (15 February 1951): 22.

Defenbacher, Daniel S. "Texas: Cosmopolitan Art Colony." *Art in America* 42:1 (Winter 1954): 58–63.

Durham, Floyd. "An Exploration of Some of the Causes of a Developing Painters' Colony in Fort Worth, Texas." *Journal of Cultural Economics* 1:2 (December 1977): 25–34.

"Exhibition, Weyhe Gallery." *Art News*. 45 (October 1946): 69.

"Exhibition, Weyhe Gallery." *Art News* 48 (October 1949): 47.

Freudenheim, Susan. "Art: the 50-Year Career of Painter Bror Utter Tracks the Artistic Revolution of His Time." *Texas Homes* 9:1 (January 1985), Dallas: Southwest Media Corp., 29–32.

Gibbs, Jo. "Bill Bomar Balances Emotion and Intellect." *Art Digest* 21 (1 October 1946): 19.

"Hayter and Studio 17." *Museum of Modern Art Bulletin* 12:1 (August 1944): 2–16.

Hickey, Dave. "Beyond Regionalism: The Fort Worth School (1945–1955)." *Artspace* 11:1 (Winter 1986–87): 45–46.

Holliday, Betty. "Veronica Helfensteller." *Art News* 49:10 (February 1951): 50.

Mitchell, Dee. "Veronica Helfensteller." *Circa, The Texas Based Journal of Contemporary Art* (Winter 1995): 31–32.

"The Passing Shows." *Art News*, 43:12 (1–14 October 1944). New York: The Art Foundation, 22–24.

T.M.C., "Bill Bomar: Remnants: An Equation," *ARTlines*, 4:5 (June 1983) Taos: ARTlines, Inc., 11.

Riley, Maude. "Six Texans." *Art Digest* 19:1 (1 October 1944): 8

"Utter's Show," *Texas Week: Texas' Own Newsmagazine*, 1:23 (18 January 1947). Dallas: Texas Week, Inc., 18

NEWSPAPER ARTICLES

With some notable exceptions, most of the literature specific to the Fort Worth Circle can be found in local newspapers of the cities of Fort Worth and Dallas, published between 1940 and 1955. The following articles are those that the authors cite as sources for their texts, though much more about the individual artists and activities of the Circle was published by the local press.

Askew, Rual. "Dallas to Host Show Evolved 'Next Door.'" *Dallas Morning News*, 2 January 1959.

Crandall, Virginia. "1944 Local Art." *Dallas Morning News*, 21 May 1944.

Dallas Morning News. "Lithograph of the Grocery Store by Georgia Artist," 4 September 1941.

——. "Chuck Wagon Art Carnival in September," 31 August 1945.

——. "DeForest Judd Debut Here; a Local Eight," 3 November 1946.

Deen, Edith. "Exhibit Attests to Couple's Good Taste." *Fort Worth Press*, 19 February 1952.

Devree, Howard. "Among the New Exhibitions." *New York Times*, 29 September 1946.

Genauer, Emily. "Maturity, Intelligence Found in Bomar's Work." *Fort Worth Star-Telegram*, 29 September 1946 (reprint of article that first appeared in the *New York World Telegram*).

Fort Worth Press. "Art Association Is 'Broke,' Needs $2500 for Year," 13 September 1942.

Fort Worth Star-Telegram. "Six of Paintings Included in the Fourth Annual Jury Show of Ft. Worth Artists Guild," 15 January 1939.

——. "First Prize in Citywide Art Exhibit Goes to Still Life," 1 June 1939.

——. "57 Artists Represented in First Citywide Exhibition," June 1939.

——. "First Prize Winner in Local Artists Show," 7 April 1940.

——. "Artist to Join Staff at TWC," 4 January 1941.

——. "Dickson Reeder Gets First Prize in Local Art Show," 13 April 1943.

——. "Right in der Fuehrer's Face – Artists Manning Battle Stations," clipping from 1943.

——. "Kelly Fearing Oil Is Chosen for Purchase," 22 April 1945.

Gossett, Robert. "Originality in the Show." *Fort Worth Star-Telegram*, 21 May 1944.

Guedry, Edith. "Modern Art May Not Be Pleasing But It Is Typical of Era in Which We're Living." *Fort Worth Press*, 13 April 1944.

——. "Fort Worth Eyes Are on Show of Five Local Painters Opening in New York Monday." *Fort Worth Press*, 15 September 1944.

Harwell, Jerry, Jr. "Fort Worth Holds Interest in Fine Art, School Proves." *Fort Worth Press*, 4 November 1932.

Hicks, Ida Belle. "Young Fort Worth Painter Has 27 Pieces of Art Displayed at T. C. U. Gallery." *Fort Worth Star-Telegram*, 12 February 1939.

——. "Art Season Nears Height." *Fort Worth Star-Telegram*, 9 November 1941.

——. "Bror Utter's 1-Man Show Opens Today." *Fort Worth Star-Telegram*, 30 November 1941.

———. "Wartime Pressure Fails to Slow Artists in Work." *Fort Worth Star-Telegram*, 12 December 1943.

———. "Works of 22 Fort Worth Artists Are on Exhibit in Local Show at Library." *Fort Worth Star-Telegram*, 9 April 1944.

———. "Business and Art Can Meet; Outstanding Work of Painter Proves It." *Fort Worth Star-Telegram*, 30 April 1944.

———. "Three Exhibitions Soon to Draw Widespread Attention to Work of Texas Artists." *Fort Worth Star-Telegram*, 10 September 1944.

———. "Six Texas Artists' Show in New York Includes Many Fort Worth Paintings." *Fort Worth Star-Telegram*, 17 September 1944.

———. "Prizes Announced for West Texas Art Show." *Fort Worth Star-Telegram*, 21 January 1945.

———. "Nonobjective Paintings Go on Exhibit Monday." *Fort Worth Star-Telegram*, 28 January 1945.

———. "Educator to Discuss Nonobjective Paintings." *Fort Worth Star-Telegram*, 4 February 1945.

———. "Two New Shows Are of Contrasting Interest." *Fort Worth Star-Telegram*, 25 February 1945.

———. "Nation's Leading Artists Are Represented in Show." *Fort Worth Star-Telegram*, 18 March 1945.

———. "Representative Works Appeal to all Types." *Fort Worth Star-Telegram*, 25 March 1945.

———. "Kelly Fearing Oil Is Chosen for Purchase." *Fort Worth Star-Telegram*, 22 April 1945.

———. "Exhibits, Not Regional, Marked by Individuality." *Fort Worth Star-Telegram*, 29 April 1945.

———. "Progress of Fort Worth Artists Gillespie Topic." *Fort Worth Star-Telegram*, 6 May 1945.

———. "Stimulating Exhibits Are in Step With Trend." *Fort Worth Star-Telegram*, 13 May 1945.

———. "Transition of an Artist Is Reflected in Exhibit." *Fort Worth Star-Telegram*, 20 May 1945.

———. "Local Works Added to Private Collections." *Fort Worth Star-Telegram*, 3 June 1945.

———. "Opportunity to Observe Young Man's Technique." *Fort Worth Star-Telegram*, 15 July 1945.

———. "Vacations and Peacetime Plans Occupy Painters." *Fort Worth Star-Telegram*, 19 August 1945.

———. "Gravure Exhibition Will Open New Art Program." *Fort Worth Star-Telegram*, 26 August 1945.

———. "Utter's Art Provocative But Highly Interesting." *Fort Worth Star-Telegram*, 27 January 1946.

———. "Bror Utter Thinks Southwest Ready to Form New School of Painting." *Fort Worth Star-Telegram*, 3 February 1946.

———. "Bill Bomar's One-Man NY Show Opens Monday." *Fort Worth Star-Telegram*, 22 September 1946.

Jenkins, Nedra. "Bomar's Works Didn't Disappoint Homefolks." *Fort Worth Star-Telegram*, 7 December 1947.

———. "'New Generation' Exhibition: Two From Here to Have Art Show in New York." *Fort Worth Star-Telegram*, 29 April 1951.

———. "Cantey Art Collection to Be Shown in Denton." *Fort Worth Star-Telegram*, 10 February 1952.

Jewell, Edward Alden. "Art Plans of Local Museums." *New York Times*, 24 September 1944.

Jones, Peggy Louise. "New Exhibit at Telenews." *Dallas Morning News*, 15 September 1945.

———. "Texas General Exhibit Opens at Museum." *Dallas Morning News*, 11 November 1945.

———. "Oils and Prints Comprise Two New Exhibits." *Dallas Morning News*, 1 February 1946.

———. "Art Galleries to Have Two New Exhibits." *Dallas Morning News*, 24 February 1946.

———. "General Art Trends Shown in Works of Texas Artists." *Dallas Morning News*, 16 June 1946.

———. "Portraits and Objective Art for Fort Worthian at Museum." *Dallas Morning News*, 1 January 1948.

———. "Fine Painting in Exhibition at McLean's." *Dallas Morning News*, 12 October 1951.

Louchheim, Aline B. "Texas Art Is Vital and Growing." *New York Times*, 15 November 1953.

Morehead, Eleanor. "Helfensteller Sold; Ft. Worth Artists Open Gotham Show." Unidentified clipping (probably Fort Worth), 1944.

Mummert, Sallie Blyth. "Fort Worth Artists Organize Guild." *Fort Worth Star-Telegram*, 3 February 1935.

———. "Art Association Receives 8 Original Drawings in Color by E. W. Deming." *Fort Worth Star-Telegram*, 20 February 1938.

———. "Art Exhibition by Fort Worth Children to Be Opened Today." *Fort Worth Star-Telegram*, 20 March 1938.

New York Herald Tribune. "In the Art Galleries," 24 September 1944.

Peck, Patricia. "Fort Worth Artist Winner Texas General's Top Prize." *Dallas Morning News*, 24 October 1943.

———. "Texas Takes to Lithography for Annual Print Exhibition." *Dallas Morning News*, 12 December 1943.

———. "Fifth Texas General Arrives as Stimulating Christmas Gift." *Dallas Morning News*, 26 December 1943.

———. "Art From the Local Painters Out Where the West Begins." *Dallas Morning News*, 16 April 1944.

——. "Fact and Fancy in Fort Worth." *Dallas Morning News*, 17 May 1944.

——. "Printmaking's Distaff Side to the Fore." *Dallas Morning News*, 29 September 1946.

——. "Critics Not Eye to Eye on MMA Show." *Dallas Morning News*, 3 October 1946.

——. "New Gouaches by Bror Utter." *Dallas Morning News*, 1 January 1947.

——. "Ladies' Month at Telenews." *Dallas Morning News*, 10 January 1947.

——. "Abstractions, Good and Bad, in Fort Worth." *Dallas Morning News*, 16 February 1947.

Preston, Stuart. "Modern Masters – Degas, Renoir, Rouault – Young Americans." *New York Times*, 9 October 1949.

Prince, Jeff. "Wanna See my Etchings?" *Fort Worth Weekly*, 11 April 2007.

Reeder, Dickson. "An Artist Views the Show." *Fort Worth Star-Telegram*, 23 March 1941.

Riley, Maude. "Art Digest Editor Says Work of 6 Texans Is Interesting And in No Sense Regional." *Fort Worth Star-Telegram*, 24 September 1944.

Rosenfield, John. "Notes on the Passing Show." *Dallas Morning News*, 17 September 1948.

Sharp, Marynell. "Fort Worth Group in Exhibition at the Telenews." *Dallas Morning News*, 19 May 1945.

——. "One-Man Show by Versatile Fort Worthian." *Dallas Morning News*, 27 May 1945.

——. "Theater Exhibits More Paintings by North Texans." *Dallas Morning News*, 14 June 1945.

——. "Regional Art Stressed in New Exhibit." *Dallas Morning News*, 8 July 1945.

Upton, Melville, "Art of Soviet Children, Modern Museum Opens with Display of It – Shows in Other Galleries." *New York Sun*, 23 September 1944.

Walker, Nadene. "'Cat in Portia's Garden' Is Worthy Winner of First Prize in Current Art Show." *Fort Worth Star-Telegram*, 23 April 1944.

——. "Popular Vote Prize Winner at Show; Already Established Artist, Exhibitor." *Fort Worth Star-Telegram*, 5 May 1944.

——. "Bror Utter Show Opening Monday Made up of Careful and Conscientious Work." *Fort Worth Star-Telegram*, 11 June 1944.

World Telegram. "Sextet from Texas Exhibit Jointly," 20 October 1944.

ARCHIVAL SOURCES

Papers of Bror Utter, Amon Carter Museum Archives, Fort Worth, Texas. Cynthia Brants, "'The Fort Worth Circle' and the 1940s," Lecture for Retrofest, 23 April 1998, transcription. Cynthia Brants, interview by Scott Barker, Amon Carter Museum, Fort Worth, 9 March 2002, transcription. Kelly Fearing, interview by Scott Barker, Austin, Texas, 26 October 2002, transcription. Panel discussion, Modern Art Museum of Fort Worth, 14 April 1992, transcription.

Archives of American Art, Smithsonian Institution, Washington, D.C. Papers of Bill Bomar, Samuel Benton Cantey, Terese Tarlton Hershey, Dickson Reeder, Bror Utter. Bror Utter Interview, the Archives of American Art Oral History Program, 1979.

Fort Worth Public Library, Fort Worth, Texas. Papers of Samuel Benton Cantey and Carlin Art Galleries.

Museum of Fine Arts, Houston. Curatorial files.

New York Public Library, Library of the Performing Arts. King-Coit School and Children's Theatre Papers.

Old Jail Art Center, Albany, Texas. Archives and curatorial files.

Reeder Papers, Special Collections, The University of Texas at Arlington Library.

CHECKLISTS

Bill Bomar. Dallas, Texas: Betty McLean Gallery, January 15 – February 7, 1952.

Bill Bomar. New York: Weyhe Gallery, October 3 – November 3, 1949.

Bill Bomar. Fort Worth, Texas: Fort Worth Art Association, December 6 – 31, 1947.

Bill Bomar. New York: Weyhe Gallery, September 23 – October 16, 1946.

Bror Utter. Fort Worth, Texas: Fort Worth Art Association, February 10 – 27, 1953.

Bror Utter. Dallas, Texas: Betty McLean Gallery, February 13 – March 10, 1952.

Bror Utter: Paintings, Prints, Drawings. Fort Worth, Texas: Fort Worth Art Association, January 26 – February 15, 1946.

Cynthia Brants. Dallas, Texas: Betty McLean Gallery, April 9 – May 4, 1953.

Exhibition of Contemporary American Paintings and Sculpture. Fort Worth, Texas: Fort Worth Art Association, March 20 – April 20, 1945.

Exhibition No. Five. Dallas, Texas: Betty McLean Gallery, September 17 – October 13, 1951.

Exhibition of Paintings, Prints and Drawings by Veronica Helfensteller. Fort Worth, Texas: Fort Worth Art Association, May 2 – 21, 1944.

Exhibition of the Work of Dickson Reeder. Fort Worth, Texas: Fort Worth Art Association, May 21 – June 15, 1945.

Fort Worth Local. The Fort Worth *Locals* began in 1939. Checklists for many, but not all, of the *Locals* that occurred during the 1940s have been identified; 1942, 1944, and 1945 are missing.

Grauer, Michael R. *Of This Vast State: Women Artists of Texas, 1900 – 1960*. Dallas, Texas: The Women's Museum, November 3, 2006 – January 28, 2007.

Kelly Fearing: The Influence of "The Fort Worth School," 1939 – 1955. Dallas, Texas: Valley House Gallery, April 20 – May 30, 1992.

Kelly Fearing. Dallas, Texas: Betty McLean Gallery, March 15 – April 14, 1952.

Newcomers: First Showing of a New Generation. New York: The Downtown Gallery, May 1 – 19, 1951.

Paintings. Marjorie Johnson. Fort Worth, Texas: Fort Worth Art Association, December 2 – 24, 1949.

Selected Works of Art from the Private Collection of Mr. & Mrs. Sam B. Cantey III of Fort Worth. Denton, Texas: Department of Art, Texas State College for Women, February 17 – March 2, 1952.

Six Texas Painters. New York: Weyhe Gallery, September 18 – October 7, 1944.

Texas Contemporary Artists. New York: Knoedler, June 10 – September 28, 1952.

Texas Fine Arts Association. An Exhibition of Oils, Gouaches, Prints & Drawings by Bror Utter. San Antonio: Elisabet Ney Museum, February 29 – March 19, 1948.

Texas General. The *Texas General* exhibitions began in 1940. Checklists exist for all.

Three Painters of the Fort Worth School. Fort Worth, Texas: Fort Worth Gallery, April 11 – May 13, 1992.

ELECTRONIC SOURCES

Barker, Scott Grant. "Travelers of the Mind: The Rise of the Fort Worth Circle, 1940 – 1955." Texas State University, San Marcos: CASETA, 2003.

ONLINE SOURCES

Texas State Handbook Online. www.tsha.utexas.edu/handbook/online. The Texas State Handbook Online is a service of the Texas State Historical Association.

LIST OF FIGURES

FIGURE **1**
Bror Utter, n.d.
Bror Utter Papers, Amon Carter Museum

FIGURE **2**
Lia Cuilty, n.d.
From *Prints of the Fort Worth Circle 1940 – 1960* exhibition catalogue

FIGURE **3**
Dickson Reeder, 1943
Courtesy, Reeder Papers, Special Collections, The University of Texas at Arlington Library

FIGURE **4**
Flora Reeder, ca. 1940
Courtesy, Reeder Papers, Special Collections, The University of Texas at Arlington Library

FIGURE **5**
Carnegie Public Library, Fort Worth, Texas, ca. 1910
Courtesy of the Genealogy, History, and Archives Unit, Fort Worth Public Library

FIGURE **6**
Fort Worth Public Library Art Gallery, ca. 1940
Courtesy of the Genealogy, History, and Archives Unit, Fort Worth Public Library

FIGURE **7**
Reeders playing instruments, 1943
Courtesy, Reeder Papers, Special Collections, The University of Texas at Arlington Library

FIGURE **8**
Front row: Veronica Helftensteller, Bror Utter; Back row: Flora Blanc Reeder, Kelly Fearing, Lia Cuilty, Dickson Reeder, n.d.
Courtesy, Reeder Papers, Special Collections, The University of Texas at Arlington Library

FIGURE **9**
Veronica Helfensteller, ca. 1945
Courtesy, Reeder Papers, Special Collections, The University of Texas at Arlington Library

FIGURE **10**
Marjorie Johnson, 1949
Collection of Pat Steel

FIGURE **11**
Bill Bomar, New York City, 1948
Collection of Pat Steel

FIGURE **12**
Kelly Fearing in Bill Bomar's Chelsea Hotel apartment, 1948
Collection of Pat Steel

FIGURE **13**
Sara Shannon, 1943
Collection of Pat Steel

FIGURE **14**
Installation photograph of *Six Texas Painters*, Weyhe Gallery, New York City, September 1944
Courtesy, Reeder Papers, Special Collections, The University of Texas at Arlington Library

FIGURE **15**
Dickson Reeder (1912 – 1970)
The Dispute, 1944
Oil on canvas, 24¾ x 30 in.
Dallas Museum of Art, Lida Hooe Memorial Fund

FIGURE **16**
Bror Utter (1913 – 1993)
Accident at Rehearsal, 1944
Location unknown
Courtesy, *Fort Worth Star-Telegram Collection*, Special Collections, The University of Texas at Arlington Library

FIGURE **17**
Cynthia Brants, 1954
Courtesy, Reeder Papers, Special Collections, The University of Texas at Arlington Library

FIGURE **18**
George Grammer, ca. 1955
Collection of George Grammer

FIGURE **19**
With Dickson and Flora looking on, a trio of actors performs in the Reeder Children's School production of *A Midsummer Night's Dream*, 1954
Courtesy, Reeder Papers, Special Collections, The University of Texas at Arlington Library

FIGURE **20**
Lia Cuilty, Marjorie Johnson, and Bill Bomar in New York City, 1949
Collection of Pat Steel

FIGURE **21**
Sam and Betsy Cantey, ca. 1950s
Collection of Ambler Cantey

FIGURE **22**
Bror Utter (1913–1993)
Cloisters, 1948
Oil on canvas, $20\frac{1}{4}$ x 24 in.
Collection of the Modern Art Museum of Fort Worth

FIGURE **23**
John Marin (1870–1953)
Tree, Maine, 1917
Watercolor on paper, $16\frac{1}{2}$ x $14\frac{1}{8}$ in.
From the Collection of the Old Jail Art Center, Albany, Texas, Gift of Bill Bomar
1981.119

FIGURE **24**
Flora Blanc as the Goddess of War and friend Helen Phillips as Peace, Paris, ca. 1937
Courtesy, Reeder Papers, Special Collections, The University of Texas at Arlington Library

FIGURE **25**
Flora Blanc, Paris, ca. 1937
Courtesy, Reeder Papers, Special Collections, The University of Texas at Arlington Library

FIGURE **26**
A drawing (1937) from one of Dickson Reeder's sketchbooks showing the influence of Picasso, Léger, and surrealism
Courtesy, Reeder Papers, Special Collections, The University of Texas at Arlington Library

FIGURE **27**
Bror Utter (1913–1993)
Colorado Springs, 1941
Lithograph, $7\frac{15}{16}$ x $15\frac{3}{4}$ in.
Amon Carter Museum, Fort Worth, Texas
1995.5

FIGURE **28**
Flora teaching, mid-1950s
Courtesy, Reeder Papers, Special Collections, The University of Texas at Arlington Library

FIGURE **29**
The program cover for the Reeder Children's School production of *A Midsummer Night's Dream*, 1954
Collection of Scott Grant Barker

FIGURE **30**
Veronica Helfensteller (1910–1964)
The Three Guardians, 1943
Lithograph, $13\frac{7}{8}$ x $17\frac{1}{8}$ in.
Dallas Museum of Art, Dallas Art Museum League Prize, Third Annual Texas Print Exhibition, 1944

FIGURE **31**
Blanche McVeigh (1895–1970)
First Methodist Church, ca. 1936
Etching, $5\frac{3}{16}$ x $3\frac{5}{8}$ in.
Amon Carter Museum, Gift of Edward and William Hudson in memory of their mother, Josephine Terrell Smith Hudson
2004.2

FIGURE **32**
El Greco (1541–1614)
Burial of Count Orgaz, 1586
Oil on canvas, 15 x $11\frac{3}{4}$ ft.
Church of Santo Tomé, Toledo, Spain

FIGURE **33**
Veronica Helfensteller (1910–1964)
The Mandrill's Tea Party, ca. 1943
Lithograph, $17\frac{1}{8}$ x $20\frac{1}{16}$ in.
Blanton Museum of Art, The University of Texas at Austin, Gift of Kelly Fearing, 1993
Photograph by Rick Hall

FIGURE **34**
Bror Utter (1913–1993)
Sketchbook *[Woman hanging clothes]*, 1952
Watercolor, ink, and graphite on paper, $8\frac{7}{8}$ x $11\frac{7}{8}$ in.
Amon Carter Museum
1996.5.4

BIOGRAPHY ILLUSTRATIONS

Bill Bomar, ca. 1950
Collection of Pat Steel

Cynthia Brants, ca. 1955
Collection of Pat Steel

Lia Cuilty, 1947
Courtesy, Reeder Papers, Special Collections, The University of Texas at Arlington Library

Kelly Fearing, 1948
Collection of Pat Steel

George Grammer, ca. 1955
Collection of George Grammer

Veronica Helfensteller, n.d.
The Jerry Bywaters Collection on Art of the Southwest, Hamon Arts Library, Southern Methodist University (*Fort Worth Star-Telegram* photograph)

Marjorie Johnson, ca. 1953
Collection of Pat Steel

Dickson Reeder, ca. 1940
Collection of Nell Reeder Branch

Flora Blanc Reeder, ca. 1940
Unattributed

Sara Shannon (Steel), ca. 1949
Collection of Pat Steel

Bror Utter, ca. 1950
Collection of Pat Steel

LIST OF PLATES

PLATE **1**
Bill Bomar (1919–1991)
Santa Fe View, 1942
Watercolor on paper, 22 7/8 x 31 1/2 in.
Amon Carter Museum
1998.6

PLATE **2**
Lia Cuilty (1908–1978)
The Day's at Morn, 1944
Gouache, watercolor, and graphite on paper, 23 1/6 x 29 in.
Jane Cranz

PLATE **3**
Kelly Fearing (b. 1918)
Jitterbuggers, 1939
Watercolor and graphite on paper, 20 1/2 x 16 1/2 in.
Mr. and Mrs. Charles Smith
Art © Kelly Fearing/Licensed by VAGA, New York, NY

PLATE **4**
Kelly Fearing (b. 1918)
Attic Piece, 1941
Oil on artist's board, 23 7/8 x 19 7/8 in.
Larry and Stephanie Boettigheimer
Art © Kelly Fearing/Licensed by VAGA, New York, NY

PLATE **5**
Frank Fisher (1907–1959)
Still Life, 1939
Oil on artist's board, 18 1/8 x 24 1/4 in.
Hock Shop Collection

PLATE **6**
Veronica Helfensteller (1910–1964)
Untitled [St. Louis Apartment House], ca. 1935–37
Watercolor and graphite on paper, 9 15/16 x 13 15/16 in.
Earl Weed and Dena Edwards, Houston, Texas

PLATE **7**
Veronica Helfensteller (1910–1964)
Untitled [Eads Bridge, St. Louis], ca. 1935–37
Watercolor on paper, 11 15/16 x 15 15/16 in.
Earl Weed and Dena Edwards, Houston, Texas

PLATE **8**
Dickson Reeder (1912–1970)
Mazy, 1937
Engraving, i/ii, 6 3/4 x 5 1/2 in.
H. Kenneth Jackson

PLATE **9**
Dickson Reeder (1912–1970)
Mazy, 1937
Engraving, etching, and soft-ground etching, ii/ii, 6 3/4 x 5 1/2 in.
Blanton Museum of Art, The University of Texas at Austin, Archer M. Huntington Museum Fund, 1988. Photograph by Rick Hall

PLATE **10**
Dickson Reeder (1912–1970)
Untitled, 1937
Engraving, 5 x 4 1/16 in.
From the Private Collection of Cy E. Barcus

PLATE **11**
Dickson Reeder (1912–1970)
Sketchbook, 1937
Graphite on paper, 8 1/4 x 5 1/8 in.
Reeder Papers, Special Collections, The University of Texas at Arlington Library

PLATE **12**
Flora Blanc Reeder (1916–1995)
The Dragon and Saint George, 1937
Engraving and soft-ground etching, 8 11/16 x 5 15/16 in.
Mr. Howard M. Ross

PLATE **13**
Bror Utter (1913–1993)
Going Home, 1944
Oil on artist's board, 16 x 20 in.
Charles and Karen Harris Cerulla

PLATE **14**
Veronica Helfensteller (1910–1964)
The Host in the Coffin, 1943
Gouache on paper, 16 1/16 x 20 1/16 in.
Mrs. W. K. Gordon Jr.

PLATE **15**
Dickson Reeder (1912–1970)
Untitled [Sara with the Ace of Spades], ca. 1942
Oil on canvas, 40 x 30 in.
Pat Steel

PLATE **16**
Dickson Reeder (1912–1970)
All Hallow's Eve, 1945
Oil on canvas, 36 1/8 x 30 1/4 in.
Permanent Collection of the Art Museum of South Texas, gift of the *Corpus Christi Caller-Times*

PLATE **17**
Dickson Reeder (1912–1970)
Masquerade, 1945
Gouache and watercolor on paper, 13 15/16 x 11 15/16 in.
Rainone Galleries, Arlington, Texas

PLATE **18**
Dickson Reeder (1912–1970)
Study for stage curtain, *The Rose and the Ring*, ca. 1946–53
Gouache and graphite on paper, 11 x 14 3/16 in.
Reeder School Records, Special Collections, The University of Texas at Arlington Library

PLATE **19**
Dickson Reeder (1912–1970)
Costume study for *The Rose and the Ring*, ca. 1946–53
Gouache and graphite on paper, 11 1/4 x 11 15/16 in.
Reeder School Records, Special Collections, The University of Texas at Arlington Library

PLATE **20**
Dickson Reeder (1912–1970)
Costume study for *A Midsummer Night's Dream*, ca. 1948–54
Gouache, ink, watercolor, and graphite on paper, 12 x 8 13/16 in.
Reeder School Records, Special Collections, The University of Texas at Arlington Library

PLATE **21**
Dickson Reeder (1912–1970)
Costume study for *A Midsummer Night's Dream*, ca. 1948–54
Gouache and watercolor on paper, 10 1/4 x 8 3/8 in.
Reeder School Records, Special Collections, The University of Texas at Arlington Library

PLATE **22**
Flora Blanc Reeder (1916–1995)
Reading the Cards, ca. 1943
Oil on canvas, 34 x 30 in.
Caroline M. Dulle

PLATE **23**
Sara Shannon (1920 – 1996)
Ballet on the Stairs, 1943
Oil on canvas, 20 x 16 in.
Shannon Steel

PLATE **24**
Emily Guthrie Smith (1909 – 1986)
The Halloween Party, 1943
Pastel and charcoal on paperboard,
$19\frac{13}{16}$ x $24\frac{13}{16}$ in.
Ms. Helen McCrimmon

PLATE **25**
Bror Utter (1913 – 1993)
Lady with a Box, 1941
Lithograph, $15\frac{3}{16}$ x $9\frac{7}{8}$ in.
Kathryn and Morris Matson

PLATE **26**
Bror Utter (1913 – 1993)
The Aerialists, 1946
Oil on canvas, $30\frac{1}{8}$ x 24 in.
W. P. McLean Middle School,
Fort Worth, Texas

PLATE **27**
Bror Utter (1913 – 1993)
Party, 1946
Oil on artist's board, 12 x $15\frac{15}{16}$ in.
Amon Carter Museum
1998.2

PLATE **28**
Bill Bomar (1919 – 1991)
Head of an Artist, 1944
Oil on canvas, 18 x $12\frac{1}{4}$ in.
Courtesy of the Old Jail Art Center,
Albany, Texas. Jewel Nail Bomar and
William P. Bomar Jr. Collection
1993.029

PLATE **29**
Bill Bomar (1919 – 1991)
Flora, 1944
Oil on canvas, $30\frac{1}{4}$ x $18\frac{1}{4}$ in.
The Museum of Fine Arts, Houston,
9th *Texas General Exhibition*,
museum purchase prize,
Marquis and Marquise d'Oyley funds

PLATE **30**
Bill Bomar (1919 – 1991)
Sara, 1946
Oil on canvas, 36 x 22 in.
Pat Steel

PLATE **31**
Bill Bomar (1919 – 1991)
Jewel's Feathered Hat, 1947
Oil on canvas, 36 x 22 in.
Courtesy of the Old Jail Art Center, Albany,
Texas. Gift of Betsy Lee Cantey
1984.046

PLATE **32**
Bill Bomar (1919 – 1991)
Lia, 1953
Oil on artist's board, $27\frac{1}{2}$ x $23\frac{1}{2}$ in.
Heirs of Lia Cuilty; Caroline M. Dulle,
Susan M. Pritchett, Steve Murrin Jr.

PLATE **33**
Dickson Reeder (1912 – 1970)
The Shannon Children, 1941
Oil on canvas, $39\frac{1}{2}$ x $31\frac{1}{2}$ in.
Mr. and Mrs. E. Ogden Whipple

PLATE **34**
Dickson Reeder (1912 – 1970)
Ellaraye, 1945
Oil on canvas, 26 x $45\frac{1}{4}$
Louise Hopkins Underwood

PLATE **35**
Dickson Reeder (1912 – 1970)
Conversation Piece, 1945
Oil on canvas, $29\frac{1}{2}$ x $36\frac{1}{2}$ in.
Mr. Howard M. Ross

PLATE **36**
Dickson Reeder (1912 – 1970)
Portrait of Bill Bomar, 1946
Oil on canvas, $26\frac{7}{8}$ x $17\frac{1}{4}$ in.
Courtesy of the Old Jail Art Center,
Albany, Texas. Gift of Bill Bomar
1989.017

PLATE **37**
Dickson Reeder (1912 – 1970)
Portrait of Veronica Helfensteller, ca. 1947
Oil on canvas, 20 x 16 in.
Earl Weed and Dena Edwards,
Houston, Texas

PLATE **38**
Dickson Reeder (1912 – 1970)
Charles, 1948
Oil on canvas, 28 x $17\frac{5}{16}$ in.
W. P. McLean Middle School,
Fort Worth, Texas

PLATE **39**
Dickson Reeder (1912 – 1970)
Joe Harris, ca. 1947 – 48
Oil on canvas, 26 x 17 in.
Earl Weed and Dena Edwards,
Houston, Texas

PLATE **40**
Cynthia Brants (1924 – 2006)
New England Harbor, ca. 1951 – 52
Aquatint and etching, 7 x $9\frac{3}{8}$ in.
Dallas Museum of Art, Richard H. McLarry
Prize, *Fifth Southwestern Exhibition of Prints and Drawings*, 1952

PLATE **41**
Lia Cuilty (1908 – 1978)
Seed Pods, 1947
Etching and soft-ground etching, 6 x $7\frac{3}{4}$ in.
Blanton Museum of Art, The University of
Texas at Austin, Gift of Kelly Fearing, 1993
Photograph by Rick Hall

PLATE **42**
Lia Cuilty (1908 – 1978)
Shells, 1950
Etching, soft-ground etching, and aquatint,
$5\frac{3}{4}$ x $7\frac{3}{8}$ in.
Heirs of Lia Cuilty; Caroline M. Dulle,
Susan M. Pritchett, Steve Murrin Jr.

PLATE **43**
Kelly Fearing (b. 1918)
Tribulations, 1944
Etching and soft-ground etching,
$4\frac{3}{8}$ x $5\frac{3}{8}$ in.
Valley House Gallery and Sculpture Garden
Art © Kelly Fearing/Licensed by VAGA,
New York, NY

PLATE **44**
Kelly Fearing (b. 1918)
Hercules and the Hydra, 1945
Etching and soft-ground etching,
$4\frac{7}{16}$ x $6\frac{5}{8}$ in.
Valley House Gallery and Sculpture Garden
Art © Kelly Fearing/Licensed by VAGA,
New York, NY

PLATE **45**
Kelly Fearing (b. 1918)
Floating Objects (Floating Above), 1945
Etching, soft-ground etching, and drypoint, 5 x 7⅞ in.
Valley House Gallery and Sculpture Garden

PLATE **46**
Kelly Fearing (b. 1918)
The Birds, 1946
Engraving and etching, 7 7/16 x 7 in.
Earl Weed and Dena Edwards, Houston, Texas

PLATE **47**
Kelly Fearing (b. 1918)
Fishermen, 1946
Etching and aquatint, 7 15/16 x 5½ in.
Courtesy of the Old Jail Art Center, Albany, Texas. Jewel Nail Bomar and William P. Bomar Jr. Collection
1993.017

PLATE **48**
Veronica Helfensteller (1910–1964)
Rock Formation, 1945
Etching, soft-ground etching, and aquatint, 5¾ x 8 1/16 in.
H. Kenneth Jackson

PLATE **49**
Veronica Helfensteller (1910–1964)
Bottles of the Sea, 1945
Etching and soft-ground etching, 5 15/16 x 6 15/16 in.
Collection of Linda Jo and Scott Grant Barker

PLATE **50**
Veronica Helfensteller (1910–1964)
Three Virgins, Three Giraffes and a Turtle, ca. 1945
Etching and soft-ground etching, 6 x 8 in.
Amon Carter Museum, Gift of Friends in memory of Bror Utter
1994.3

PLATE **51**
Veronica Helfensteller (1910–1964)
The House that Jack Built, 1947
Etching, 7⅜ x 6¼ in.
Dallas Museum of Art, Junior League Prize, *Sixth Annual Texas Print Exhibition*, 1947

PLATE **52**
Marjorie Johnson (1911–1997)
Untitled [Woman at Table], 1946
Etching and aquatint, 8⅞ x 6⅞ in.
Blanton Museum of Art, The University of Texas at Austin, Gift of Kelly Fearing, 1993
Photograph by Rick Hall

PLATE **53**
Dickson Reeder (1912–1970)
Mysterious Pool, 1941
Etching and soft-ground etching, 8 x 6 15/16 in.
From the Private Collection of Cy E. Barcus

PLATE **54**
Dickson Reeder (1912–1970)
The Keyhole Extraordinary (Extraordinary Keyhole), 1944
Etching and soft-ground etching, 7 1/16 x 4 7/16 in.
Amon Carter Museum
1995.7

PLATE **55**
Dickson Reeder (1912–1970)
Fish, 1944
Etching, soft-ground etching, and aquatint, 5⅞ x 8⅞ in.
Valley House Gallery and Sculpture Garden

PLATE **56**
Dickson Reeder (1912–1970)
Graffitage, 1944
Etching and soft-ground etching, 7 x 4 15/16 in.
Collection of Linda Jo and Scott Grant Barker

PLATE **57**
Bror Utter (1913–1993)
Man in the Pit, ca. 1943
Etching and aquatint, 7½ x 6 13/16 in.
Valley House Gallery and Sculpture Garden

PLATE **58**
Bror Utter (1913–1993)
Cacti, 1945
Etching and soft-ground etching, 5 15/16 x 4 15/16 in.
Amon Carter Museum
1990.31

PLATE **59**
Bror Utter (1913–1993)
Cells, 1945
Etching and soft-ground etching, 3 15/16 x 4⅞ in.
Amon Carter Museum
1990.32

PLATE **60**
Bror Utter (1913–1993)
Woman Combing Her Hair (Lady Combing Her Hair), 1945
Etching, soft-ground etching, and aquatint, 7 15/16 x 6 13/16 in.
Amon Carter Museum
1995.4

PLATE **61**
Bror Utter (1913–1993)
Tree of Knowledge, 1945
Etching, soft-ground etching, and aquatint, 8 1/16 x 6 13/16 in.
Amon Carter Museum
1990.30

PLATE **62**
Bill Bomar (1919–1991)
Jay's Pool, 1944
Oil on canvas, 30 x 35 in.
Courtesy of the Old Jail Art Center. Bequest of Linda Reimers Mixson
2007.009

PLATE **63**
Bill Bomar (1919–1991)
Day Observation for a Harlequin, 1947
Oil on canvas, 24 x 28 in.
Matilda Peeler

PLATE **64**
Bill Bomar (1919–1991)
Web and Roses, ca. 1947–48
Oil on canvas, 24 x 28⅛ in.
Collection of the Modern Art Museum of Fort Worth, Purchase Prize, 1948, Leonard Brothers Exhibition

PLATE **65**
Bill Bomar (1919–1991)
Burial in Spain, 1949
Oil on canvas, 52 x 27 in.
Mr. and Mrs. John E. Merrifield

PLATE **66**
Cynthia Brants (1924–2006)
The Cocktail Party, 1947
Oil on canvas, 40 3/4 x 47 5/8 in.
Kimbell and Mitch Wynne

PLATE **67**
Cynthia Brants (1924–2006)
The Centaur, 1953
Oil on canvas, 50 x 40 in.
Robert T. Brousseau

PLATE **68**
Lia Cuilty (1908–1978)
Arrested Flight, ca. 1943
Gouache and watercolor on paper,
15 5/16 x 10 13/16 in.
Heirs of Lia Cuilty; Caroline M. Dulle,
Susan M. Pritchett, Steve Murrin Jr.

PLATE **69**
Kelly Fearing (b. 1918)
The Kite Flyers, 1945
Oil on artist's board, 16 x 22 in.
Collection of the Modern Art Museum of
Fort Worth, Leonard Brothers Prize Award
Art © Kelly Fearing/Licensed by VAGA,
New York, NY

PLATE **70**
Kelly Fearing (b. 1918)
The Lifters, 1946
Oil on canvas, 24 x 32 1/4 in.
From the Private Collection of Cy E. Barcus
Art © Kelly Fearing/Licensed by VAGA,
New York, NY

PLATE **71**
Kelly Fearing (b. 1918)
The Collector, 1945
Etching and soft-ground etching,
7 13/16 x 6 11/16 in.
Amon Carter Museum, Gift in memory of
Donald S. Vogel
2004.20
Art © Kelly Fearing/Licensed by VAGA,
New York, NY

PLATE **72**
Kelly Fearing (b. 1918)
The Aquarist, 1945
Oil on canvas, 16 x 23 7/8 in.
Collection of David Lackey and
Russell Prince
Art © Kelly Fearing/Licensed by VAGA,
New York, NY

PLATE **73**
Kelly Fearing (b. 1918)
The Collector, 1946
Oil and wax on panel, 11 5/8 x 9 5/8 in.
Private Collection, Dallas, Texas
Art © Kelly Fearing/Licensed by VAGA,
New York, NY

PLATE **74**
George Grammer (b. 1928)
Oil Wells at Night, 1950
Oil on canvas, 20 x 16 in.
C. Brants Trust

PLATE **75**
Veronica Helfensteller (1910–1964)
Untitled [Animals at the Zoo], ca. 1945
Pastel and charcoal on paper,
18 15/16 x 23 15/16 in.
From the collection of the late
Lorraine Sherley

PLATE **76**
Veronica Helfensteller (1910–1964)
Animals at the Zoo, 1946
Etching, soft-ground etching, and aquatint,
6 15/16 x 7 7/8 in.
Collection of the Modern Art Museum of
Fort Worth, Museum Purchase, *Exhibition of
Fort Worth Artists*

PLATE **77**
Veronica Helfensteller (1910–1964)
Doorway Aviary, 1948
Watercolor, gouache, graphite, and ink on
paper, 20 15/16 x 14 1/2 in.
Courtesy of the Old Jail Art Center,
Albany, Texas. Gift of Reilly Nail
2006.036

PLATE **78**
Veronica Helfensteller (1910–1964)
Poor Little Girl Who Swallowed the Seeds,
ca. 1947–48
Lithograph, 9 7/8 x 13 3/4 in.
Alan Propper

PLATE **79**
Veronica Helfensteller (1910–1964)
*"Reclining under a tree (they) played at chess
and cards...,"* 1944
Gouache on paper, illustration for "The
Centaur Plays Croquet," 12 5/8 x 16 7/8 in.
Private Collection

PLATE **80**
Veronica Helfensteller (1910–1964)
"'Horace,' she cried ...," 1944
Gouache on paper, illustration for "The
Centaur Plays Croquet," 12 11/16 x 16 15/16 in.
Private Collection

PLATE **81**
Marjorie Johnson (1911–1997)
Studio Corner, 1949
Oil on canvas, 30 x 25 in.
Beth and David Dike Collection,
Dallas, Texas

PLATE **82**
Bror Utter (1913–1993)
The Dreamer (Embellished Forms No. 2), 1946
Gouache and graphite on paper,
14 15/16 x 20 15/16 in.
Collection of the Modern Art Museum of
Fort Worth, Leonard Brothers Prize Award,
Exhibition of Fort Worth Artists

PLATE **83**
Bror Utter (1913–1993)
Garden of Earthly Delights, 1946
Gouache on paper, 12 x 13 in.
Mr. and Mrs. John H. James

PLATE **84**
Bror Utter (1913–1993)
Untitled, 1946
Gouache and watercolor on paper,
13 7/16 x 12 5/16 in.
Amon Carter Museum
1991.5

PLATE **85**
Bror Utter (1913–1993)
Untitled, 1946
Gouache and watercolor on paper,
12 15/16 x 15 1/2 in.
Tom and Tamsen Kiehnhoff

PLATE **86**
Bror Utter (1913–1993)
Untitled, 1946
Gouache and watercolor on paper,
12 5/8 x 14 9/16 in.
Randolph Tibbits and Richard Bebermeyer

PLATE **87**
Bror Utter (1913–1993)
Presence, 1947
Gouache and watercolor on paper,
11 15/16 x 9 1/8 in.
Amon Carter Museum
1990.33

PLATE **88**
Bror Utter (1913–1993)
Untitled, 1947
Gouache and watercolor on paper,
13 x 13 7/8 in.
Tom and Tamsen Kiehnhoff

PLATE **89**
Bror Utter (1913–1993)
Untitled, 1947
Gouache on paper, 14 15/16 x 11 in.
From the collection of the late
Lorraine Sherley

PLATE **90**
Bror Utter (1913–1993)
Untitled [Two Women], 1948
Gouache on paper, 11 x 9 in.
Bill and Mary Cheek Family Collection

PLATE **91**
Bror Utter (1913–1993)
Untitled, 1948
Gouache and watercolor on paper,
10 7/8 x 16 1/16 in.
Amon Carter Museum
1991.6

PLATE **92**
Bror Utter (1913–1993)
Evening Reflections, 1949
Gouache and watercolor on paper,
10 1/2 x 13 1/2 in.
Amon Carter Museum
1991.4

PLATE **93**
Bror Utter (1913–1993)
Near and Farsighted Readers, 1950
Oil on canvas, 22 3/16 x 19 1/8 in.
Barry and Elizabeth Cook

PLATE **94**
Bror Utter (1913–1993)
The Altar of the Dead, 1951
Etching, soft-ground etching, and aquatint,
5 15/16 x 8 5/16 in.
Valley House Gallery and Sculpture Garden

PLATE **95**
Bror Utter (1913-1993)
Sketchbook, 1952
Watercolor, ink, and graphite on paper,
8 7/8 x 11 13/16 in.
Amon Carter Museum
1996.5.10

PLATE **96**
Bror Utter (1913–1993)
Metamorphosis III (Assembly of Birds), 1953
Oil on artist's board, 20 x 26 in.
Amon Carter Museum
1996.6

PLATE **97**
Bror Utter (1913–1993)
Signals, 1953
Oil on canvas, 50 x 40 in.
Robert T. Brousseau

PLATE **98**
Bror Utter (1913-1993)
Trio, 1953
Oil on canvas, 30 x 40 in.
Collection of the Modern Art Museum of
Fort Worth, Gift of Bertram M. Newhouse in
honor of Sallie M. Gillespie

THE AMON CARTER MUSEUM was established through the generosity of Amon G. Carter (1879–1955) to house his collection of paintings and sculpture by Frederic Remington and Charles M. Russell; to collect, preserve, and exhibit the finest examples of American art; and to serve an educational role through exhibitions, publications, and programs devoted to the study of American art.

FOR THE AMON CARTER MUSEUM

Mary Jane Crook
Editor

Timothy Gambell
Graphic Design

Will Gillham
Director of Publications

Miriam Hermann
Publications Assistant

Christine Valentine
and Ginger Watson
Proofreaders

Steven Watson
Manager of Photographic Services

First edition; printed in Fort Worth, Texas.

Amon Carter Museum
3501 Camp Bowie Boulevard
Fort Worth, Texas 76107
www.cartermuseum.org

LIBRARY OF CONGRESS CATALOGING-IN-PUBLICATION DATA

Barker, Scott Grant.
Intimate modernism: Fort Worth Circle artists in the 1940s / by Scott Barker and Jane Myers. — 1st ed.
p. cm.
Issued in connection with an exhibition held Feb. 16 – May 11, 2008, Amon Carter Museum, Fort Worth, Texas.
ISBN 978-0-88360-103-7 (clothbound) — ISBN 978-0-88360-104-4 (limited edition)
1. Fort Worth Circle (Group of artists) — Exhibitions. 2. Modernism (Art) — Texas — Fort Worth — Exhibitions. 3. Art, American — Texas — Fort Worth — 20th century — Exhibitions. I. Myers, Jane, 1955- II. Amon Carter Museum of Western Art. III. Title.
N6512.5.F66B37 2008
709'.7645315 — dc22

2007045695